WPA Outcomes for First-Year Composition	Where *The Allyn & Bacon Guide* Addresses These Outcomes
KNOWLEDGE OF CONVENTIONS By the end of first-year composition, students should • Learn common formats for different kinds of texts • Develop knowledge of genre conventions ranging from structure and paragraphing to tone and mechanics • Practice appropriate means of documenting their work • Control such surface features as syntax, grammar, punctuation, and spelling	Part 1, "A Rhetoric for Writers," Concepts 7, 11, and 12 Chapter 12, "Incorporating Sources into Your Own Writing" Chapter 13, "Citing and Documenting Sources" Handbook (Regular Edition) Additionally, all Writing Project chapters in Part 2 explain appropriate format, tone, and style.
COMPOSING IN ELECTRONIC ENVIRONMENTS By the end of first-year composition, students should • Use electronic environments for drafting, reviewing, revising, editing, and sharing texts • Locate, evaluate, organize, and use research material collected from electronic sources, including scholarly library databases; other official databases (e.g., federal government databases); and informal electronic networks and Internet sources • Understand and exploit the difference in the rhetorical strategies and in the affordances available for both print and electronic composing processes and texts	Additionally, the Writing Project chapters in Part 2 make frequent reference to electronic formats and processes, including desktop-published material, posters, advocacy ads, and PowerPoint presentations.

The Allyn & Bacon Guide to Writing

Sixth Custom Edition
University of Houston

Taken from:
The Allyn & Bacon Guide to Writing, Sixth Edition
by John D. Ramage, John C. Bean, and June Johnson

The New Century Handbook, Fifth Edition
by Christine A. Hult and Thomas N. Huckin

The Successful Writer's Handbook, Second Edition
by Kathleen T. McWhorter and Jane E. Aaron

The Longman Handbook for Writers and Readers,
Sixth Edition
by Chris M. Anson and Robert A. Schwegler

Cover Art: Courtesy of Purestock/Getty Images

Taken from:

The Allyn & Bacon Guide to Writing, Sixth Edition
by John D. Ramage, John C. Bean, and June Johnson
Copyright © 2012, 2009, 2006 by Pearson Education, Inc.
Published by Longman
New York, New York 10036

The New Century Handbook, Fifth Edition
by Christine A. Hult and Thomas N. Huckin
Copyright © 2011, 2008, 2005 by Pearson Education, Inc.
Published by Longman

The Allyn & Bacon Guide to Writing, Sixth Edition
by John D. Ramage, John C. Bean, and June Johnson
Copyright © 2012, 2009 by Pearson Education, Inc.
Published by Longman

The Longman Handbook for Writers and Readers, Sixth Edition
by Chris M. Anson and Robert A. Schwegler
Copyright © 2011 by Pearson Education, Inc.
Published by Longman

This special edition published in cooperation with Pearson Learning Solutions.

All trademarks, service marks, registered trademarks, and registered service marks are the
property of their respective owners and are used herein for identification purposes only.

Pearson Learning Solutions, 501 Boylston Street, Suite 900, Boston, MA 02116
A Pearson Education Company
www.pearsoned.com

Printed in the United States of America

1 2 3 4 5 6 7 8 9 10 V354 16 15 14 13 12 11

000200010270761776

BK

ISBN 10: 1-256-34813-9
ISBN 13: 978-1-256-34813-9

DETAILED CONTENTS

PART 1   A RHETORIC FOR WRITERS

PART 2   WRITING PROJECTS

WRITING TO LEARN

WRITING TO EXPLORE

6   WRITING AN AUTOBIOGRAPHICAL NARRATIVE   144

PART 3   A GUIDE TO COMPOSING AND REVISING

PART 4   A RHETORICAL GUIDE TO RESEARCH

15   PUNCTUATION   393

Chapter 14 taken from *The New Century Handbook,* Fifth Edition by Christine A. Hult and Thomas N. Huckin. Chapter 15 taken from *The Successful Writer's Handbook,* Second Edition by Kathleen T. McWhorter and Jane E. Aaron. Chapter 16 taken from *The Longman Handbook for Writers and Readers,* Sixth Edition by Chris M. Anson and Robert A. Schwegler. All else taken from The Allyn & Bacon Guide to Writing, Sixth Edition by John D. Ramage, John C. Bean, and June Johnson.

WRITING PROJECTS

THEMATIC CONTENTS

The Allyn & Bacon Guide to Writing contains readings by professional writers and students. In addition, the text has visual texts (such as advertisements, news photographs, posters, and Web sites) that can lead to productive thematic discussions. These readings and visual texts can be clustered thematically in the following ways.

NATURE AND ECOLOGY

PREFACE

Through five editions of *The Allyn & Bacon Guide to Writing*, users and reviewers have praised the book's ability to explain rhetorical concepts clearly, engage students in critical thinking, and teach reading and composing strategies that lead to thoughtful, interesting, and meaningful student work. In regular, brief, and concise editions, the text has been adopted at a wide range of two- and four-year institutions, where instructors admire its appeal to students, its focus on problem posing, its distinctive emphasis on writing and reading as rhetorical acts, its engaging classroom activities, and its effective writing assignments. Its flexibility enables composition teachers to capitalize on their own strengths and interests to create intellectually stimulating and pedagogically effective courses.

What's New in the Sixth Edition?

While retaining the signature strengths of earlier editions, the sixth edition features the following key changes and improvements:

- **Expanded coverage of integrating researched sources effectively and ethically** includes new instruction, visual presentations, and examples to help students improve skills fundamental to college readiness and success throughout their academic careers (Chapters 12 and 13).

- **A thoroughly revised chapter on image analysis** helps students work effectively with a wide variety of the visual texts they will encounter in other course areas and outside of college.

- **Five new student models and three new professional texts** offer engaging and contemporary topics for discussion, written response, and exploratory research—including banning laptops and cell phones from classes, sustainable environmental practices, and the growing gap between the rich and the poor.

- **MLA and APA coverage is thoroughly updated** according to the most recent citation guidelines from each organization, ensuring that students are learning concepts formatted according to the most current guidelines (Chapter 13).

- **New visual pedagogy presents complex topics clearly** and at-a-glance to better suit today's learners and includes new Strategies Charts and new color-coded examples and explanations of incorporating sources using summary, paraphrase, and quotation (Chapters 12 and 13).

- **A new section on presenting data visually** to reach different kinds of readers helps students create effective tables, graphs, and charts to support their arguments (Chapter 10).

- **New instruction helps writers think rhetorically about introductions** (Chapter 2, Concept 6).
- **Chapters 3 and 4 have been extensively revised** to include the previous edition's Chapter 5 and to consolidate the presentation of angle of vision, the ladder of abstraction, and the value of sensory detail.
- **A revised Concept 2 helps writers develop meaningful thesis statements** by showing them how to start by investigating problems rather than topics (Chapter 1).

Distinctive Approach of *The Allyn & Bacon Guide to Writing*

The improvements in the sixth edition enhance the enduring strengths of *The Allyn & Bacon Guide to Writing* that have made this text pedagogically effective for students and intellectually satisfying for instructors. What follows are the distinctive elements of our approach to teaching composition:

- **Integration of rhetorical theory with composition research.** The authors of this text are scholars in rhetoric, composition studies, writing across the curriculum, critical thinking, global cultural studies, and active learning pedagogy. Together, they bring to *The Allyn & Bacon Guide to Writing* a distinctive pedagogical approach that integrates rhetorical theory with composition research by treating writing and reading as rhetorical acts and as processes of inquiry, problem posing, and critical thinking. The text helps students learn important skills that transfer across disciplines and professional fields.
- **Classroom-tested assignments that guide students through all phases of the reading and writing processes and make frequent use of collaboration and peer review.** The Writing Projects promote intellectual growth and stimulate the kind of critical thinking valued in college courses. Numerous "For Writing and Discussion" exercises make it easy to incorporate active learning into a course while deepening students' understanding of concepts. The text's focus on the subject-matter question that precedes the thesis helps students see academic disciplines as fields of inquiry rather than as data banks of right answers.
- **Coverage of a wide range of genres and aims including academic, civic, and professional genres as well as personal and narrative forms.** By placing nonfiction writing on a continuum from closed-form prose (thesis-based) to open-form prose (narrative-based), the text presents students with a wide range of genres and aims, and clearly explains the rhetorical function and stylistic features of different genres. The text focuses on closed-form writing for entering most academic, civic, and professional conversations, and on open-form writing for narrating ideas and experiences that resist closed-form structures and for creating stylistic surprise and pleasure.
- **Instructional emphases meet the Council of Writing Program Administrators (WPA) guidelines** for outcome goals in first-year

composition courses. The correlation of the WPA Outcomes Statement with the sixth edition of *The Allyn & Bacon Guide to Writing* appears on the front endpapers, part opening pages, and in the *Instructor's Resource Manual*. In addition to helping instructors plan their courses, these correlations help with program-wide internal and external assessments.

- **Great flexibility for instructors.** Because the chapters on rhetoric, on Writing Projects, and on composing and research strategies have been designed with self-contained modules, users praise the ease with which they can select chapters and sections and order them to fit the goals of their own courses.

- **Use of reader-expectation theory to explain how closed-form prose achieves maximum clarity and how open-form prose achieves its distinctive pleasures.** The skills explained in Chapter 10 on composing and revising closed-form prose (such as the reader's need for understanding the problem before encountering the thesis, for forecasting and signposts, for points before particulars, and for old information before new information) are taught as self-contained Skill Lessons that can be easily integrated into a variety of course structures. These explanations show students why certain principles of closed-form prose (such as unified and coherent paragraphs with topic sentences) derive from the psychology of cognition rather than from the rule-making penchant of English teachers. The skills explained in Chapter 18 on open-form prose show how writers create pleasurable surprise through purposeful disruptions and violations of the conventions of closed-form prose.

- **Emphasis on teaching students to read rhetorically.** An often-noted strength of *The Allyn & Bacon Guide to Writing* is its method for teaching students to read rhetorically so that they can summarize complex readings and speak back to them armed with their own powers of analysis and critical thinking. This skill is crucial for undergraduate research in any discipline. In its focus on rhetorical reading, the text teaches students to understand the differences between print and cyberspace sources; to analyze the rhetorical occasion, genre, context, intended audience, and angle of vision of sources; to evaluate sources according to appropriate criteria; and to negotiate the World Wide Web with confidence.

- **A sequenced skill-based approach to research** teaches students expert strategies for conducting academic research in a rhetorical environment.

- **Coverage of visual rhetoric and document design** focuses on Web sites, advertisements, posters, and other texts where words and images work together for rhetorical effect.

- **A friendly, encouraging tone** respects students and treats them as serious learners.

Key Features of *The Allyn & Bacon Guide to Writing*

- **An organization that emphasizes concepts and skills and promotes active learning.** The modular organization offers instructors great flexibility in designing courses and allows students to quickly navigate the text.

- **Twelve rhetorical "Concepts" in Part 1** provide students with memorable takeaway ideas that enable them to situate verbal and visual texts in a rhetorical context and to think critically about how any text tries to persuade its audience.

- **Writing Projects in Part 2,** arranged according to rhetorical aim, teach students the features of a genre while promoting new ways of seeing and thinking. The exploratory exercises for each Writing Project help students develop their skills at posing problems, generating ideas, delaying closure, valuing alternative points of view, and thinking dialectically.

- **Numbered "Skills" in Parts 3 and 4,** designed as modular mini-lessons, teach the compositional and research skills that can be applied to any writing project.

- **Professional and student readings on current and enduring questions** that illustrate rhetorical principles, invite thematic grouping, and provide models for students' own writing.

- **"For Writing and Discussion" exercises,** which appear regularly throughout the text, provide class-tested critical thinking activities that promote conceptual learning or active exploration of ideas.

- **Strategies charts** present suggestions for approaching reading, writing, and research tasks in a handy format for student reference and use.

- **Framework charts for genres and writing assignments** help students understand the structural features of different genres, and serve as flowcharts that promote both idea generation and more purposeful structure.

- **Peer review guidelines for major assignments** help students conduct effective peer reviews of each other's drafts.

Strategies for Using *The Allyn & Bacon Guide to Writing*

The text's organization makes it easy to design a new syllabus or adapt the text to your current syllabus. Although there are many ways to use *The Allyn & Bacon Guide to Writing,* the most typical course design has students reading and discussing selected concepts from Chapters 1–4 (Part 1) during the opening weeks. The brief, informal write-to-learn projects in these chapters can be used either for homework assignments or for in-class discussion. In the rest of the course, instructors typically assign Writing Projects chapters from the array of options available in Part 2. While students are engaged with the Writing Projects in these chapters, instructors can work in mini-lessons on the writing and research "skills" in Parts 3 and 4. Typically during class sessions, instructors move back and forth between classroom exercises related directly to the current Writing Project (invention exercises, group brainstorming, peer review workshops) and discussions focused on instructional matter from the rest of the text. (For more specific suggestions on how to select and sequence materials, see the sample syllabi in the *Instructor's Resource Manual.*)

Supplements for *The Allyn & Bacon Guide to Writing*

The Instructor's Resource Manual, **Sixth Edition,** has been revised by Susanmarie Harrington of the University of Vermont. The *Instructor's Resource Manual* integrates emphases for meeting the Council of Writing Program Administrators' guidelines for outcome goals in first-year composition courses. It continues to offer detailed teaching suggestions to help both experienced and new instructors; practical teaching strategies for composition instructors in a question-and-answer format; suggested syllabi for courses of various lengths and emphases; chapter-by-chapter teaching suggestions; answers to Handbook exercises; suggestions for using the text with nonnative speakers; suggestions for using the text in an electronic classroom; transparency masters for class use; and annotated bibliographies.

 **MyCompLab.** The only online application that integrates a writing environment with proven resources for grammar, writing, and research, MyCompLab gives students help at their fingertips as they draft and revise. Instructors have access to a variety of assessment tools including commenting capabilities, diagnostics and study plans, and an e-portfolio. Created after years of extensive research and in partnership with faculty and students across the country, MyCompLab offers a seamless and flexible teaching and learning environment built specifically for writers.

Interactive Pearson eText. An e-book version of *The Allyn & Bacon Guide to Writing,* Sixth Edition, is also available in MyCompLab. This dynamic, online version of the text is integrated throughout MyCompLab to create an enriched, interactive learning experience for writing students.

CourseSmart. Students can subscribe to *The Allyn & Bacon Guide to Writing,* Sixth Edition, as a CourseSmart eText (at CourseSmart.com). The site includes all of the book's content in a format that enables students to search the text, bookmark passages, save their own notes, and print reading assignments that incorporate lecture notes.

Acknowledgments

We wish to give special thanks to the following composition scholars and teachers, who reviewed the fifth-edition text or the manuscript for the sixth edition, helping us understand how they use *The Allyn & Bacon Guide to Writing* in the classroom and offering valuable suggestions for improving the text: Ann Marie Ade, Embry-Riddle Aeronautical University; Terri A. Amlong, De Sales University; Larry Beason, University of Southern Alabama; Lisa Beckelhimer, University of Cincinnati; Linda Bingham, Hawkeye Community College; Rita M. Brown, Sanford-Brown College, Collinsville; Lizbeth A. Bryant, Purdue University Calumet; Allison Carr, University of Cincinnati; Laura Carroll, Abilene Christian University; Virginia Chappell, Marquette University; Jim Dervin, Winston-Salem State University; Robert Grindy, Richland Community College; Kimberly Harrison, Florida International University; Jen Hazel, Owens Community College; Melissa Ianetta, University of Delaware; Gilda Kelsey,

University of Delaware; Lindsay Lewan, Arapahoe Community College; Theresa P. Maue, Embry-Riddle Aeronautical University; Amanda McGuire Rzicznek, Bowling Green State University; MaryGrace N. Paden, John Tyler Community College; Deirdre Pettipiece, University of the Sciences in Philadelphia; Jeanne Purtell, Harrisburg Area Community College, York; Jamey Trotter, Arapahoe Community College; Scott Warnock, Drexel University; and Derand Wright, Southern Illinois University Carbondale.

Thank you also to the students who reviewed *The Allyn & Bacon Guide to Writing,* telling us about their experiences using the fifth edition: Joseph Derosier, Embry-Riddle Aeronautical University; Roxanne Malick, Harrisburg Area Community College; Lindsey Shiflett, Richland Community College; Chelsea Stevenson, Richland Community College; and Heidi Thomas, Harrisburg Area Community College.

Thanks also to various scholars who have written commissioned sections of *The Allyn & Bacon Guide to Writing* for previous editions and whose work remains in the sixth edition. Thanks to Tim McGee of Philadelphia University, whose work still influences our material on oral presentation. Thanks also to Alice Gillam of the University of Wisconsin–Milwaukee, who authored the chapter on self-reflective writing, and to Virginia Chappell of Marquette University, who contributed significantly on analyzing a short story. Finally, we wish to thank again Christy Friend of the University of South Carolina, Columbia, who wrote the chapter on essay examinations for the first edition.

Our deepest thanks and appreciation go to our editor, Lauren Finn, whose comprehensive view of the field, keen insights, and excellent people and communication skills make her a pleasure to work with. We are also particularly grateful to our development editor, Marion Castellucci, who has worked with us through multiple revisions and has become an invaluable part of our team. Her insight, sense of humor, professional experience, and extensive editorial knowledge have once again kept us on track and made the intense work of this revision possible.

We owe special thanks to three people whose expertise inform our new approaches to image analysis: to Naomi Hume for her experience in teaching the analysis of paintings; to Claire Garoutte for her work on documentary photography; and to Kristopher Johnson for his insights from the fields of advertising and marketing.

We would also like to thank three Seattle University students who provided special research assistance for this edition as well as their perspective on important issues: Jon Carr, Kyle Madsen, and Lydia Wheeler. We'd also like to thank Stephen and Sarah Bean for their research help. Most of all, we are indebted to all our students, who have made the teaching of composition such a joy. We thank them for their insights and for their willingness to engage with problems, discuss ideas, and, as they compose and revise, share with us their frustrations and their triumphs. They have sustained our love of teaching and inspired us to write this book.

Finally, John Bean thanks his wife, Kit, also a professional composition teacher, whose dedication to her students as writers and individuals manifests the sustaining values of our unique profession. John also thanks his children, Matthew, Andrew, Stephen, and Sarah, who have grown to adulthood since he began writing textbooks. June Johnson thanks her husband, Kenneth Bube, for his loving support, his interest in teaching, and his expert understanding of the importance of writing in mathematics and the sciences. Finally, she thanks her daughter, Jane Ellen, who has offered encouragement and support in countless ways.

JOHN D. RAMAGE
JOHN C. BEAN
JUNE JOHNSON

A RHETORIC
FOR WRITERS

As the search for clean, renewable energy to relieve the pressure on oil gains momentum, photographs of wind turbines are appearing more frequently in magazines and newspapers. However, because this source of energy is controversial, *how* these massive technological windmills are depicted varies widely. Do they blend into the landscape or mar it with their industrial presence? Photographers and writers, conscious of the rhetorical effect of photos, carefully plan the impression they want photos of wind power to convey. This low-angle shot of wind turbines, emphasizing their size and power and hinting at barren hills in the background, participates in this public controversy.

This photograph is part of a discussion in Chapter 3 on the way that visuals make appeals to *logos*, *ethos*, and *pathos*.

3

PART 1 A RHETORIC FOR COLLEGE WRITERS

Part 1 addresses the following outcomes for first-year composition from the Council of Writing Program Administrators.

RHETORICAL KNOWLEDGE	• Focus on a purpose (Concepts 2 and 3) • Respond to the needs of different audiences (Concepts 1, 3, 8, 11, 12) • Respond appropriately to different kinds of rhetorical situations (Concepts 1, 3, 8, 9, 11, and 12; Brief Writing Projects) • Use conventions of format and structure appropriate to the rhetorical situation (Concepts 1, 3, 5-7, 11, 12; Brief Writing Projects) • Adopt appropriate voice, tone, and level of formality (Concepts 11 and 12; Brief Writing Projects) • Understand how genres shape reading and writing (Concepts 1 and 3, 11, 12; Brief Writing Projects) • Write in several genres (Brief Writing Projects)
CRITICAL THINKING, READING, AND WRITING	• Use writing and reading for inquiry, learning, thinking, and communicating (Concept 2, 4-6; Brief Writing Projects) • Understand a writing assignment as a series of tasks, including finding, evaluating, analyzing, and synthesizing appropriate primary and secondary sources (Concepts 4-7) • Integrate their own ideas with those of others (Concepts 2 and 4) • Understand the relationships among language, knowledge, and power (Concepts 8 and 9; Brief Writing Projects)
PROCESSES	• Understand writing as an open process that permits writers to use later invention and rethinking to revise their work (Concepts 2, 4, 5) • Use a variety of technologies to address a range of audiences (Concepts 10 and 12)
KNOWLEDGE OF CONVENTIONS	• Learn common formats for different kinds of texts (Concepts 1, 3, 12; Brief Writing Projects) • Develop knowledge of genre conventions ranging from structure and paragraphing to tone and mechanics (Concepts 1, 3, 11, 12; Brief Writing Projects)
COMPOSING IN ELECTRONIC ENVIRONMENTS	• Use electronic environments for drafting, reviewing, revising, editing, and sharing texts (Brief Writing Projects) • Understand and exploit the differences in the rhetorical strategies and in the affordances available for both print and electronic composing processes and texts (Concept 12)

THINKING RHETORICALLY ABOUT GOOD WRITING

It seems to me, then, that the way to help people become better writers is not to tell them that they must first learn the rules of grammar, that they must develop a four-part outline, that they must consult the experts and collect all the useful information. These things may have their place. But none of them is as crucial as having a good, interesting question.

—*Rodney Kilcup, Historian*

When new students ask us about the rules for good college writing, they are often surprised by history professor Rodney Kilcup's unexpected advice in the epigraph above. To become a better writer, says Kilcup, the most crucial thing is to have "a good, interesting question." We love Professor Kilcup's advice because we'd like you to think of good writers as critical thinkers who pose questions and problems.

As we show throughout this text, writing is closely allied to critical thinking and to the innate satisfaction you take in exercising your curiosity, creativity, and problem-solving ability. Writing helps you discover and express ideas that you would otherwise never think or say. Unlike speaking, writing gives you time to think deeply and long about an idea. Because you can revise writing, it lets you pursue a problem in stages, with each draft reflecting a deeper, clearer, or more complex level of thought. Moreover, the skills you learn in a writing course are transferable to all majors and to your professional careers. Research has shown that managers, accountants, lawyers, engineers, and other professionals spend, on average, forty-four percent of their professional time writing. In sum, writing has lifelong importance: It stimulates, challenges, and stretches your mental powers while giving you a voice in important academic, civic, and professional conversations.

In this chapter, you will learn three important concepts about writing:

- **CONCEPT 1** Good writing can vary from closed to open forms.
- **CONCEPT 2** Good writers address problems rather than topics.
- **CONCEPT 3** Good writers think rhetorically about purpose, audience, and genre.

CONCEPT I Good writing can vary from closed to open forms.

In our experience, beginning college writers are often discomforted by the ambiguity of the rules governing writing. They often wish for some consistent rules: "Never use 'I' in a formal paper" or "Start every paragraph with a topic sentence." The problem is that different kinds of writing have different criteria for effectiveness, leaving the writer with rhetorical choices rather than with hard-and-fast formulas for success. You'll be able to appreciate this insight for yourself through the following exercise.

Read the following short pieces of nonfiction prose. The first is a letter to the editor written by a professional civil engineer in response to a newspaper editorial arguing for the development of wind-generated electricity. The second short piece is entitled "A Festival of Rain." It was written by the American poet and religious writer Thomas Merton, a Trappist monk. After reading the two samples carefully, proceed to the discussion questions that follow.

David Rockwood
A Letter to the Editor

1   Your editorial on November 16, "Get Bullish on Wind Power," is based on fantasy rather than fact. There are several basic reasons why wind-generated power can in no way serve as a reasonable major alternative to other electrical energy supply alternatives for the Pacific Northwest power system.

2   First and foremost, wind power is unreliable. Electric power generation is evaluated not only on the amount of energy provided, but also on its ability to meet system peak load requirements on an hourly, daily, and weekly basis. In other words, an effective power system would have to provide enough electricity to meet peak demands in a situation when the wind energy would be unavailable—either in no wind situations or in severe blizzard conditions, which would shut down the wind generators. Because wind power cannot be relied on at times of peak needs, it would have to be backed up by other power generation resources at great expense and duplication of facilities.

3   Secondly, there are major unsolved problems involved in the design of wind generation facilities, particularly for those located in rugged mountain areas. Ice storms, in particular, can cause sudden dynamic problems for the rotating blades and mechanisms which could well result in breakdown or failure of the generators. Furthermore, the design of the facilities to meet the stresses imposed by high winds in these remote mountain regions, in the order of 125 miles per hour, would indeed escalate the costs.

4   Thirdly, the environmental impact of constructing wind generation facilities amounting to 28 percent of the region's electrical supply system (as proposed in your editorial) would be tremendous. The Northwest Electrical Power system presently has

a capacity of about 37,000 megawatts of hydro power and 10,300 megawatts of thermal, for a total of about 48,000 megawatts. Meeting 28 percent of this capacity by wind power generators would, most optimistically, require about 13,400 wind towers, each with about 1,000 kilowatt (one megawatt) generating capacity. These towers, some 100 to 200 feet high, would have to be located in the mountains of Oregon and Washington. These would encompass hundreds of square miles of pristine mountain area, which, together with interconnecting transmission facilities, control works, and roads, would indeed have major adverse environmental impacts on the region.

5   There are many other lesser problems of control and maintenance of such a system. Let it be said that, from my experience and knowledge as a professional engineer, the use of wind power as a major resource in the Pacific Northwest power system is strictly a pipe dream.

Thomas Merton
A Festival of Rain

1   Let me say this before rain becomes a utility that they can plan and distribute for money. By "they" I mean the people who cannot understand that rain is a festival, who do not appreciate its gratuity, who think that what has no price has no value, that what cannot be sold is not real, so that the only way to make something *actual* is to place it on the market. The time will come when they will sell you even your rain. At the moment it is still free, and I am in it. I celebrate its gratuity and its meaninglessness.

2   The rain I am in is not like the rain of cities. It fills the woods with an immense and confused sound. It covers the flat roof of the cabin and its porch with insistent and controlled rhythms. And I listen, because it reminds me again and again that the whole world runs by rhythms I have not yet learned to recognize, rhythms that are not those of the engineer.

3   I came up here from the monastery last night, sloshing through the corn fields, said Vespers, and put some oatmeal on the Coleman stove for supper. ... The night became very dark. The rain surrounded the whole cabin with its enormous virginal myth, a whole world of meaning, of secrecy, of silence, of rumor. Think of it: all that speech pouring down, selling nothing, judging nobody, drenching the thick mulch of dead leaves, soaking the trees, filling the gullies and crannies of the wood with water, washing out the places where men have stripped the hillside! What a thing it is to sit absolutely alone, in a forest, at night, cherished by this wonderful, unintelligible, perfectly innocent speech, the most comforting speech in the world, the talk that rain makes by itself all over the ridges, and the talk of the watercourses everywhere in the hollows!

4   Nobody started it, nobody is going to stop it. It will talk as long as it wants, this rain. As long as it talks I am going to listen.

5   But I am also going to sleep, because here in this wilderness I have learned how to sleep again. Here I am not alien. The trees I know, the night I know, the rain I know. I close my eyes and instantly sink into the whole rainy world of which I am a part, and the world goes on with me in it, for I am not alien to it.

Comparing Rockwood's and Merton's Writing

Working in small groups or as a whole class, try to reach consensus on the following specific tasks:

1. What are the main differences between the two types of writing? If you are working in groups, help your recorder prepare a presentation describing the differences between Rockwood's writing and Merton's writing.
2. Create a metaphor, simile, or analogy that best sums up your feelings about the most important differences between Rockwood's and Merton's writing: "Rockwood's writing is like . . ., but Merton's writing is like. . . ."
3. Explain why your metaphors are apt. How do your metaphors help clarify or illuminate the differences between the two pieces of writing?

Now that you have done some thinking on your own about the differences between these two examples, turn to our brief analysis.

Distinctions between Closed and Open Forms of Writing

David Rockwood's letter and Thomas Merton's mini-essay are both examples of nonfiction prose. But as these examples illustrate, nonfiction prose can vary enormously in form and style. From the perspective of structure, we can place nonfiction prose along a continuum that goes from closed to open forms of writing (see Figure 1.1).

Closed-Form Prose Of our two pieces of prose, Rockwood's letter illustrates tightly closed writing and falls at the far left end of the continuum because it has these elements:

- An explicit thesis in the introduction that informs readers of the point of the whole essay (i.e., wind-generated power isn't a reasonable alternative energy source in the Pacific Northwest)

FIGURE 1.1
A Continuum of Essay Types: Closed to Open Forms

Closed Forms

Top-down thesis-based prose
- thesis explicitly stated in introduction
- all parts of essay linked clearly to thesis
- body paragraphs develop thesis
- body paragraphs have topic sentences
- structure forecasted

Delayed-thesis prose
- thesis appears near end
- text reads as a mystery
- reader held in suspense

- Unified and coherent paragraphs (i.e., "First and foremost, wind power is unreliable. ... Secondly, there are major unsolved problems. ... Thirdly, ...")
- Sustained development of that thesis without digressions

Once the thesis is stated, readers know the point of the essay and can predict its structure. (You might note that the five-paragraph essay sometimes taught in high school is a by-the-numbers way to teach closed-form prose.) Because its structure is transparent and predictable, the success of closed-form prose rests entirely on its ideas, which must "surprise" readers by asserting something new, challenging, doubtful, or controversial. It aims to change readers' view of the subject through the power of reason, logic, and evidence. Closed-form prose is what most college professors write in their scholarly research, what they most often expect from their students, and what is most common in professional and business contexts.

Open-Form Prose In contrast, Merton's "A Festival of Rain" falls toward the right end of the closed-to-open continuum because it exhibits these features:

- No reduction to a single, summarizable thesis (Merton clearly opposes the consumer culture that will try to "sell" you the rain, but what exactly does Merton mean by "festival" or by rain's "gratuity and its meaninglessness"?)
- The use of story or narrative as an organizing principle (i.e., the story of Merton's leaving the monastery to sleep in the rain-drenched cabin) through which a point emerges suggestively

Although open-form prose does not announce its thesis and support it with reasons and evidence, it does have a focus. As Merton's piece illustrates, the focus is more like a theme in fiction that readers might discuss and even dispute than like a thesis in argument.

Consider also the extent to which Merton violates the rules for closed-form prose. Instead of using transitions between paragraphs, Merton juxtaposes passages that tell the story of his camping trip ("I came up here from the monastery last night ...") with passages that make cryptic, interpretive comments about his experience ("The rain I am in is not like the rain of cities"). Unlike paragraphs in

Open Forms

Thesis-seeking prose
- essay organized around a question rather than a thesis
- essay explores the problem or question, looking at it in many ways
- writer may or may not arrive at thesis

Theme-based narrative
- often organized chronologically or has storylike elements
- often used to heighten or deepen a problem, or show its human significance
- often has an implicit theme rather than a thesis
- often violates rules of closed-form prose by using literary techniques

closed-form prose, which typically begin with topic sentences and are developed with supporting details, the paragraphs in Merton's piece have no clear hierarchical structure; paragraph 4, in fact, is only two lines long. These open-form elements often appear in personal essays, in blogs, in newspaper or magazine feature stories or character profiles, or in professional nonfiction.

Flexibility of "Rules" along the Continuum As you can see from the continuum in Figure 1.1, essays can fall anywhere along the scale. Not all thesis-with-support writing has to be top down, stating its thesis explicitly in the introduction. In some cases writers choose to delay the thesis, creating a more exploratory, open-ended, "let's think through this together" feeling before finally stating the main point late in the essay. In some cases writers explore a problem without *ever* finding a satisfactory thesis, creating an essay that is thesis seeking rather than thesis supporting, an essay aimed at deepening the question, refusing to accept an easy answer. Such essays may replicate their authors' process of exploring a problem and include digressions, speculations, conjectures, multiple perspectives, and occasional invitations to the reader to help solve the problem. When writers reach the far right-hand position on the continuum, they no longer state an explicit thesis. Instead, like novelists or short story writers, they embed their points in plot, imagery, dialogue, and so forth, leaving their readers to *infer* a theme from the text. This kind of writing is often called "literary nonfiction."

Where to Place Your Writing along the Continuum

Clearly, essays at opposite ends of this continuum operate in different ways and obey different rules. Because each position on the continuum has its appropriate uses, the writer's challenge is to determine which sort of writing is most appropriate in a given situation. Most college papers (but not all) and much professional writing are written in closed form. Thus if you were writing a business proposal, a legal brief, or an academic paper for a scholarly audience, you would typically choose a closed-form structure, and your finished product would include elements such as the following:

- An explicit thesis in the introduction
- Forecasting of structure
- Cohesive and unified paragraphs with topic sentences
- Clear transitions between sentences and between parts
- No digressions

But if you were writing to express your conflicted relationship with, say, a parent or friend or to reflect on your first discovery of racism or homophobia, you would probably move toward the open end of the continuum and violate one or more of these conventions. Instead of a thesis-support structure, you might use the power of compelling stories, vivid characterization, dialogue, and evocative language to convey your ideas.

If we return now to the question about good writing posed at the beginning of this chapter, we can see that having a thesis statement, topic sentences, good transitions, and unified and coherent paragraphs are not qualities of "good prose" but simply of "closed-form prose." What makes a piece of closed-form prose "good," as we will see in the next section, is the extent to which it addresses a problem or question that matters to the reader and brings to the reader something new, surprising, or provocative. In contrast, we have seen that open-form prose can be "good" without having a thesis-driven, hierarchical structure. Open-form prose conveys its pleasures and insights through narrative strategies rather than through thesis-with-support strategies.

Thinking Personally about Closed and Open Forms

FOR WRITING AND DISCUSSION

Do you and your classmates most enjoy writing prose at the closed or at the more open end of the continuum?

Individual task: Recall a favorite piece of writing that you have done in the past. Jot down a brief description of the kind of writing this was (a poem, a personal-experience essay, a piece of workplace writing, a research paper, a newspaper story, a persuasive argument). Where would you place this piece of writing on the closed-to-open continuum? Explore why you like this piece of writing. Are you at your best in closed-form writing that calls for an explicit thesis statement and logical support? Or are you at your best in more open and personal forms?

Small-group or whole-class task: Share the results of the individual tasks. Is there a wide range of preferences in your class? If so, how do you account for this variance? If not, how do you account for the narrow range?

CONCEPT 2 Good writers address problems rather than topics.

In the previous section, we explained how the rules for good writing vary along a continuum from closed to open forms. In this section, we return to the close connection between writing and critical thinking. From your previous schooling, you are probably familiar with the term **thesis statement**, which is the main point a writer wants to make in an essay. However, you may not have thought much about the *question* that lies behind the thesis, which is the problem or issue that the writer is wrestling with. Behind every thesis statement is an explicit or implied **thesis question**, which is the problem or issue to which the thesis responds. An essay's thesis statement is actually the writer's proposed answer to this question, and it is this question that has propelled the writer's thinking.

Thus, the problem that matters to engineer David Rockwood is whether wind power can be a viable alternative energy source. Rockwood writes to make his answer ("No!") persuasive to readers. Thomas Merton's question is more complex and subtle, one that leads him to use open-form narrative strategies. His question seems to be: What is the effect of a consumer economy on our understanding of meaning and value? He wants to raise readers' awareness of a problem with corporate capitalism (where corporations want to sell you even the rain), which alienates us from nature and from our deepest selves.

This focus on a writer's motivating problem or question differs somewhat from the common view that writers first choose a topic and then narrow it down. Of course, writers have broad areas of interest (which we might call topics), but what they are seeking isn't the topic itself but a cluster of problems or questions within the topic. Instead of "narrowing a topic," they seek a problem that grips their curiosity and gets them thinking.

Shared Problems Unite Writers and Readers

For college professors, "a good, interesting question" is at the heart of good writing. Professors want students to become gripped by problems because they themselves are gripped by problems. For example, at a workshop for new faculty members, we asked participants to write a brief description of the question or problem that motivated their Ph.D. dissertation or a recent conference paper or article. Here is how a biochemistry professor responded:

> During periods of starvation, the human body makes physiological adaptations to preserve essential protein mass. Unfortunately, these adaptations don't work well during long-term starvation. After the body depletes its carbohydrate storage, it must shift to depleting protein in order to produce glucose. Eventually, this loss of functional protein leads to metabolic dysfunction and death. Interestingly, several animal species are capable of surviving for extensive periods without food and water while conserving protein and maintaining glucose levels. How do the bodies of these animals accomplish this feat? I wanted to investigate the metabolic functioning of these animals, which might lead to insights into the human situation.

As you progress through your college career, you will find yourself increasingly engaged with the kinds of questions that motivate your professors. All around college campuses you'll find clusters of professors and students asking questions about all manner of problems ranging from puzzles in the reproductive cycles of worms and bugs to the use of nanotechnology to fight global warming, from the changing portrayal of race and gender in American films to the impact of digital technology on the dissemination of news. At the heart of all these communities of writers and readers is an interest in common questions and the hope for better or different answers. Writers write because they have something new or surprising or challenging to say in response to a question. Readers read because they share the writer's interest in the problem and want to deepen their understanding.

Where Do Problems Come From?

So where do these problems come from? How does a writer get hooked on a problem? Although this question is complex at a philosophical level, we can offer two relatively simple and helpful answers: Sometimes you encounter a problem that is already "out there" in a conversation already in progress in some human community. Some enduring problems have been sparking conversations that have lasted for thousands of years: Do humans have free will? What constitutes ethical action? What is the origin of the universe? Why do good people have to suffer? Thousands of less sweeping problems are being discussed by human communities all the time. In many of your college courses, you'll be introduced to long-standing problems that you hadn't encountered before and that may hook you and draw you into their spell. In these cases, a problem that is already "out there" initiates your search for a possible answer and invites you to join the conversation.

But sometimes you actually find, pose, or articulate a problem yourself, fresh from your own brain. In this case you start a conversation, rather than join an existing one. (It may turn out later that other people have asked the same question, but you didn't know that at the time.) For example, you find your own problem whenever you see something puzzling in the natural world, note curious or unexplained features in a cultural phenomenon or artifact, or discover conflicts or contradictions within your own way of looking at the world.

In the table below we describe some of the ways that writers can become gripped by a problem that may lead to engaged writing.

TABLE 1.1   How Writers Become Gripped by a Problem

Occasion That Leads to Problem	Your Interior Mental State	Example
	The problem is already "out there." *(You enter a conversation already in progress)*	
You encounter others arguing about a problem, and you don't know where you stand.	• You are equally persuaded by different views or dissatisfied with all the views • Part of you thinks X but another part thinks Y (you feel divided)	I don't know where I stand on the question of whether health care should be rationed. In *To Kill a Mockingbird*, I can't decide whether Atticus Finch is a good father.
You aren't satisfied with a common view of something or you disagree with someone on an issue.	• Your skepticism or intuition pushes against some popular view • You are committed to a view different from someone else's • *Note: You must go beyond simply having an opinion. You aren't gripped by a problem until you have seen the possible strengths of other views and the possible weaknesses of your own.*	My teacher's explanation of the causes for anorexia doesn't seem quite right to me. Shanita says that we should build more nuclear power plants to combat global warming, but I say nuclear power is too dangerous.
Someone gives you a question that you can't yet answer.	• You feel overwhelmed with unknowns • You feel that you can't begin to answer until you do more exploration and research • If you know enough to start proposing hypotheses, you aren't satisfied with any of your approaches	Your boss asks you whether the company should enact the proposed marketing plan. Your history professor asks you, "To what extent does Frederick Jackson Turner's frontier hypothesis reflect a Euro-centric world view?"

(continued)

TABLE 1.1   *continued*

Occasion That Leads to Problem	Your Interior Mental State	Example
	You pose the problem yourself. *(You initiate the conversation)*	
You see something puzzling in a natural or cultural phenomenon.	• Something deviates from what you would expect or is otherwise unexplainable • You begin testing possible solutions or answers. (Often you want to talk to someone—to start a conversation about the problem)	Why is this fungus appearing on some of these tomatoes but not on the others? Why is Twitter more popular among middle-aged adults than teenagers?
You see something unexpected, puzzling, or unexplained in a poem, painting, or other human artifact.	• You can't see why the artist/maker did something in such a way • You wonder why this particular artifact is different from other artifacts that you thought would be similar	Why does Merton call rain "meaningless"? If Hamlet really loves Ophelia, then why does he treat her like a whore in the nunnery scene?
You articulate something inconsistent or contradictory in your own view of the world.	• You feel unsettled by your own inconsistent views or values • You probe more deeply into your own identity and place in the world	I agree with Merton's argument against consumerism, but I really want a large plasma TV. Is consumerism really bad? Am I a materialist?

In each of these cases, the problem starts to spark critical thinking. As we'll explain in more detail in Chapter 2, you are starting to "wallow in complexity."

FOR WRITING AND DISCUSSION

Finding a Problem

This classroom exercise, based on the image in Figure 1.2, will give you the experience of posing a problem for yourself and then participating in a conversation initiated by shared questions from the class. It is designed to help you think about your own thinking as you ask questions and formulate problems that you might want to explore. Figure 1.2 is a photograph of a sculpture, called *The Foundling*, by Australian artist Patricia Piccinini. (The photograph is taken in an art museum; note the spectator walking by in the background.) The sculpture, which is made of silicone, fiberglass, human hair, leather, plywood, and clothing, is part of a larger Piccinini exhibit of similar life-size figures. Imagine that you came across this sculpture while visiting a museum. Consider the sculpture's title as well as its appearance and its effect on viewers.

Individual task: Working individually, spend several minutes writing down one or more thought-provoking questions that emerge from your looking

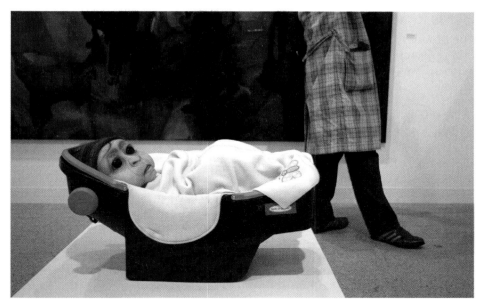

FIGURE 1.2 The Foundling

at the photo of the front view of this sculpture. By "thought-provoking," we mean questions that don't have simple "right answers" but that invite "possible answers" supported by different lines of reasoning, speculation, and argument.

Task for group or whole class discussion: Working in small groups or as a whole class, share your individual questions. Then speculate about possible answers to several of them. The best questions will lead to alternative responses—the feeling of a genuine conversation with different points of view. Each individual should now write down new questions that emerge from the conversation.

Individual reflection: To what extent did the activities provoked by this exercise help you think about where questions come from? How did the questions that you initially posed for yourself evolve as you participated in a conversation about the sculpture? Identify one question that now particularly intrigues you and explain why you find it a good question. (If you would like to find out more about Patricia Piccinini, a quick Web search will yield many results, including statements of her philosophy of art and photographs of her other works.)

CONCEPT 3   Good writers think rhetorically about purpose, audience, and genre.

So far, we have used the term "rhetoric"—as in "A Rhetoric for Writers" (the title of Part 1 of this text) or "thinking rhetorically"—without defining it. Now is the time for us to explain what we mean by *rhetoric*.

What Is Rhetoric?

At the broadest level, **rhetoric** is the study of how human beings use language and other symbols to influence the attitudes, beliefs, and actions of others. One prominent twentieth-century rhetorician, Kenneth Burke, calls rhetoric "a symbolic means of inducing cooperation in beings that by nature respond to symbols." To understand what Burke means by "symbols," consider the difference in flirting behavior between peacocks and humans. When male peacocks flirt, they spread their fantastic tail feathers, do mating dances, and screech weirdly to attract females, but the whole process is governed by instinct. Peacocks don't have to choose among different symbolic actions such as buying an Armani tail versus buying a knockoff from Wal-Mart or driving to the mating grounds in the right car. Unlike a peacock, however, a flirting human must make symbolic choices, all of which have meaning. Consider the different flirting messages humans send to each other by their choice of clothes, their method of transportation, their choice of major, their favorite music. Even word choices (for example, academic jargon words versus street slang) or texting behavior give further hints of a person's identity, values, and social groups. Rhetoricians study, among other things, how these symbols arise within a given culture and how they influence others.

In a narrower sense, rhetoric is the art of making messages persuasive. Perhaps the most famous definition of rhetoric comes from the Greek philosopher Aristotle, who defined rhetoric as "the ability to see, in any particular case, all the available means of persuasion." An effective speaker's task, in Aristotle's view, is to persuade listeners to accept the speaker's views on a question of action or belief. But to do so, the speaker must first understand all the arguments on all sides of the question ("all the available means of persuasion"). If we imagine the interaction of several speakers, each proposing different answers to a question, and if we imagine all the speakers listening to each other respectfully and open-mindedly, we can see how productive human conversation could emerge. The study of rhetoric can therefore help people write, speak, read, and listen more effectively.

At an operational level, writers can be said to "think rhetorically" whenever they are consciously aware of writing to an audience for a purpose within a genre. (A *genre*, to be explained in more detail shortly, is a recurring type of writing with distinguishing features and conventions such as a letter to the editor, a scholarly article, a business memo, or a blog.) To think rhetorically, writers consider questions like these:

- *Purpose:* What am I trying to accomplish in this paper? What do I want my readers to know, believe, see, or do?
- *Audience:* Who are my intended readers, and what are their values and assumptions? What do they already know or believe about my subject? How much do they care about it?
- *Genre:* What kind of document am I writing? What are its requirements for structure, style, and document design?

Let's look more closely at each of these components of a writer's rhetorical context.

How Writers Think about Purpose

In this section, we want to help you think more productively about your purpose for writing, which can be examined from several different perspectives: your rhetorical aim, the motivating occasion that gets you going, and your desire to change your reader's view. All three perspectives will help you make your awareness of purpose work for you and increase your savvy as a writer. Let's look at each in turn.

Purpose as Rhetorical Aim   One powerful way to think about purpose is through the general concept of "rhetorical aim." In this text, we identify six different rhetorical aims of writing: to express, to explore, to inform, to analyze and synthesize, to persuade, and to reflect. Thinking of each piece of writing in terms of one or more of these rhetorical aims can help you understand typical ways that your essay can be structured and developed and can help you clarify your relationship with your audience. The writing projects in Part 2 of this text are based on these rhetorical aims. Table 1.2 gives you an overview of each of the six rhetorical

TABLE 1.2 **Purpose as Rhetorical Aim**			
Rhetorical Aim	**Focus of Writing**	**Relationship to Audience**	**Forms and Genres**
Express or share (Chapter 6) May also include an artistic aim (Chapter 11)	Your own life, personal experiences, reflections	You share aspects of your life; you invite readers to walk in your shoes, to experience your insights	**Form:** Has many open-form features **Sample genres:** journal, blog, personal Web site, or online profile; personal essays or literacy narratives, often with artistic features
Explore or inquire	A significant subject-matter problem that puzzles you	You take readers on your own intellectual journey by showing your inquiry process (raising questions, seeking evidence, considering alternative views)	**Form:** Follows open form in being narrative based; is thesis seeking rather than thesis supporting **Sample genres:** freewriting; research logs; articles and books focused on process of discovery
Inform or explain (Chapter 7)	Factual knowledge addressing a reader's need or curiosity	You provide knowledge that your readers need or want, or you arouse curiosity and provide new, surprising information. You expect readers to trust your authority	**Form:** Usually has a closed-form structure **Sample genres:** encyclopedia articles; instruction booklets; sales reports; technical reports; informative magazine articles; informative Web sites

(continued)

TABLE 1.2 *continued*

Rhetorical Aim	Focus of Writing	Relationship to Audience	Forms and Genres
Analyze, synthesize, or interpret (Chapter 8)	Complex subject matter that you can break down into parts and put together in new ways for greater understanding	Using critical thinking and possibly research, you challenge readers with a new way of understanding your subject. Skeptical readers expect you to support your thesis with good particulars.	**Form:** Typically has a closed-form structure **Sample genres:** scholarly articles; experimental reports; many kinds of college research papers; public affairs magazine articles; many kinds of blogs
Persuade	Subject-matter questions that have multiple controversial answers	You try to convince readers, who may not share your values and beliefs, to accept your stance on an issue by providing good reasons and evidence and attending to alternative views.	**Form:** Usually closed form, but may employ many open-form features for persuasive effect **Sample genres:** letters to the editor; op-ed pieces; advocacy pieces in public affairs magazines; advocacy Web sites; researched academic arguments
Reflect	Subject matter closely connected to your interests and experience; often involves self-evaluation of an experience	Writing for yourself as well as for a reader, you seek to find personal meaning and value in an experience or course of study. You assume a sympathetic and interested reader.	**Form:** Anywhere on the closed-to-open-form continuum **Sample genres:** memoirs, workplace self-evaluations; introductory letter for a portfolio; personal essays looking back on an experience

aims and sketches out how the subject matter differs from aim to aim, how the writer's task and relationship to readers differ according to aim, and how a chosen aim affects the writing's genre and its position on the spectrum from open to closed forms.

Purpose as a Response to a Motivating Occasion Another important way to think about purpose is to think about each piece of writing as a response to a particular motivating occasion. Almost all writing is compelled by some sort of motivating occasion or exigency.* This exigency can be external (someone giving you a task and setting a deadline) or internal (your awareness of a problem stimulating your desire to bring about some change in people's views). Thus, when engineer David Rockwood read a newspaper editorial supporting wind-power projects, his own belief in the impracticality of wind power motivated him to write a letter to

---

*An *exigency* is an urgent or pressing situation requiring immediate attention. Rhetoricians use the term to describe the event or occasion that causes a writer to begin writing.

the editor in rebuttal (see pp. 6–7). But he also knew that he had to write the letter within one or two days or else it stood no chance of being published. His exigency thus included both internal and external factors.

College students' motivations for writing can be equally mixed: In part, you write to meet an assignment deadline; in part, you write to please the teacher and get a good grade. But ideally you also write because you have become engaged with an intellectual problem and want to say something significant about it. Our point here is that your purposes for writing are always more complex than the simple desire to meet an assignment deadline.

Purpose as a Desire to Change Your Reader's View Perhaps the most useful way to think about purpose is to focus on the change you want to bring about in your audience's view of the subject. When you are given a college writing assignment, this view of purpose engages you directly with the intellectual problem specified in the assignment. This view of purpose will be developed further in Concept 5 when we explain the importance of surprise as a measure of what is new or challenging in your essay. For most essays, you can write a one-sentence, nutshell statement about your purpose.

See Chapter 2, Concept 5, for an explanation of surprise in thesis statements.

> My purpose is to give my readers a vivid picture of my difficult struggle with Graves' disease.
>
> My purpose is to explain how Thoreau's view of nature differs in important ways from that of contemporary environmentalists.
>
> My purpose is to persuade the general public that wind-generated electricity is not a practical energy alternative in the Pacific Northwest.

In closed-form academic articles, technical reports, and other business and professional pieces, writers often place explicit purpose statements in their introductions along with the thesis. In most other forms of writing, the writer uses a behind-the-scenes purpose statement to achieve focus and direction but seldom states the purpose explicitly. Writing an explicit purpose statement for a paper is a powerful way to nutshell the kind of change you want to bring about in your reader's view of the subject.

Chapter 10, Skill 10.4, shows you how purpose statements can be included in closed-form introductions.

How Writers Think about Audience

In our discussion of purpose, we have already had a lot to say about audience. What you know about your readers—their familiarity with your subject matter, their reasons for reading, their closeness to you, their values and beliefs—affects most of the choices you make as a writer.

In assessing your audience, you must first determine who that audience is— a single reader (for example, your boss), a select group (a scholarship committee; attendees at an undergraduate research conference), or a general audience. If you imagine a general audience, you will need to make some initial assumptions about their views and values. Doing so creates an "implied audience," giving you a stable rather than a moving target so that you can make decisions about your own essay. Once you have identified your audience, you can use the following strategies for analysis.

Strategies for Analyzing Audience

Questions to Ask about Your Audience	Reasons for Asking the Question
How busy are my readers?	• Helps you decide on length, document design, and open versus closed features • In workplace writing, busy readers often require closed-form prose with headings that allow for skimming
What are my readers' motives for reading?	• If the reader has requested the document, you need only a short introduction • In most cases, your opening must hook your reader's interest
What is my relationship with my readers?	• Helps you decide on a formal or informal style • Helps you select tone—polite and serious or loose and slangy
What do my readers already know about my topic? Do my readers have more or less expertise than I have, or about the same expertise?	• Helps you determine what will be old/familiar information for your audience versus new/unfamiliar information • Helps you decide how much background and context to include • Helps you decide to use or avoid in-group jargon and specialized knowledge
How interested are my readers in my topic? Do my readers already care about it?	• Helps you decide how to write the introduction • Helps you determine how to make the problem you address interesting and significant to your reader
What are my readers' attitudes toward my thesis? Do my readers share my beliefs and values?	• Helps you make numerous decisions about tone, structure, reference to alternative views, and use of evidence • Helps you decide on the voice and persona you want to project

To appreciate the importance of audience, consider how a change in audience can affect the content of a piece. Suppose you want voters to approve a bond issue to build a new baseball stadium. If most voters are baseball fans, you can appeal to their love of the game, the pleasure of a new facility, and so forth. But non-baseball fans won't be moved by these arguments. To reach them, you must tie the new stadium to their values. You can argue that it will bring new tax revenues, clean up a run-down area, revitalize local businesses, or stimulate tourism.

Your purpose remains the same—to persuade taxpayers to fund the stadium—but the content of your argument changes if your audience changes.

In college, you often seem to be writing for an audience of one—your instructor. However, most instructors try to read as a representative of a broader audience. To help college writers imagine these readers, many instructors try to design writing assignments that provide a fuller sense of audience. They may ask you to write for the readers of a particular magazine or journal, or they may create case assignments with built-in audiences (for example, "You are an accountant in the firm of Numbers and Fudge; one day you receive a letter from ..."). If your instructor does not specify an audience, you can generally assume the audience to be what we like to call "the generic academic audience"—student peers who have approximately the same level of knowledge and expertise in the field as you do, who are engaged by the question you address, and who want to read your writing and be surprised in some way.

How Writers Think about Genre

The term *genre* refers to categories of writing that follow certain conventions of style, structure, approach to subject matter, and document design. Table 1.3 shows different kinds of genres.

The concept of genre creates strong reader expectations and places specific demands on writers. How you write any given letter, report, or article is influenced by the structure and style of hundreds of previous letters, reports, or articles written in the same genre. If you wanted to write for *Reader's Digest*, for example, you would have to use the conventions that appeal to its older, conservative readers: simple language, subjects with strong human interest, heavy reliance on anecdotal evidence in arguments, an upbeat and optimistic perspective, and an approach that reinforces the conservative *ethos* of individualism, self-discipline, and family.

TABLE 1.3   Examples of Genres

Personal Writing	Academic Writing	Popular Culture	Public Affairs, Civic Writing	Professional Writing	Literature
Letter	Scholarly article	Articles for magazines such as *Seventeen, Ebony*, or *Vibe*	Letter to the editor	Cover letter for a job application	Short story
Diary/journal	Research paper	Advertisements	Newspaper editorial	Résumé	Novel
Memoir	Scientific report	Hip-hop lyrics	Op-ed piece	Business memo	Graphic novel
Blog	Abstract or summary	Fan Web sites	Advocacy Web site	Legal brief	Play
Text message	Book review	Bumper stickers	Political blog	Brochure	Sonnet
E-mail	Essay exam	Reviews of books, films, plays, music	Magazine article on civic issue	Technical manual	Epic poem
Facebook profile	Annotated bibliography			Instruction booklet	Literary podcast
Personal essay	Textual analysis			Proposal	
Literacy narrative				Report	
				Press release	

If you wanted to write for *Seventeen* or *Rolling Stone*, however, you would need to use quite different conventions.

To illustrate the relationship of a writer to a genre, we sometimes draw an analogy with clothing. Although most people have a variety of different types of clothing in their wardrobes, the genre of activity for which they are dressing (Saturday night movie date, job interview, wedding) severely constrains their choice and expression of individuality. A man dressing for a job interview might express his personality through choice of tie or quality and style of business suit; he probably wouldn't express it by wearing a Hawaiian shirt and sandals. Even when people deviate from a convention, they tend to do so in a conventional way. For example, teenagers who do not want to follow the genre of "teenager admired by adults" form their own genre of purple hair and pierced body parts. The concept of genre raises intriguing and sometimes unsettling questions about the relationship of the unique self to a social convention or tradition.

These same kinds of questions and constraints perplex writers. For example, academic writers usually follow the genre of the closed-form scholarly article. This highly functional form achieves maximum clarity for readers by orienting them quickly to the article's purpose, content, and structure. Readers expect this format, and writers have the greatest chance of being published if they meet these expectations. In some disciplines, however, scholars are beginning to publish more experimental, open-form articles. They may slowly alter the conventions of the scholarly article, just as fashion designers alter styles of dress.

FOR WRITING AND

Thinking about Purpose, Audience, and Genre

1. This exercise, which is based on Table 1.2 on page 17, will help you appreciate how rhetorical aim connects to choices about subject matter as well as to audience and genre. As a class, choose one of the following topic areas or another provided by your instructor. Then imagine six different writing situations in which a hypothetical writer would compose an essay about the selected topic. Let each situation call for a different aim. How might a person write about the selected topic with an expressive aim? An exploratory aim? An informative aim? An analytic aim? A persuasive aim? A reflective aim? How would each essay surprise its readers?

automobiles	animals	hospices or nursing homes
homelessness	music	dating or marriage
advertising	energy crisis	sports injuries

Working on your own or in small groups, create six realistic scenarios, each of which calls for prose in a different category of aim. Then share your results as a whole class. Here are two examples based on the topic "hospices."

Expressive Aim   Working one summer as a volunteer in a hospice for dying cancer patients, you befriend a woman whose attitude toward death changes your life. You write an autobiographical essay about your experiences with this remarkable woman.

Analytic Aim   You are a hospice nurse working in a home care setting. You and your colleagues note that sometimes family members cannot adjust psychologically to the burden of living with a dying person. You decide to investigate this phenomenon. You interview "reluctant" family members in an attempt to understand the causes of their psychological discomfort so that you can provide better counseling services as a possible solution. You write a paper for a professional audience analyzing the results of your interviews.

2. Working in small groups or as a whole class, develop a list of the conventions for one or more of the following genres:
   • Cell phone text messages as typically created by teenagers
   • A Facebook profile
   • The home page for a college or university Web site

Chapter Summary

This chapter has introduced you to three transferable rhetorical concepts aimed at deepening your thinking about "good writing" in college.

* ***Concept 1: Good writing can vary from closed to open forms.*** Closed-form prose has an explicit thesis statement, topic sentences, unified and coherent paragraphs, and good transitions. At the other end of the continuum is open-form prose, which often uses narrative techniques such as storytelling, evocative language, surprising juxtapositions, and other features that violate the conventions of closed-form prose. Closed-form prose is "good" only if its ideas bring something new, provocative, or challenging to the reader.

* ***Concept 2: Good writers address problems rather than topics.*** Writers write because they have something surprising or challenging to say in response to a question that matters to the reader. Writers can pose their own problematic questions about a subject or become engaged in controversies or issues that are already "out there."

* ***Concept 3: Good writers think rhetorically about purpose, audience, and genre.*** In thinking about purpose, writers consider their rhetorical aim, their motivating occasion, or their desire to bring about change in their readers' view. They also think about their audience, analyzing how much their readers already know about (and care about) their subject and assessing their readers' values, beliefs, and assumptions. Writers attend to genre by thinking about the conventions of content, structure, and style associated with the kind of document they are writing.

Two Messages for Different Purposes, Audiences, and Genres

BRIEF WRITING PROJECT I

The purpose of this brief write-to-learn assignment is to let you experience first-hand how rhetorical context influences a writer's choices. The whole assignment, which has three parts, should not be more than two double-spaced pages long.

1. ***A Text Message to a Friend.*** Write a text message to a friend using the abbreviations, capitalization, and punctuation style typically used for text messages. Explain that you are going to miss an upcoming social event (movie, football game, dance, trip to the local diner or coffee house) because you are feeling sick. Then ask your friend to text you during the event to schedule another get-together. (Make up details as you need them.)

2. ***An E-Mail Message to a Professor.*** Compose an e-mail message to your professor explaining that you cannot meet an assignment deadline because you are sick and asking for an extension. (Use the same sickness details from Part 1.) Create a subject line appropriate for this new context.

3. ***Reflection on the Two Messages.*** Using items 1 and 2 as illustrative examples, explain to someone who has not read Chapter 1 of this text why a difference in your rhetorical context caused you to make different choices in these two messages. In your explanation, use the terms "purpose," "audience," and "genre." Your goal is to teach your audience the meanings of these terms.

BRIEF WRITING PROJECT 2

A Letter to Your Professor about What Was New in Chapter I

Write a letter to your instructor in which you reflect on the extent to which the ideas in this opening chapter are new to you or have caused you to think about writing in new or different ways. Structure your letter in the following way:

- Describe for your instructor a piece of writing you did in high school or elsewhere that represents your most engaged work or about which you are most proud. Explain the context of this piece of writing (class or professional setting, nature of the assignment, length, and so forth) and provide a brief summary of your intentions and argument. Explain why this piece of writing particularly engaged you.

- Then analyze this piece of writing and your own thinking processes in producing it in light of the following three questions from this chapter:
  - Where would you place this piece of writing on the continuum from closed to open forms? Why?
  - To what extent was this piece of writing rooted in a "good, interesting question"? Explain.
  - To what extent did you think about purpose, audience, and genre as you wrote this piece?

- Finally, explain to your instructor the extent to which this chapter caused you to think about writing in any new or different ways.

 For additional help with writing, reading, and research, go to **www.mycomplab.com.**

THINKING RHETORICALLY ABOUT YOUR SUBJECT MATTER

2

"In management, people don't merely 'write papers,' they solve problems," said [business professor A. Kimbrough Sherman]. . . . He explained that he wanted to construct situations where students would have to **"wallow in complexity"** and work their way out, as managers must.

—A. Kimbrough Sherman, Management Professor, Quoted by
Barbara E. Walvoord and Lucille P. McCarthy

In the previous chapter we explained how the rules for good writing vary along a continuum from closed to open forms, how writers become engaged with subject-matter questions, and how they think rhetorically about their purpose, audience, and genre. In this chapter we show how writers think rhetorically about their "subject matter"—that is, how they think about what is unknown, puzzling, or controversial in their subject matter and about how their view of the subject might be different from their audience's.

Because this chapter concerns academic writing, we focus on closed-form prose—the kind of thesis-governed writing most often required in college courses and often required in civic and professional life. As we will show, thesis-governed writing requires a behind-the-scenes ability to think rigorously about a problem and then to make a claim* based on your own solution to the problem. This claim should bring something new, interesting, useful, or challenging to readers.

In this chapter, you will learn four concepts of significant explanatory power:

- **CONCEPT 4**   To determine their thesis, writers must often "wallow in complexity."
- **CONCEPT 5**   A strong thesis surprises readers with something new or challenging.
- **CONCEPT 6**   In closed-form prose, a typical introduction starts with the problem, not the thesis.
- **CONCEPT 7**   Thesis statements in closed-form prose are supported hierarchically with points and particulars.

*In this text we use the words *claim* and *thesis statement* interchangeably. In courses across the curriculum, instructors typically use one or the other of these terms. Other synonyms for *thesis statement* include *proposition, main point,* or *thesis sentence.*

CONCEPT 4 **To determine their thesis, writers must often "wallow in complexity."**

As we explained in the previous chapter, the starting point of academic writing is a "good, interesting question." At the outset, we should say that these questions may lead you toward new and unfamiliar ways of thinking. Beginning college students typically value questions that have right answers. Students ask their professors questions because they are puzzled by confusing parts of a textbook, a lecture, or an assigned reading. They hope their professors will explain the confusing material clearly. Their purpose in asking these questions is to eliminate misunderstandings, not to open up controversy and debate. Although basic comprehension questions are important, they are not the kinds of inquiry questions that lead to strong college-level writing and thinking.

Instead, the kinds of questions that stimulate the writing most valued in college are open-ended questions that focus on unknowns or uncertainties (what educational researcher Ken Bain calls "beautiful problems") rather than factual questions that have single, correct answers.* Good open-ended questions invite multiple points of view or alternative hypotheses; they stimulate critical thinking and research. We don't mean to make this focus on problems sound scary. Indeed, humans pose and solve problems all the time and often take great pleasure in doing so. Psychologists who study critical and creative thinking see problem solving as a productive and positive activity. According to one psychologist, "Critical thinkers are actively engaged with life. . . . They appreciate creativity, they are innovators, and they exude a sense that life is full of possibilities."** Our way of thinking about problems has been motivated by the South American educator Paulo Freire, who wanted his students (often poor, illiterate villagers) to become *problematizers* instead of memorizers. Freire opposed what he called "the banking method" of education, in which students deposit knowledge in their memory banks and then make withdrawals during exams. The banking method, Freire believed, left third world villagers passive and helpless to improve their situations in life. Using the banking method, students being taught to read and write might learn the word *water* through drill-and-skill workbook sentences such as, "The water is in the well." With Freire's problematizing method, students might learn the word *water* by asking, "Why is the water dirty and who is responsible?" Freire believed that good questions have stakes and that answering them can make a difference in the world.

---

*Cognitive psychologists call these beautiful problems "ill-structured." An ill-structured problem has competing solutions, requiring the thinker to argue for the best solution in the absence of full and complete data or in the presence of stakeholders with different backgrounds, assumptions, beliefs, and values. In contrast, a "well-structured" problem eventually yields a correct answer. Math problems that can be solved by applying the right formulae and processes are well structured. That's why you can have the correct answers in the back of the book.

**Academic writers regularly document their sources. Two standard methods for documenting sources in student papers and in many professional scholarly articles are the MLA and APA citation systems explained in Chapter 13. In this text we have cited our sources in an "Acknowledgments" section. To find our source for this quotation (or the quotations from Kilcup or Kimbrough in the epigraphs or the "beautiful problem" quotation from Ken Bain), see the Acknowledgments at the end of the text.

Learning to Wallow in Complexity

This focus on important problems explains why college professors want students to go beyond simply understanding course concepts as taught in textbooks and lectures. Such comprehension is important, but it is only a starting point. As management professor A. Kimbrough Sherman explains in the epigraph to this chapter, college instructors expect students to wrestle with problems by applying the concepts, data, and thought processes they learn in a course to new situations. As Sherman puts it, students must learn to "wallow in complexity" and work their way out. To put it another way, college professors want students to "earn" their thesis. (Earning a thesis is very different from simply stating your opinion, which might not be deeply examined at all.) Because college professors value this kind of complex thinking, they often phrase essay exam questions or writing assignments as open-ended problems that can be answered in more than one way. They are looking not for the right answer, but for well-supported arguments that acknowledge alternative views. A C paper and an A paper may have the same "answer" (identical thesis statements), but the C writer may have waded only ankle deep into the mud of complexity, whereas the A writer wallowed in it and worked a way out.

What skills are required for successful wallowing? Specialists in critical thinking have identified the following:

CRITICAL THINKING SKILLS NEEDED FOR "WALLOWING IN COMPLEXITY"

- The ability to pose problematic questions
- The ability to analyze a problem in all its dimensions—to define its key terms, determine its causes, understand its history, appreciate its human dimension and its connection to one's own personal experience, and appreciate what makes it problematic or complex
- The ability (and determination) to find, gather, and interpret facts, data, and other information relevant to the problem (often involving library, Internet, or field research)
- The ability to imagine alternative solutions to the problem, to see different ways in which the question might be answered and different perspectives for viewing it
- The ability to analyze competing approaches and answers, to construct arguments for and against alternatives, and to choose the best solution in light of values, objectives, and other criteria that you determine and articulate
- The ability to write an effective argument justifying your choice while acknowledging counterarguments

We discuss and develop these skills throughout this text.

Seeing Each Academic Discipline as a Field of Inquiry and Argument

In addition to these general thinking abilities, critical thinking requires what psychologists call "domain-specific" skills. Each academic discipline has its own characteristic ways of approaching knowledge and its own specialized habits of mind. The questions asked by psychologists differ from those asked by historians or anthropologists; the evidence and assumptions used to support arguments in literary analysis differ from those in philosophy or sociology. As illustrations, here are some examples of how different disciplines might pose different questions about hip-hop:

- *Psychology:* To what extent do hip-hop lyrics increase misogynistic or homophobic attitudes in male listeners?
- *History:* What was the role of urban housing projects in the early development of hip-hop?
- *Sociology:* How does the level of an individual's appreciation for rap music vary by ethnicity, class, age, geographic region, and gender?
- *Rhetoric/Composition:* What images of urban life do the lyrics of rap songs portray?
- *Marketing and Management:* How did the white media turn a black, urban phenomenon into corporate profits?
- *Women's Studies:* What influence does hip-hop music have on the self-image of African-American women?
- *Global Studies:* How are other countries adapting hip-hop to their cultures?

As these questions suggest, when you study a new discipline, you must learn not only the knowledge that scholars in that discipline have acquired over the years, but also the processes they used to discover that knowledge. It is useful to think of each academic discipline as a network of conversations in which participants exchange information, respond to each other's questions, and express agreement and disagreement. As each discipline evolves and changes, its central questions evolve also, creating a fascinating, dynamic conversation that defines the discipline. Table 2.1 provides examples of questions that scholars have debated over the years as well as questions they are addressing today.

TABLE 2.1	Scholarly Questions in Different Disciplines	
Field	Examples of Current Cutting-Edge Questions	Examples of Historical Controversies
Anatomy	What is the effect of a pregnant rat's alcohol ingestion on the development of fetal eye tissue?	In 1628, William Harvey produced a treatise arguing that the heart, through repeated contractions, causes blood to circulate through the body. His views were attacked by followers of the Greek physician Galen.
Literature	To what extent does the structure of a work of literature, for example, Conrad's *Heart of Darkness*, reflect the class and gender bias of the author?	In the 1920s, a group of New Critics argued that the interpretation of a work of literature should be based on close examination of the work's imagery and form and that the intentions of the writer and the biases of the reader were not important. These views held sway in U.S. universities until the late 1960s, when they came increasingly under attack by deconstructionists and other postmoderns, who claimed that author intentions and reader's bias were important parts of the work's meaning.

TABLE 2.1 *continued*		
Field	**Examples of Current Cutting-Edge Questions**	**Examples of Historical Controversies**
Rhetoric/ Composition	How does hypertext structure and increased attention to visual images in Web-based writing affect the composing processes of writers?	Prior to the 1970s, college writing courses in the United States were typically organized around the rhetorical modes (description, narration, exemplification, comparison and contrast, and so forth). This approach was criticized by the expressivist school associated with the British composition researcher James Britton. Since the 1980s, composition scholars have proposed various alternative strategies for designing and sequencing assignments.
Psychology	What are the underlying causes of gender identification? To what extent are differences between male and female behavior explainable by nature (genetics, body chemistry) versus nurture (social learning)?	In the early 1900s under the influence of Sigmund Freud, psychoanalytic psychologists began explaining human behavior in terms of unconscious drives and mental processes that stemmed from repressed childhood experiences. Later, psychoanalysts were opposed by behaviorists, who rejected the notion of the unconscious and explained behavior as responses to environmental stimuli.

Using Exploratory Writing to Help You Wallow in Complexity

One of the important discoveries of research in rhetoric and composition is the extent to which experienced writers use writing to generate and discover ideas. Not all writing, in other words, is initially intended as a final product for readers. The very act of writing—often without concern for audience, structure, or correctness—can stimulate the mind to produce ideas. Moreover, when you write down your thoughts, you'll have a record of your thinking that you can draw on later. In Chapter 9 we explain this phenomenon more fully, showing you how to take full advantage of the writing process for invention of ideas and revision for readers. In this section we describe five strategies of exploratory writing and talking: freewriting; focused freewriting; idea mapping; dialectic talk in person, in class discussions, or in electronic discussion boards; and playing the believing and doubting game.

Freewriting   *Freewriting*, also sometimes called *nonstop writing* or *silent, sustained writing*, asks you to record your thinking directly. To freewrite, put pen to paper (or sit at your computer screen, perhaps turning *off* the monitor so that you can't see what you are writing) and write rapidly, *nonstop*, for ten to fifteen minutes at a stretch. Don't worry about grammar, spelling, organization, transitions, or other features of edited writing. The object is to think of as many ideas as possible. Some freewriting looks like stream of consciousness. Some is more organized and focused, although it lacks the logical connections and development that would make it suitable for an audience of strangers.

Many freewriters find that their initial reservoir of ideas runs out in three to five minutes. If this happens, force yourself to keep your fingers moving. If you can't think of anything to say, write, "Relax" over and over (or "This is stupid" or "I'm stuck") until new ideas emerge.

What do you write about? The answer varies according to your situation. Often you will freewrite in response to a question or problem posed by your instructor. Sometimes you will pose your own questions and use freewriting to explore possible answers or simply generate ideas.

The following freewrite, by student writer James Gardiner, formed the starting point for his later exploration of issues connected to online social networks such as MySpace.com and Facebook.com. It was written in response to the prompt "What puzzles you about the new digital age?" We will return to James's story occasionally throughout this text. You can read his final paper in Chapter 13, pages 340–348, where he argues that online social networks can have unexpected detrimental effects on many users. You can also read his earlier exploratory paper, which narrates the evolution of his thinking as he explored the popularity of MySpace and Facebook.

JAMES GARDINER'S INITIAL FREEWRITE

Hmm, what puzzles me about the new digital age? Let's see, let's see, OK I'm puzzled by what life used to be like before there was so much technology. I'm amazed by the growing role that technology has on the lives of people my age. It seems that my generation is spending an increasing amount of time surfing the net, talking on cell phones, listening to MP3 players, playing video games, and watching digital television. I wonder what type of effect these new technologies will have on our society as a whole and if the positive aspects that they bring into the lives of their users outweigh the negative aspects. Are kids happier now that they have all this technology? Hmm. What is the effect of text-messaging rather than talking directly to people? Also what about online social networks like Myspace and Facebook? A lot of my friends have a profile on these sites. I've never joined one of these networks or created a profile. What is my reason for avoiding them? Think. Think. OK, for one thing, I have seen how much time people can spend on these sites and I already feel that I spend enough time checking emails and voicemails. Here's another thing—I am a little hesitant to display personal information about myself on a website that can be viewed by anyone in the world. I feel I am a generally private person and there is something about posting personal details of my life in cyberspace that makes me a little uneasy. As these online social networks increase in popularity and membership, I am puzzled by how my generation will be affected by them. Although people use the sites to communicate with one another, they are usually (physically) alone at their computer. I wonder how this new type of online communication will affect other forms of interpersonal communication skills in the "real world." I also question whether young people should be encouraged to limit their time on these networks and what specifically they should use these sites for. [out of time]

Note how this freewrite rambles, moving associatively from one topic or question to the next. Freewrites often have this kind of loose, associative structure. The value of such freewrites is that they help writers discover areas of interest or rudimentary beginnings of ideas. When you read back over one of your freewrites, try to find places that seem worth pursuing. Freewriters call these places "hot spots," "centers of interest," "centers of gravity," or simply "nuggets" or "seeds." Because we believe this technique is of great value to writers, we suggest that you use it to generate ideas for class discussions and essays.

Focused Freewriting Freewriting, as we have just described it, can be quick and associational, like brainstorming aloud on paper. Focused freewriting, in contrast, is less associational and aimed more at developing a line of thought. You wrestle with a specific problem or question, trying to think and write your way into its complexity and multiple points of view. Because the writing is still informal, with the emphasis on your ideas and not on making your writing grammatically or stylistically polished, you don't have to worry about spelling, punctuation, grammar, or organizational structure. Your purpose is to deepen and extend your thinking on the problem. Some instructors will create prompts or give you specific questions to ponder, and they may call this kind of exploratory writing "focused freewriting," "learning log responses," "writer's notebook entries," or "thinking pieces."

Examples of focused freewriting can be found in the learning log entries on pp. 200–206 in Chapter 8.

Idea Mapping Another good technique for exploring ideas is *idea mapping*, a more visual method than freewriting. To make an idea map, draw a circle in the center of a page and write down your broad topic area (or a triggering question or your thesis) inside the circle. Then record your ideas on branches and subbranches that extend out from the center circle. As long as you pursue one train of thought, keep recording your ideas on subbranches off the main branch. But as soon as that chain of ideas runs dry, go back and start a new branch.

Often your thoughts will jump back and forth between one branch and another. This technique will help you see them as part of an emerging design rather than as strings of unrelated ideas. Additionally, idea mapping establishes at an early stage a sense of hierarchy in your ideas. If you enter an idea on a subbranch, you can see that you are more fully developing a previous idea. If you return to the hub and start a new branch, you can see that you are beginning a new train of thought.

An idea map usually records more ideas than a freewrite, but the ideas are not as fully developed. Writers who practice both techniques report that they can vary the kinds of ideas they generate depending on which technique they choose. Figure 2.1 shows a student's idea map made while he was exploring issues related to the grading system.

Dialectic Talk Another effective way to explore the complexity of a topic is through face-to-face discussions with others, whether in class, over coffee in the student union, or late at night in bull sessions. Not all discussions are productive; some are too superficial and scattered, others too heated. Good ones are *dialectic*—participants with differing views on a topic try to understand each other and resolve their differences by examining contradictions in each person's position. The key to dialectic conversation is careful listening, which is made possible by an openness to each other's views. A dialectic discussion differs from

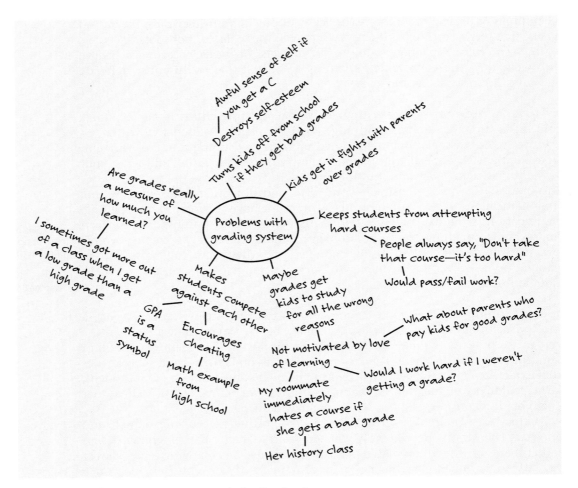

FIGURE 2.1 Idea Map on Problems with the Grading System

a talk show shouting match or a pro/con debate in which proponents of opposing positions, their views set in stone, attempt to win the argument. In a dialectic discussion, participants assume that each position has strengths and weaknesses and that even the strongest position contains inconsistencies, which should be exposed and examined. When dialectic conversation works well, participants scrutinize their own positions more critically and deeply, and often alter their views. True dialectic conversation implies growth and change, not a hardening of positions.

Dialectic discussion can also take place in electronic discussion boards, chat rooms, blogs, or other digital sites for informal exchange of ideas. If your goal is to generate ideas, your stance should be the exact opposite of the flamer's stance. A flamer's intention is to use brute rhetorical power (sometimes mindlessly obscene or mean, sometimes clever and humorous) to humiliate another writer and shut off further discussion. In contrast, the dialectician's goal is to listen respectfully to other ideas, to test new ways of thinking, to modify ideas in the face of other views, and to see an issue as fully and complexly as possible. If you go on to a discussion board to learn and change, rather than to defend your own position and shut off other views, you will be surprised at how powerful this medium can be.

Playing the Believing and Doubting Game   One of the best ways to explore a question is to play what writing theorist Peter Elbow calls the "believing and doubting game." This game helps you appreciate the power of alternative arguments and points of view by urging you to formulate and explore alternative positions. To play the game, you imagine a possible answer to a problematic question and then systematically try first to believe that answer and then to doubt it. The game stimulates your critical thinking, helping you wallow in complexity and resist early closure.

When you play the believing side of this game, you try to become sympathetic to an idea or point of view. You listen carefully to it, opening yourself to the possibility that it is true. You try to appreciate why the idea has force for so many people; you try to accept it by discovering as many reasons as you can for believing it. It is easy to play the believing game with ideas you already believe in, but the game becomes more difficult, sometimes even frightening and dangerous, when you try believing ideas that seem untrue or disturbing.

The doubting game is the opposite of the believing game. It calls for you to be judgmental and critical, to find fault with an idea rather than to accept it. When you doubt a new idea, you try your best to falsify it, to find counterexamples that disprove it, to find flaws in its logic. Again, it is easy to play the doubting game with ideas you don't like, but it, too, can be threatening when you try to doubt ideas that are dear to your heart or central to your own worldview.

Here is how one student played the believing and doubting game with the following assertion from professional writer Paul Theroux that emphasizing sports is harmful to boys.

> Just as high school basketball teaches you how to be a poor loser, the manly attitude towards sports seems to be little more than a recipe for creating bad marriages, social misfits, moral degenerates, sadists, latent rapists and just plain louts. I regard high school sports as a drug far worse than marijuana.

Believing and Doubting Paul Theroux's Negative View of Sports

Believe

1   Although I am a woman I have a hard time believing this because I was a high school basketball player and believe high school sports are *very* important. But here goes. I will try to believe this statement even though I hate it. Let's see. It would seem that I wouldn't have much first-hand experience with how society turns boys

(continued)

into men. I do see though that Theroux is right about some major problems. Through my observations, I've seen many young boys go through humiliating experiences with sports that have left them scarred. For example, a 7-year-old boy, Matt, isn't very athletic and when kids in our neighborhood choose teams, they usually choose girls before they choose Matt. I wonder if he sees himself as a sissy and what this does to him? I have also experienced some first-hand adverse effects of society's methods of turning boys into men. In our family, my dad spent much of his time playing football, basketball, and baseball with my brother. I've loved sports since I was very young so I was eager to play. In order to play with them, I had to play like a boy. Being told you threw or played like a girl was the worst possible insult you could receive. The phrase, "be tough" was something I heard repeatedly while I was growing up. Whenever I got hurt, my dad would say, "Be tough." It didn't matter how badly I was hurt, I always heard the same message. Today, I think, I have a very, very difficult time opening up and letting people get to know me, because for so long I was taught to keep everything inside. Maybe sports does have some bad effects.

Doubt

2   I am glad I get to doubt this too because I have been really mad at all the sports bashing that has been going on in class. I think much of what Theroux says is just a crock. I know that the statement "sports builds character" is a cliché, but I really believe it. It seems to me that the people who lash out at sports clichés are those who never experienced these aspects of athletics and therefore don't understand them. No one can tell me that sports didn't contribute to some of my best and most meaningful friendships and growing experiences. I am convinced that I am a better person because through sports I have had to deal with failure, defeat, frustration, sacrificing individual desires for the benefit of the team, and so on. After my last high school basketball game when after many years of mind games, of hating my coach one minute and the next having deep respect for him, of big games lost on my mistakes, of hours spent alone in the gym, of wondering if the end justifies the means, my coach put his arm around me and told me he was proud. Everything, all the pain, frustration, anxiety, fear, and sacrifice of the past years seemed so worthwhile. You might try to tell me that this story is hackneyed and trite, but I won't listen because it is a part of me, and some thing you will never be able to damage or take away. I think athletes share a special bond. They know what it is like to go through the physical pain of practice time and again. They understand the wide variety of emotions felt (but rarely expressed). They also know what a big role the friendships of teammates and coaches play in an athlete's life.

We admire this writer a great deal—both for the passion with which she defends sports in her doubting section and for the courage of walking in a sports basher's shoes in the believing section. This exercise clearly engaged and stretched her thinking.

Using Exploratory Writing and Talking to Generate Ideas

Background: In our discussion of problem posing in the last chapter (Concept 2: "Good writers address problems rather than topics," pp. 11–15), we explain two main ways that you can become gripped by a problem: (1) You can become engaged by a question or issue that is already "out there"—that is, already being examined or debated in some academic or civic community; or (2) you can pose your own question based on your observation of a puzzling phenomenon or artifact. You might have tried out these strategies in your thinking about the sculpture in Figure 1.2, page 15. Now in Concept 4, we have shown how exploratory writing and talking can help you learn to wallow in complexity. For this exercise we give you for analysis a poem by e. e. cummings and a pair of historical graphs on life expectancy and causes of death in the twentieth century.

next to of course god america i

"next to of course god america i
love you land of the pilgrims' and so forth oh
say can you see by the dawn's early my
country 'tis of centuries come and go

and are no more what of it we should worry
in every language even deafanddumb
thy sons acclaim your glorious name by gorry
by jingo by gee by gosh by gum
why talk of beauty what could be more beautiful than these heroic happy dead
who rushed like lions to the roaring slaughter
they did not stop to think they died instead
then shall the voice of liberty be mute?"

He spoke. And drank rapidly a glass of water

—e. e. cummings

1. ***Generating questions using freewriting and discussion***
   Individual task: Read e. e. cummings' poem three or four times, trying to make as much sense of it as you can. Then freewrite for five minutes in response to this prompt: *What do you find puzzling or thought provoking about this poem?* Let the ideas flow through your fingers. You are trying to identify aspects of the poem that you personally find puzzling or thought provoking while also trying to recall memories of conversations already "out there" about issues raised in the poem. While freewriting, you can also explore how you might try to "answer" some of these questions.
   Small-group or whole-class task: Share some of the questions or ideas raised in your freewrites and see how such "dialectic conversation" inspires more ideas.

(continued)

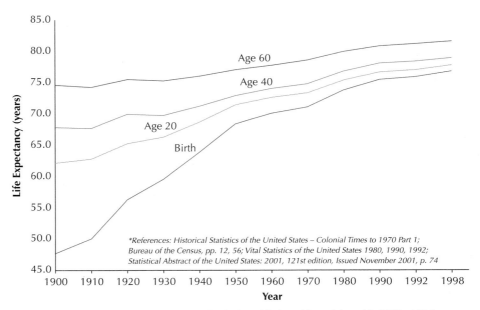

References: Historical Statistics of the United States – Colonial Times to 1970 Part 1; Bureau of the Census, pp. 12, 56; Vital Statistics of the United States 1980, 1990, 1992; Statistical Abstract of the United States: 2001, 121st edition, Issued November 2001, p. 74

FIGURE 2.2 U.S. Life Expectancy at Birth, Age 20, Age 40, and Age 60, 1900–1998

2. ***Generating questions using idea mapping and discussion***
   Repeat the same process, but this time look at the graphs in Figures 2.2 and 2.3, and use idea mapping rather than freewriting. Address the question, *What do you find puzzling or thought provoking in these graphs about changes in life expectancy and causes of death in the twentieth century?* On spokes coming out from the center of the idea map, write some questions or ideas raised by

FIGURE 2.3 U.S. Death Rates for Selected Causes, 1900–2000

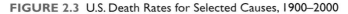
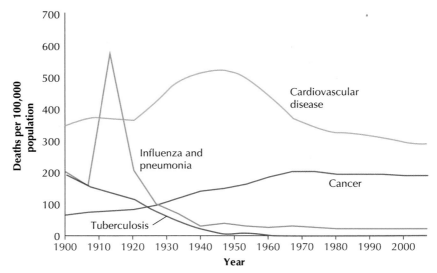

the graphs. Then pursue ideas from each of these spokes so that you begin making a branching map of thoughts. Then share your maps with classmates, using them to spark problem-centered conversations. Finally, discuss which technique works better for you, freewriting or idea mapping. How are they similar or different in the way they stimulate thinking?

3. ***Using freewriting or idea mapping to move from topics to problems***
Another valuable use of exploratory writing and talking is to turn broad topic areas such as "poverty," "music," "globalization," "climate change," "animal rights," or "food" into problematic questions that invite alternative points of view and opportunities for analysis or argument. Using freewriting or idea mapping, start with a broad topic area (either something that interests you or something that your instructor assigns) and explore it in search of questions or problems. Try to recall all the conversations about this topic that you have heard where people expressed confusion or disagreement. Also think of puzzling questions that might emerge from your own personal experiences with the topic area. Your goal is to find a question that interests you and eventually to discover a thesis that gives you an entry into the conversation.

CONCEPT 5   A strong thesis statement surprises readers with something new or challenging.

The strategies for exploring ideas that we offered in the previous section can prepare you to move from posing problems to proposing your own solutions. Your answer to your subject-matter question becomes your **thesis statement**. In this section we show that a good thesis surprises its readers either by bringing something new to the reader or by pushing against other possible ways to answer the writer's question.

Thus a strong thesis usually contains an element of uncertainty, risk, or challenge. A strong thesis implies a naysayer who could disagree with you. According to composition theorist Peter Elbow, a thesis has "got to stick its neck out, not just hedge or wander. [It is] something that can be quarreled with." Elbow's sticking-its-neck-out metaphor is a good one, but we prefer to say that a strong thesis *surprises* the reader with a new, unexpected, different, or challenging view of the writer's topic. By surprise, we intend to connote, first of all, freshness or newness for the reader. Many kinds of closed-form prose don't have a sharply contestable thesis of the sticking-its-neck-out kind highlighted by Elbow. A geology report, for example, may provide readers with desired information about rock strata in an exposed cliff, or a Web page for diabetics may explain how to coordinate meals and insulin injections during a plane trip across time zones. In these cases, the information is surprising because it brings something new and significant to intended readers.

In other kinds of closed-form prose, especially academic or civic prose addressing a problematic question or a disputed issue, surprise requires an argumentative, risky, or contestable thesis. In these cases also, surprise is not inherent in the material but in the intended readers' reception; it comes from the writer's providing an adequate or appropriate response to the readers' presumed question or problem.

In this section, we present two ways of creating a surprising thesis: (1) trying to change your reader's view of your subject; and (2) giving your thesis tension.

Trying to Change Your Reader's View of Your Subject

To change your reader's view of your subject, you must first imagine how the reader would view the subject *before* reading your essay. Then you can articulate how you aim to change that view. A useful exercise is to write out the "before" and "after" views of your imagined readers:

Before reading my essay, my readers think this way about my topic: _____

_____

After reading my essay, my readers will think this different way about my topic:

_____

You can change your reader's view of a subject in several ways.* First, you can enlarge it. Writing that enlarges a view is primarily informational; it provides new ideas and data to add to a reader's store of knowledge about the subject. For example, suppose you are interested in the problem of storing nuclear waste (a highly controversial issue in the United States) and decide to investigate how Japan stores radioactive waste from its nuclear power plants. You could report your findings on this problem in an informative research paper. (Before reading my paper, readers would be uncertain how Japan stores nuclear waste. After reading my paper, my readers would understand the Japanese methods, possibly helping us better understand our options in the United States.)

Second, you can clarify your reader's view of something that was previously fuzzy, tentative, or uncertain. Writing of this kind often explains, analyzes, or interprets. This is the kind of writing you do when analyzing a short story, a painting, an historical document, a set of economic data, or other puzzling phenomena or when speculating on the causes, consequences, purpose, or function of something. Suppose, for example, that you are analyzing the persuasive strategies used in various clothing ads. You are intrigued by a jeans ad that you "read" differently from your classmates. (Before reading my paper, my readers will think that this jeans ad reveals a liberated woman, but after reading my paper they will see that the ad fulfills traditional gender stereotypes.)

Another kind of change occurs when an essay actually restructures a reader's whole view of a subject. Such essays persuade readers to change their minds or make decisions. For example, engineer David Rockwood, in his letter to the editor that we reprinted in Chapter 1 (pp. 6–7), wants to change readers' views about

---

*Our discussion of how writing changes a reader's view of the world is indebted to Richard Young, Alton Becker, and Kenneth Pike, *Rhetoric: Discovery and Change* (New York: Harcourt Brace & Company, 1971).

wind power. (Before reading my letter, readers will believe that wind-generated electricity can solve our energy crisis, but after reading my letter they will see that the hope of wind power is a pipe dream.)

Surprise, then, is the measure of change an essay brings about in a reader. Of course, to bring about such change requires more than just a surprising thesis; the essay itself must persuade the reader that the thesis is sound as well as novel. Later in this chapter (Concept 7), we talk about how writers support a thesis through a network of points and particulars.

Giving Your Thesis Tension through "Surprising Reversal"

Another element of a surprising thesis is tension. By *tension* we mean the reader's sensation of being pulled away from familiar ideas toward new, unfamiliar ones. A strategy for creating this tension—a strategy we call "surprising reversal"—is to contrast your surprising answer to a question with your targeted audience's common answer, creating tension between your own thesis and one or more alternative views. Its basic template is as follows:

"Many people believe X (common view), but I am going to show Y (new, surprising view)."

The concept of surprising reversal spurs the writer to go beyond the commonplace to change the reader's view of a topic.

One of the best ways to employ this strategy is to begin your thesis statement with an "although" clause that summarizes the reader's "before" view or the counterclaim that your essay opposes; the main clause states the surprising view or position that your essay will support. You may choose to omit the *although* clause from your actual essay, but formulating it first will help you achieve focus and surprise in your thesis. The examples that follow illustrate the kinds of tension we have been discussing and show why tension is a key requirement for a good thesis.

Question	What effect has the cell phone had on our culture?
Thesis without Tension	The invention of the cell phone has brought many advantages to our culture.
Thesis with Tension	Although the cell phone has brought many advantages to our culture, it may also have contributed to an increase in risky behavior among boaters and hikers.
Question	Do reservations serve a useful role in contemporary Native American culture?
Thesis without Tension	Reservations have good points and bad points.
Thesis with Tension	Although my friend Wilson Real Bird believes that reservations are necessary for Native Americans to preserve their heritage, the continuation of reservations actually degrades Native American culture.

In the first example, the thesis without tension (cell phones have brought advantages to our culture) is a truism with which everyone would agree and hence lacks surprise. The thesis with tension places this truism (the reader's "before" view) in an *although* clause and goes on to make a surprising or contestable assertion. The idea that the cell phone contributes to risky behavior among outdoor enthusiasts alters our initial, complacent view of the cell phone and gives us new ideas to think about.

In the second example, the thesis without tension may not at first seem tensionless because the writer sets up an opposition between good and bad points. But *almost anything* has good and bad points, so the opposition is not meaningful, and the thesis offers no element of surprise. Substitute virtually any other social institution (marriage, the postal service, the military, prisons), and the statement that it has good and bad points would be equally true. The thesis with tension, in contrast, is risky. It commits the writer to argue that reservations have degraded Native American culture and to oppose the counterthesis that reservations are needed to *preserve* Native American culture. The reader now feels genuine tension between two opposing views.

Tension, then, is a component of surprise. The writer's goal is to surprise the reader in some way, thereby bringing about some kind of change in the reader's view. As you are wallowing in complexity about your subject-matter problem, try the following strategies for bringing something new, surprising, or challenging to your targeted readers:

Strategies for Creating a Thesis with Tension or Surprise

How You Became Gripped with a Problem	Example of a Problem	Your Strategy While You "Wallow in Complexity"	Possible Thesis with Tension or Surprise
The problem is already "out there." *(You enter a conversation already in progress)*			
You don't know where you stand on an issue.	Should health care be rationed?	Look at all sides of the issue, including all the available data, to determine where you stand based on your own examined values.	Although rationing health care at first seems inhumane, it may be the only ethical way to provide affordable health care to all citizens.
You do know where you stand on an issue. *[You need to move from an opinion to an earned thesis.]*	Shanita says that we should build more nuclear power plants to combat global warming, but I say nuclear power is too dangerous.	Research the strengths of the opposing views and the weaknesses of your own view. (*Note: You may change your mind.*)	Although nuclear power poses danger from storage of waste or possible meltdown, the benefits of reducing greenhouse gases and cutting coal pollution outweigh the dangers.

How You Became Gripped with a Problem	Example of a Problem	Your Strategy While You "Wallow in Complexity"	Possible Thesis with Tension or Surprise
Someone gives you a question that you can't yet answer.	Your boss asks you whether the company should enact the proposed marketing plan.	Do the research, critical thinking, and analysis needed to propose the "best solution" to the boss's question.	The marketing team's proposal, despite its creative use of advertising, is too risky to undertake at this time.
You pose the problem yourself. *(You initiate the conversation)*			
You see something puzzling in a natural phenomenon or a cultural activity or artifact.	Why does Merton call rain "meaningless"?	Through critical thinking and research, try to figure out a plausible "best solution" to your question.	Merton's puzzling use of "meaningless" in reference to the rain can perhaps be explained by his admiration for Buddhism.
You discover something inconsistent or contradictory in your own view of the world.	I agree with Merton's argument against consumerism, but I really want a large plasma TV. Is consumerism really bad? Am I a materialist?	Reflect on your own values and beliefs; try to achieve a consistent stand with regard to enduring social or ethical issues.	Although Merton makes me consider the potential shallowness of my desire for a huge plasma TV, I don't think I'm necessarily a materialist.

Developing Thesis Statements Out of Questions

FOR WRITING AND DISCUSSION

It is difficult to create thesis statements on the spot because a writer's thesis grows out of an exploratory struggle with a problem. However, in response to a question one can often propose a claim and treat it as a tentative thesis statement for testing. You may have already done some exploratory talking and writing in response to a problem provided by your instructor or about problems supplied so far in this text: the sculpture in Figure 1.2 (p. 15), the e. e. cummings poem (p. 35), or the graphs in Figures 2.2 and 2.3 (p. 36). Working individually, spend ten minutes considering possible thesis statements that you might make in response to one or more of the questions you have already been thinking about. (Remember that these are tentative thesis statements, done for practice, that you might abandon after doing research or more critical thinking.) Identify a possible audience for your thesis statement,

(continued)

and try to explain why this audience would find your thesis new, surprising, or challenging. Then, working in small groups or as a whole class, share your thesis statements. Select one or two thesis statements that your small group or class thinks are particularly effective and brainstorm the kinds of evidence that would be required to support the thesis.

Alternatively, your instructor might use the following exercises:

1. To what extent should the public support genetically modified foods? (possible audiences: readers of health food magazines; general public concerned about food choices; investors in companies that produce genetically modified seeds)
2. Should the government mandate more fuel-efficient cars? If so, how? (possible audiences: SUV owners; conservative legislators generally in favor of free markets; investors in the automobile industry)

Here is an example:

Problematic question: What can cities do to prevent traffic congestion?

One possible thesis: Although many people think that building light-rail systems won't get people out of their cars, new light-rail systems in many cities have attracted new riders and alleviated traffic problems.

Intended audience: Residents of cities concerned about traffic congestion but skeptical about light-rail

Kinds of evidence needed to support thesis: Examples of cities with successful light-rail systems; evidence that many riders switched from driving cars; evidence that light-rail alleviated traffic problems

CONCEPT 6 **In closed-form prose, a typical introduction starts with the problem, not the thesis.**

So far we've talked about the importance of finding a good problem and exploring its complexity. Eventually, however, your goal is to contribute to the conversation by stating and supporting your own thesis. First, however, readers need to know what problem your thesis addresses. One of the principles of closed-form prose—which we describe in detail later in this text—is that readers' need to attach new information to old information. In other words, before they can understand an answer, they must first understand the question. One function of the introduction in most closed-form prose is to show your readers what the problem is and to motivate their interest in it. This introduction can be long or short depending on whether your targeted audience is already familiar with the problem or already cares about it. Once readers know what problem you intend to address, they are prepared for your thesis statement.

For more on the old/new contract, see Chapter 10, Skill 10.7.

A Protypical Introduction

To show you how academic writers typically begin by asking a question, we will illustrate with several "prototype" examples.* In the following introduction by student writer Jackie Wyngaard, note how the author first presents a question and then moves, at the end of the introduction, to her thesis statement.

EMP: MUSIC HISTORY OR MUSIC TRIVIA?

Along with other college students new to Seattle, I wanted to see what cultural opportunities the area offers. I especially wanted to see billionaire Paul Allen's controversial Experience Music Project (known as EMP), a huge, bizarre, shiny, multicolored structure that is supposed to resemble a smashed guitar. Brochures say that EMP celebrates the creativity of American popular music, but it has prompted heated discussions among architects, Seattle residents, museum goers, and music lovers, who have questioned its commercialism and the real value of its exhibits. My sister recommended this museum to me because she knows I am a big music lover and a rock and roll fan. Also, as an active choir member since the sixth grade, I have always been intrigued by the history of music. I went to EMP expecting to learn more about music history from exhibits that showed a range of popular musical styles, that traced historical connections and influences, and that enjoyably conveyed useful information. However, as a museum of rock history, EMP is a disappointing failure.

Provides background on EMP

Begins to turn topic area (EMP) into a problem by showing that it has been controversial

Establishes her own purposes and expectations: She expects EMP to teach her about music history.

Implies her question: Is EMP a good place to learn about the history of rock music?

States her thesis

Features of a Good Introduction

Wyngaard's introduction, which shares the structure of many professionally written closed-form introductions, includes the following prototypical features:

- ***Background needed to identify the topic area and provide context.*** Readers need early on to know the specific topic area of the paper they are about to read—in this case a paper about the Experience Music Project in Seattle rather than, say, shower mold or medieval queenship. Sometimes writers also use a startling scene or statistic as an "attention grabber" as part of the opening background.
- ***A direct or implied question.*** As soon as possible, readers need to sense the problem, question, or issue that the writer will examine. In this case, Jackie Wyngaard implies her question: Will my expectations about EMP be fulfilled? Note that her question appears directly in her title: "EMP: Music History [her expectations] or Music Trivia [her claim]?"
- ***An indication of how the question invites tension or is otherwise problematic.*** An effective question or problem supposes the possibility of

*A *prototype* is the most typical or generic instance of a class and doesn't constitute a value judgment. For example, a prototype bird might be a robin or blackbird (rather than an ostrich, chicken, hummingbird, or pelican) because these birds seem to exhibit the most typical features of "birdiness." Likewise, a prototype dog would be a medium-sized mutt rather than a St. Bernard or toy poodle.

alternative points of view, different perspectives in tension with each other. In many cases, a writer summarizes alternative arguments sparked by the question or summarizes a particular point of view that the writer intends to oppose. Because Jackie initiates the conversation about EMP's status as a rock museum, she evokes this tension by contrasting her initial expectations with her later disappointment.

- ***An indication of how the question is significant or worth examining.*** In order to avoid a "so what?" response, writers must motivate readers' interest in the question. Somebody might say, "Who cares about EMP anyway?" Jackie's strategy is to imagine an audience who shares her interest in rock and roll music and her love of music history. These are the readers who will care whether it is worth big bucks to spend an afternoon in EMP. Readers who identify with Jackie's enthusiasm for rock history will share her engagement with the question. Other strategies for showing a question's significance include pointing to the good or bad consequences of a particular way of answering the question ("If we could understand why the crime rate in New York City dropped dramatically in the 1990s, we could apply these same principles to other cities today") or by showing how an answer to a smaller question might help readers begin to answer a larger question ("If we could better understand the role of the witches in *Macbeth*, we would better understand the ways gender was constructed in Shakespeare's time").

For more on thesis statements, purpose statements, and blueprint statements, see Skill 10.4. See also James Gardiner's full essay on pp. 340–348.

- ***The writer's thesis, which brings something new to the audience.*** Once readers are hooked on the writer's question, they are ready for the writer's answer. In this case, Jackie makes the claim that EMP fails as a rock history museum.
- ***[optional] A purpose statement ("The purpose of this paper is … ") along with a mapping statement forecasting the content and shape of the rest of the article ("First I discuss X, then Y, and finally Z").*** Because her paper is short, Jackie ends the introduction with her thesis. An alternative strategy, common among longer closed-form essays, is to include a purpose statement along with a forecasting passage that maps what is coming. This strategy is used by student writer James Gardiner at the end of his introduction to a paper about the consequences of using online social networks like Facebook. Note how he poses his problematic question and then moves to a purpose statement and mapping statement.

States directly the question his paper will address

Purpose statement

Maps out the argument's structure while motivating readers' interest in question

… While "Facebook Trance" might describe only an occasional and therefore harmless phenomenon, it gives rise to an important question: What are the possible negative consequences of OSNs [online social networks]? What should youthful users be watchful for and guard against? The purpose of this paper is to identify the possible harms of OSNs. I will suggest that overuse of OSNs can be a contributing factor to a decline in grades as well as to other problems such as a superficial view of relationships, an increase in narcissism, and possible future embarrassment.

For a fuller look at the ways a writer can introduce readers to the problem he or she is addressing, consider the following strategies chart:

Strategies for Introducing Your Problem to Targeted Readers	
Situation	**Strategies**
The problem is already "out there" *(You enter a conversation already in progress)*	*If readers are already familiar with the problem and care about it, use a mix of the following strategies:* • Provide background where needed • State the problem directly (often as a grammatical question ending with a question mark) or imply the question through context • Summarize the different points of view on the problem (or) • Summarize the particular point of view you intend to "push against" *If readers are less familiar with the problem:* • Summarize controversy in more depth • Explain why the problem is problematic (show why there are no easy answers to the problem; point out weaknesses in proposed answers; show the history of attempts to solve the problem) *If readers don't already care about the problem:* • Show why the problem is important (answer the "so what?" question) • Show how solving the problem will bring good consequences (or) • Show how answering the question will help us begin to answer a larger question

You pose the problem yourself *(You initiate the conversation)*	• Describe the artifact or phenomenon you are writing about and point to the specific features where you see an inconsistency, gap, or puzzle
	• State the problem directly (often as a grammatical question ending with a question mark)
	• Show how there isn't any immediate, easy answer to the question or problem or how the question can invite controversy/discussion; you can often employ a template such as the following:
	  • Some people might think…, but closer observation shows that….
	  • At first I thought…, but later I saw that….
	  • Part of me thinks…, but another part of me thinks that….
	  • I expected … ; but what I actually found was….
	• Show why the problem is important (answer the "so what?" question)
	• Show how solving the problem will bring good consequences (or)
	• Show how answering this question will help us begin to answer a larger question

Examining Problem-Thesis Structure of Introductions

Background: As we explained in Concept 1, good writing can vary along a continuum from closed to open forms. Although academic essays are typically closed form, they can vary significantly along the continuum. Likewise, the introductions to closed-form essays don't always follow the prototypical structure we just described. But many do. In this exercise, we invite you to analyze additional introductions.

Task: Look at the following introductions. In each case, analyze the extent to which the introduction follows or varies from the prototypical introductions we have described in Concept 6.

1. Paragraphs 1–2 of Ross Taylor's "Paintball: Promoter of Violence or Healthy Fun?"
2. Paragraphs 1–4 of "No to Nukes," a *Los Angeles Times* editorial
3. Paragraphs 1–6 of Shannon King's "How Clean and Green Are Hydrogen Fuel-Cell Cars?"

CONCEPT 7 Thesis statements in closed-form prose are supported hierarchically with points and particulars.

Of course, a surprising thesis is only one aspect of an effective essay. An essay must also persuade the reader that the thesis is believable as well as surprising. Although tabloid newspapers have shocking headlines ("Cloning Produces Three-Headed Sheep"), skepticism quickly replaces surprise when you look inside and find the article's claims unsupported. A strong thesis, then, must both surprise the reader and be supported with convincing particulars.

In fact, the particulars are the flesh and muscle of writing and comprise most of the sentences. In closed-form prose, these particulars are connected clearly to points, and the points precede the particulars. In this section, we explain this principle more fully.

How Points Convert Information to Meaning

When particulars are clearly related to a point, the point gives meaning to the particulars, and the particulars give force and validity to the point. Particulars constitute the evidence, data, details, examples, and subarguments that develop a point and make it convincing. By themselves, particulars are simply information—mere data without meaning.

In the following example, you can see for yourself the difference between information and meaning. Here is a list of information:*

- In almost all species on earth, males are more aggressive than females.
- Male chimpanzees win dominance by brawling.

*The data in this exercise are adapted from Deborah Blum, "The Gender Blur," *Utne Reader* Sept. 1998: 45–48.

- To terrorize rival troops, they kill females and infants.
- The level of aggression among monkeys can be manipulated by adjusting their testosterone levels.
- Among humans, preliminary research suggests that male fetuses are more active in the uterus than female fetuses.
- Little boys play more aggressively than little girls despite parental efforts to teach gentleness to boys and aggression to girls.

To make meaning out of this list of information, the writer needs to state a point—the idea, generalization, or claim—that this information supports. Once the point is stated, a meaningful unit (point with particulars) springs into being:

> Aggression in human males may be a function of biology rather than culture. *Point*
> In almost all species on earth, males are more aggressive than females. Male chimpanzees win dominance by brawling; to terrorize rival troops, they kill females and infants. Researchers have shown that the level of aggression among monkeys can be manipulated by adjusting their testosterone levels. Among humans, preliminary research suggests that male fetuses are more active in the uterus than female fetuses. Also, little boys play more aggressively than little girls despite parental efforts to teach gentleness to boys and aggression to girls.   *Particulars*

Once the writer states this point, readers familiar with the biology/culture debate about gender differences immediately feel its surprise and tension. This writer believes that biology determines gender identity more than does culture. The writer now uses the details as evidence to support a point.

To appreciate the reader's need for a logical connection between points and particulars, note how readers would get lost if, in the preceding example, the writer included a particular that seemed unrelated to the point ("Males also tend to be taller and heavier than women"—a factual statement, but what does it have to do with aggression?) or if, without explanation, the writer added a particular that seemed to contradict the point ("Fathers play more roughly with baby boys than with baby girls"—another fact, but one that points to culture rather than biology as a determiner of aggression).

Obviously, reasonable people seek some kind of coordination between points and particulars, some sort of weaving back and forth between them. Writing teachers use a number of nearly synonymous terms for expressing this paired relationship: *points/particulars, generalizations/specifics, claims/evidence, ideas/ details, interpretations/data, meaning/support.*

How Removing Particulars Creates a Summary

What we have shown, then, is that skilled writers weave back and forth between generalizations and specifics. The generalizations form a network of higher-level and lower-level points that develop the thesis; the particulars (specifics) support each of the points and subpoints in turn. In closed-form prose, the network of points is easily discernible because points are clearly highlighted with transitions, and main points are placed prominently at the heads of paragraphs. (In open-form prose, generalizations are often left unstated, creating gaps where the reader must actively fill in meaning.)

Being able to write summaries and abstracts of articles is an important academic skill. See Chapter 5 on strategies for writing summaries and strong responses, pp. 105–116.

If you remove most of the particulars from a closed-form essay, leaving only the network of points, you will have written a summary or abstract of the essay. As an example, reread the civil engineer's letter to the editor arguing against the feasibility of wind-generated power (pp. 6–7). The writer's argument can be summarized in a single sentence:

> Wind-generated power is not a reasonable alternative to other forms of power in the Pacific Northwest because wind power is unreliable, because there are major unsolved problems involved in the design of wind-generation facilities, and because the environmental impact of building thousands of wind towers would be enormous.

What we have done in this summary is remove the particulars, leaving only the high-level points that form the skeleton of the argument. The writer's thesis remains surprising and contains tension, but without the particulars the reader has no idea whether to believe the generalizations or not. The presence of the particulars is thus essential to the success of the argument.

FOR WRITING AND DISCUSSION

Analyzing Supporting Particulars

Compare the civil engineer's original letter with the one-sentence summary just given and then note how the engineer uses specific details to support each point. How do these particulars differ from paragraph to paragraph? How are they chosen to support each point?

How to Use Points and Particulars When You Revise

The lesson to learn here is that in closed-form prose, writers regularly place a point sentence in front of detail sentences. When a writer begins with a point, readers interpret the ensuing particulars not as random data but rather as *evidence* in support of that point. The writer depends on the particulars to make the point credible and persuasive.

This insight may help you understand two of the most common kinds of marginal comments that readers (or teachers) place on writers' early drafts. If your draft has a string of sentences giving data or information unconnected to any stated point, your reader is apt to write in the margin, "What's your point here?" or "Why are you telling me this information?" or "How does this information relate to your thesis?" Conversely, if your draft tries to make a point that isn't developed with particulars, your reader is apt to write marginal comments such as "Evidence?" or "Development?" or "Could you give an example?" or "More details needed."

Don't be put off by these requests; they are a gift. It is common in first drafts for main points to be unstated, buried, or otherwise disconnected from their details and for supporting information to be scattered confusingly throughout the draft or missing entirely. Having to write point sentences obliges you to wrestle with your intended meaning: Just what am I trying to say here? How can I nutshell that in a point? Likewise, having to support your points with particulars causes you to wrestle with the content and shape of your argument: What particulars will make this point convincing? What further research do I need to do to find these particulars? In Part 3 of this text, which is devoted to advice about composing and revising, we show how the construction and location of point sentences are essential for reader clarity. Part 3 also explains various composing and revising strategies that will help you create effective networks of points and particulars.

Chapter Summary

This chapter has introduced you to four concepts that will enable you to think about your subject matter from a rhetorical perspective.

- *Concept 4: To determine their thesis, writers must often "wallow in complexity."* What typically initiates the writing process is a problematic question that invites the writer to explore the problem's complexity. To do so, experienced writers often use exploratory techniques such as freewriting, idea mapping, dialectic talk, and the believing and doubting game to generate ideas.
- *Concept 5: A strong thesis surprises readers with something new or challenging.* A good thesis tries to change the reader's view of the subject and often creates tension by pushing against alternative views.
- *Concept 6: In closed-form prose, a typical introduction starts with the problem, not the thesis.* Readers need to be engaged with the writer's question before they can understand the thesis.
- *Concept 7: Thesis statements in closed-form prose are supported hierarchically with points and particulars.* Points give meaning to particulars; particulars make points persuasive. If you remove the particulars from a writer's argument and keep the points, you will have created a summary.

Playing the Believing and Doubting Game

BRIEF WRITING PROJECT

Part 1. The Game. Play the believing and doubting game with one of the assertions listed here (or with another assertion provided by your instructor) by freewriting your believing and doubting responses. Spend ten minutes believing and then ten minutes doubting the assertion, for a total of twenty minutes. When you believe an assertion, you agree, support, illustrate, extend, and apply the idea. When you doubt an assertion, you question, challenge, rebut, and offer counterreasons and counterexamples to the assertion. Note that when students first learn to do exploratory writing, they often run out of ideas quickly and want to stop. But the best ideas often happen when you push through that wall. If you run out of ideas, let your mind follow a tangent. Particularly explore your personal experiences with the subject. Eventually you will get back on track with new ideas.

1. Grades are an effective means of motivating students to do their best work.
2. Facebook is a good way to make new friends.
3. In recent years, advertising has made enormous gains in portraying women as strong, independent, and intelligent.
4. If there is only one kidney available for transplant and two sick persons need it, one in her thirties and one in her sixties, the kidney should go to the younger person.
5. The United States should reinstate the draft.
6. Humans have free will.
7. Fencing at the U.S.–Mexico border is not an effective immigration policy.
8. If students in a large lecture course can listen to a lecture and surf the Web or check e-mail at the same time, then they should be allowed to do so.

Part 2. Reflection. Write a reflective paragraph in which you assess the extent to which the believing and doubting game extended or stretched your thinking. Particularly, answer these questions:

- What was difficult about this writing activity?
- To what extent did it make you take an unfamiliar or uncomfortable stance?
- How can believing and doubting help you wallow in complexity?

 For additional help with writing, reading, and research, go to **www.mycomplab.com.**

THINKING RHETORICALLY ABOUT HOW MESSAGES PERSUADE

3

A way of seeing is also a way of not seeing.

—Kenneth Burke, Rhetorician

Every time an Indian villager watches the community TV and sees an ad for soap or shampoo, what they notice are not the soap and shampoo but the lifestyle of the people using them, the kind of motorbikes they ride, their dress and their homes.

—Nayan Chanda, Indian-Born Editor of YaleGlobal Online Magazine

In Chapters 1 and 2 we have focused on writing as a rhetorical act: When writers think rhetorically, they write to an audience for a purpose within a genre. We have also shown how academic writers pose subject-matter questions that engage their audience's interests, and then propose solutions to those problems that bring something new, surprising, or challenging to their audiences.

In this chapter we expand your understanding of a writer's choices by showing how messages persuade. We'll use the word *message* in its broadest sense to include verbal texts and nonverbal texts such as photographs and paintings or consumer artifacts such as clothing. When you understand how messages achieve their effects, you will be better prepared to analyze and evaluate those messages and to make your own choices about whether to resist them or accede to them.

In this chapter, you will learn three more important rhetorical concepts:

- CONCEPT 8   Messages persuade through their angle of vision.
- CONCEPT 9   Messages persuade through appeals to *logos, ethos,* and *pathos*.
- CONCEPT 10 Nonverbal messages persuade through visual strategies that can be analyzed rhetorically.

CONCEPT 8 Messages persuade through their angle of vision.

One way that messages persuade is through their **angle of vision**, which causes a reader to see a subject from one perspective only—the writer's. Writers create an angle of vision through strategies such as the following:

- Stating point of view directly
- Selecting some details while omitting others
- Choosing words or figures of speech with intended connotations
- Creating emphasis or de-emphasis through sentence structure and organization

The writer's angle of vision—which might also be called a lens, a filter, a perspective, or a point of view—is persuasive because it controls what the reader "sees." Unless readers are rhetorically savvy, they can lose awareness that they are seeing the writer's subject matter through a lens that both reveals and conceals.

A classic illustration of angle of vision is the following thought exercise:

THOUGHT EXERCISE ON ANGLE OF VISION

Suppose you attended a fun party on Saturday night. (You get to choose what constitutes "fun" for you.) Now imagine that two people ask what you did on Saturday night. Person A is a close friend who missed the party. Person B is your parent. How would your descriptions of Saturday night differ?

Clearly there isn't just one way to describe this party. Your description will be influenced by your purpose and audience. You will have to decide:

- What image of myself should I project? (For your friend you might construct yourself as a party animal; for your parent, as a more detached observer.)
- How much emphasis do I give the party? (You might describe the party in detail for your friend while mentioning it only in passing to your parent, emphasizing instead all the homework you did over the weekend.)
- What details should I include or leave out? (Does my parent really need to know that the neighbors called the police?)
- What words should I choose? (The slang you use with your friend might not be appropriate for your parent.)

You'll note that our comments about your rhetorical choices reflect common assumptions about friends and parents. You might actually have a party-loving parent and a geeky friend, in which case your party descriptions would be altered accordingly. In any case, you are in rhetorical control; you choose what your audience "sees" and how they see it.

Recognizing the Angle of Vision in a Text

This thought exercise illustrates a key insight of rhetoric: There is always more than one way to tell a story, and no single way of telling it constitutes the whole truth. By saying that a writer writes from an "angle of vision," we mean that the writer cannot take a godlike stance that allows a universal, unfiltered, totally unbiased or objective way of knowing. Rather, the writer looks at the subject from a certain location, or, to use another metaphor, the writer wears a lens that colors or filters the topic in a certain way. The angle of vision, lens, or filter determines what part of a topic gets "seen" and what remains "unseen," what gets included or excluded, what gets emphasized or de-emphasized, and so forth. It even determines what words get chosen out of an array of options—for example, whether the writer says "panhandler" or "homeless person," "torture" or "enhanced interrogation," "universal health care" or "socialized medicine."

As an illustration of angle of vision, consider the cartoon in Figure 3.1, which shows different ways that stakeholders "see" sweatshops. For each stakeholder, some aspects of sweatshops surge into view, while other aspects remain unseen or invisible. An alert reader needs to be aware that none of these stakeholders can portray sweatshops in a completely "true" way. Stockholders and corporate leaders emphasize reduced labor costs and enhanced corporate profits and retirement portfolios while de-emphasizing (or omitting entirely) the working conditions in

FIGURE 3.1 Different Angles of Vision on "Sweatshops"

sweatshops or the plight of American workers whose jobs have been outsourced to developing countries. Consumers enjoy abundant low-cost goods made possible by sweatshops and may not even think about where or how the products are made. Opponents of sweatshops focus on the miserable conditions of sweatshop workers, their low wages, the use of child labor, and the "obscene" profits of corporations. Meanwhile, as the American union worker laments the loss of jobs in the United States, third world workers and their children may welcome sweatshops as a source of income superior to the other harsh alternatives such as scavenging in dumps or prostitution. The multiple angles of vision show how complex the issue of sweatshops is. In fact, most issues are equally complex, and any one view of the issue is controlled by the writer's angle of vision.

To get a hands-on feel for how a writer creates an angle of vision, try doing the following U. R. Riddle activity, which invites you to write a letter of recommendation for a student.

FOR WRITING AND DISCUSSION

U. R. Riddle Letter

Background: Suppose that you are a management professor who regularly writes letters of recommendation for former students. One day you receive a letter from a local bank requesting a confidential evaluation of a former student, Uriah Rudy Riddle (U. R. Riddle), who has applied for a job as a management trainee. The bank wants your assessment of Riddle's intelligence, aptitude, dependability, and ability to work with people. You haven't seen U. R. for several years, but you remember him well. Here are the facts and impressions you recall about Riddle:

- Very temperamental student, seemed moody, something of a loner
- Long hair and very sloppy dress—seemed like a misplaced street person; often twitchy and hyperactive
- Absolutely brilliant mind; took lots of liberal arts courses and applied them to business
- Wrote a term paper relating different management styles to modern theories of psychology—the best undergraduate paper you ever received. You gave it an A+ and remember learning a lot from it yourself.
- Had a strong command of language—the paper was very well written
- Good at mathematics; could easily handle all the statistical aspects of the course
- Frequently missed class and once told you that your class was boring
- Didn't show up for the midterm. When he returned to class later, he said only that he had been out of town. You let him make up the midterm, and he got an A.
- Didn't participate in a group project required for your course. He said the other students in his group were idiots.
- You thought at the time that Riddle didn't have a chance of making it in the business world because he had no talent for getting along with people.
- Other professors held similar views of Riddle—brilliant, but rather strange and hard to like; an odd duck.

You are in a dilemma because you want to give Riddle a chance (he's still young and may have had a personality transformation of some sort), but you also don't want to damage your own professional reputation by falsifying your true impressions.

Individual task: Working individually for ten minutes or so, compose a brief letter of recommendation assessing Riddle; use details from the list to support your assessment. Role-play that you have decided to take a gamble with Riddle and give him a chance at this career. Write as strong a recommendation as possible while remaining honest. (To make this exercise more complex, your instructor might ask half the class to role-play a negative angle of vision in which you want to warn the bank against hiring Riddle without hiding his strengths or good points.)

Task for group or whole-class discussion: Working in small groups or as a whole class, share your letters. Then pick representative examples ranging from the most positive to the least positive and discuss how the letters achieve their different rhetorical effects. If your intent is to support Riddle, to what extent does honesty compel you to mention some or all of your negative memories? Is it possible to mention negative items without emphasizing them? How?

Analyzing Angle of Vision

Just as there is more than one way to describe the party you went to on Saturday night or to write about sweatshops, there is more than one way to write a letter of recommendation for U. R. Riddle. The writer's angle of vision determines what is "seen" or "not seen" in a given piece of writing—what gets slanted in a positive or negative direction, what gets highlighted, what gets thrown into the shadows. As rhetorician Kenneth Burke claims in the first epigraph for the chapter, "A way of seeing is also a way of not seeing." Note how the writer controls what the reader "sees." As Riddle's former professor, you might in your mind's eye see Riddle as long-haired and sloppy, but if you don't mention these details in your letter, they remain unseen to the reader. Note too that your own terms "long-haired and sloppy" interpret Riddle's appearance through the lens of your own characteristic way of seeing— a way that perhaps values business attire and clean-cut tidiness. Another observer might describe Riddle's appearance quite differently, thus seeing what you don't see.

In an effective piece of writing, the author's angle of vision often works so subtly that unsuspecting readers—unless they learn to think rhetorically—will be drawn into the writer's spell and believe that the writer's prose conveys the "whole picture" of its subject rather than a limited picture filtered through the screen of the writer's perspective.

Contrasting Angles of Vision in Two Texts Consider the differences in what gets seen in the following two descriptions of the Arctic National Wildlife Refuge in Alaska (the ANWR), where proponents of oil exploration are locked in a fierce battle with anti-exploration conservationists. The first passage is from a pro-exploration advocacy group called Arctic Power; the second is from former President Jimmy Carter.

ARCTIC POWER'S DESCRIPTION OF THE ANWR

On the coastal plain [of the ANWR], the Arctic winter lasts for 9 months. It is dark continuously for 56 days in midwinter. Temperatures with the wind chill can reach –110 degrees F. It's not pristine. There are villages, roads, houses, schools, and military installations. It's not a unique Arctic ecosystem. The coastal plain is only a small fraction of the 88,000 square miles that make up the North Slope. The same tundra environment and wildlife can be found throughout the circumpolar Arctic regions. The 1002 Area [the legal term for the plot of coastal plain being contested] is flat. That's why they call it a plain. [...]

Some groups want to make the 1002 Area a wilderness. But a vote for wilderness is a vote against American jobs.

JIMMY CARTER'S DESCRIPTION OF THE ANWR

Rosalynn [Carter's wife] and I always look for opportunities to visit parks and wildlife areas in our travels. But nothing matches the spectacle of wildlife we found on the coastal plain of America's Arctic National Wildlife Refuge in Alaska. To the north lay the Arctic Ocean; to the south rolling foothills rose toward the glaciated peaks of the Brooks Range. At our feet was a mat of low tundra plant life, bursting with new growth, perched atop the permafrost.

As we watched, 80,000 caribou surged across the vast expanse around us. Called by instinct older than history, this Porcupine (River) caribou herd was in the midst of its annual migration. To witness this vast sea of caribou in an uncorrupted wilderness home, and the wolves, ptarmigan, grizzlies, polar bears, musk oxen and millions of migratory birds, was a profoundly humbling experience. We were reminded of our human dependence on the natural world.

Sadly, we were also forced to imagine what we might see if the caribou were replaced by smoke-belching oil rigs, highways and a pipeline that would destroy forever the plain's delicate and precious ecosystem.

How Angle of Vision Persuades To understand more clearly how angle of vision persuades, you can analyze the language strategies at work. Some of these strategies—which writers employ consciously or unconsciously to achieve their intended effects—are described in the following strategies chart.

Strategies for Constructing an Angle of Vision

Strategy	ANWR Example	U. R. Riddle Example
State your intention directly.	• Earlier passages directly state Arctic Powers' pro-drilling and Carter's anti-drilling stances.	• You might say "Riddle would make an excellent manager" or "Riddle doesn't have the personality to be a bank manager."
Select details that support your intentions; omit or de-emphasize others.	• Arctic Power writer (AP) "sees" the cold, barren darkness of the ANWR; Carter sees the beauty.	• A positive view of Riddle would select and emphasize Riddle's good traits and de-emphasize or omit his bad ones.

Strategy	ANWR Example	U. R. Riddle Example
	• AP spotlights the people who live on the coastal plain while making the animals invisible; Carter spotlights the caribou while omitting the people. • To AP, drilling means jobs; to Carter it means destructive oil rigs.	• A negative view would take opposite the tack.
Choose words that frame your subject in the desired way or have desired connotations.	• AP frames the ANWR as the dreary "1002 Area"; Carter frames it as a "spectacle of wildlife," a unique "delicate and precious ecosystem." • Arctic Power uses words with negative connotations ("wind chill"); Carter uses words connoting life and growth ("a mat of low tundra plant life").	• "Riddle is an independent thinker who doesn't follow the crowd" (frames him positively in value system that favors individualism). • "Riddle is a loner who thinks egocentrically" (frames him negatively in value system favoring consensus and social skills). • You could say, "Riddle is forthright" or "Riddle is rude"—positive versus negative connotations.
Use figurative language (metaphors, similes, and analogies) that conveys your intended effect.	• AP avoids figurative language, claiming objective presentation of facts. • Carter uses positive metaphors to convey ANWR's vitality (tundra "bursting with new growth") and negative metaphors for drilling ("smoke-belching oil rigs").	• To suggest that Riddle has outgrown his alienating behavior, you could say, "Riddle is a social late bloomer." • To recommend against hiring Riddle while still being positive, you could say, "Riddle's independent spirit would feel caged in by the routine of a bank."
Use sentence structure to emphasize and de-emphasize your ideas. (*Emphasize an idea by placing it at the end of a long sentence, in a short sentence, or in a main clause.*)	• AP uses short sentences to emphasize main points: "It's not pristine." It's not a unique ecosystem." "That's why they call it a plain." • Carter uses longer sentences for description, with an occasional short sentence to make a point: "We were reminded of our human dependence on the natural world."	Consider the difference between the following: • "Although Riddle had problems relating to other students, he is a brilliant thinker." • "Although Riddle is a brilliant thinker, he had problems relating to other students in the class."

Jacob Sarfati
Professor Thekkiam
15 October 2010
English 1303

My Convenience Is Our Loss of Rights

My wife and I are non-smokers. In our thirties, we still consider ourselves to be young. We workout four to five times a week and do our best to eat foods that will keep our bodies running at optimal performance so that we can get through our week of work and school. We do the things that we do because it is what we feel is best for our lives. We are Americans, and incorrectly, we always thought that it was our right to lead our lives as we saw best fit.

In 2007, Many Houstonians lost what they felt was an inherent and unalienable right: the right to smoke in public. The law was instituted as a city ordinance, with the rights of the people in mind. However, who gave the city the right to make this choice for us?

I can honestly tell you, as non-smokers, my wife and I are happy to walk into a restaurant and to not be overpowered by the smell of smoke. The city of Houston has seemingly made life easier on us both. By vilifying and segregating smokers, and their disgusting habit, my wife and I get to more completely enjoy life. We no longer have to think about where we want to eat before we leave the house. On Saturday night, we no longer have to wait in the long line for a table inside of the small non-smoking section. We no longer have to shop for a bar that suits our needs. All bars inside of the city now have to conform to us. Furthermore, when we get home after a night out, we no longer have to change and leave our clothes in the bathroom or toss them immediately into the washing machine. We no longer have to worry about the house filling with the smell of the smoke that has saturated our clothing during our evening out. At first glance, the City of Houston is seemingly catering to us, and our needs. In a city of 2.2 million, everyone now has a law that makes life easier for me and mine. Oh, the convenience, correct? INCORRECT!

There are two sides to every story, and this world of ours was not painted in black and white. With color, is how we perceive the world. It is through color and variance that we come to learn of our surroundings and it is with color that we should learn that every law given is also a right revoked. Are we happier with the city conforming to us, or are we worse off with the loss of rights to do what we want when we want? It is important to take a step back and properly assess our modern history. Understanding the economic direction of the last several decades will show that these new decisions, made for Americans, are out of line.

The 1990's flourished as the post Reagan era of the United States still believed in a market driven economy. A market economy is one based on the power of specialization in which the process of both goods and services are determined by a free price system set by supply and demand. I truly believe that this market, guided by Adam Smith's invisible hand, is what was originally intended by our founding fathers.

It is with these concepts in mind that the City of Houston should have acted in 2007. Rather than an increase in regulation, leading to a loss of American rights, we should have seen our government step aside to let the market drive the smokers and the non-smokers to an individual or mutual location based on market decisions. Businesses should be allowed to run themselves. A market driven system cannot simply cater to one side or the other, this would be ridiculous. Although a large percentage of Houstonians are smokers, their numbers are under 50% of the population. If a business were allowed to run on its own free will, why would they only cater to percentage of potential clientele? The answer is, they would not. If the population was demanding smoke free environments and non-smokers did not want to be around smokers, then bars, restaurants, and public areas that did not have clean air designated areas for non-smokers would lose revenue.

As Houston becomes more health conscience, business owners would start to see their shops with fewer and fewer customers. Owners would take it upon themselves to figure out why patrons have stopped spending their money and visiting their businesses. Businesses cater to patrons and do what is needed to get customers inside to spend money. If more then half of patrons demand a smoke free environment in order to be comfortable enough to spend their money, then this would have happened under the direction of business owners to facilitate the influx of more customers, without additional government regulation.

In addition, as the average citizen increases their knowledge of tobacco products and the effects of tobacco on the body, not only to smokers but also to those receiving their second hand smoke, they would have taken more individual action. Health conscious citizens in attendance to a smoke filled environment would have eventually slowed, if it were important to them. The upcoming awareness of the health conscious citizen is only a small step from the realization that a city the size of Houston has thousands of other bars, each with their own individual atmosphere. When enough of the population comes to this recognition, when shop owners start to lose money, it is human nature, and the nature of the market to investigate why this is happening. With the current law in hand, the city has not only revoked the rights of the business owners to provide their clients with their preferred environment but they have denied the citizens of previously accepted rights.

When Thomas Jefferson signed the Declaration of Independence on July 4th, 1776 it is my belief that it was his intention to prevent these specific types of regulation from being dictated by the government. Jefferson wrote:

> We hold these truths to be self-evident, that all men are created equal, that they are endowed by their Creator with certain unalienable rights, that among these are life, liberty, and the pursuit of happiness.

What we have been told here specifically is that we have the right to the "pursuit of happiness." Nowhere, in any founding documents did we as citizens of the United States, or residents of any individual state, receive the right to absolute comfort and satisfaction. We have not been promised a life of luxury and comfort, only the ability to step out in to the world and achieve if the effort is put forth. In addition, this law revokes the pursuit of happiness if you are a smoker.

The black and white version of the City of Houston's smoking ordinance is that non-smokers have received the right to not be around smokers. In addition, smokers have lost the right to smoke in public. The color version is that we have all lost rights as the government grows in strength. We have lost the right to make our own decision and we have gained an arm of regulation around us as citizens. As a non-smoker, in a twisted way, I am able to see some benefit in this increase regulation. But as a veteran and an American, I have to ask myself, what is next? In the news today I see that the City of Boston is attempting to eliminate sodas from being sold in government building. Their concern is that government employee's sugar intake is too high. Who gave them this right to have this concern? There is currently a crack down on bake sales in New York City schools. In an effort to limit the sugar and fat intake of students the Education Department has limited fund-raising tools. In Santa Clara, California county officials have voted to ban toys and other promotions that restaurants offer with high calorie children's meals. Bye-bye Happy Meal. Who gave these people the right to regulate what I put in my body, or what I feed my children? These problems are all symptoms of a larger illness. When smokers lost their right to smoke in public, a door opened that has created a new avenue of governmental control.

My frustration here is focused. The government is growing in both size and power. The rights that Americans took in the Declaration of Independence are now being eliminated by our own elected governing officials. Every new law providing you with comfort takes away the declared right of another citizen. I simply ask one thing of my readers, when assessing laws and rights, please put our freedom ahead of your own individual comfort.

CONCEPT 9 Messages persuade through appeals to *logos, ethos*, and *pathos.*

Another way to think about the persuasive power of texts is to examine the strategies writers or speakers use to sway their audiences toward a certain position on an issue. To win people's consideration of their ideas, writers or speakers can appeal to what the classical philosopher Aristotle called *logos, ethos*, and *pathos*. Developing the habit of examining how these appeals are functioning in texts and being able to employ these appeals in your own writing will enhance your ability to read and write rhetorically. Let's look briefly at each:

* ***Logos* is the appeal to reason.** It refers to the quality of the message itself—to its internal consistency, to its clarity in asserting a thesis or point, and to the quality of reasons and evidence used to support the point.
* ***Ethos* is the appeal to the character of the speaker/writer.** It refers to the speaker/writer's trustworthiness and credibility. One can often increase one's *ethos* in a message by being knowledgeable about the issue, by appearing thoughtful and fair, by listening well, and by being respectful of alternative points of view. A writer's accuracy and thoroughness in crediting sources and

professionalism in caring about the format, grammar, and neat appearance of a document are part of the appeal to *ethos.*

- ***Pathos* is the appeal to the sympathies, values, beliefs, and emotions of the audience.** Appeals to *pathos* can be made in many ways. *Pathos* can often be enhanced through evocative visual images, frequently used in Web sites, posters, and magazine or newspaper articles. In written texts, the same effects can be created through vivid examples and details, through connotative language, and through empathy with the audience's beliefs and values.

To see how these three appeals are interrelated, you can visualize a triangle with points labeled *Message, Audience,* and *Writer* or *Speaker.* Rhetoricians study how effective communicators consider all three points of this *rhetorical triangle.* (See Figure 3.2.)

We encourage you to ask questions about the appeals to *logos, ethos,* and *pathos* every time you examine a text. For example, is the appeal to *logos* weakened by the writer's use of scanty and questionable evidence? Has the writer made a powerful appeal to *ethos* by documenting her sources and showing that she is an authority on the issue? Has the writer relied too heavily on appeals to *pathos* by using numerous heart-wringing examples? Later chapters in this textbook will help you use these appeals competently in your own writing as well as analyze these appeals in others' messages.

Message
Logos: *How can I make my ideas internally consistent and logical? How can I find the best reasons and support them with the best evidence?*

Audience
Pathos: *How can I make the readers open to my message? How can I best engage my readers' emotions and imaginations? How can I appeal to my readers' values and interests?*

Writer or Speaker
Ethos: *How can I present myself effectively? How can I enhance my credibility and trustworthiness?*

FIGURE 3.2 Rhetorical Triangle

CONCEPT 10 **Nonverbal messages persuade through visual strategies that can be analyzed rhetorically.**

Just as you can think rhetorically about texts, you can think rhetorically about photographs, drawings, and other images as well as artifacts such as clothing or cars.

Visual Rhetoric

Consider, for example, the persuasive power of famous photographs from the war in Iraq. Early in the war, several widely publicized images, particularly the film footage of the toppling of the statue of Saddam Hussein and the "Mission Accomplished" photograph of former President George W. Bush wearing a pilot's flight suit on the deck of the aircraft carrier *Abraham Lincoln*, served to consolidate public support of the war. Later, certain images began eating away at public support. For example, an unauthorized picture of flag-draped coffins filling the freight deck of a military transport plane focused attention on those killed in the war. Particularly devastating for supporters of the war were the images of American guards sexually humiliating Iraqi prisoners in the Abu Ghraib prison. Images like these stick in viewers' memories long after specific texts are forgotten.

What gives images this persuasive power? For one thing, they can be apprehended at a glance, condensing an argument into a memorable scene or symbol that taps deeply into our emotions and values. Images also persuade by appealing to *logos*, *ethos*, and *pathos*. They make implicit arguments (*logos*) while also appealing to our values and emotions (*pathos*) and causing us to respond favorably or unfavorably to the artist or photographer (*ethos*). Like verbal texts, images have an angle of vision, which can be crafted by selecting, manipulating, and often photoshopping images to control what viewers see and thus influence what they think. (Note that "angle of vision" is itself a visual metaphor.) Through the location and angle of the camera, the distance from the subject, and the framing, cropping, and filtering of the image, the photographer steers us toward a particular view of the subject, influencing us to forget, at least momentarily, that there are other ways of seeing the same subject.

Although images can have powerful rhetorical effects, these effects may be less controllable and more audience-dependent than those of verbal texts. Consider, for example, the wind farm photograph on page 3. In this striking image, the dominance of the whirling turbines could convey several implicit arguments. Some viewers might find that this photo fuels their objections to wind farms. They might zero in on how intrusive, massive, and unattractive wind turbines are. The blurred blades of the gigantic turbines might strike them as frightening or menacing. These same viewers, though, might respond more positively to a longdistance photo of wind turbines against a scarlet sunset over the hills. In contrast, other viewers might interpret these wind turbines in motion as an argument for the plentiful energy that wind farms generate. For these viewers, the photograph's angle of vision, which emphasizes the size and power of these wind towers against a background of barren hills and blue sky, could be used to counter David Rockwood's argument in his letter to the editor in

Chapter 1 (pp. 6–7) that wind power is unreliable and destroys the "pristine wilderness." Instead, to these viewers the photograph suggests that wind farms make productive use of arid or barren land. Interpreted this way, this photo could be seen to use *pathos* to appeal to environmentalists' concerns (preserve beautiful landscape; don't harm wildlife) while evoking positive feelings about technology. In either case, viewers would agree that the photographer is obviously a professional, who uses an upward camera placement to emphasize the technological power of the wind turbines. One's feelings toward the photograph and the photographer may also depend on how much the photograph seems "natural" as opposed to being framed for artistic or political effect. Because images are somewhat open in the way they create visual arguments, writers of texts that include images should anticipate viewers' possible alternative interpretations.

Analyzing Visual Messages

FOR
WRITING
AND
DISCUSSION

The following exercise asks you to think about how rhetorical effects of images can create implicit arguments. Figures 3.3–3.6 depict the controversial northernmost part of Alaska—the Arctic National Wildlife Refuge and the North Slope near the Brooks Range that Arctic Power and Jimmy Carter described on page 56. This region figures prominently in public debates about the United States' energy independence, climate change, environmental preservation, and unexplored sources of oil. Note that oil drilling has long been established in the North Slope but is currently forbidden in the adjacent ANWR. Working in small groups or as a whole class, explore the rhetorical effect of images by doing the following two tasks.

1. ***Analyzing the Photos.*** Explore the rhetorical effect of these images, noting how the effect may differ from person to person.
   a. In each photograph, on what details has the photographer chosen to focus? How do the details contribute to a dominant impression conveyed by the whole photograph? How does the photograph affect you emotionally? How does it make you feel about the ANWR/North Slope?
   b. Place your impression of the ANWR/North Slope, as conveyed by each of these images, on a continuum from ugly/forbidding to beautiful/fascinating or from barren/empty of animal life to biologically rich.
2. ***Using the Photos.*** Now imagine that you are creating a flyer for each of the following audiences and purposes. Which photo would you use to make the most compelling argument (consider *logos*, *ethos*, and *pathos*) for each audience? Explain your reasoning. Note that there is no "right answer" for these questions. If you think that none of the photographs would be appropriate for the designated audience and purpose, what kind of photograph would be more effective?
   a. *Audience:* tourists
      Purpose: to invite people to buy tour packages to the Arctic National Wildlife Refuge and the North Slope

(*continued*)

FIGURE 3.3 Caribou Crossing a River in the Arctic National Wildlife Refuge

FIGURE 3.4 Caribou Grazing Near Oil Pipeline in the Arctic North Slope

FIGURE 3.5 The ANWR Coastal Plain in Winter

FIGURE 3.6 Oil-Extraction Plant, North Slope

b. *Audience*: political leaders and voters
   Purpose: to persuade decision makers to take a pro-environment, anti-business stand on this region
c. *Audience*: political leaders and voters
   Purpose: to persuade decision makers to see this region as remote, empty, and therefore available for oil exploration and business development
d. *Audience*: undecided voters who want both more oil and a preserved environment
   Purpose: to persuade people to see that economic development in the ANWR can be compatible with preserving the region's unique natural beauty and wildlife

The Rhetoric of Clothing and Other Consumer Items

Not only do photographs, paintings, and drawings have rhetorical power, but so do the images projected by many of our consumer choices. Consider, for example, the rhetorical thinking that goes into our choice of clothes. We choose our clothes not only to keep ourselves covered and warm but also to project visually our identification with certain social groups and subcultures. For example, if you want to be identified as a skateboarder, a preppy socialite, a geek, a NASCAR fan, or a junior partner in a corporate law firm, you know how to select clothes and accessories that convey that identification. The way you dress is a code that communicates where you fit (or how you want to be perceived as fitting) within a class and social structure.

How do these symbolic codes get established? They can be set by fashion designers, by advertisers, or by trendy groups or individuals. The key to any new clothing code is to make it look different in some distinctive way from an earlier code or from a code of another group. Sometimes clothing codes develop to show rebellion against the values of parents or authority figures. At other times they develop to show new kinds of group identities.

Clothing codes are played on in conscious ways in fashion advertisements so that consumers become very aware of what identifications are signaled by different styles and brands. This aspect of consumer society is so ubiquitous that one of the marks of growing affluence in third world countries is people's attention to the rhetoric of consumer goods. Consider the second epigraph to this chapter, which indicates that villagers in India watching TV ads notice not only the soap or shampoo being advertised but also the brands of motorbikes and the lifestyles of the people in the ads. Buying a certain kind of consumer good projects a certain kind of status or group or class identity. Our point, from a rhetorical perspective, is that in making a consumer choice, many people are concerned not only with the quality of the item itself but also with its rhetorical symbolism. Note that the same item can send quite different messages to different groups: A Rolex watch might enhance one's credibility at a corporate board meeting while undercutting it at a barbecue for union workers.

Clothing as Visual Arguments

FOR WRITING AND DISCUSSION

The rhetorical power of clothing especially comes into play in the workplace. This exercise asks to you think about workplace dress codes, which are enforced by peer pressure and peer modeling as well as by company policies. Figures 3.7 to 3.10 show four different workplace environments. Working in small groups or as a whole class, consider the rhetoric of workplace clothing by sharing your responses to the following questions:

1. How would you describe the differences in dress codes in each of these environments?
2. If you were employed in one of these workplaces, how much do you think you could vary your style of dress without violating workplace codes?

(*continued*)

FIGURE 3.7 Engineering firm

FIGURE 3.8 Warehouse

FIGURE 3.9 Associates, Law Firm

FIGURE 3.10 Espresso Bar

3. Suppose that you are interviewing for a job in one of these workplaces. What clothing would be appropriate for your interview and why? (Note that how you dress for an interview might be different from how you dress once you have the job.) Share your rhetorical thinking about clothing choices aimed at making the best first impression on the people who interview you. Be as specific as possible for all items of clothing including shoes and accessories.

4. To what extent are dress codes for women more complex than those for men?

Chapter Summary

In this chapter we have looked briefly at rhetorical theory in order to explain the persuasive power of both verbal and visual texts.

- *Concept 8: Messages persuade through their angle of vision.* Any text necessarily looks at its subject from a perspective—an angle of vision—that selects and emphasizes some details while omitting or minimizing others. You can analyze writers' angle of vision by considering their direct statements of intention, their selection of details, their word choice, their figures of speech, and their manipulation of sentence structure to control emphasis.
- *Concept 9: Messages persuade through appeals to* **logos**, **ethos**, *and* **pathos.** *Logos* refers to the power of the writer's reasons and evidence; *pathos* to the way the writer connects to the reader's sympathies, emotions, values, and beliefs; and *ethos* to the way the writer portrays himself or herself as trustworthy and credible.
- *Concept 10: Nonverbal messages persuade through visual strategies that can be analyzed rhetorically.* Like verbal texts, visual texts have an angle of vision created by the way the image is framed and by the perspective from which it is viewed. Images also make implicit arguments (*logos*), appeal to the viewer's emotions and values (*pathos*), and suggest the creator's character and trustworthiness (*ethos*). One can also analyze consumer choices (clothing, jewelry, cars) rhetorically because such choices make implicit arguments about the consumer's desired identity.

Analyzing Angle of Vision in Two Passages about Nuclear Energy

BRIEF

WRITING PROJECT

Background and Readings

This brief writing project will give you practice at analyzing the angle of vision in different texts. The assignment focuses on two passages about nuclear power plants.

The first passage is from the home page of NuclearPowerNow, a nuclear power advocacy site. It was posted in 2008.

PASSAGE 1

Nuclear Power Now

Nuclear power is the world's largest source of emission-free energy. Nuclear power plants produce no controlled air pollutants, such as sulfur and particulates, or greenhouse gases. The use of nuclear power in place of other energy sources helps to keep the air clean, preserve the Earth's climate, avoid ground-level ozone formation and prevent acid rain.

Nuclear power has important implications for our national security. Inexpensive nuclear power, in combination with fuel cell technology, could significantly reduce our dependency on foreign oil.

Nuclear power plants have experienced an admirable safety record. About 20% of electricity generated in the U.S. comes from nuclear power, and in the last forty years of this production, not one single fatality has occurred as a result of the operation of a civilian nuclear power plant in the United States. In comparison, many people die in coal mining accidents every year and approximately ten thousand Americans die every year from pollution related to coal burning.

The nuclear power industry generates approximately 2,000 tons of solid waste annually in the United States. In comparison, coal fueled power plants produce 100,000,000 tons of ash and sludge annually, and this ash is laced with poisons such as mercury and nitric oxide.

Even this 2,000 tons of nuclear waste is not a technical problem. Reprocessing of nuclear fuel, and the implementation of Integral Fast Reactor technology, will enable us to turn the vast majority of what is currently considered waste into energy.

Unfortunately, the voting public has been victimized by forty years of misinformation regarding the safety of nuclear power. The graphs on nuclear energy showing it to be safe, economical, and in our national interest are countered by anti-nuclear activists using fear tactics to frighten the electorate into inaction.

Until we can successfully educate the American electorate on the real pros and cons of nuclear power, we will not be able to engage in a healthy national discussion on the topic.

The second passage is by Carl Pope, the executive director of the Sierra Club. This brief article was posted in September 2009 on the "Great Debate" blog site hosted by Reuters, a news service focused on business and industry.

PASSAGE 2

Nuclear Power Is Not the Way Forward

Nuclear power is not a responsible choice and makes no sense as part of America's clean energy future. We can meet our energy needs through energy efficiency and renewable energy, and have a clean and healthy world without nuclear power.

There are four insurmountable problems with nuclear power.

First, nuclear power produces highly dangerous radioactive waste. Every nuclear reactor generates about 20 tons of highly radioactive spent nuclear fuel and additional low-level radioactive waste per year. The waste can kill at high doses and cause cancer and birth defects at low doses. Nuclear waste remains dangerous to humans for 200 thousand years.

Worse, we don't know what to do with this waste once it is generated. Some propose dumping nuclear waste in Yucca Mountain, NV; however, the mountain is seismically active. An earthquake in the 1990's caused over $1 million damage to a Department of Energy (DOE) facility at the site. In addition, a Department of Energy panel of scientists has found that the nuclear material may leak from the containment vessels over time and will contaminate groundwater. On its way to Yucca Mountain, the waste would also pass through thousands of cities and towns and present multiple exposure risks.

Second, nuclear power is prohibitively expensive. The method is not anywhere near cost effective; nuclear plants in the states of Oregon, New York, Maine, Illinois, and Connecticut have been shut down because the owners found it was too expensive to keep them going.

American taxpayers are also subsidizing the nuclear industry. According to the Congressional Research Service, the industry has cost taxpayers tens of billions of dollars in research and development subsidies.

Third, an accident at a coal plant is a problem, but an accident at a nuclear plant can be a disaster. Because human beings operate plants and drive the trucks that transport nuclear waste, accidents can and will happen. The danger with nuclear power is that the stakes in accidents are extremely high. Anyone exposed to radiation leaks or accidents will likely sicken or die from that exposure.

And finally, there is a risk that nuclear material will fall into the wrong hands. Some have recommended that we consider "reprocessing" of spent nuclear fuel, a method that consolidates waste into weapons-usable plutonium. The government has elaborate plans to prevent rogue nations and terrorists from stealing the nuclear fuel or waste to make nuclear bombs. The more nuclear reactors, the more risk of radioactive material being stolen to make bombs.

Nuclear power is not the way forward. America deserves a safer, cleaner, and cheaper energy future.

Your task: Contrast the differences in angle of vision in these two passages by analyzing how they create their different rhetorical effects. Consider factors such as overt statements of meaning, selection/omission of details, connotations of words and figures of speech, and sentence emphasis. To help guide your analysis, review the strategies chart ("Strategies for Constructing an Angle of Vision"). Your goal here is to explain to your readers how these two passages create different impressions of nuclear power.

Cabrera 1

Racchel Cabrera
E. Rosenblum
ENGL 1303
15 October 2010

How Much Thought Goes Into Ads

The United States has adopted a modified free market economy that allows and at times requires businesses that produce similar merchandise to compete and out-do the other. This constant rivalry benefits the consumer directly since it's the manufacturers' mission to create the next best product, or a better version of it. But with so much competition, how is a business to attract the necessary attention and publicity of this new and improved product to the masses? Advertising is any determined company's sole tool in maximizing profits. Take a stroll on campus, or a drive down 45, or even as you wait in the theatres for the movie to begin, you're bound to be bombarded with more than just a few advertisements. Advertisers use lighting techniques, camera angles and placement tactics to meticulously construct a commercial that appeals to specific audiences. A better understanding of how such techniques can influence a purchase can be achieved through the dissection of chewing gum competitors', Trident and Orbit, ads.

The Trident White ad displays a man casually standing in a business suit waiting in an elevator between two women. The woman to the right of the man is blonde and is wearing a conservative blue dress and necklace to match her eyes. The woman to his left is brunette and wearing a white ruffled shirt and a salmon cardigan. In one hand, she holds a coffee cup and the other grips the railing behind her. Both ladies are looking up at the grinning businessman with closed-mouth, approving smirks. The text above the man's head reads in pure white "35% More Officecrushable" and at the bottom, the ad informs that "Trident White prevents over 35% of stains for a smile that's very convincing." The elevator is mostly mahogany brown with two strips of white on either side of the smiling man.

The Orbit ad is set up in two parts. In the top half, a smiling blonde woman stands with excellent posture in a sailor-esque white suit with blue detailing and a scarf wrapped around her neck to match. She's gesturing towards a gigantic pack of Orbit gum unraveling from its plastic covering. The bottom half shows the same blonde woman in the same posture and position now exposed in her undergarments (scarf still attached). The enormous pack of gum that the half-naked lady is still gesturing to is now free of its plastic skin. The ad reads "When you remove the outer wrapper, there's something surprising underneath."

The Trident ad is obviously geared towards the male audience as it captures the ego boosting moment of two very attractive women ogling at one average man. The brunette is even gripping the railing as if to show her struggle at resisting the enchanting pearly whites. It also simultaneously appeals to the nine to five cubicle inhabitants, who are notorious for being coffee addicts. Anyone who drinks coffee on a regular basis can testify the stains it leaves on the enamel, so a product that advocates 35% stain prevention would definitely be a point of interest for a coffee addict. The advertisers attract attention to the man's smile by, first, positioning his face dead center of the ad, and then eliminating any means of comparing the brightness of his teeth to the other members of the elevator as they only smirk at him with pursed lips. The brown walls of the elevator as a background subtly aids in emphasizing the illumination of his grin, along with the white lettering above his head. The lighting is relatively normal and realistic for an elevator but the angle of the camera is set a little lower to make the man seem taller and more superior. Men can relate to/admire a character of superiority and power.

Cabrera 3

In the Orbit ad, the presentation of conservativeness and "cleanness" not only contribute to the promotion of white teeth but also establishes the intended audience: women. Cleanliness and neatness allures the female gender because it's also associated with stability and assurance, which are important attributes for women look for, even in gum. The ad does call for the removal of the spokeswoman's suit but her undergarments are tasteful and cover all the important areas from above her bosom to her mid-thigh. The lighting is moderate as well in this but the creators of this advertisement did make sure to shoot a full body view of the blonde from a slightly lower angle to show slight superiority to (perhaps) yellow or stained teeth. White is a common theme from the back drop to the spokeswoman's clothes to her perfect ivory teeth. The gum pack is the main focus, positioned in the center and blown up to a size larger than the woman standing next to it.

Both ads used the colors white and blue. White symbolizes cleanliness, spotlessness, and novelty for the two commercials. The Trident ad used the blonde's blue dress for calmness, it's a peaceful/neutral color that serves purely to match (in neutrality) with the brunette's passive color schemes. Orbit uses blue to symbolize ice and snow which is then associated with the color white, and so, through circular symbolization, blue represents the same elements as white. They both depict the gum-chewing models as happy, brightly shining independents, except Trident uses an unorthodox method of displaying independency. Females are surrounding the man, but because he seems to pay no attention to the gazing, even looking up to the ceiling, it leads the audience to assume he either doesn't need the attention or care for it.

Advertisers use a medley of techniques to coax their audience into purchasing their product. And even after knowing full well the tactics businesses utilize to their advantage, we the audience, will fall victim to their tricks time and time again because without gullible consumerism, our free market economy would not survive.

THINKING RHETORICALLY ABOUT STYLE AND DOCUMENT DESIGN

4

Style is everything, and nothing. It is not that, as is commonly supposed, you get your content and soup it up with style; style is absolutely embedded in the way you perceive.

—*Martin Amis, Author*

... [C]larity and excellence in thinking is very much like clarity and excellence in the display of data. When principles of design replicate principles of thought, the act of arranging information becomes an act of thought.

—*Edward Tufte, Visual Design Researcher and Consultant*

In Chapters 1, 2, and 3, we explained the importance of rhetorical thinking for writers. In this chapter, we focus on the rhetorical effect of different writing styles and document designs and suggest ways to increase the power and effectiveness of your prose. As our two epigraphs suggest, style and document design are not decorative add-ons to jazz up dull content but rather means of guiding an audience to see what matters. Style and document design are thus "acts of thought."

To build on your understanding of rhetorical effectiveness, in this chapter you will learn two new concepts:

- **CONCEPT 11** Good writers make purposeful stylistic choices.
- **CONCEPT 12** Good writers make purposeful document design choices.

CONCEPT 11 Good writers make purposeful stylistic choices.

You can gain power as a writer by understanding the rhetorical effect of different writing styles.

Factors That Affect Style

Style refers to analyzable features of language that work together to create different effects. As shown in Figure 4.1, style can be thought of as a mixture of four factors:

- ***Ways of shaping sentences,*** such as length or complexity of sentence structure
- ***Word choice,*** such as abstract versus concrete or formal versus colloquial
- ***Voice, or persona,*** which refers to the reader's impression of the writer as projected from the page: expert versus layperson or scholarly voice versus popular voice
- ***Tone,*** which refers to the writer's attitude toward the subject matter or toward the reader, such as cold or warm, humorous or serious, detached or passionate

What style you adopt depends on your purpose, audience, and genre. Consider, for example, the differences in style in two articles about the animated sitcom *South Park*. The first passage comes from an academic journal in which the author analyzes how race is portrayed in *South Park*. The second passage is from a popular magazine, where the author argues that despite *South Park*'s vulgarity, the sitcom has a redeeming social value.

PASSAGE FROM SCHOLARLY JOURNAL

In these cartoons, multiplicity encodes a set of nonwhite identities to be appropriated and commodified by whiteness. In the cartoon world, obscene humor and satire mediate this commodification. The whiteness that appropriates typically does so by virtue of its mobile positioning between and through imagined boundaries contrarily shown as impassible to black characters or agents marked as black. Let me briefly turn to an appropriately confusing example of such a character in *South Park*'s

FIGURE 4.1 Ingredients of Style

Ways of shaping sentences	Types of words	Voice or persona	Tone
Long/short	Abstract/concrete	Expert/layperson	Intimate/distant
Simple/complex	Formal/colloquial	Scholar/student	Personal/impersonal
Many modifiers/few modifiers	Unusual/ordinary	Outsider/insider	Angry/calm
Normal word order/frequent inversions or interruptions	Specialized/general	Political liberal/ conservative	Browbeating/sharing
Mostly main clauses/many embedded phrases and subordinate clauses	Metaphorical/literal	Neutral observer/ active participant	Informative/ entertaining
	Scientific/literary		Humorous/serious
			Ironic/literal
			Passionately involved/aloof

scatological hero extraordinaire, Eric Cartman. ... Eric Cartman's yen for breaking into Black English and interactions with black identities also fashion him an appropriator. However, Cartman's voice and persona may be seen as only an avatar, one layer of textual identity for creator Trey Parker, who may be regarded in one sense as a "blackvoice" performer.

—Michael A. Chaney, "Representations of Race and Place in
Static Shock, King of the Hill, and *South Park*"

PASSAGE FROM POPULAR MAGAZINE

Despite the theme song's chamber of commerce puffery, *South Park* is the closest television has ever come to depicting hell on earth. Its inhabitants are, almost without exception, stupid, ignorant or venal—usually all three. Its central characters are four eight-year-olds: Stan, the high-achiever, Kyle, the sensitive Jew, Kenny, whose grisly death each week prompts the tortured cry, "Oh my God! They've killed Kenny! Those bastards!" and Eric Cartman, who has become the Archie Bunker of the '90s, beloved by millions. My 12-year-old son informs me that many of his schoolmates have taken to speaking permanently in Cartman's bigoted and usually furiously inarticulate manner. A (mild) sample: any display of human sensitivity is usually met by him with the rejoinder: "Tree-hugging hippie crap!" This has led to predictable calls for *South Park*, which is usually programmed late in the evening, to be banned altogether.

—Kevin Michael Grace, "*South Park* Is a Snort of Defiance
Against a World Gone to Hell"

Analyzing Differences in Style

FOR WRITING AND DISCUSSION

Working in small groups or as a whole class, analyze the differences in the styles of these two samples.

1. How would you describe differences in the length and complexity of sentences, in the level of vocabulary, and in the degree of formality?
2. How do the differences in styles create different voices, personas, and tones?
3. Based on clues from style and genre, who is the intended audience of each piece? What is the writer's purpose? How does each writer hope to surprise the intended audience with something new, challenging, or valuable?
4. How are the differences in content and style influenced by differences in purpose, audience, and genre?

In the sections that follow, we highlight some ways of thinking about style that will be particularly relevant to you in your college writing.

Four Powerful Strategies for Improving Your Style

The preceding section has given you an overview of vocabulary and concepts for analyzing style. In this section we offer four powerful tips for making your own style forceful, clear, and effective. Of all the advice given about style in various handbooks, these four tips are usually regarded as essential—so much so that they rise to the level of rhetorical principles.

Streamline Your Prose by Cutting Deadwood In early drafts, writers often produce wordy, convoluted prose where unneeded words and roundabout expressions take up space without adding meaning. When they revise, experienced writers cut deadwood and use other strategies to make their prose as efficient and economical as possible. Their aim is to create streamlined sentences that keep the reader on track. In the following examples, consider how cutting words creates a leaner, more streamlined style:

Wordy/Verbose	Streamlined
As a result of the labor policies established by Bismarck, the working-class people in Germany were convinced that revolution was unnecessary for the attainment of their goals and purposes.	Bismarck's labor policies convinced the German working class that revolution was unnecessary.
In recent times a new interest has been apparent among many writers to make the language as it is used by specialists in the areas of government, law, and medicine more available to be understood and appreciated by readers who are not specialists in the aforementioned areas.	Recently writers have tried to make the language of government, law, and medicine more accessible to nonspecialist readers.

Control Emphasis with Sentence Structure Experienced writers vary the length and structure of their sentences to create a rhythm that emphasizes main ideas. For example, you can emphasize an idea by placing it in a main clause or by placing it in a short sentence surrounded by longer sentences. We illustrated this phenomenon in our discussion of the U. R. Riddle exercise (pp. 54–55), where variations in sentence structure created different emphases on Riddle's good or bad points:

> Although Riddle is a brilliant thinker, he had problems relating to other students in my class. (Emphasizes Riddle's personal shortcomings.)
> Although Riddle had problems relating to other students in my class, he is a brilliant thinker. (Emphasizes Riddle's intelligence.)

Neither of these effects would have been possible had the writer simply strung together two simple sentences:

> Riddle had problems relating to other students in my class. He is also a brilliant thinker.

In this version, both points about Riddle are equally emphasized, leaving the reader uncertain about the writer's intended meaning.

Our point is that subordinate structures help the reader distinguish between main and subordinate ideas. If you string together a long sequence of short sentences—or simply join them with words like *and, or, so,* or *but*—you create a choppy effect that fails to distinguish between more important and less important material. Consider the differences in the following examples.

Every Idea Equally Emphasized	Main Ideas Emphasized	Comment
Hisako usually attends each lab meeting. However, she missed the last one. She took the train to Boston to meet her sister. Her sister was arriving from Tokyo.	Although Hisako usually attends each lab meeting, she missed the last one because she took the train to Boston to meet her sister, who was arriving from Tokyo.	Sentence now focuses on main idea—why Hisako missed the lab.
I am a student at Sycamore College, and I live in Watkins Hall, and I am enclosing a proposal that concerns a problem with dorm life. There is too much drinking, so nondrinking students don't have an alcohol-free place to go, and so the university should create an alcohol-free dorm, and they should strictly enforce this no-alcohol policy.	As a Sycamore College student living in Watkins Hall, I am enclosing a proposal to improve dorm life. Because there is too much drinking on campus, there is no place for nondrinking students to go. I propose that the university create an alcohol-free dorm and strictly enforce the no-alcohol policy.	The fact that the writer is a Sycamore College student living in Watkins Hall is needed background information but not a main point. Focus of passage is now a crisp summary of the problem and her proposed solution.

In each of the above examples, the revised passage is easier to process because it subordinates less important material, focusing the reader's attention on main ideas.

Use Specific Details, Where Appropriate, to Stay Low on the Ladder of Abstraction In previous writing courses, you might have been offered advice such as "Show, don't tell" or "Use concrete, specific language." Our advice in this section follows the same spirit: to write as low on the ladder of abstraction as your context allows.

We use the metaphor of a ladder to show how words can vary along a continuum from the abstract ("crime") to the more specific and concrete ("aggravated assault with brass knuckles"). As a general rule, when you move from points to particulars in your prose, the more specific you can make these particulars, the more vivid the rhetorical effect on a reader. As an illustration, consider Figure 4.2, which depicts a "ladder of abstraction" descending from abstract terms at the top toward more specific ones at the bottom.

Choosing words low on the ladder of abstraction is particularly effective for descriptive writing, where your goal is to create a vivid mental image for readers. Writing teachers often express this advice through the maxim "Show, don't tell." *Tell* words interpret a scene or tell readers what to feel about a scene without describing it. ("The dog looked angry.") In contrast, *show* words describe a scene through sensory details. ("The neighbor's Doberman, growling and baring his

Level on Ladder	Clothing Example	Global Problem Example	Gendered Play Example
High level: Abstract or general	• She chose new footwear.	• Should farmers in developing countries produce traditional crops or commercial crops?	• Sam exhibited traditionally gendered play behavior.
Middle level	• She chose new flip-flops.	• In India, should farmers plant traditional crops or genetically engineered crops?	• Sam played with trucks and fire engines.
Low level: Specific or concrete	• She chose new purple platform flip-flops with rhinestones.	• For sale on the global market, should farmers of Northern India plant traditional mandua and jhangora or genetically modified soy beans?	• Sam gleefully smashed his toy Tonka fire engine into the coffee table.

FIGURE 4.2 The Ladder of Abstraction: From Abstract to Specific

teeth, lunged against his chain.") The description itself evokes the desired effect without requiring the writer to interpret it overtly. This difference in rhetorical effect can be seen in the following examples of descriptive writing:

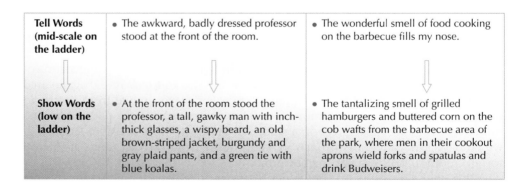

Tell Words (mid-scale on the ladder)	• The awkward, badly dressed professor stood at the front of the room.	• The wonderful smell of food cooking on the barbecue fills my nose.
Show Words (low on the ladder)	• At the front of the room stood the professor, a tall, gawky man with inch-thick glasses, a wispy beard, an old brown-striped jacket, burgundy and gray plaid pants, and a green tie with blue koalas.	• The tantalizing smell of grilled hamburgers and buttered corn on the cob wafts from the barbecue area of the park, where men in their cookout aprons wield forks and spatulas and drink Budweisers.

Of course, not all writing needs to be this low on the ladder of abstraction. Our advice, rather, is to descend as low on the ladder as your context allows. Even the most abstract kind of prose will move up and down between several rungs on the ladder. In closed-form prose writers need to make choices about the level of specificity that will be most effective based on their purpose, audience, and genre. Note the differences in the levels of abstraction in the following passages:

PASSAGE 1: FAIRLY HIGH ON LADDER OF ABSTRACTION

Although lightning produces the most deaths and injuries of all weather-related accidents, the rate of danger varies considerably from state to state. Florida has twice as many deaths and injuries from lightning strikes as any other state. Hawaii and Alaska have the fewest.

Point sentence

Particulars high on ladder of abstraction

—Passage from a general interest informative article on weather-related accidents

PASSAGE 2: LOWER ON LADDER OF ABSTRACTION

Florida has twice as many deaths and injuries from lightning strikes as any other state, with many of these casualties occurring on the open spaces of golf courses. Florida golfers should carefully note the signals of dangerous weather conditions such as darkening skies, a sudden drop in temperature, an increase in wind, flashes of light and claps of thunder, and the sensation of an electric charge on one's hair or body. In the event of an electric storm, golfers should run into a forest, get under a shelter, get into a car, or assume the safest body position. To avoid being the tallest object in an area, if caught in open areas, golfers should find a low spot, spread out, and crouch into a curled position with feet together to create minimal body contact with the ground.

Point sentence

Particulars at midlevel on ladder

Particulars at lower level on ladder

—Passage from a safety article aimed at Florida golfers

Both of these passages are effective for their audience and purpose. The first passage might be compared to a distant shot with a camera, giving an overview of lightning deaths in the United States, while the second zooms in for a more detailed look at a specific case, Florida golf courses. Sometimes, low-on-the-ladder particulars consist of statistics or quotations rather than sensory details. For example, civil engineer David Rockwood uses low-on-the-ladder numerical data about the size and number of wind towers to convince readers that wind generation of electricity entails environmental damage. Your rhetorical decisions about level of abstraction are important because too much high-on-the-scale writing can become dull for readers, while too much low-on-the-scale writing can seem overwhelming or pointless.

See Rockwood's letter to the editor, pp. 6–7.

Choosing Details for Different Levels on the Ladder of Abstraction

FOR WRITING AND DISCUSSION

The following exercise will help you appreciate how details can be chosen at different levels of abstraction to serve different purposes and audiences. Working in small groups or as a whole class, invent details at appropriate positions on the ladder of abstraction for each of the following point sentences.

1. *Yesterday's game was a major disappointment.* You are writing an e-mail message to a friend who is a fan (of baseball, football, basketball, another sport) and missed the game; use midlevel details to explain what was disappointing.

(continued)

2. *Although the game stank, there were some great moments.* Switch to low-on-the-ladder specific details to describe one of these "great moments."
3. *Advertising in women's fashion magazines creates a distorted and unhealthy view of beauty.* You are writing an analysis for a college course on popular culture; use high-to-midlevel details to give a one-paragraph overview of several ways these ads create an unhealthy view of beauty.
4. *One recent ad, in particular, conveys an especially destructive message about beauty.* Choose a particular ad and describe it with low-on-the-ladder, very specific details.

Use a Voice Matched to Your Purpose, Audience, and Genre College students often wonder what style—and particularly, what voice—is appropriate for college papers. For most college assignments, we recommend that you approximate your natural speaking voice to give your writing a conversational academic style. By "natural," we mean a voice that strives to be plain and clear while retaining the engaging quality of a person who is enthusiastic about the subject.

Of course, as you become an expert in a discipline, you may need to move toward a more scholarly voice. For example, the prose in an academic journal article can be extremely dense with technical terms and complex sentence structure, but expert readers in that field understand and expect this voice. Students sometimes try to imitate a dense academic style before they have achieved the disciplinary expertise to make the style sound natural. The result can seem pretentiously stilted and phony—an "inflated" style. At the other extreme, students sometimes adopt an overly informal or street slang voice that doesn't fit an academic context. Writing with clarity and directness within your natural range will usually create the most effective and powerful voice. Consider the difference in the following examples:

Inflated Voice	Natural Speaking Voice	Overly Informal Voice
As people advance in age, they experience time-dependent alterations in their ability to adapt to environmental change. However, much prior research on the aging process has failed to differentiate between detrimental changes that result from an organism's aging process itself and detrimental changes resulting from a disease process that is often associated with aging.	As people get older, they are less able to adapt to changes in their environment. Research on aging, however, hasn't always distinguished between loss of function caused by aging itself and loss caused by diseases common among older people.	Old folks don't adapt well to changes in their environments. Some scientists who studied the cane and walker crowd found out that it was hard to tell the difference between bad stuff caused by age versus bad stuff caused by disease.

Although the "natural voice" style is appropriate for most college papers, especially those written for lower-division courses, many professors construct assignments asking you to adopt different voices and different styles. It is thus important to understand the professor's assignment and to adopt the style and voice appropriate for the assigned rhetorical situation.

Revising Passages to Create a More Effective Style

Working individually or in small groups, try to improve the style of the following passages by cutting deadwood, by combining sentences to subordinate less important ideas and emphasize main points, or by achieving a more natural voice.

1. It is unfortunate that the mayor acted in this manner. The mayor settled the issue. But before he settled the issue he made a mistake. He fostered a public debate that was very bitter. The debate pitted some of his subordinates against each other. These subordinates were in fact key subordinates. It also caused many other people to feel inflamed passions and fears as a result of the way the mayor handled the issue.

2. Cheerleading should be seen as a sport. It should not be regarded as just sexy dancing. This issue is especially important to women. It is often the desire of junior high school girls to want to become cheerleaders, but their role models for achieving this desire are the Dallas Cowboys cheerleaders, but instead the vision they should strive to achieve is a vision of cheerleaders as athletes. Such athletes in order to become cheerleaders must be able to do very athletic moves and stunts such as handstands, cartwheels, handsprings, high jumps, and the splits. A great cheerleader is not a girl who makes suggestive moves like a pop star in an MTV video, but instead it is a girl who can participate in routines that are complex like lifts, tosses, flips, catches, and other gymnastic moves.

FOR WRITING AND DISCUSSION

CONCEPT 12 **Good writers make purposeful document design choices.**

Document design refers to the format of a text including use of charts, illustrations, or visual images. The "look" of a document can signal to readers its purpose, its genre, its intended audience, and the writer's intended (or unintended!) *ethos*. Writers need to distinguish between document design appropriate for manuscripts—a category that includes most of the kinds of writing you will do in college—and document design for published works.

Document Design for Manuscripts and Papers

As a writer in an academic setting, you will usually be producing manuscript (keyboarded pages of typed text held together with a staple or folder, or submitted electronically) rather than a publication-ready document. Your document design choices mainly concern margins, font style and size, material in headers or footers (page number, document identification), and line spacing. Generally these choices are dictated by the style guidelines of an academic discipline such as the Modern

Language Association (MLA) or by the conventions established in a business or professional setting. If you deviate from the expected document design, readers will assume that you are doing so on purpose and will wonder what that purpose is. (If you use scripted font or design a personalized cover page for an academic paper, you'd make a "notice me" statement, analogous to wearing a green jumpsuit to a business meeting—you might want to do so, but there's a risk.)

Attention to document design and the appearance of your manuscripts thus signals your membership in an academic or professional community. An inappropriately formatted or sloppy paper can hurt your *ethos* and may send a message that you are unprofessional. Figure 4.3 illustrates the first- and second-page manuscript formats for MLA and APA (American Psychological Association) style papers.

Document Design for Published Works

In contrast to manuscripts and college papers, published works require elaborate decisions about document design. The original manuscripts for a scholarly article, an article for a popular magazine, a newspaper op-ed piece, and a Web page may have all been double-spaced, typed documents with one-inch margins, but the published products look totally different, as you can see in Figure 4.4. Today's writers, especially in professional settings, often use desktop-publishing software to produce print-ready or Web-ready documents that have a professional visual appeal. For published documents, design is closely related to genre and involves decisions about type, use of space and layout, color, and graphics or images. Let's look at each in turn.

Type Type comes in different typeface styles, or **fonts**, that are commonly grouped in three font families:

1. **Serif fonts** have tiny extensions on the letters, which make them easier to read in long documents.
2. **Sans serif fonts** lack the extensions on the letters and are good for labels, headings, and short documents.
3. **Specialty fonts,** often used for decorative effect, include script fonts and special symbols.

Fonts also come in different sizes and can be formatted with **boldface**, *italics*, <u>underlining</u>, or shading.

In published documents, font use varies by genre. Scholarly print publications usually employ conservative typography: a consistently sized, plain, highly readable font like Times New Roman with variations mainly reserved for titles, headings, notes, and bibliography. Popular magazines, on the other hand, tend to use fonts playfully and artistically; they vary font styles and sizes to attract readers' attention and to make articles look pleasingly decorative on the page. Although the body text of articles is usually the same font throughout, the opening page often uses a variety of fonts and sizes. Font variations may highlight key ideas for readers who are reading casually or rapidly.

FIGURE 4.3 Manuscript Format for MLA and APA Papers

MLA Manuscript, page 1

Gardiner 1

James Gardiner

Professor Johnson

Writing Seminar: Inquiry and Argument

15 May 2007

Why *Facebook* Might Not Be Good For You:

Some Dangers of Online Social Networks

Walk into any computer lab located at any college campus across the country and you'll see dozens of students logged onto an online social network (OSN). In the last few years, the use of these networks has skyrocketed among Internet users, especially young adults. These new virtual communities are significantly influencing the way young people communicate and interact with one another. A report titled "E-Expectations: The Class of 2007" went so far as to label upcoming college freshmen "the Social-Networking Generation" (qtd. in Joly).

In late 2006, the Pew Internet Project, a nonpartisan, nonprofit research group that examines the social impact of the Internet, reported that 55 percent of online teens have created a personal profile on OSNs and that 48 percent of teens visit social networking Web sites daily, with 22 percent visiting several times a day (Lenhart and Madden 2). The two most popular OSNs are *MySpace* and *Facebook*. *MySpace* is a general networking site that allows anyone to join, develop a profile, and display personal information. In less than four years of existence, *MySpace* has exploded to become the third most visited Web site on the Internet behind only *Google* and *Yahoo* ("Top Sites") with more than 100 million members (Joly). *Facebook* is geared more toward college students (until recently it required that a person attend a university to join the network) and is the number one site accessed by 18- to 24-year-olds. According to research studies cited in an article in the *Toronto Star*, 90 percent of all undergraduates

APA Manuscript, page 1

A Comparison of Gender Stereotypes in *SpongeBob SquarePants* and a 1930s

Mickey Mouse Cartoon

Lauren Campbell, Charlie Bourain, and Tyler Nishida

November 10, 2006

MLA Manuscript, page 2

Gardiner 2

has also experienced unprecedented growth in its relatively short existence and now ranks as the seventh most visited site on the Internet ("Top Sites") and has a member base of more than 19 million (Joly).

With the use of OSNs increasing among young people, the term "Facebook trance" has emerged to describe a person who loses track of all time and stares at the screen for hours (Copeland). While "Facebook trance" might describe only an occasional and therefore harmless phenomenon, it gives rise to important questions: What are the possible negative consequences of OSNs? What should youthful users be watchful for and guard against? The purpose of this paper is to identify the possible harms of OSNs. I will suggest that overuse of OSNs can be a contributing factor to a decline in grades as well as to other problems such as a superficial view of relationships, an increase in narcissism, and possible future embarrassment.

I don't mean to deny that OSNs have positive consequences for young people. For one thing, they provide a "virtual hangout" that acts as a convenient and cost-effective way to stay in close contact with friends and family. According to the Pew survey, 91 percent of users use OSNs to keep in touch with their regularly seen friends, while 82 percent use the sites to stay in touch with distant friends (Lenhart and Madden). OSNs let young people regularly view their friends' profiles, leave short messages or comments, and share personal information. OSN researcher Danah Boyd also claims that these sites give young people a platform on which to experiment with identities, voice their opinions, and practice how they present themselves through personal data, pictures, and music placed in their profiles (Bowley). OSNs also assist them in learning more about people they've met offline. Used as an investigative tool, OSNs offer quick ways to get additional background information on someone. For example, a student could use an OSN to decide whom

APA Manuscript, page 2

Abstract

Researchers in gender identity have continually argued whether gender differences are biological or social. Because television is a prime place for teaching children gender differences through socialization, we studied the extent of gender stereotyping in two 1930s Mickey Mouse cartoons and two recent *SpongeBob SquarePants* cartoons. We analyzed the cartoons in one-minute increments and recorded the number of gender stereotypical and gender-non-stereotypical actions in each increment. Our results confirmed our hypothesis that *SpongeBob SquarePants* would have fewer gender stereotypes than Mickey Mouse. This study is significant because it shows that in at least one contemporary cartoon males and females have a range of acceptable behaviors that go beyond traditional gender stereotypes.

FIGURE 4.4 Examples of Published Documents

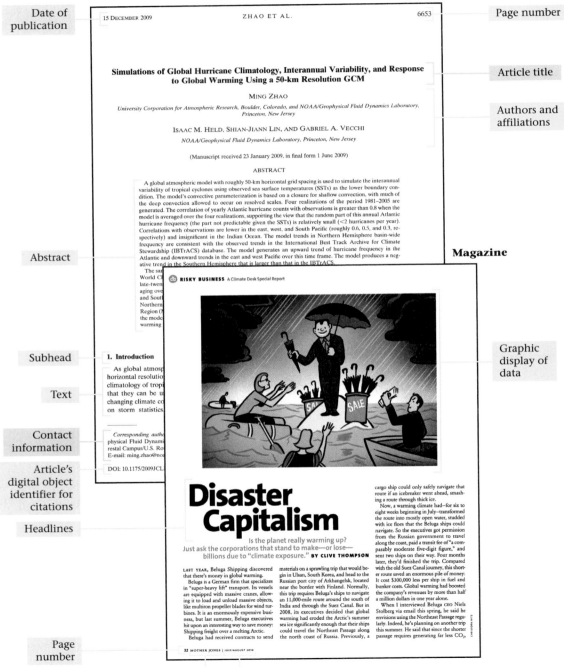

Scholarly Journal

Date of publication

Page number

Article title

Authors and affiliations

Abstract

Magazine

Subhead

Text

Graphic display of data

Contact information

Article's digital object identifier for citations

Headlines

Page number

Publication   Date

Newspaper

Op Ed Page

The Providence Sunday Journal

COMMENTARY

Sunday, February 21, 2010   B3

Date and page number

There's no 'sensible middle' in America

FROMA HARROP

Are the stars aligned to bring America's Cup back to Newport?

TOWNSEND GODDARD

Author biography

Climate evangelism undermines global-warming solutions

BJØRN LOMBORG

Headline

Author

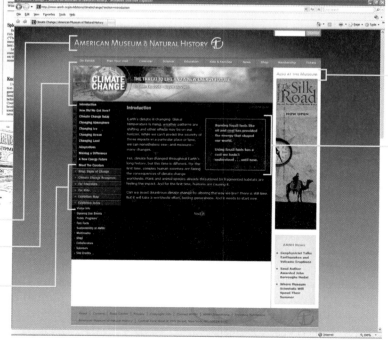

Web Page

Links to main section of museum's site

Link to blog

Site sponsor

Site title

Links to sections of site

Space and Layout **Layout** refers to how the text is formatted on the page. Layout includes the following elements:

- Page size, margin size, proportion of text to white space
- Arrangement of text on the page (single or multiple columns, spaces between paragraphs)
- Use of justification (alignment of text with the left or right margins or both margins)
- Placement of titles, use of headings and subheadings, and spacing before and after headings
- Use of numbered or bulleted lists or of boxes and sidebars to highlight ideas or break text into visual units

Academic and scholarly publications, both in print and on the Web, use simple, highly functional document layouts. Most scholarly print journals use single or double columns of text that are justified at both margins to create a regular, even look. The layout of scholarly journals strikes a balance between maximizing the amount of text that fits on a page and ensuring readability.

In contrast, text layout in popular magazines and Web sites is more varied and playful, with text often wrapped around charts, sidebars, photographs, or drawings. While readability is important, so is visual appeal and entertainment: Readers must enjoy looking at the pages. For example, many popular print magazines try to blur the distinction between content and advertising so that ads become part of the visual appeal. This is why the table of contents is often buried a dozen or more pages into the magazine. The publisher wants to coax readers to think of the ads as part of the content. In contrast, the table of contents for most academic print journals is on the cover.

Color Colors make powerful appeals, even affecting moods. Whereas manuscripts are printed entirely in black ink, published documents often use color to identify and set off main ideas or important information. Color-tinted boxes can indicate special features or allow different but related articles to appear on the same page.

Academic and scholarly articles, books, and Web sites use color minimally, relying instead on different font styles and sizes to make distinctions in content. Popular magazines and Web sites, on the other hand, use colors playfully, artistically, decoratively, and strategically to enhance their appeal. They often vary colors of type or background for different kinds of content to give variety to the whole publication.

Graphics and Images **Graphics** include visual displays of information such as tables, line graphs, bar graphs, pie charts, maps, cartoons, illustrations, and photos.

As with the use of type, space, and color, the use of graphics indicates the focus, seriousness, function, and complexity of the writing. In scientific articles and books, many of the important findings may be displayed in complex, technical graphs and tables. Sources of information for these graphics are usually prominently stated, with key variables clearly labeled. In the humanities and social sciences, content-rich photos and drawings also tend to be vital parts of an article, even the subject of the analysis.

Popular publications typically use simple numeric visuals (for example, a colorful pie chart or a dramatic graph) combined with decorative use of **images**, especially photos. If photos appear, it is worthwhile to consider their rhetorical function. For example, some photos may be unscripted, realistic, and spontaneous, like news photos of a disaster scene or a sports highlight. Some may aim to look like news photos, but are in fact scripted and posed. Still others are concept (thematic) photos meant to illustrate an idea in an article. For example, an article on health care costs may include a photoshopped picture of a woman in a hospital gown surrounded by images of pills, doctors, expensive medical equipment, and wrangling employers and insurance agents.

Analyzing Rhetorical Effect

FOR WRITING AND DISCUSSION

Working individually or in small groups, analyze how genre and document design are interrelated in the examples shown in Figure 4.4.

1. How does the design of each document—its use of fonts, layout, color, and graphics—identify each piece as a scholarly article, an article in a popular magazine, a newspaper op-ed piece, or a Web page?
2. When you download an article from an electronic database (unless it is in pdf format), you often lose visual cues about the article's original genre. Even when an article is in pdf format, you lose cues about its original print context—the kind of magazine or journal the article appeared in, the magazine's layout and advertisements, and its targeted audience. Likewise, when you print a document from a Web site, you lose contextual cues about the original Web environment. How do document design and other visual features in the original print or Web source provide important contextual information for reading the article and using it in your own research?

Chapter Summary

In this chapter we have looked at how writers think rhetorically about style and document design.

- *Concept 11: Good writers make purposeful stylistic choices.* Style refers to analyzable language features—such as sentence structure, word choice, voice, and tone—that work together to create different rhetorical effects. You can improve your style by learning to cut deadwood, use sentence structure for emphasis, write low on the ladder of abstraction, and achieve a natural voice in your writing.
- *Concept 12: Good writers make purposeful document design choices.* Document design issues differ for manuscripts and published works. In producing manuscripts, expert writers follow the guidelines of their academic or professional communities, thereby signaling insider status. Design features for published documents concern type sizes and styles; layout and spacing; use of color; and use of graphics or images. Academic articles generally adopt a conservative design while more popular genres approach design playfully and artistically.

| **Two Contrasting Descriptions of the Same Scene**

This brief writing project is a write-to-learn task that will help you appreciate how writers construct an "angle of vision" (see Concept 8) and how aspects of style (particularly writing low on the ladder of abstraction) have strong rhetorical effects (Concept 11).

> Write two descriptions of the same scene, from contrasting angles of vision. Here is the catch: Your first description must convey a favorable impression of the scene, making it appear pleasing or attractive. The second description must convey a negative or unfavorable impression, making the scene appear unpleasant or unattractive. Both descriptions must contain only factual details and must describe exactly the same scene from the same location at the same time. It's not fair, in other words, to describe the scene in sunny weather and then in the rain or otherwise to alter factual details. Each description should be one paragraph long (approximately 125–175 words).
>
> Your instructor may ask you to discuss how you sought to create different rhetorical effects in these descriptions.

Establishing a Context

To get into the spirit of this unusual assignment, you need to create a personal rationale for why you are writing two opposing descriptions. Our students have been successful imagining any one of the following three rationales:

- ***Different moods.*** Pretend that you are observing this scene in different moods. How could you reflect a "happy" view of this scene and then a "sad" view? Let the mood determine your selection and framing of details, but don't put yourself into the scene. The reader should infer your mood from the description.
- ***Verbal game.*** Here you see yourself as a word wizard trying consciously to create two different rhetorical effects for readers. In this scenario, you don't worry how you feel about the scene but how you want your readers to feel. Your focus is on crafting the language to influence your audience in different ways.
- ***Different rhetorical purposes.*** In this scenario, you imagine your description in service of some desired action. You might dislike a certain space (for example, a poorly designed library reading room) and describe it in a way that highlights its bad features. This description is *the way you really feel.* Your next task is to see this same scene from an opposing perspective—perhaps that of the architect who designed the reading room.

Observing and Taking Notes

Once you have chosen your scene, you'll need to observe and take notes for fifteen or twenty minutes in preparation for writing the focused descriptions of the scene using specific, concrete, sensory details. You need to compose descriptions that are rich in sensory detail—sights, sounds, smells, textures, even on occasion tastes—all contributing to a dominant impression that gives the description focus.

You can train yourself to notice sensory details by creating a two-column sensory chart and noting details that appeal to each of the senses. Then try describing them, first positively (left column) and then negatively (right column). One student, observing a scene in a local tavern, made these notes in her sensory chart:

Positive Description	**Negative Description**
Taste	
salted and buttered popcorn	salty, greasy popcorn
frosty pitchers of beer	half-drunk pitchers of stale, warm beer
big bowls of salted-in-the-shell peanuts on the tables	mess of peanut shells and discarded pretzel wrappers on tables and floor
Sound	
hum of students laughing and chatting	din of high-pitched giggles and various obnoxious frat guys shouting at each other
the jukebox playing oldies but goodies from the early Beatles	jukebox blaring out-of-date music

Student Example

We conclude with a student example of this assignment.

DESCRIPTION 1—POSITIVE EFFECT

Light rain gently drops into the puddles that have formed along the curb as I look out my apartment window at the corner of 14th and East John. Pedestrians layered in sweaters, raincoats, and scarves and guarded with shiny rubber boots and colorful umbrellas sip their steaming hot triple-tall lattes. Some share smiles and pleasant exchanges as they hurry down the street, hastening to work where it is warm and dry. Others, smelling the aroma of French roast espresso coming from the coffee bar next to the bus stop, listen for the familiar rumbling sound that will mean the 56 bus has arrived. Radiant orange, yellow, and red leaves blanket the sidewalk in the areas next to the maple trees that line the road. Along the curb a mother holds the hand of her toddler, dressed like a miniature tugboat captain in yellow raincoat and pants, who splashes happily in a puddle.

DESCRIPTION 2—NEGATIVE EFFECT

A solemn grayness hangs in the air, as I peer out the window of my apartment at the corner of 14th and East John. A steady drizzle of rain leaves boot-drenching puddles for pedestrians to avoid. Bundled in rubber boots, sweaters, coats, and rain-soaked scarves, commuters clutch Styrofoam cups of coffee as a defense against the biting cold. They lift their heads every so often to take a small sip of caffeine, but look sleep-swollen nevertheless. Pedestrians hurry past each other, moving quickly to get away from the dismal weather, the dull grayness. Some nod a brief hello to a familiar face, but most clutch their overcoats and tread grimly on, looking to avoid puddles or spray from passing cars. Others stand at the bus stop, hunched over, waiting in the drab early morning for the smell of diesel that means the 56 bus has arrived. Along the curb an impatient mother jerks the hand of a toddler to keep him from stomping in an oil-streaked puddle.

 For additional help with writing, reading, and research, go to **www.mycomplab.com.**

WRITING PROJECTS

This poster, one of hundreds created by the United States' Office of War Information during World War II, enlisted Americans' communal efforts, particularly women's help at home, in conserving resources to support the production for the war being fought on two fronts—the Pacific and Europe. This poster taps the urgency of that historical moment just as Michael Pollan's article, "Why Bother?", in Chapter 5 speaks to our current environmental problems. Think about how choice of words, images, color, and design in this poster work together to create an emotionally intense argument. Consider how you would design a poster to convey Pollan's argument or some other timely environmental message.

PART 2 WRITING PROJECTS

Part 2 addresses the following outcomes for first-year composition from the Council of Writing Program Administrators.

RHETORICAL KNOWLEDGE	• Focus on a purpose: • To learn (Ch. 5) • To explore (Ch. 6) • To inform (Ch. 8) • To analyze/synthesize (Ch. 8) • Respond to the needs of different audiences • Respond appropriately to different kinds of rhetorical situations • Use conventions of format and structure appropriate to the rhetorical situation • Adopt appropriate voice, tone, and level of formality • Understand how genres shape reading and writing (Readings and Thinking Critically activities) • Write in several genres: • Summary and Strong Response (Ch. 5) • Autobiographical Narrative, Literacy Narrative (Ch. 6) • Informative Report, Informative and Surprising Article (Ch. 7) • Synthesis Essay (Ch. 8)
CRITICAL THINKING, READING, AND WRITING	• Use writing and reading for inquiry, learning, thinking, and communicating (Exploratory activities, For Writing and Discussion activities, Readings, and Thinking Critically activities) • Understand a writing assignment as a series of tasks, including finding, evaluating, analyzing, and synthesizing appropriate primary and secondary sources • Integrate their own ideas with those of others (Ch. 5, Summary/Strong Response; Ch. 8, Synthesis Essay)
PROCESSES	• Be aware that it usually takes multiple drafts to create a successful text • Develop flexible strategies for generating, revising, editing, and proofreading • Understand writing as an open process that permits writers to use later invention and re-thinking to revise their work • Learn to critique their own and others' work (Question for Peer Review)
KNOWLEDGE OF CONVENTIONS	• Develop knowledge of genre conventions ranging from structure and paragraphing to tone and mechanics • Practice appropriate means of documenting their work (Ch. 5, Summary/Strong Response; Ch. 8, Synthesis Essay)
COMPOSING IN ELECTRONIC ENVIRONMENTS	• Understand and exploit the differences in the rhetorical strategies and in the affordances available for both print and electronic composing processes and texts (Ch. 7, Desktop-published Article)

READING
RHETORICALLY
The Writer as Strong Reader

5

Many new college students are surprised by the amount, range, and difficulty of reading they have to do in college. Every day they are challenged by reading assignments ranging from scholarly articles and textbooks on complex subject matter to primary sources such as Plato's dialogues or Darwin's *Voyage of the Beagle*.

To interact strongly with challenging texts, you must learn how to read them both with and against the grain. When you read *with the grain* of a text, you see the world through its author's perspective, open yourself to the author's argument, apply the text's insights to new contexts, and connect its ideas to your own experiences and personal knowledge. When you read *against the grain* of a text, you resist it by questioning its points, raising doubts, analyzing the limits of its perspective, or even refuting its argument.

We say that readers read *rhetorically* when they are aware of the effect a text is intended to have on them. Strong rhetorical readers analyze how a text works persuasively and they think critically about whether to enter into or challenge the text's intentions. The two writing projects in this chapter, both of which demand rhetorical reading, introduce you to several of the most common genres of academic writing: the summary, and various kinds of strong response essays, which usually incorporate a summary of the text to which the writer is responding. Thus our goal is to help you become a more powerful reader of academic texts, prepared to take part in the conversations of the disciplines you study.

In this chapter, you will learn to:

- listen carefully to a text, recognize its parts and their functions, and summarize its ideas
- formulate strong responses to texts by interacting with them, either by agreeing with, interrogating, or actively opposing them

Exploring Rhetorical Reading

As an introduction to rhetorical reading, we ask you to imagine that you are investigating different strategies that individual Americans might take to protect the environment. You have come across the 2008 article "Why Bother?" by Michael Pollan in the *New York Times Magazine*. Pollan, a professor of journalism at the

University of California Berkeley's Graduate School of Journalism, is known for his popular books on reforming our food-production system for the benefit of humans, animals, and the environment: *The Omnivore's Dilemma: A Natural History of Four Meals* (2007), *In Defense of Food: An Eater's Manifesto* (2009), and *Food Rules* (2010). Before reading Pollan's article, respond to the following opinion survey, using a 1 to 5 scale, with 1 meaning "strongly agree" and 5 meaning "strongly disagree."

Item	Strongly agree	Agree	Neutral	Disagree	Strongly disagree
1. Global warming is a very serious problem.	1	2	3	4	5
2. Going green in my own lifestyle will have no effect on climate change—the magnitude of the problem is too great.	1	2	3	4	5
3. The only way to make a real difference in climate change is through hugely expensive actions taken by governments and businesses.	1	2	3	4	5
4. The best way to combat global warming is for individual Americans to go green in their own consumer choices.	1	2	3	4	5
5. Environmentally conscious people should change the way they eat.	1	2	3	4	5

When you have finished rating your degree of agreement with these statements, read Pollan's article, using whatever note-taking, underlining, or highlighting strategies you normally use when reading for a class. When you have finished reading, complete the exercises that follow.

Michael Pollan
Why Bother?

1   **Why bother?** That really is the big question facing us as individuals hoping to do something about climate change, and it's not an easy one to answer. I don't know about you, but for me the most upsetting moment in *An Inconvenient Truth* came long after Al Gore scared the hell out of me, constructing an utterly convincing case that the very survival of life on earth as we know it is threatened by climate change. No, the really dark moment came during the closing credits, when we are asked to … change our light bulbs. That's when it got really depressing. The immense disproportion

between the magnitude of the problem Gore had described and the puniness of what he was asking us to do about it was enough to sink your heart.

2   But the drop-in-the-bucket issue is not the only problem lurking behind the "why bother" question. Let's say I do bother, big time. I turn my life upside-down, start biking to work, plant a big garden, turn down the thermostat so low I need the Jimmy Carter* signature cardigan, forsake the clothes dryer for a laundry line across the yard, trade in the station wagon for a hybrid, get off the beef, go completely local. I could theoretically do all that, but what would be the point when I know full well that halfway around the world there lives my evil twin, some carbon-footprint *doppelgänger* in Shanghai or Chongqing who has just bought his first car (Chinese car ownership is where ours was back in 1918), is eager to swallow every bite of meat I forswear and who's positively itching to replace every last pound of CO2 I'm struggling no longer to emit. So what exactly would I have to show for all my trouble?

3   A sense of personal virtue, you might suggest, somewhat sheepishly. But what good is that when virtue itself is quickly becoming a term of derision? And not just on the editorial pages of the *Wall Street Journal* or on the lips of the vice president,* who famously dismissed energy conservation as a "sign of personal virtue." No, even in the pages of the *New York Times* and the *New Yorker*, it seems the epithet "virtuous," when applied to an act of personal environmental responsibility, may be used only ironically. Tell me: How did it come to pass that virtue—a quality that for most of history has generally been deemed, well, a virtue—became a mark of liberal softheadedness? How peculiar, that doing the right thing by the environment—buying the hybrid, eating like a locavore—should now set you up for the Ed Begley Jr.* treatment.

4   And even if in the face of this derision I decide I am going to bother, there arises the whole vexed question of getting it right. Is eating local or walking to work really going to reduce my carbon footprint? According to one analysis, if walking to work increases your appetite and you consume more meat or milk as a result, walking might actually emit more carbon than driving. A handful of studies have recently suggested that in certain cases under certain conditions, produce from places as far away as New Zealand might account for less carbon than comparable domestic products. True, at least one of these studies was co-written by a representative of agribusiness interests in (surprise!) New Zealand, but even so, they make you wonder. If determining the carbon footprint of food is really this complicated, and I've got to consider not only "food miles" but also whether the food came by ship or truck and how lushly the grass grows in New Zealand, then maybe on second thought I'll just buy the imported chops at Costco, at least until the experts get their footprints sorted out.

5   There are so many stories we can tell ourselves to justify doing nothing, but perhaps the most insidious is that, whatever we do manage to do, it will be too little too late. Climate change is upon us, and it has arrived well ahead of schedule.

*Jimmy Carter was the Democratic president (1977–1981) who supported environmental policies, world peace, and human rights.
*Pollan is referring to Dick Cheney who served as George W. Bush's vice president from 2001–2009.
*Ed Begley, Jr., is a prominent television star who has his own green living reality TV show, *Living with Ed*. Begley has explored such topics as tapping the energy produced by people using exercise equipment.

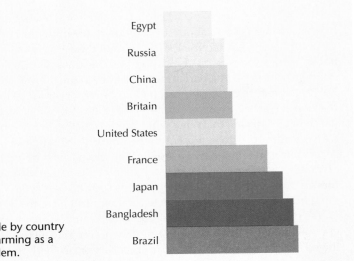

High Anxiety?
Percentage of people by country
who view global warming as a
"very serious" problem.

Scientists' projections that seemed dire a decade ago turn out to have been unduly optimistic: the warming and the melting is occurring much faster than the models predicted. Now truly terrifying feedback loops threaten to boost the rate of change exponentially, as the shift from white ice to blue water in the Arctic absorbs more sunlight and warming soils everywhere become more biologically active, causing them to release their vast stores of carbon into the air. Have you looked into the eyes of a climate scientist recently? They look really scared.

So do you still want to talk about planting gardens?

I do.

Whatever we can do as individuals to change the way we live at this suddenly very late date does seem utterly inadequate to the challenge. It's hard to argue with Michael Specter*, in a recent *New Yorker* piece on carbon footprints, when he says: "Personal choices, no matter how virtuous [N.B.!], cannot do enough. It will also take laws and money." So it will. Yet it is no less accurate or hardheaded to say that laws and money cannot do enough, either; that it will also take profound changes in the way we live. Why? Because the climate-change crisis is at its very bottom a crisis of lifestyle—of character, even. The Big Problem is nothing more or less than the sum total of countless little everyday choices, most of them made by us (consumer spending represents 70 percent of our economy), and most of the rest of them made in the name of our needs and desires and preferences.

For us to wait for legislation or technology to solve the problem of how we're living our lives suggests we're not really serious about changing—something our politicians cannot fail to notice. They will not move until we do. Indeed, to look to leaders and experts, to laws and money and grand schemes, to save us from our predicament represents precisely the sort of thinking—passive, delegated, dependent

*Michael Specter is a staff writer for the *New Yorker* and a national science reporter, who has most recently written a book, *Denialism*, about people's refusal to accept scientific evidence.

for solutions on specialists—that helped get us into this mess in the first place. It's hard to believe that the same sort of thinking could now get us out of it.

10   Thirty years ago, Wendell Berry, the Kentucky farmer and writer, put forward a blunt analysis of precisely this mentality. He argued that the environmental crisis of the 1970s—an era innocent of climate change; what we would give to have back *that* environmental crisis!—was at its heart a crisis of character and would have to be addressed first at that level: at home, as it were. He was impatient with people who wrote checks to environmental organizations while thoughtlessly squandering fossil fuel in their everyday lives—the 1970s equivalent of people buying carbon offsets to atone for their Tahoes and Durangos. Nothing was likely to change until we healed the "split between what we think and what we do." For Berry, the "why bother" question came down to a moral imperative: "Once our personal connection to what is wrong becomes clear, then we have to choose: we can go on as before, recognizing our dishonesty and living with it the best we can, or we can begin the effort to change the way we think and live."

11   For Berry, the deep problem standing behind all the other problems of industrial civilization is "specialization," which he regards as the "disease of the modern character." Our society assigns us a tiny number of roles: we're producers (of one thing) at work, consumers of a great many other things the rest of the time, and then once a year or so we vote as citizens. Virtually all of our needs and desires we delegate to specialists of one kind or another—our meals to agribusiness, health to the doctor, education to the teacher, entertainment to the media, care for the environment to the environmentalist, political action to the politician.

12   As Adam Smith and many others have pointed out, this division of labor has given us many of the blessings of civilization. Specialization is what allows me to sit at a computer thinking about climate change. Yet this same division of labor obscures the lines of connection—and responsibility—linking our everyday acts to their real-world consequences, making it easy for me to overlook the coal-fired power plant that is lighting my screen, or the mountaintop in Kentucky that had to be destroyed to provide the coal to that plant, or the streams running crimson with heavy metals as a result.

13   Of course, what made this sort of specialization possible in the first place was cheap energy. Cheap fossil fuel allows us to pay distant others to process our food for us, to entertain us and to (try to) solve our problems, with the result that there is very little we know how to accomplish for ourselves. Think for a moment of all the things you suddenly need to do for yourself when the power goes out—up to and including entertaining yourself. Think, too, about how a power failure causes your neighbors—your community—to suddenly loom so much larger in your life. Cheap energy allowed us to leapfrog community by making it possible to sell our specialty over great distances as well as summon into our lives the specialties of countless distant others.

14   Here's the point: Cheap energy, which gives us climate change, fosters precisely the mentality that makes dealing with climate change in our own lives seem impossibly difficult. Specialists ourselves, we can no longer imagine anyone but an expert, or anything but a new technology or law, solving our problems. Al Gore asks us to change the light bulbs because he probably can't imagine us doing anything much more challenging, like, say, growing some portion of our own food. We can't imagine it, either, which is probably why we prefer to cross our fingers and talk about the

promise of ethanol and nuclear power—new liquids and electrons to power the same old cars and houses and lives.

15   The "cheap-energy mind," as Wendell Berry called it, is the mind that asks, "Why bother?" because it is helpless to imagine—much less attempt—a different sort of life, one less divided, less reliant. Since the cheap-energy mind translates everything into money, its proxy, it prefers to put its faith in market-based solutions—carbon taxes and pollution-trading schemes. If we could just get the incentives right, it believes, the economy will properly value everything that matters and nudge our self-interest down the proper channels. The best we can hope for is a greener version of the old invisible hand. Visible hands it has no use for.

16   But while some such grand scheme may well be necessary, it's doubtful that it will be sufficient or that it will be politically sustainable before we've demonstrated to ourselves that change is possible. Merely to give, to spend, even to vote, is not to do, and there is so much that needs to be done—without further delay. In the judgment of James Hansen, the NASA climate scientist who began sounding the alarm on global warming 20 years ago, we have only 10 years left to start cutting—not just slowing—the amount of carbon we're emitting or face a "different planet." Hansen said this more than two years ago, however; two years have gone by, and nothing of consequence has been done. So: eight years left to go and a great deal left to do.

17   Which brings us back to the "why bother" question and how we might better answer it. The reasons not to bother are many and compelling, at least to the cheap-energy mind. But let me offer a few admittedly tentative reasons that we might put on the other side of the scale:

18   If you do bother, you will set an example for other people. If enough other people bother, each one influencing yet another in a chain reaction of behavioral change, markets for all manner of green products and alternative technologies will prosper and expand. (Just look at the market for hybrid cars.) Consciousness will be raised, perhaps even changed: new moral imperatives and new taboos might take root in the culture. Driving an S.U.V. or eating a 24-ounce steak or illuminating your McMansion like an airport runway at night might come to be regarded as outrages to human conscience. Not having things might become cooler than having them. And those who did change the way they live would acquire the moral standing to demand changes in behavior from others—from other people, other corporations, even other countries.

19   All of this could, theoretically, happen. What I'm describing (imagining would probably be more accurate) is a process of viral social change, and change of this kind, which is nonlinear, is never something anyone can plan or predict or count on. Who knows, maybe the virus will reach all the way to Chongqing and infect my Chinese evil twin. Or not. Maybe going green will prove a passing fad and will lose steam after a few years, just as it did in the 1980s, when Ronald Reagan took down Jimmy Carter's solar panels from the roof of the White House.

20   Going personally green is a bet, nothing more or less, though it's one we probably all should make, even if the odds of it paying off aren't great. Sometimes you have to act as if acting will make a difference, even when you can't prove that it will. That, after all, was precisely what happened in Communist Czechoslovakia and Poland, when a handful of individuals like Václav Havel and Adam Michnik resolved that they would

simply conduct their lives "as if" they lived in a free society. That improbable bet created a tiny space of liberty that, in time, expanded to take in, and then help take down, the whole of the Eastern bloc.

21   So what would be a comparable bet that the individual might make in the case of the environmental crisis? Havel himself has suggested that people begin to "conduct themselves as if they were to live on this earth forever and be answerable for its condition one day." Fair enough, but let me propose a slightly less abstract and daunting wager. The idea is to find one thing to do in your life that doesn't involve spending or voting, that may or may not virally rock the world but is real and particular (as well as symbolic) and that, come what may, will offer its own rewards. Maybe you decide to give up meat, an act that would reduce your carbon footprint by as much as a quarter. Or you could try this: determine to observe the Sabbath. For one day a week, abstain completely from economic activity: no shopping, no driving, no electronics.

22   But the act I want to talk about is growing some—even just a little—of your own food. Rip out your lawn, if you have one, and if you don't—if you live in a high-rise, or have a yard shrouded in shade—look into getting a plot in a community garden. Measured against the Problem We Face, planting a garden sounds pretty benign, I know, but in fact it's one of the most powerful things an individual can do—to reduce your carbon footprint, sure, but more important, to reduce your sense of dependence and dividedness: to change the cheap-energy mind.

23   A great many things happen when you plant a vegetable garden, some of them directly related to climate change, others indirect but related nevertheless. Growing food, we forget, comprises the original solar technology: calories produced by means of photosynthesis. Years ago the cheap-energy mind discovered that more food could be produced with less effort by replacing sunlight with fossil-fuel fertilizers and pesticides, with a result that the typical calorie of food energy in your diet now requires about 10 calories of fossil-fuel energy to produce. It's estimated that the way we feed ourselves (or rather, allow ourselves to be fed) accounts for about a fifth of the greenhouse gas for which each of us is responsible.

24   Yet the sun still shines down on your yard, and photosynthesis still works so abundantly that in a thoughtfully organized vegetable garden (one planted from seed,

nourished by compost from the kitchen and involving not too many drives to the garden center), you can grow the proverbial free lunch—CO2-free and dollar-free. This is the most-local food you can possibly eat (not to mention the freshest, tastiest and most nutritious), with a carbon footprint so faint that even the New Zealand lamb council dares not challenge it. And while we're counting carbon, consider too your compost pile, which shrinks the heap of garbage your household needs trucked away even as it feeds your vegetables and sequesters carbon in your soil. What else? Well, you will probably notice that you're getting a pretty good workout there in your garden, burning calories without having to get into the car to drive to the gym. (It is one of the absurdities of the modern division of labor that, having replaced physical labor with fossil fuel, we now have to burn even more fossil fuel to keep our unemployed bodies in shape.) Also, by engaging both body and mind, time spent in the garden is time (and energy) subtracted from electronic forms of entertainment.

25   You begin to see that growing even a little of your own food is, as Wendell Berry pointed out 30 years ago, one of those solutions that, instead of begetting a new set of problems—the way "solutions" like ethanol or nuclear power inevitably do—actually beget other solutions, and not only of the kind that save carbon. Still more valuable are the habits of mind that growing a little of your own food can yield. You quickly learn that you need not be dependent on specialists to provide for yourself—that your body is still good for something and may actually be enlisted in its own support. If the experts are right, if both oil and time are running out, these are skills and habits of mind we're all very soon going to need. We may also need the food. Could gardens provide it? Well, during World War II, victory gardens supplied as much as 40 percent of the produce Americans ate.

26   **But there are sweeter** reasons to plant that garden, to bother. At least in this one corner of your yard and life, you will have begun to heal the split between what you think and what you do, to commingle your identities as consumer and producer and citizen. Chances are, your garden will re-engage you with your neighbors, for you will have produce to give away and the need to borrow their tools. You will have reduced the power of the cheap-energy mind by personally overcoming its most debilitating weakness: its helplessness and the fact that it can't do much of anything that doesn't involve division or subtraction. The garden's season-long transit from seed to ripe fruit—*will you get a load of that zucchini?!*—suggests that the operations of addition and multiplication still obtain, that the abundance of nature is not exhausted. The single greatest lesson the garden teaches is that our relationship to the planet need not be zero-sum, and that as long as the sun still shines and people still can plan and plant, think and do, we can, if we bother to try, find ways to provide for ourselves without diminishing the world.

THINKING CRITICALLY
about "Why Bother?"

1. In three to four sentences, summarize Pollan's main points.

2. Freewrite a response to this question: In what way has Pollan's article caused me to reconsider one or more of my answers to the opinion survey on page 88?

3. Working in small groups or as a whole class, compare the note-taking strategies you used while reading this piece. (a) How many people wrote marginal notes? How many underlined or highlighted? (b) Compare the contents of these notes. Did people highlight the same passages or different ones? (c) Individually, look at your annotations and highlights and try to decide why you wrote or marked what you did. Share your reasons for making these annotations. The goal of this exercise is to make you more aware of your thinking processes as you read.

4. Working as a whole class or in small groups, share your responses to the questionnaire and to the postreading questions. What were the most insightful or provocative points in this article? To what extent did this article change people's thinking about the value of individual actions or about the impact of our individual lifestyles on climate change? As a result of Pollan's argument, are you more apt to try growing some of your own vegetables either now or in the future?

Understanding Rhetorical Reading

In this section, we explain why college-level reading is often difficult for new students and offer suggestions for improving your reading process based on the reading strategies of experts.

What Makes College-Level Reading Difficult?

The difficulty of college-level reading stems in part from the complexity of new subject matter. Whatever the subject—from international monetary policies to the intricacies of photosynthesis—you have to wrestle with new and complex materials that might perplex anyone. But in addition to the daunting subject matter, several other factors contribute to the difficulty of college-level reading:

- **Vocabulary.** Many college-level readings contain unfamiliar technical language such as the economic terms *assets, opportunity costs,* or *export subsidy* or the philosophic terms *hermeneutics* or *Neo-Platonism.* Even nontechnical readings and civic writing for the general public can contain unfamiliar terms. For example, in the Pollan article, the literary term *doppelgänger* or the ecological terms *feedback loops* or *pollution-trading systems* may have given you pause. In academia, words often carry specialized meanings that evoke a whole history of conversation and debate that may be inaccessible, even through a specialized dictionary. Good examples might be *postmodernism, string theory,* or *cultural materialism.* You will not fully understand these terms until you are initiated into the disciplinary conversations that gave rise to them.
- **Unfamiliar rhetorical context.** As we explained in Part 1, writers write to an audience for a purpose arising from some motivating occasion. Knowing an author's purpose, occasion, and audience will often clarify confusing parts

of a text. For example, Pollan's article was published in the *New York Times Magazine*, which attracts a liberal, well-educated audience. Pollan assumes that his audience already believes in global warming and takes climate change seriously. In fact, they may be so overwhelmed with the problem that they are ready to give up, shrug, and say, "Why bother?" His purpose is to motivate them to action. A text's internal clues can sometimes help you fill in the rhetorical context, but often you may need to do outside research.

- *Unfamiliar genre.* In your college reading, you will encounter a range of genres such as textbooks, trade books, scholarly articles, scientific reports, historical documents, newspaper articles, op-ed pieces, and so forth. Each of these makes different demands on readers and requires a different reading strategy.

- *Lack of background knowledge.* Writers necessarily make assumptions about what their readers already know. For example, Pollan makes numerous references to popular culture (Al Gore's *An Inconvenient Truth*; "the Ed Begley Jr. treatment"; "imported chops at Costco") or to general liberal arts knowledge (references to the economist Adam Smith or to the recent history of Communist Czechoslovakia and Poland). The more familiar you are with this cultural background, the more you will understand Pollan's argument on first reading.

FOR WRITING AND DISCUSSION

Appreciating the Importance of Background Knowledge

The importance of background knowledge is easily demonstrated any time you dip into past issues of a newsmagazine or try to read articles about an unfamiliar culture. Consider the following passage from a 1986 *Newsweek* article. How much background knowledge do you need before you can fully comprehend this passage? What cultural knowledge about the United States would a student from Ethiopia or Indonesia need?

> Throughout the NATO countries last week, there were second thoughts about the prospect of a nuclear-free world. For 40 years nuclear weapons have been the backbone of the West's defense. For almost as long American presidents have ritually affirmed their desire to see the world rid of them. Then, suddenly, Ronald Reagan and Mikhail Gorbachev came close to actually doing it. Let's abolish all nuclear ballistic missiles in the next 10 years, Reagan said. Why not all nuclear weapons, countered Gorbachev. OK, the president responded, like a man agreeing to throw in the washer-dryer along with the house.
>
> What if the deal had gone through? On the one hand, Gorbachev would have returned to Moscow a hero. There is a belief in the United States that the Soviets need nuclear arms because nuclear weapons are what make them a superpower. But according to Marxist-Leninist doctrine, capitalism's nuclear capability (unforeseen by Marx and Lenin) is the only thing that can prevent the inevitable triumph of communism. Therefore, an end to nuclear arms would put the engine of history back on its track.
>
> On the other hand, Europeans fear, a nonnuclear United States would be tempted to retreat into neo-isolationism.
>
> —Robert B. Cullen, "Dangers of Disarming," *Newsweek*

Working in small groups or as a class, identify words and passages in this text that depend on background information or knowledge of culture for complete comprehension.

Using the Reading Strategies of Experts

In Chapter 9, we describe the differences between the writing processes of experts and those of beginning college writers. There are parallel differences between the reading processes of experienced and inexperienced readers, especially when they encounter complex materials. In this strategies chart we describe some expert reading strategies that you can begin applying to your reading of any kind of college-level material.

Strategies for Reading Like an Expert		
Strategies	**What to Do**	**Comments**
Reconstruct the rhetorical context.	Ask questions about purpose, audience, genre, and motivating occasion.	If you read an article that has been anthologized (as in the readings in this textbook), note any information you are given about the author, publication, and genre. Try to reconstruct the author's original motivation for writing.
Take notes.	Make extensive marginal notes as you read.	Expert readers seldom use highlighters, which encourage passive, inefficient reading.
Get in the dictionary habit.	Look up words whose meaning you can't get from context.	If you don't want to interrupt your reading, check off words to look up when you are done.
Match your reading speed to your goals.	Speed up when skimming or scanning for information. Slow down for complete comprehension or detailed analysis.	Robert Sternberg, a cognitive psychologist, discovered that novice readers tend to read everything at about the same pace, no matter what their purpose. Experienced readers know when to slow down or speed up.

(continued)

Strategies	What to Do	Comments
Read a complex text in a "multidraft" way.	Read a text two or three times. The first time, read quickly, skimming ahead rapidly, looking at the opening sentences of paragraphs and at any passages that sum up the writer's argument or clarify the argument's structure. Pay particular attention to the conclusion, which often ties the whole argument together.	Rapid "first-draft reading" helps you see the text's main points and structure, thus providing background for a second reading. Often, experienced readers reread a text two or three times. They hold confusing passages in mental suspension, hoping that later parts of the essay will clarify earlier parts.

Reading with the Grain and Against the Grain

For an explanation of the believing and doubting game, see Chapter 2, Concept 4.

The reading and thinking strategies that we have just described enable skilled readers to interact strongly with texts. Your purpose in using these strategies is to read texts both *with the grain* and *against the grain*, a way of reading that is analogous to the believing and doubting game we introduced in Chapter 2. This concept is so important that we have chosen to highlight it separately here.

When you read with the grain of a text, you practice what psychologist Carl Rogers calls "empathic listening," in which you try to see the world through the author's eyes, role-playing as much as possible the author's intended readers by adopting their beliefs and values and acquiring their background knowledge. Reading with the grain is the main strategy you use when you summarize a text, but it comes into play also when you develop a strong response. When making with-the-grain points, you support the author's thesis with your own arguments and examples, or apply or extend the author's argument in new ways.

When you read against the grain of a text, you question and perhaps even rebut the author's ideas. You are a resistant reader who asks unanticipated questions, pushes back, and reads the text in ways unforeseen by the author. Reading against the grain is a key part of creating a strong response. When you make against-the-grain points, you challenge the author's reasoning, sources, examples, or choices of language. You present alternative lines of reasoning, deny the writer's values, or raise points or specific data that the writer has omitted. Strategies for thinking with the grain and against the grain are shown in the following chart, along with particular occasions when each is helpful.

Strategies for Reading with and Against the Grain

Reading with the Grain	Reading Against the Grain
• Listen to the text, follow the author's reasoning, and withhold judgment.	• Challenge, question, and resist the author's ideas.

Reading with the Grain	Reading Against the Grain
• Try to see the subject and the world from the author's perspective. • Add further support to the author's thesis with your own points and examples. • Apply the author's argument in new ways.	• Point out what the author has left out or overlooked; note what the author has *not* said. • Identify what assumptions, ideas, or facts seem unsupported or inaccurate. • Rebut the author's ideas with counterreasoning and counterexamples.
Occasions When Most Useful	**Occasions When Most Useful**
• In writing summaries, you listen to a text without judgment to identify the main ideas. • In writing analyses, you seek to understand a text to determine points to elaborate on and discuss. • In synthesizing ideas from sources, you determine what ideas to adopt and build on. • In writing arguments, you inhabit an author's viewpoint to deepen your understanding of an issue and to understand alternative views so you can represent them fairly.	• In writing an initial strong response, you determine the ways in which your beliefs, values, and views might be different from the author's. • In writing analyses, you identify limitations in the author's view. • In synthesizing, you determine which ideas to reject, replace, or go beyond. • In writing arguments, you develop refutations and rebuttals to the author's views.

Strong readers develop their ability to read in both ways—with the grain and against the grain. Some readers prefer to separate these approaches by first reading a text with the grain and then rereading it with more against-the-grain resistance. Throughout the rest of this chapter, we show you different ways to apply these strategies in your reading and writing.

Understanding Summary Writing

A **summary** (often called an **abstract**) is a condensed version of a text that extracts and presents main ideas in a way that does justice to the author's intentions. As fairly and objectively as possible, a summary states the main ideas of a longer text, such as an article or even a book. Although the words "summary" and "abstract" are often used interchangeably, the term "abstract" is usually used for a stand-alone summary at the head of a published article. Scholars often present "abstracts" of their own work (that is, a summary of their argument) for publication in a conference program.

Usefulness of Summaries

Students often report later in their academic careers how valuable summary writing skills are. Summary writing fosters a close engagement between you and the text and demonstrates your understanding of it. By forcing you to distinguish between main and subordinate points, summary writing is a valuable tool for improving your reading comprehension. Summary writing is also useful in other ways. For example, summaries at the beginning of articles, in prefaces to books, and on book jackets help readers determine if they want to read the article or book. To participate in conferences, your professors—and perhaps you also—send abstracts of proposed papers to conference committees in hopes of getting the paper accepted for presentation. Engineers and business executives place "executive summaries" at the beginning of proposals of major reports. In the "literature review" section of scientific papers, summaries of previous research are used to demonstrate gaps in knowledge that the present researchers will try to fill. Finally, writing summaries is a particularly important part of research writing, where you often present condensed views of other writers' arguments, either in support of your own view or as alternative views that you are analyzing or responding to.

The Demands that Summary Writing Makes on Writers

Even though summaries are short, they are challenging to write. You must distinguish between the main and subordinate points in a text, and you must provide even coverage of the text. You must also convey clearly the main ideas—ideas that are often complex—in a limited number of words. Often, summaries are written to certain specifications, say, one-tenth of the original article, or 200 words, or 100 words.

One of the biggest challenges of summarizing is framing the summary so that readers can easily tell your own ideas from those of the author you are summarizing. Often, you are incorporating a summary into a piece of writing as a basis of your own analysis or argument, so this distinction is particularly important. You make this distinction by using frequent **attributive tags** (sometimes called "signal phrases") such as "Pollan claims," "according to Pollan," or "Pollan says"; by putting quotation marks around any passages that use the writer's original wording; and by citing the article using the appropriate documentation style. Typically, writers also introduce the summary with appropriate contextual information giving the author's name and perhaps also the title and genre (in research writing, this information is repeated in the "Works Cited" or "References" list). The first sentence of the summary typically presents the main idea or thesis of the entire article. Here is an example summary of the Pollan article using MLA citation and documentation style.

Chapter 12 provides additional instruction in summarizing, paraphrasing, and quoting sources. It also explains how to incorporate sources smoothly into your own writing and avoid plagiarism.

Identification of the article, journal, and author

Gives overview summary of whole article

Summary of "Why Bother?"

In "Why Bother?" published in the *New York Times Magazine*, environmental journalist Michael Pollan asks why, given the magnitude of the climate change problem, any individual should bother to go green, and argues that an individual's actions can bring multiple rewards for individuals, society, and the environment. Explaining that "the warming and the melting" (90) are occurring much faster than earlier models had predicted, Pollan acknowledges the apparent powerlessness of individuals to make a difference. Not only are we uncertain what actions to take to preserve the planet, but we realize that whatever we do will be offset by growing carbon emissions from emerging nations. Our actions will be "too little too late" (89). He asserts that our environmental problem is a "crisis of lifestyle"—"the sum total of countless little everyday choices" (90) made possible by cheap fossil fuel, which has led to our increasingly specialized jobs. Nevertheless, to counteract our practical and moral distance from the environment caused by this specialization, Pollan urges individuals to go green. Although he concedes that "'laws and money'" (90) are necessary, he still believes that individual actions may be influential by setting off a "process of viral social change" (92). A particularly powerful act, he claims, is to convert yards into vegetable gardens. Growing your own vegetables, he argues, will help us overcome "specialization," eat locally, reduce carbon emissions, get healthy exercise, reconnect with neighbors, and restore our relationship with the earth. (227 words)

Attributive tag

Short quotations from article, MLA documentation style; number in parentheses indicates page number of original article where quotation is found

Work Cited

Pollan, Michael. "Why Bother?" *New York Times Magazine* 20 Apr. 2008: 19+. Rpt. in *The Allyn and Bacon Guide to Writing*. John D. Ramage, John C. Bean, and June Johnson. 6th ed. New York: Pearson, 2012. 88–94. Print.

Bibliographic citation for Pollan's article using MLA style. In a formal paper, the "Works Cited" list begins on a new page at the end of the paper.

Note in this example how the use of attributive tags, quotation marks, and citations makes it easy to tell that the writer is summarizing Pollan's ideas rather than presenting his own. Note too the writer's attempt to remain neutral and objective and not to impose his own views. To avoid interjecting your own opinions, you need to choose your verbs in attributive tags carefully. Consider the difference between "Smith argues" and "Smith rants" or between "Brown asserts" and "Brown leaps to the conclusion that. . . . " In each pair, the second verb, by moving beyond neutrality, reveals the writer's judgment of the author's ideas.

In an academic setting, then, think of summaries as short, tightly written pieces that retain an author's main ideas while eliminating the supporting details. In the writing projects for this chapter, we'll explain the strategies you can use to write a good summary. The following chart lists the criteria for incorporating a summary effectively into your own prose.

CRITERIA FOR AN EFFECTIVE SUMMARY INCORPORATED INTO YOUR OWN PROSE

- Represents the original article accurately and fairly.
- Is direct and concise, using words economically.
- Remains objective and neutral, not revealing the writer's own ideas on the subject, but, rather, only the original author's points.
- Gives the original article balanced and proportional coverage.
- Uses the writer's own words to express the original author's ideas.
- Distinguishes the summary writer's ideas from the original author's ideas by using attributive tags (such as "according to Pollan" or "Pollan argues that").
- Uses quotations sparingly, if at all, to present the original author's key terms or to convey the flavor of the original.
- Is a unified, coherent piece of writing in its own right.
- Cites and documents the text the writer is summarizing and any quotations used according to an appropriate documentation system.

FOR WRITING AND DISCUSSION

Determining What Is a Good Summary

This exercise asks you to work with the "Criteria for an Effective Summary Incorporated into Your Own Prose" (above) as you analyze the strengths and weaknesses of three summaries of the same article: "Protect Workers' Rights" by Bruce Raynor, published in the *Washington Post* on September 1, 2003. Imagine three student writers assigned to summarize this editorial in approximately 200 words. The first of the summaries below we have rated as excellent. Read the excellent summary first and then determine how successful the other summaries are.

SUMMARY 1 (AN EXCELLENT SUMMARY OF THE RAYNOR ARTICLE)

In Bruce Raynor's op-ed article "Protect Workers' Rights," originally published in the *Washington Post* on September 1, 2003, union official Raynor argues that workers everywhere are threatened by the current rules of globalization that allow corporations and governments to seek out the cheapest and least regulated labor around the world. Using the example of the Pillowtex Corporation that recently shut down its plant in Kannapolis, North Carolina, he shows how ending manufacturing that has played a long and major role in the economies of towns leaves workers without severance pay, medical insurance, money to pay taxes and mortgages, and other options for employment. According to Raynor, in the last three years, millions of jobs have been lost in all branches of American manufacturing. While policymakers advise these workers to seek education to retool for white-collar jobs, Raynor points out that fields such as telemarketing and the computer industry are also losing millions of jobs. Furthermore, outsourcing has caused a drop in wages in the United States. The same dynamic of jobs moving to countries with cheaper and less stringent safety and health regulation has recently caused Mexican and Bangladeshi workers to lose their jobs to Chinese workers. Raynor concludes with a call to protect the rights of workers everywhere by rewriting the "rules for the global economy" (A25). (214 words)

Work Cited

Raynor, Bruce. "Protect Workers' Rights." *Washington Post* 1 Sept. 2003: A25. Print.

SUMMARY 2

The closing of the Pillowtex Corporation's factories in the United States represents a loss of sixteen textile plants and about 6,500 jobs, according to Bruce Raynor, president of UNITE, a union of textile workers.

The workers left in Kannapolis, North Carolina, former home of one of the largest Pillowtex plants, are experiencing financial problems as they are unable to buy medical insurance, pay their taxes or mortgages or find other jobs.

Raynor argues that the case of the Pillowtex workers is representative of workers in other industries such as metals, papers, and electronics and that "this is the longest decline since the Great Depression" with about three million jobs gone in the last three years.

He then explains that white-collar jobs are not safe either because millions of jobs in telemarketing, claims adjusting, and even government are predicted to go overseas in the next five years. Furthermore, Raynor states that the possibility of outsourcing jobs leads to lowering of wages within the United States, as "outsourcing has forced down hourly wage rates by 10 percent to 40 percent for many U.S. computer consultants" (A25).

However, according to Raynor, the developing countries like Mexico and Bangladesh that have acquired manufacturing jobs are also threatened by countries like China who can offer employees who are willing to work for even lower wages and under worse conditions.

Raynor concludes that "a prosperous economy requires that workers be able to buy the products that they produce" (A25) and that workers everywhere need to be protected. (251 words)

Work Cited

Raynor, Bruce. "Protect Workers' Rights." *Washington Post* 1 Sept. 2003: A25. Print.

SUMMARY 3

In his article "Protect Workers' Rights," Bruce Raynor, president of UNITE, a textile workers' union, criticizes free trade and globalization for taking away workers' jobs. Using the Pillowtex Corporation's closing of its plant in Kannapolis, North Carolina, as his prime example, Raynor claims that outsourcing has destroyed the economy of this town and harmed workers across the United States. Raynor threatens that millions of white-collar jobs are also being lost and going to be lost in the next five years. Raynor complains that the whole national and global economy is falling apart and is going to get worse. He implies that the only solution is to keep jobs here in the United States. He maintains that workers around the world are also suffering when factories are moved from one developing country to another that has even more favorable conditions for the corporations. Raynor naively fails to factor in the role of consumers and the pressures on corporations into his defense of workers' rights. Clearly, Raynor loves unions and hates corporations; he probably fears that he is going to lose his own job soon. (183 words)

Understanding Strong Response Writing

We have said that the summary or abstract is an important academic genre and that summary writing is an essential academic skill. Equally important is strong response writing in which you identify and probe points in a text, sometimes by examining how a piece is written and often by inserting your own ideas into the text's conversation. "Strong response" is an umbrella term that incorporates a wide variety of ways that you can speak back to a text. In all cases, you are called on to do your own critical thinking by generating and asserting your own responses to the text.

In this section we will explain four different genres of strong response writing:

- Rhetorical critique
- Ideas critique
- Reflection
- Blended version of all three of these

Strong Response as Rhetorical Critique

A strong response as **rhetorical critique** analyzes a text's rhetorical strategies and evaluates how effectively the author achieves his or her intended goals. When writing a rhetorical critique, you discuss how a text is constructed, what rhetorical strategies it employs, and how effectively it appeals to *logos*, *ethos*, and *pathos*. In other words, you closely analyze the text itself, giving it the same close attention that an art critic gives a painting, a football coach gives a game video, or a biologist gives a cell formation. The close attention can be with the grain, noting the effectiveness of the text's rhetorical strategies, or against the grain, discussing what is ineffective or problematic about these strategies. Or an analysis might point out both the strengths and weaknesses of the text's rhetorical strategies.

For example, suppose that you are writing a rhetorical critique of an article from a conservative business journal advocating oil exploration in the Arctic National Wildlife Refuge (ANWR). You might analyze the article's rhetorical strategies by asking questions like these:

- How is the argument shaped to appeal to a conservative, business-oriented audience?
- How has the writer's angle of vision influenced the selection of evidence for his or her argument?
- How does the writer make himself or herself seem credible to this audience?

You would also evaluate the *logos* of the argument:

- How sound is the logic of the argument?
- Is the evidence accurate and current?
- What are the underlying assumptions and beliefs on which the argument is based?

Rhetorical critiques are usually closed-form, thesis-driven essays. The essay has a thesis that captures the writer's overall assessment of the text and maps out the specific points that the writer will develop in the analysis. When you are writing a rhetorical critique, your goal is to find a few rhetorical points that you find particularly intriguing, important, or disturbing to discuss and probe. Typically, your analysis zeroes in on some key features that you, the writer, find noteworthy. In the following strategies chart, we suggest the kinds of questions you can ask about a text to construct a rhetorical critique.

Question-Asking Strategies for Writing a Rhetorical Critique

Ask Questions about Any of the Following:	Examples
Audience and purpose: • Who is the intended audience? • What is the writer's purpose? • How well does the text suit its particular audience and purpose?	Examine how Michael Pollan writes to the well-educated audience of the *New York Times Magazine*, who are aware of climate change debates and most likely concerned about the problems ahead. Consider how Pollan writes to move these readers beyond good intentions to action. Examine how the text's structure, language, and evidence support this purpose.
Influence of genre on the shape of the text: • How has the genre affected the author's style, structure, and use of evidence?	Examine how the genre of the feature editorial for a highbrow magazine accounts for the length, structure, and depth of Pollan's argument. Examine how his references to political and intellectual figures (Al Gore, then Vice President Cheney, Adam Smith, Wendell Berry, and so forth) carry weight in this magazine's investigation of contemporary issues.
Author's style: • How do the author's language choices and sentence length and complexity contribute to the impact of the text?	Examine how Pollan's casual and cordial connections with readers (use of "I," "you," and "we"), his urgency, and his use of questions contribute to the article's effect.
Appeal to *logos*, the logic of the argument: • How well has the author created a reasonable, logically structured argument?	Examine how well Pollan uses logical points to support his claim and make his claim persuasive.

(continued)

Ask Questions about Any of the Following:	Examples
Use of evidence: • How reputable, relevant, current, sufficient, and representative is the evidence?	Examine how Pollan uses references to scientific articles, newspaper accounts, and his own experiences to develop his points.
Appeal to *ethos* and the credibility of the author: • How well does the author persuade readers that he/she is knowledgeable, reliable, credible, and trustworthy?	Examine how Pollan conveys his knowledge of environmentalism, economics, and social trends. Examine the effects of genre and style in creating this *ethos*. Examine whether this *ethos* is effective for readers who are not familiar with Pollan's other writing, are skeptical of climate change, or are less in tune with environmental activism.
Appeal to *pathos*: • How well does the writer appeal to readers' emotions, sympathies, and values?	Examine how Pollan seeks to tap his audience's values and feelings. Consider how he conveys his familiarity with the everyday choices and decisions facing his readers.
Author's angle of vision: • How much does the author's angle of vision or interpretive filter dominate the text, influencing what is emphasized or omitted?	Examine how Pollan's angle of vision shapes his perspective on climate change, his choice of activist solutions, and his development of solutions. Consider how Pollan's reputation as the author of a number of books on food system reform influences his focus in this argument.

For a rhetorical critique, you would probably not choose all of these questions but would instead select three or four to highlight. Your goal is to make insightful observations about how a text works rhetorically and to support your points with examples and short quotations from the text.

Strong Response as Ideas Critique

A second kind of strong response, the **ideas critique,** focuses on the ideas at stake in the text. Rather than treat the text as an artifact to analyze rhetorically (as in a rhetorical critique), you treat it as a voice in a conversation—one perspective on an issue or one solution to a problem or question. Your strong response examines how the ideas of the original author mesh or conflict with your own. Based on your own critical thinking, personal experiences, and research, to what extent do you agree or disagree with the writer's thesis? A with-the-grain reading of a text would support all or some of the text's ideas, while also supplying additional evidence or extending the argument, perhaps applying it in a new context. An against-the-grain reading would challenge the writer's ideas, point out flaws and holes in the writer's thinking, and provide counterexamples and rebuttals. You might agree with some ideas and disagree with others in the text. In any case, in an ideas critique you speak back to the text from your own experience, background, reading, and thoughtful wrestling with the writer's ideas.

As an example, let's return to the article from the conservative business journal on drilling for oil in the ANWR. For an ideas critique, you would give your own views on oil exploration in the ANWR to support or challenge the writer's views, to raise new questions, and otherwise to add your voice to the ANWR conversation.

- You might supply additional reasons and evidence for drilling.
- You might oppose drilling in the ANWR by providing counterreasoning and counterexamples.
- You might propose some kind of synthesis or middle ground, where you would allow drilling in the ANWR but only under certain conditions.

When you write an ideas critique you are thus joining an important conversation about the actual subject matter of a text. Because much academic and professional writing focuses on finding the best solution to complex problems, this kind of strong response is very common. Usually this genre requires closed-form, thesis-governed prose. The following strategies chart suggests questions you can ask about a text to enter into its conversation of ideas.

Question-Asking Strategies for Writing an Ideas Critique	
Questions to Ask	**Examples**
Where do I agree with this author? (with the grain)	Consider how you might amplify or extend Pollan's ideas. Build on his ideas by discussing examples where you or acquaintances have tried to change your lifestyle to lower carbon emissions. Show how these changes might have inspired others to do so.
What new insights has this text given me? (with the grain)	Explore Pollan's ideas that the environmental crisis is at heart a "crisis of lifestyle" or that specialization leads to a disjuncture between our everyday acts and their environmental consequences. Explore Pollan's argument that individual actions may lead to a social revolution. Think of how your eating habits or relationship to gardens has or could contribute to reform.

(continued)

Questions to Ask	Examples
Where do I disagree with this author? (against the grain)	Challenge Pollan's assumptions about the magnitude of the problem. Challenge Pollan's idea that individuals can make a difference. Challenge his assumptions that technological solutions won't work because we still will face a crisis of lifestyle. Challenge the practicality and value of his main solution—growing gardens.
What points has the author overlooked or omitted? (against the grain)	Recognize that Pollan overlooks the constraints that would keep people from gardening. Consider that Pollan chooses not to focus on problems of overpopulation, water shortage, or economic disruption caused by environmentalism.
What new questions or problems has the text raised? (with or against the grain)	Explain how Pollan minimizes the economic impact of environmental action and downplays the role of government and business. Consider how we might need to "change the system" rather than just change ourselves. Consider his apparent lack of interest in technological solutions to the energy crisis.
What are the limitations or consequences of this text? (with or against the grain)	Consider ways that Pollan excludes some of his readers even while reaching out to others. Consider how Pollan, given his books on food and his passion for replacing industrial food production with local food, has written a predictable argument. Consider what new ideas he brings to his readers.

Because critiques of ideas appear in many contexts where writers search for the best solutions to problems, this kind of thinking is essential for academic research. In writing research papers, writers typically follow the template "This other writer has argued A, but I am going to argue B." Often the writer's own view (labeled "B") results from the writer's having wrestled with the views of others. Because this kind of dialectic thinking is so important to academic and professional life, we treat it further in Chapter 8 on analysis and synthesis. This chapter encourages you to articulate alternative views and respond to them.

Strong Response as Reflection

A third kind of strong response is often called a "reflection" or a "reflection paper." (An instructor might say, for example, "Read Michael Pollan's article on climate change and write a reflection about it.") Generally, a **reflection** is an introspective genre; it invites you to connect the reading to your own personal experiences, beliefs, and values. In a reflection paper, the instructor is particularly interested in how the reading has affected you personally—what memories it has triggered, what personal experiences it relates to, what values and beliefs it has challenged, what dilemmas it poses, and so forth. A **reflection paper** is often more exploratory, open-ended, musing, and tentative than a rhetorical critique or an ideas critique, which is usually closed form and thesis governed.

To illustrate, let's consider how you might write a reflection in response to the article in the conservative business journal on drilling for oil in the ANWR. One approach might be to build a reflection around a personal conflict in values by exploring how the reading creates a personal dilemma:

- You might write about your own wilderness experiences, musing about the importance of nature in your own life.
- But at the same time, you might reflect on the extent to which your own life depends on cheap oil and acknowledge your own reluctance to give up owning a car.

In short, you want pristine nature and the benefits of cheap oil at the same time. Another quite different approach might be to reflect on how this article connects to discussions you are having in your other courses, say, the economic cost of individuals' and companies' going green.. Here are some strategies you can use to generate ideas for a reflective strong response:

Question-Asking Strategies for Writing a Reflective Strong Response	
Questions to Ask	Examples
What personal memories or experiences does this text trigger?	Explore how Pollan's article evokes memories of your own frustrations about or successes with "green" living. Have you ever tried to change your habits for environmental reasons? If so, how did you go about doing it? Would your changes have met Berry's and Pollan's criteria for a change of "lifestyle"?
What personal values or beliefs does this text reinforce or challenge?	Explore the extent to which you can or can't identify with Pollan, Al Gore, and others who are proclaiming the seriousness of climate change and advocating changes in lifestyle. To what extent does Pollan as a person of conviction spark your admiration?

(continued)

Questions to Ask	Examples
What questions, dilemmas, or problems does this text raise for me?	Explore how Pollan has challenged readers to take actions that may be difficult for them. For instance, you may have arrived at other solutions or know groups or organizations that are contributing positively in other ways. Perhaps Pollan's level of commitment or his particular approach to living green disturbs you in some way.
What new insights, ideas, or thoughts of my own have been stimulated by this text?	Explore any moments of enlightenment you had while reading Pollan. For example, perhaps his focus on individual action rather than on "laws and money" seems problematic to you. Perhaps there are other causes besides the environment that spur you to concern or to action. Perhaps you are now interested in exploring what inspires people to make major changes in how they live.

As you can tell from these questions, a reflective strong response highlights your own personal experiences and beliefs in conversation with the text. Whereas the focus of a rhetorical critique is on analyzing the way the text works rhetorically and the focus of an ideas critique is on taking a stance on the ideas at stake in the text, a reflective response focuses on the personal dimension of reading the text. Reflections call for a degree of self-disclosure or self-exploration that would be largely absent from the other kinds of strong responses.

Strong Response as a Blend

It should be evident that the boundaries among the rhetorical critique, ideas critique, and reflection overlap and that a strong response could easily blend features of each. In trying to decide how to respond strongly to a text, you often don't have to confine yourself to a pure genre but can mix and match different kinds of responses. You can analyze and critique a text's rhetorical strategies, show how the text challenges your own personal values and beliefs, and also develop your own stance on the text's ideas. In writing a blended response, you can emphasize what is most important to you, while not limiting yourself to only one approach.

Before we turn to the writing project for this chapter, we show you an example of a student's summary/strong response that is a blend of rhetorical critique, ideas critique, and personal reflection. Note that the essay begins by conveying the writer's investment in environmental conservation. It then summarizes Pollan's article. Following the summary, the student writer states his thesis, followed by his strong response, which contains both rhetorical points and points engaging Pollan's ideas.

Kyle Madsen (student)
Can a Green Thumb Save the Planet?
A Response to Michael Pollan

When I was a child, our household had one garbage can, in which my family and I would deposit all of our cardboard, plastic, glass, and paper waste. No one on my block had ever heard of recycling or using energy saving bulbs, and we never considered turning down our thermostats during the frozen winters and ice storms that swept our region from November to March. It wasn't that we didn't care about what we were doing to our environment. We just didn't know any better. However, once I got to college all that changed. My university's policies requested that students separate glass bottles and pizza boxes from plastic candy wrappers and old food containers. Thanks in large part to the chilling success of Al Gore's documentary *An Inconvenient Truth*, many of my old neighbors were starting to catch on as well, and now my home town is as devoted to its recycling as any major metropolitan area. Still, even though we as a country have come a long way in just a few years, there is a long way to go. Environmental journalist Michael Pollan in his article "Why Bother?" for the *New York Times Magazine* examines why working to slow the threat of climate change is such a daunting task.

In "Why Bother?" Michael Pollan explores how we have arrived at our current climate change crisis and argues why and how we should try to change our individual actions. Pollan sums up the recent scientific evidence for rapid climate change and then focuses on people's feeling overwhelmed in the face of this vast environmental problem. He presents his interpretation of how we have contributed to the problem and why we feel powerless. Pollan asserts that the climate-change crisis is "the sum total of countless everyday choices" made by consumers globally and that it is "at its very bottom a crisis of lifestyle—of character, even" (90). Our reliance on "cheap fossil fuel" has contributed to both the problem and to our sense of helplessness. In the final part of his article, Pollan concedes that "laws and money" (90) are necessary to create change, but he still advocates acting on our values and setting an example, which might launch a green social revolution. According to Pollan, "The idea is to find one thing to do in your life that does not involve spending or voting … that will offer its own rewards" (93). He concludes by encouraging readers to plant gardens in order to reduce carbon emissions, to lessen our "sense of dependence and dividedness" (93)—to empower ourselves to contribute positively to our environment.

Although Pollan has created an argument with strong logical, ethical, and emotional appeals, his very dominant angle of vision—seen in his assumptions, alarmist language, and exclusive focus on garden-growing—may fail to win neutral readers. I also think Pollan's argument loses impact by not discussing more realistic alternatives such as pursuing smart consumerism and better environmental education for children.

Pollan builds a forceful case in his well-argued and knowledgeable interpretation of our climate-change problem as a "crisis of lifestyle—of character, even" (90).

Introduces topic/problem and shows writer's investment in caring for the environment

Identifies Pollan's article and Pollan's purpose

Summary of Pollan's article

Thesis statement focused on rhetorical points

Second part of thesis focused on ideas critique

With-the-grain rhetorical point focused on the logos and ethos of Pollan's argument

His frank confrontation of the problem of how to motivate people is compelling, especially when he admits the contrast between "the magnitude of the problem" and the "puniness" of individual action (89). Pollan both deepens his argument and constructs a positive ethos by drawing on the ideas of environmental ethicist Wendell Berry and classical economist Adam Smith to explain how modern civilization has developed through the division of labor (specialization), which has brought us many advantages but also cut us off from community and environmental responsibility. In this part of his argument, Pollan helps readers understand how our dependence on cheap oil and our lifestyle choices have enhanced our roles as limited, specialized producers and major consumers. Pollan's development of his theory of the "cheap-energy mind" (92) and his reasonable support of this idea are the strongest part of his argument and the most relevant to readers like me. I have thought that we have become small cogs in an overbearing machine of consumption and only larger cogs such as the government can have enough influence on the overall system to make change happen. From time to time, I have wondered what I as one person could really do. This sense of insignificance, which Pollan theorizes, has made me wait until my regular light bulbs burned out before considering replacing them with energy-efficient ones.

Brief reflective comment

With-the-grain rhetorical point focused on the pathos of Pollan's argument

Another strength of Pollan's argument is the way he builds bridges to his audience through his appeals to *pathos*. He understands how overwhelmed the average person can feel when confronted with the climate-change problem. Pollan never criticizes his readers for not being as concerned as he is. Instead he engages them in learning with him. He explores with readers the suggestion of walking to work, a task on par with light bulb changing, when he writes, even if "I decide that I am going to bother, there arises the whole vexed question of getting it right. Is eating local or walking to work really going to reduce my carbon footprint?" (89). By asking questions like these, he speaks as a concerned citizen who tries to create a dialogue with his audience about the problem of climate change and what individuals can do.

Against-the-grain rhetorical point focused on angle of vision

However, despite his outreach to readers, Pollan's angle of vision may be too dominant and intense for some readers. He assumes that his *New York Times Magazine* readers already share his agreement with the most serious views of climate change held by many scientists and environmentalists, people who are focusing on the "truly terrifying feedback loops" (90) in weather and climate. He also assumes that his readers hold similar values about local food and gardening. This intense angle of vision may leave out some readers. For example, I am left wondering why gardening is more effective than, say, converting to solar power. He also tries to shock his readers into action with his occasional alarmist or overly dramatic use of language. For example, he tries to invoke fear: "Have you looked into the eyes of a climate scientist recently? They look really scared" (90). However, how many regular people have run-ins with climate scientists?

Transition to ideas critique, an against-the-grain point critiquing Pollan's ideas—Pollan

In addition, after appearing very in tune with readers in the first part of his argument, in the final part he does not address his readers' practical concerns. He describes in great detail the joys of gardening—specifically how it will connect readers not only to the earth, but to friends and neighbors as well—yet he glosses over the amount of work necessary to grow a garden. He writes, "Photosynthesis still works so abundantly that in a thoughtfully organized vegetable garden (one planted from seed, nourished by compost from the kitchen and involving not too many drives to the gardening center), you can grow the proverbial free lunch" (93–4). However, not everyone has a space for a garden or access to a public one to grow tomatoes themselves, and it takes hours of backbreaking labor to grow a productive vegetable garden—hardly a free lunch. Average Americans work upwards of sixty hours per week, so it is unrealistic to expect them to spend their free time working in a garden. In not addressing readers' objections to gardening or suggesting other ways to mend our cheap oil values, I think Pollan proposes simply another situation for semi-concerned individuals to again say, "Why bother?"

doesn't acknowledge the impracticality of expecting people to grow their own vegetables.

Also, besides gardens, I think Pollan could emphasize other avenues of change such as sustainable consumerism. In different places in the article, he mentions that individuals can use their consumer lifestyles to achieve a more sustainable way of life, but he chooses to insist that gardening be the main means. I would have liked him to discuss how we as consumers could buy more fuel-efficient cars, avoid plastic packaging, drink tap water, and buy products from green industries. This "going green" trend has already taken root in many of America's top industries—at least in their advertising and public relations campaigns. We can't leave a Starbucks without inadvertently learning about what they are doing to offset global warming. But we consumers need to know which industries really are going green in a significant way so that we can spend our shopping dollars there. If Pollan is correct, environmentally conscientious consumers can demand a change from the corporations they rely on, so why not use the same consumerism that got us into this mess to get us out?

Another point critiquing Pollan's ideas. Madsen proposes sustainable consumerism as an alternative to gardening.

Besides sustainable consumerism, I think we should emphasize the promotion of better environmental education for our children. Curriculum in K–12 classrooms presented by teachers rather than information from television or newspapers will shape children's commitment to the environment. A good example is the impact of Recycle Now, an organization aimed at implementing recycling and global awareness in schools. According to Dave Lawrie, a curriculum expert featured on their Web site, "Recycling at school is a hands-on way to show pupils that every single person can help to improve the environment. Everyone in our school has played a part in making a difference." With serious education, kids will learn the habits of respecting the earth, working in gardens, and using energy-saving halogen bulbs, making sustainability and environmental stewardship a way of life.

Another point addressing Pollan's ideas— environmental education in the schools as an alternative to gardening.

While Pollan is correct in pushing us into action now, asking Americans to grow a garden, when changing a light bulb seems daunting, is an unrealistic and limited approach. However, Pollan persuasively addresses the underlying issues in our attitudes toward the climate crisis and works to empower readers to become responsible and involved. Whether it be through gardening, supporting green businesses, or education, I agree with Pollan that the important thing is that you learn to bother for yourself.

Short conclusion bringing closure to the essay.

Works Cited

Lawrie, Dave. "Bringing the Curriculum to Life." *School Success Stories. RecycleNow* 11 Nov. 2009. Web. 28 Feb. 2010.

Pollan, Michael. "Why Bother?" *New York Times Magazine* 20 Apr. 2008: 19+. Rpt. in *The Allyn and Bacon Guide to Writing.* John D. Ramage, John C. Bean, and June Johnson. 6th ed. New York: Pearson, 2012. 88–94. Print.

Citation of works cited in the essay using MLA format

In the student example just shown, Kyle Madsen illustrates a blended strong response that includes both a rhetorical critique of the article and some of his own views. He analyzes Pollan's article rhetorically by pointing out both the persuasive features of the argument and the limiting angle of vision of a worried environmentalist and extremely committed gardening enthusiast. He seconds some of Pollan's points with his own examples, but he also reads Pollan against the grain by suggesting how Pollan's word choice and fixation on gardening as a solution prevent him from developing ideas that might seem more compelling to some readers.

WRITING PROJECT

A Summary

Write a summary of an article assigned by your instructor for an audience who has not read the article. Write the summary using attributive tags and providing an introductory context as if you were inserting it into your own longer paper (see the model on p. 106). The word count for your summary will be specified by your instructor. Try to follow all the criteria for a successful summary listed on page 106, and use MLA documentation style, including a Works Cited entry for the article that you are summarizing. (Note: Instead of an article, your instructor may ask you to summarize a longer text such as a book or a visual-verbal text such as a Web page or an advocacy brochure. We address these special cases at the end of this section.)

Generating Ideas: Reading for Structure and Content

Once you have been assigned an article to summarize, your first task is to read it carefully a number of times to get an accurate understanding of it. Remember that summarizing involves the essential act of reading with the grain as you figure out exactly what the article is saying. In writing a summary, you must focus on both a text's structure and its content. In the following steps, we recommend a process that will help you condense a text's ideas into an accurate summary. As you become a more experienced reader and writer, you'll follow these steps without thinking about them.

Step 1: The first time through, read the text fairly quickly for general meaning. If you get confused, keep going; later parts of the text might clarify earlier parts.

Step 2: Read the text carefully paragraph by paragraph. As you read, write gist statements in the margins for each paragraph. A *gist statement* is a brief indication of a paragraph's function in the text or a brief summary of a paragraph's content. Sometimes it is helpful to think of these two kinds of gist statements as "what it does" statements and "what it says" statements.* A "what

---

*For our treatment of "what it does" and "what it says" statements, we are indebted to Kenneth A. Bruffee, *A Short Course in Writing*, 2nd ed. (Cambridge, MA: Winthrop, 1980).

it does" statement specifies the paragraph's function—for example, "summarizes an opposing view," "introduces another reason," "presents a supporting example," "provides statistical data in support of a point," and so on. A "what it says" statement captures the main idea of a paragraph by summarizing the paragraph's content. The "what it says" statement is the paragraph's main point, in contrast to its supporting ideas and examples.

When you first practice detailed readings of a text, you might find it helpful to write complete *does* and *says* statements on a separate sheet of paper rather than in the margins until you develop the internal habit of appreciating both the function and content of parts of an essay. Here are *does* and *says* statements for selected paragraphs of Michael Pollan's article on climate change activism.

Paragraph 1: *Does*: Introduces the need for environmental action as a current problem that readers know and care about and sets up the argument. ***Says***: We as individuals often wonder if our small, minor actions are worth doing in light of the magnitude of the climate change problem.

Paragraph 2: *Does*: Explores another reason why individuals may doubt whether individual actions could make a difference. ***Says***: People willing to change their lifestyles to combat climate change may be discouraged by the increase in a carbon-emissions lifestyle in other parts of the world such as China.

Paragraph 8: *Does*: Expresses an alternative view, partially concedes to it, and asserts a counterview. ***Says***: Although big money and legislation will be important in reversing climate change, the problem at its heart is a "crisis of lifestyle—of character" (90), and therefore will require the effort of individuals.

Paragraph 18: *Does*: Presents and develops one of Pollan's main reasons that concerned individuals should take personal action to fight climate change. ***Says***: Setting an example through our own good environmental choices could exert moral influence here and abroad, on individuals and big business.

Writing a *says* statement for a paragraph is sometimes difficult. You might have trouble, for example, deciding what the main idea of a paragraph is, especially if the paragraph doesn't begin with a closed-form topic sentence. One way to respond to this problem is to formulate the question that you think the paragraph answers. If you think of chunks of the text as answers to a logical progression of questions, you can often follow the main ideas more easily. Rather than writing *says* statements in the margins, therefore, some readers prefer writing *says* questions. *Says* questions for the Pollan text may include the following:

- What are some of the biggest obstacles that discourage people from undertaking individual actions to fight climate change?
- Despite our excuses not to act, why is individual action still necessary?
- How is the problem of climate a "crisis of lifestyle"?
- What are the reasons we should "bother"?
- Why is growing one's own vegetable garden a particularly powerful individual act?

No matter which method you use—*says* statements or *says* questions—writing gist statements in the margins is far more effective than underlining or highlighting in helping you recall the text's structure and argument.

Step 3: Locate the article's main divisions or parts. In longer closed-form articles, writers often forecast the shape of their essays in their introductions or use their conclusions to sum up main points. For example, Pollan's article uses some forecasting and transitional statements to direct readers through its parts and main points. The article is divided into several main chunks as follows:

- Introductory paragraphs, which establish the problem to be addressed and describe the reasons that people don't take action to help slow climate change (paragraphs 1–5)
- Two short transitional paragraphs (a one-sentence question and a two-word answer) stating the author's intention to call for individual action in spite of the obstacles. These two paragraphs prepare the move into the second part of the article (paragraphs 6 and 7).
- A paragraph conceding to the need for action beyond the individual (laws and money) followed by a counterclaim that the climate change problem is a "crisis of lifestyle" (paragraph 8)
- Eight paragraphs developing Pollan's "crisis of lifestyle" claim, drawing on Wendell Berry and explaining the concepts of specialization and the "cheap-energy mind" that have led us into both the climate change problem and our feelings of inadequacy to tackle it (paragraphs 9–16)
- A transitional paragraph conceding that reasons against individual action are "many and compelling," but proposing better ways to answer the "why bother" question. (paragraph 17)
- Two paragraphs developing Pollan's reasons for individual action—how individuals will influence each other and broader communities and lead to "viral social change" (paragraphs 18–19)
- Two paragraphs elaborating on the possibility of viral social change based on analogy to the end of Communism in Czechoslovakia and Poland and to various ways individuals might make significant changes in their lifestyles (paragraphs 20–21)
- Five paragraphs detailing Pollan's choice for the best solution for people to reduce their carbon emissions and make a significant environmental statement: grow gardens (paragraphs 22–26)

Instead of listing the sections of your article, you might prefer to make an outline or tree diagram of the article showing its main parts.

Drafting and Revising

Once you have determined the main points and grasped the structure of the article you are summarizing, combine and condense your *says* statements into clear sentences that capture the gist of the article. These shortened versions of your *says* statements will make up most of your summary, although you might mention the structure of the article to help organize the points. For example, you might say, "[Author's name] makes four main points in this article. … The article concludes with a call to action. ... " Because representing an article in your own words in a greatly abbreviated form is a challenge, most writers revise their sentences to find the clearest, most concise way to express the article's ideas accurately. Choose and use your words carefully to stay within your word limit.

The procedures for summarizing articles can work for book-length texts and visual-verbal texts as well. For book-length texts, your *does* and *says* statements may cover chapters or parts of the book. Book introductions and conclusions as well as chapter titles and introductions may provide clues to the author's thesis and subthesis to help you identify the main ideas to include in a book summary. For verbal-visual texts such as a public affairs advocacy ad, product advertisement, Web page, or brochure, examine the parts to see what each contributes to the whole. In your summary, help your readers visualize the images, comprehend the parts, and understand the main points of the text's message.

Plan to create several drafts of all summaries to refine your presentation and wording of ideas. Group work may be helpful in these steps.

Finding Key Points in an Article

FOR WRITING AND DISCUSSION

If the whole class or a group of students is summarizing the same article, brainstorm together and then reach consensus on the main ideas that you think a summary of that article should include to be accurate and complete. Then reread your own summary and check off each idea.

When you revise your summary, consult the criteria on page 102 in this chapter as well as the Questions for Peer Review that follow.

Questions for Peer Review

In addition to the generic peer review questions explained in, Skill 16.4, ask your peer reviewers to address these questions:

1. In what way do the opening sentences provide needed contextual information and then express the overall thesis of the text? What information could be added or more clearly stated?
2. How would you evaluate the writer's representation and coverage of the text's main ideas in terms of accuracy, balance, and proportion? What ideas have been omitted or overemphasized?
3. Has the writer treated the article fairly and neutrally? If judgments have crept in, where could the writer revise?
4. How could the summary use attributive tags more effectively to keep the focus on the original author's ideas?
5. Has the writer used quotations sparingly and cited them accurately? Has the writer translated points into his or her own words? Has the writer included a Works Cited?
6. Where might the writer's choice of words and phrasing of sentences be revised to improve the clarity, conciseness, and coherence of the summary?

A Summary/Strong Response Essay

In response to a text assigned by your instructor, write a "summary/strong response" essay that incorporates a 150–250-word summary of the article. In your strong response to that reading, speak back to its author from your own critical thinking, personal experience, values, and, perhaps, further reading or research. Unless your instructor assigns a specific kind of strong response (rhetorical critique, ideas critique, or reflection), write a blended response in which you are free to consider the author's rhetorical strategies, your own agreement or disagreement with the author's ideas, and your personal response to the text. Think of your response as your analysis of how the text tries to influence its readers rhetorically and how your wrestling with the text has expanded and deepened your thinking about its ideas. As you work with ideas from the text, remember to use attributive tags, quotation marks for any quoted passages, and MLA documentation to distinguish your own points about the text from the author's ideas and language.

Exploring Ideas for Your Strong Response

Earlier in the chapter we presented the kinds of strong responses you may be asked to write in college. We also provided examples of the questions you can ask to generate ideas for different kinds of strong response. Your goal now is to figure out what you want to say. Your first step, of course, is to read your assigned text with the grain, listening to the text so well that you can write a summary of its argument. Use the strategies described in the previous writing project to compose your summary of the assigned text.

After you have written your summary, which demonstrates your full understanding of the text, you are ready to write a strong response. Because your essay cannot discuss every feature of the text or every idea the text has evoked, you will want to focus on a small group of points that enable you to bring readers a new, enlarged, or deepened understanding of the text. You may decide to write a primarily with-the-grain response, praising, building on, or applying the text to a new context, or a primarily against-the-grain response, challenging, questioning, and refuting the text. If your strong response primarily agrees with the text, you must be sure to extend it and apply the ideas rather than simply make your essay one long summary of the article. If your strong response primarily disagrees with the text and criticizes it, you must be sure to be fair and accurate in your criticisms. Here we give you some specific rereading strategies that will stimulate ideas for your strong response, as well as an example of Kyle Madsen's marginal response notes to Pollan's article (Figure 5.1).

See Chapter 1, Concept 3, for a discussion of audience analysis.

Strategies for Rereading to Stimulate Ideas for a Strong Response

Strategies	What to Do	Comments
Take notes.	Make copious marginal notes while rereading, recording both with-the-grain and against-the-grain responses.	Writing a strong response requires a deep engagement with texts. For example, in Figure 5.1, observe how Kyle Madsen's notes incorporate with-the-grain and against-the-grain responses and show him truly talking back to and interacting with Pollan's text.
Identify "hot spots" in the text.	Mark all hot spots with marginal notes. After you've finished reading, find these hot spots and freewrite your responses to them in a reading journal.	By "hot spot" we mean a quotation or passage that you notice because you agree or disagree with it or because it triggers memories or other associations. Perhaps the hot spot strikes you as thought provoking. Perhaps it raises a problem or is confusing yet suggestive.
Ask questions.	Write several questions that the text caused you to think about. Then explore your responses to those questions through freewriting, which may trigger more questions.	Almost any text triggers questions as you read. A good way to begin formulating a strong response is to note these questions.
Articulate your difference from the intended audience.	Decide who the writer's intended audience is. If you differ significantly from this audience, use this difference to question the author's underlying assumptions, values, and beliefs.	Your gender, age, class, ethnicity, sexual orientation, political and religious beliefs, interests, values, and so forth, may cause you to feel estranged from the author's imagined audience. If the text seems written for straight people and you are gay, or for Christians and you are a Muslim or an atheist, or for environmentalists and you grew up in a small logging community, you may well resist the text. Sometimes your sense of exclusion from the intended audience makes it difficult to read a text at all.

Michael Pollan
Why Bother?

This idea is very direct and clear.

Short sentence sounds casual.

Another very informal statement.

Good word choice? Sounds prejudiced and alarmist.

This paragraph shows Pollan's liberal perspective.

Informal speech.

Sounds like Pollan is talking to readers.

How I felt when I saw this film.

Helpful examples.

Look up this word.

Exaggerated statement?

Former Vice President Cheney?

What's the definition of this term?

Why bother? That really is the big question facing us as individuals hoping to do something about climate change, and it's not an easy one to answer. I don't know about you, but for me the most upsetting moment in *An Inconvenient Truth* came long after Al Gore scared the hell out of me, constructing an utterly convincing case that the very survival of life on earth as we know it is threatened by climate change. No, the really dark moment came during the closing credits, when we are asked to … change our light bulbs. That's when it got really depressing. The immense disproportion between the magnitude of the problem Gore had described and the puniness of what he was asking us to do about it was enough to sink your heart.

But the drop-in-the-bucket issue is not the only problem lurking behind the "why bother" question. Let's say I do bother, big time. I turn my life upside-down, start biking to work, plant a big garden, turn down the thermostat so low I need the Jimmy Carter signature cardigan, forsake the clothes dryer for a laundry line across the yard, trade in the station wagon for a hybrid, get off the beef, go completely local. I could theoretically do all that, but what would be the point when I know full well that halfway around the world there lives my evil twin, some carbon-footprint *doppelgänger* in Shanghai or Chongqing who has just bought his first car (Chinese car ownership is where ours was back in 1918), is eager to swallow every bite of meat I forswear and who's positively itching to replace every last pound of CO2 I'm struggling no longer to emit. So what exactly would I have to show for all my trouble?

A sense of personal virtue, you might suggest, somewhat sheepishly. But what good is that when virtue itself is quickly becoming a term of derision? And not just on the editorial pages of the *Wall Street Journal* or on the lips of the vice president, who famously dismissed energy conservation as a "sign of personal virtue." No, even in the pages of the *New York Times* and the *New Yorker*, it seems the epithet "virtuous," when applied to an act of personal environmental responsibility, may be used only ironically. Tell me: How did it come to pass that virtue—a quality that for most of history has generally been deemed, well, a virtue—became a mark of liberal softheadedness? How peculiar, that doing the right thing by the environment—buying the hybrid, eating like a locavore— should now set you up for the Ed Begley Jr.* treatment.

FIGURE 5.1   Kyle Madsen's Marginal Response Notes

Practicing Strong Response Reading Strategies

What follows is a short passage by writer Annie Dillard in response to a question about how she chooses to spend her time. This passage often evokes heated responses from our students.

> I don't do housework. Life is too short. ... I let almost all my indoor plants die from neglect while I was writing the book. There are all kinds of ways to live. You can take your choice. You can keep a tidy house, and when St. Peter asks you what you did with your life, you can say, "I kept a tidy house, I made my own cheese balls."

Individual task: Read the passage and then briefly freewrite your reaction to it.

Group task: Working in groups or as a whole class, develop answers to the following questions:

1. What values does Dillard assume her audience holds?
2. What kinds of readers are apt to feel excluded from that audience?
3. If you are not part of the intended audience for this passage, what in the text evokes resistance?

Articulate Your Own Purpose for Reading

Although you usually read a text because you are joining the author's conversation, you might occasionally read a text for an entirely different purpose from what the author intended. For example, you might read the writings of nineteenth-century scientists to figure out what they assumed about nature (or women, or God, or race, or capitalism). Or suppose that you examine a politician's metaphors to see what they reveal about her values, or analyze *National Geographic* for evidence of political bias. Understanding your own purpose will help you read deeply both with and against the grain.

Writing a Thesis for a Strong Response Essay

A thesis for a strong response essay should map out for readers the points that you want to develop and discuss. These points should be risky and contestable; your thesis should surprise your readers with something new or challenging. Your thesis might focus entirely on with-the-grain points or entirely on against-the-grain points, but most likely it will include some of both. Avoid tensionless thesis statements such as "This article has both good and bad points."

See Chapter 2, Concept 5, for a discussion of surprising thesis statements.

Here are some thesis statements that students have written for strong responses in our classes. Note that each thesis includes at least one point about the rhetorical strategies of the text.

EXAMPLES OF SUMMARY/STRONG RESPONSE THESIS STATEMENTS

- In "The Beauty Myth," Naomi Wolf makes a very good case for her idea that the beauty myth prevents women from ever feeling that they are good enough;

however, Wolf's argument is geared too much toward feminists to be persuasive for a general audience, and she neglects to acknowledge the strong social pressures that I and other men feel to live up to male standards of physical perfection.

- Although Naomi Wolf in "The Beauty Myth" uses rhetorical strategies persuasively to argue that the beauty industry oppresses women, I think that she overlooks women's individual resistance and responsibility.
- Although the images and figures of speech that Thoreau uses in his chapter "Where I Lived, and What I Lived For" from *Walden* wonderfully support his argument that nature is spiritually renewing, I disagree with his antitechnology stance and with his extreme emphasis on isolation as a means to self-discovery.
- In "Where I Lived, and What I Lived For" from *Walden*, Thoreau's argument that society is missing spiritual reality through its preoccupation with details and its frantic pace is convincing, especially to twenty-first century audiences; however, Thoreau weakens his message by criticizing his readers and by completely dismissing technological advances.
- Although the booklet *Compassionate Living* by People for the Ethical Treatment of Animals (PETA) uses the design features of layout, color, and image powerfully, its extreme examples, its quick dismissal of alternative views, and its failure to document the sources of its information weaken its appeal to *ethos* and its overall persuasiveness.

FOR WRITING AND DISCUSSION

Examining Thesis Statements for Strong Response Critiques

Working individually or in groups, identify the points in each of the thesis statements in the preceding section and briefly state them. Think in terms of the ideas you are expecting the writers to develop in the body of the essay. As a follow-up to this exercise, you might share in your groups your own thesis statements for your strong response essays. How clearly does each thesis statement lay out points that the writer will probe? As a group, discuss what new, important perspectives each thesis statement promises to bring to readers and how each thesis suits a rhetorical critique, ideas critique, or some combination of these.

Shaping and Drafting

Most strong response essays call for a short contextualizing introduction to set up your analysis. In the essay on pages 117–119, student writer Kyle Madsen begins by reflecting on personal and societal changes in environmental awareness and then raises the question that Pollan will address: What challenges confront us in changing how we live? Student writer Stephanie Malinowski uses a similar strategy. She begins by tapping into her readers' experiences with outsourcing, and then poses the question that Thomas Friedman addresses in his op-ed piece: Should Americans support or question the practice of outsourcing?

Both student writers introduce the question addressed by the article they are critiquing, and both include a short summary of the article that gives readers a foundation for the critique before they present the points of the article they will address in their strong responses.

Each of the thesis statements in the preceding section as well as Kyle's and Stephanie's thesis statements identifies and maps out two or more points that readers will expect to see developed and explained in the body of the essay. In a closed-form, thesis-driven strong response, readers will also expect the points to follow the order in which they are presented in the thesis. If your strong response is primarily a rhetorical critique, your evidence will come mainly from the text you are analyzing. If your strong response is primarily an ideas critique, your evidence is apt to come from personal knowledge of the issue or from further reading or research. If your strong response is primarily reflective, much of your evidence will be based on your own personal experiences and inner thoughts. A blended response, of course, can combine points from any of these perspectives.

Each point in your thesis calls for a lively discussion, combining general statements and specifics that will encourage readers to see this text your way. Just as you do in your summary, you must use attributive tags to distinguish between the author's ideas and your own points and responses. In addition, you must document all ideas gotten from other sources as well as place all borrowed language in quotation marks or block indentations according to MLA format and include a Works Cited in MLA format. Most strong response essays have short conclusions, just enough commentary to bring closure to the essay.

Revising

In a summary/strong response essay, you may want to work on the summary separately before you incorporate it into your whole essay. Use the peer review questions for summaries (p. 123) for that part of your essay. You will definitely want to get feedback from readers to make your strong response as clear, thorough, and compelling as possible.

Questions for Peer Review

In addition to the generic peer review questions explained in Skill 16.4, ask your peer reviewers to address these questions:

1. How appealingly do the title and introduction of the essay set up the topic of critique, convey the writer's interest, and lay a foundation for the summary of the article and the writer's thesis?
2. How could the writer's thesis statement be clearer in presenting several focused points about the text's rhetorical strategies and ideas?
3. How could the body of the strong response follow the thesis more closely?
4. Where do you, the reader, need more clarification or support for the writer's points? How could the writer develop with-the-grain or against-the-grain points more appropriately?
5. Where could the writer work on the effectiveness of attributive tags, quotations, and documentation?

The readings for this chapter address the issue of outsourcing, the practice of moving jobs from developed countries like the United States to developing countries, which have a cheaper workforce. This practice affects available jobs for college graduates and American workers as well as the progress and vitality of the economies of many countries. Outsourcing continues to spark fiery debates about job creation and unemployment in the United States, about the distribution of benefits and harm, and about global economic competition. The readings that follow address these points from multiple perspectives. The questions for analysis have been omitted from all but the student essay by Stephanie Malinowski so that you can do your own independent thinking in preparation for writing your own summary/strong response essay.

Our first reading is an op-ed piece by prominent journalist Thomas L. Friedman, published in the *New York Times* on February 29, 2004. Friedman is known for his pro–free trade enthusiasm and his three books on globalization, *The Lexus and the Olive Tree* (1999), *The World Is Flat: A Brief History of the Twenty-First Century* (2005), and *Hot, Flat, and Crowded* (2008).

Thomas L. Friedman
30 Little Turtles

1   Indians are so hospitable. I got an ovation the other day from a roomful of Indian 20-year-olds just for reading perfectly the following paragraph: "A bottle of bottled water held 30 little turtles. It didn't matter that each turtle had to rattle a metal ladle in order to get a little bit of noodles, a total turtle delicacy. The problem was that there were many turtle battles for less than oodles of noodles."

2   I was sitting in on an "accent neutralization" class at the Indian call center 24/7 Customer. The instructor was teaching the would-be Indian call center operators to suppress their native Indian accents and speak with a Canadian one—she teaches British and U.S. accents as well, but these youths will be serving the Canadian market. Since I'm originally from Minnesota, near Canada, and still speak like someone out of the movie "Fargo," I gave these young Indians an authentic rendition of "30 Little Turtles," which is designed to teach them the proper Canadian pronunciations. Hence the rousing applause.

3   Watching these incredibly enthusiastic young Indians preparing for their call center jobs—earnestly trying to soften their t's and roll their r's—is an uplifting experience, especially when you hear from their friends already working these jobs how they have transformed their lives. Most of them still live at home and turn over part of their salaries to their parents, so the whole family benefits. Many have credit cards and have become real consumers, including of U.S. goods, for the first time. All of them seem to have gained self-confidence and self-worth.

4   A lot of these Indian young men and women have college degrees, but would never get a local job that starts at $200 to $300 a month were it not for the call centers. Some do "outbound" calls, selling things from credit cards to phone services to Americans and Europeans. Others deal with "inbound" calls—everything from tracing lost luggage for U.S. airline passengers to solving computer problems for U.S. customers. The calls are transferred here by satellite or fiber optic cable.

5   I was most taken by a young Indian engineer doing tech support for a U.S. software giant, who spoke with pride about how cool it is to tell his friends that he just spent the day helping Americans navigate their software. A majority of these call center workers are young women, who not only have been liberated by earning a decent local wage (and therefore have more choice in whom they marry), but are using the job to get M.B.A.'s and other degrees on the side.

6   I gathered a group together, and here's what they sound like: M. Dinesh, who does tech support, says his day is made when some American calls in with a problem and is actually happy to hear an Indian voice: "They say you people are really good at what you do. I am glad I reached an Indian." Kiran Menon, when asked who his role model was, shot back: "Bill Gates—[I dream of] starting my own company and making it that big." I asked C. M. Meghna what she got most out of the work: "Self-confidence," she said, "a lot of self-confidence, when people come to you with a problem and you can solve it—and having a lot of independence." Because the call center teams work through India's night—which corresponds to America's day—"your biological clock goes haywire," she added. "Besides that, it's great."

7   There is nothing more positive than the self-confidence, dignity and optimism that comes from a society knowing it is producing wealth by tapping its own brains—men's and women's—as opposed to one just tapping its own oil, let alone one that is so lost it can find dignity only through suicide and "martyrdom."

8   Indeed, listening to these Indian young people, I had a déjà vu. Five months ago, I was in Ramallah, on the West Bank, talking to three young Palestinian men, also in their 20's, one of whom was studying engineering. Their hero was Yasir Arafat. They talked about having no hope, no jobs and no dignity, and they each nodded when one of them said they were all "suicide bombers in waiting."

9   What am I saying here? That it's more important for young Indians to have jobs than Americans? Never. But I am saying that there is more to outsourcing than just economics. There's also geopolitics. It is inevitable in a networked world that our economy is going to shed certain low-wage, low-prestige jobs. To the extent that they go to places like India or Pakistan—where they are viewed as high-wage, high-prestige jobs—we make not only a more prosperous world, but a safer world for our own 20-year-olds.

Our second reading is a summary/strong response essay by student writer Stephanie Malinowski in response to the Friedman article. It follows primarily a "rhetorical critique" strategy for the strong response.

Stephanie Malinowski
Questioning Thomas L. Friedman's Optimism in "30 Little Turtles"

1   You are struggling to fix a problem that arises when you are downloading new computer software on to your computer. You're about to give up on the whole thing when an idea hits you: call the software company itself to ask for assistance. Should

you be surprised when the person who answers the phone to help you is based in India? Should Americans support or question outsourcing?

2   In "30 Little Turtles," an op-ed piece that appeared in the *New York Times* on February 29, 2004, journalist and foreign affairs columnist Thomas L. Friedman argues that outsourcing call center jobs from the Western world to India is transforming the lives of Indian workers and benefiting geopolitics. Friedman supports his argument by detailing his experience visiting a call center in India. He claims that the Indians working to serve Canadian and American markets are happy with how their work has improved their lives. Friedman points out that the working Indian women feel liberated now that they are making a decent wage and can afford such things as a college education. He describes Indian workers' view of their jobs, using words such as "self-confidence" and "independence." At the end of his article, Friedman states that he doesn't favor Indian employment over American employment but that outsourced jobs in countries like India or Pakistan create both prosperity and global security. Although Friedman's article clearly conveys to its audience how some Indian workers are benefiting from outsourcing, his argument relies heavily on personal experience and generalizations. I also think his condescending attitude hurts his argument, and he concludes his article too abruptly, leaving readers with questions.

3   Friedman succeeds in portraying the positive side of outsourcing to his *New York Times* readers who may be questioning the rationale for outsourcing. Friedman interviews the recipients of American jobs to see outsourcing from their perspective and enlightens Americans trying to understand how outsourcing is benefiting workers in other countries. Friedman's opening is vivid and captures the readers' interest by detailing his experience inside an Indian call center. He quotes the Indian workers expressing the joys of working for American and Canadian people. These workers testify to the financial and personal gains these jobs have brought. One woman says that she feels good about her job and herself "when people come to you with a problem and you can solve it" (125). The article is so full of optimism that the reader can't help but empathize with the Indians and feel happy that outsourcing has transformed their lives. Through these emotional appeals, Friedman succeeds in making readers who may have big reservations about outsourcing think about the human dimension of outsourcing.

4   However, Friedman also makes large generalizations based on his few personal experiences, lessening the credibility of his article. The first sentence of the article reads, "Indians are so hospitable." So are *all* Indians "so hospitable"? Friedman seems to make this generalization about national character based on the fact that he was applauded by a room full of Indians after reading a tongue twister paragraph in a perfect Canadian accent. I can see why Friedman appreciates his warm reception, but "feel good" moments can hardly provide evidence for the soundness of global economic policies. Friedman generalizes further about what he sees and hears in the call center room. He talks about the Indian employees in these terms: "All of them seem to have gained self-confidence and self-worth" (124). From this single observation, Friedman makes the assumption that almost every Indian working an outsourcing job must be gaining, and that the overall experience has done wonders for their lives. However, other articles that I have read have mentioned that call center work is basically a

deadend job and that $200 a month is not a big salary. Later in his conclusion, Friedman states that "we make not only a more prosperous world, but a safer world for our own 20-year-olds" (125). Can this conclusion be drawn from one visit to a call center where Indians expressed gratitude for their outsourcing work?

5   An even bigger problem with Friedman's article is the condescending way in which he describes the Indian workers. I think he portrays the culture as being incompetent before the American and Canadian outsourcing jobs came to improve their accents and their lives. One statement that conveys condescension is this remark: "Watching these incredibly enthusiastic young Indians preparing for their call center jobs—earnestly trying to soften their t's and roll their r's—is an uplifting experience … " (124). This passage reminds me of the delight and pride of parents witnessing their children's growth milestones. Friedman is casting the accent neutralization of the Indian workers as overcoming a barrier in order to reach success. Friedman's condescending tone is apparent again when he restates the words of one American caller to an Indian worker, "They say you people are really good at what you do. I am glad I reached an Indian" (125). I see Friedman's reason for including this quote; he wants the reader to know that Indian workers are being valued for their work. However, the words that the American uses, which Friedman deliberately chooses to include in his article, "you people," suggest that Indians are a whole other kind of people different from American workers in their skills. Friedman's condescension also appears when he says that these are "low-wage, low-prestige jobs" (125). This remark is full of problems because it puts down the Indians taking the jobs and the Americans who have lost them, and it misrepresents the outsourcing scene that now includes many highly skilled prestigious jobs.

6   I also think that Friedman weakens his article by concluding abruptly and introducing new ideas to readers that leave them with unanswered questions. Friedman asks the reader, "What am I saying here? That it's more important for young Indians to have jobs than Americans?" (125). This point seems like a relevant question to investigate, but its weakness is that Friedman never even mentions any place in his article the loss that American workers are experiencing. At the end of the article, readers are left with questions. For example, the last sentence reads, "we make not only a more prosperous world, but a safer world for our own 20-year-olds" (125). Although Friedman is implying that outsourcing improves our relationships with other countries and enhances our national safety, nowhere in the article does he substantiate this claim. He seems to have thrown this statement into the conclusion just to end the article on a happy note.

7   Giving a human face to outsourcing is a good idea; however, Friedman does not support his main argument well, and this article comes across as a simplistic, unexplored view of outsourcing. I and other readers are left needing to look for answers to serious questions about outsourcing elsewhere.

Work Cited

Friedman, Thomas L. "30 Little Turtles." *New York Times* 29 Feb. 2004. Rpt. in *The Allyn & Bacon Guide to Writing.* John D. Ramage, John C. Bean, and June Johnson. 6th ed. New York: Pearson, 2012. 124–5. Print.

THINKING CRITICALLY
about "Questioning Thomas L. Friedman's Optimism in '30 Little Turtles'"

1. What rhetorical points has Stephanie Malinowski chosen to analyze in her strong response essay?

2. What examples and quotations from Friedman's article work particularly well as support for her points? Where might she have included more support?

3. Where does Stephanie use attributive tags effectively?

4. If you were to write a rhetorical critique of Friedman's article, what points would you select to analyze?

5. If you were to write an ideas critique, what would you choose to focus on? Where would you agree and disagree with Friedman?

Our third and fourth readings consist of two political cartoons that tell stories about employment and U.S. involvement in outsourcing. As you read these cartoons, identify the characters, the story line, the angle of vision, and the argument each presents.

David Horsey is a two-time Pulitzer Prize winner for editorial cartoons. This cartoon was originally published the *Seattle Post-Intelligencer* on June 4, 2003.

David Horsey
Today's Economic Indicator

The second cartoon, by Mike Lane, appeared in the *Baltimore Sun* in 2003 and was posted on Cagle Cartoons on August 27, 2003. Lane, a prize-winning and well-known liberal editorial cartoonist, left the Baltimore newspaper in 2004 after thirty-two years.

Mike Lane
Labor Day Blues

Our fifth reading is an op-ed piece by editorial writer and syndicated columnist Froma Harrop, who writes regularly for the *Providence Journal* and whose columns appear frequently in newspapers around the country. She is known for the articulate, forthright expression of her liberal views on current issues. This piece appeared in the *Seattle Times* on April 17, 2007.

Froma Harrop
New Threat to Skilled U.S. Workers

1   The master plan, it seems, is to move perhaps 40 million high-skill American jobs to other countries. U.S. workers have not been consulted.

2   Princeton economist Alan Blinder predicts that these choice jobs could be lost in a mere decade or two. We speak of computer programming, bookkeeping, graphic design and other careers once thought firmly planted in American soil. For perspective, 40 million is more than twice the total number of people now employed in manufacturing.

3   Blinder was taken aback when, sitting in at the business summit in Davos, Switzerland, he heard U.S. executives talk enthusiastically about all the professional jobs they could outsource to lower-wage countries. And he's a free trader.

4   What America can do to stop this is unclear, but it certainly doesn't have to *speed up* the process through a government program. We refer to the H-1B visa program, which allows educated foreigners to work in the United States, usually for three years. Many in Congress want to nearly double the number of H-1B visas, to 115,000 a year.

5   To the extent that the program helps talented foreign graduates of U.S. universities stay in this country while they await their green cards, it performs a useful service. But for many companies, the visa has become just a tool for transferring American jobs offshore.

6   Ron Hira has studied the dark side of the H-1B program. A professor of public policy at the Rochester Institute of Technology, he notes that the top applicants for visas are outsourcing companies, such as Wipro Technologies of India and Bermuda-based Accenture.

7   The companies bring recruits in from, say, India to learn about American business. After three years here, the workers go home better able to interact with their U.S. customers.

8   In other cases, companies ask their U.S. employees to train H-1B workers who then replace them at lower pay. "This is euphemistically called, 'knowledge transfer,'" Hira says. "I call it 'knowledge extraction.' "

9   Another rap against the program is that it's used to depress the wages of American workers. The program's defenders argue that the law requires companies to pay "the prevailing wage."

10   But "prevailing wage" is a legalism, Hira says. It does not translate into "market wage."

11   The median pay for H-1B computing professionals in fiscal 2005 was $50,000, which means half earn less than that. An American information-technology worker with a bachelor's degree makes more than $50,000 in an entry-level job.

12   Businesses bemoan the alleged shortage of Americans trained to do the work. But wait a second—the law of supply and demand states that a shortage of something causes its price to rise. Wages in information technology have been flat.

13   The companies fret that not enough young Americans are studying science and technology. Well, cutting the pay in those fields isn't much of an incentive, is it?

14   The threat that they will outsource if they can't bring in foreign temps is a hollow one. "There's nothing stopping those companies from working offshore anyway," Hira says. "They're not patriotic."

15   This vision for a competitive America seems to be a few rich U.S. executives commandeering armies of foreign workers. They don't have to train their domestic workforce. They don't have to raise pay to American standards.

16   A provision for revving up the H-1B program is contained in the immigration bill that last year passed the Senate. The co-sponsors, Democrat Ted Kennedy of Massachusetts and Republican John McCain of Arizona, have contended that their legislation requires employers to search for U.S. workers first. It does not.

17   Skilled U.S. workers had better start looking out for their interests. No one else is.

Christopher Szymanski
Professor Porter
Engl 1303
11 May 2011

Identity: The Components

In history we have defined race as either being black or white. With increasing immigration, we have to ask the question: are nationality and/or ethnicity the only things that define us? This question is up for some strong debate and through analyzing Barbara Ehrenreich's article, "Cultural Baggage," and Richard Rodriguez's article, "'Blaxicans' and Other Reinvented Americans," both having complete opposite viewpoints on how to define your identity, I have come up with an answer to the question at hand.

Barbara Ehrenreich wrote an article in the New York Times about what she calls "Cultural Baggage." When asked about her racial or ethnic back ground she simply claimed that she had none. She did not believe that being part Scottish, Irish, and English did not qualify as a single one.

While other people that she knows and has dealt with have always talked about their background with much enthusiasm, the author was always left out. She claims that she was actually raised with no ethnicity. Due to this the author decides to go on a search for her identity.

She tries Scottish, and plays on the bagpipes. However, this does not work for her, she just did not believe it felt like she was being authentic. By marrying an eastern European Jew she thought she could possibly bring back ethnicity back into her family genes. This however, did not happen, due to the fact that her husband also did not feel strongly towards his racial and ethnic background. Ehrenreich even subjected her children to the tradition of Passover, but her children just laughed at her and told her that she did not believe in God.

The best philosophy is to think for yourself rather than to just always try new things. She realizes that her family is the family of no traditions. This allows her to stay open minded, and to try new things. Ehrenreich, along with her children advocate that "none" is the best thing for everyone, and that the world would be a better place if everyone believed that as well. The most important part to be happy is to stay loyal to your beliefs and values.

Richard Rodriguez wrote an article titled "'Blaxicans' and other reinvented Americans" talking about the following points. The western Europeans who came to America first are now questioning their identities due to all the new immigrants. Due to the fact that eventually the grandchildren of the immigrants will romanticize with the western Europeans, they will be teaching us what it means to be American.

Throughout history the talk about race in America has been between blacks and whites. However, that now has to change. People began to mix with different races and now we have "impure-Americans" or "Ambiguous-Americans". Rodriguez says that he is mixed, and Mexico is mixed, and that America is "multicultural". He believes that America should adopt a mixed concept called mestizaje. Americans are not fond of these racial mixes, they are all for diversity, as long as their elbows do not touch.

Under President Nixon, the Office of Management and Budget split the country into 5 main races. This gave a stop to everyone but named all Central Americans as Hispanics. There are only Hispanics in America, everywhere else there are Chileans, Peruvians, Mexicans and so forth. Latin Americans identify themselves as Hispanics only by the basis of language, fashion, and cuisine; not by blood. "Hispanic" now transcends borders.

"Assimilation happens," is what the author is saying (Rodriguez B10). He also says that he is not for or against it, it just happens. Culture is the same way, it just comes to you, and you do not force it. People do not just decide what culture they are today, it mixes together and with time it will come to you as a mixture of many cultures. Culture is now separate from ethnicity; we can adopt any culture we want.

The author's purpose is to "demythologize identity" (Rodriguez B10). He wants to make it a bigger decision than just black and white.

The author is an Indian, Spanish, Californian, Irish English speaking but considers himself Chinese because he lives in a Chinese neighborhood and associates himself with the Chinese culture. To understand what the author means in this passage, s/he must understand that he is Chinese. Due to the fact that we are mixing and making new identities, the author believes that you are who you associate yourself with, and ultimately who you believe you are.

Although Barbara Ehrenreich believes that if you are of mixed racial background, you do not have enough of one race so you are "none," and Richard Rodriguez believes that no matter how many different racial backgrounds you have you are all of then and ultimately you are what you believe you are. I, however, support Richard Rodriguez' claim and further believe that nationality and/or ethnicity are not the only things that define us.

In both articles: *Cultural Baggage* written by Barbara Ehrenreich and *'Blaxicans' and Other Reinvented Americans* written by Richard Rodriguez, the authors use rhetorical strategies and syntax to further emphasize the points they respectively make.

In both articles they use direct statements and repetition multiple times. For instance Ehrenreich writes on page 155 "'None.'" when asked about her ethnic background. This is written in the second paragraph and it is one of the main points she makes in her article. Respectfully, Rodriguez has multiple places where he uses this rhetorical strategy. On page 3 of his article he says, "Some Hispanics have accepted the fiction". And twice on page 4 while talking about the immigrants coming across the border, "It's over. The border is over." And when talking about culture, "Culture is fluid. Culture is Smoke. You breathe it. You eat it. You can't help hearing it." When they say these things, they are making very important points in their articles.

When the authors use repetition in their articles, they use it to evoke an emotional effect, it is almost poetic when they do so, and you subconsciously remember it. Ehrenreich uses it when talking about how her and her family do not carry down their past traditions, "I realized – whatever our distant ancestors' religions – who do not believe, who do not carry on traditions, who do not do things just because someone has done them before" (Ehrenreich 157). This again is an important point that she was the reader to have embedded in their head, that this is how her family was. When Rodriguez uses this rhetorical strategy, he uses it to evoke sympathy towards the nonwhite and nonblack Americans, "No question was put to the aforementioned Vietnamese man. There was certainly no question for the Chinese grocer, none for the Guatemalan barber, none for the tribe of Mexican Indians who reroofed your neighbor's house" (Rodriguez B10).

A strategy that only Ehrenreich uses is flashbacks. She uses this strategy multiple times in her writing to explain to the reader how she was brought up and to evoke some emotions towards her childhood. The first flashback she mentions on page 156 about how she was effected by not being proud of one ethnicity, "Throughout the 1960's and 70's I watched one group after another… stand up and proudly reclaim their roots while I just sank back ever deeper into my seat." Another time she uses it is when she talks about what her father used to always say to her, "'Think for yourself,' Dad used to say. 'Always ask why'." She is explaining to the reader why she has this thought process of having no ethnicity and such, and that is because of how she was raised as a child.

Rodriguez uses a couple more different rhetorical strategies as well that include, irony and paragraph structure evoke readers' emotions and emphasize his arguments. He begins and ends his article in a satirical statement. On page 1 he says, "There is something unsettling about immigrant because… well, because they chatter incomprehensibly, and get in everyone's way" then he ends the article with saying "I come to you as Chinese. Unless you understand that I am Chinese, then you have not understood anything I have said." He begins his article this way to attract the reader and to evoke either the readers' agreement to this or opposition to it. The ending statement really make the reader think about his intentions of writing this article are. Rodriguez wants to make sure the reader understands that his viewpoint on the issue is that you are what you believe you are; that there is more to your identity than just your ethnic background.

Rodriguez' use of paragraph structure shows that he has many different ideas that he wants to portray to the reader. Some of his paragraphs are only a sentence long such as on page 1, "The American conversation about race has always been a black-and-white conversation, but the conversation has become bloodless as badminton." This paragraph is a very important one, he tells the reader what his main purpose of writing this article was. He even uses a simile at the end of this sentence to possibly make the reader stop and think about what he means. Basically what he means is that the black-and-white conversation is meaningless and it is not the way the conversation should be directed. Throughout the article, the shorter the sentence, the more impact it has on the reader.

Both Ehrenreich and Rodriguez use similar methods of rhetoric tools to evoke certain emotions from the reader. Ehrenreich, unlike Rodriguez, uses flashback to explain to the reader how she came up with her ideas on ethnicity, and how they make sense. Rodriguez uses sarcasm and paragraph structure to convey his ideas to the reader in a way that makes him or her stop and analyze the meaning. While Ehrenreich believes that when a person has multiple ethnicities they cannot consider themselves a single one, therefore they are none. While Rodriguez believes that when a person has multiple ethnicities that he is all of them. However, both Ehrenreich and Rodriguez believe that the way you are brought up and the different experiences you are exposed to, have a significant influence on how you identify yourself.

Both Authors use rhetoric strategies to enforce their ideas respectively. In doing so, they unintentionally came to the same conclusion that there are more things that define our identities than just nationality and/or ethnicity.

Although Ehrenreich and Rodriguez have completely opposite views on ethnicity and identity, those both unknowingly come to the same conclusion on some aspects. They both agree that what creates your personal identity stems not just from your actual ethnicity or race but rather from many different aspects. These aspects include: Culture/religion, customs, what you do, where you live, philosophical outlook, political identification, friends, accomplishments, actions, clothing, family, class and economic status, and stereotypes. These are some of the ways that I personally can identify myself by and people around me can identify me. Both Ehrenreich and Rodriguez do not directly state that outside reasons define how they see themselves, but they do mention some specific examples that have helped shape their identity.

Ehrenreich indirectly says that her childhood experiences and how her family raised her have directly affected her outlook on her identity. Ehrenreich mentions in the 1960's and 70's how many of her fellow classmates would proclaim their ethnicity very proudly while she sank deeper into her seat (Ehrenreich 156). This was a past experience that clearly she remembers and it still bothers her if she is mentioning it so many years after the fact. When her father tells her to "Think for yourself" and to "always ask why" is another thing that has shaped her outlook on herself (Ehrenreich 157). This is the way she was brought up; she was also brought up to not keep tradition. Ehrenreich "recalled that [her] mother never introduced a procedure for cooking or cleaning by telling [her], 'Grandma did it this way'" (Ehrenreich 157). She was brought up with never having tradition; she had experiences where she was left out because she did not have a definite ethnicity, and both her father and mother had the same views on this all. Her family and past experiences shaped her to the way she is. Her children were also influenced by how she raised them they also believe their ethnicity is " 'none'," and go on further to say, " 'and the world would be a better place if nobody else did, either'" (Ehrenreich 158). Your family has a very strong deciding factor as to how you see yourself.

Rodriguez is more obvious that he has this thought process. He bluntly says, "[young people are] already moving into a world in which tattoo or ornament or movement or commune or sexuality or drug or rave or electronic bombast are the organizing principles of their identity" (Rodriguez B10). He agrees with my conclusion that there is much more to a person's identity than just simply his ethnicity or race. Rodriguez even says, "The notion that they are white or black simply doesn't occur" (Rodriguez B10). People do not only identify themselves with their color or their background, they use their everyday influences and experiences to express who they are as individuals. Rodriguez half-sarcastically says that he is Chinese because [he has] lived in a Chinese city for so long that [his] eye has taken on that palette, has come to prefer lime greens and rose reds and all the inventions of this Chinese Mediterranean. [He] sees photographs in magazines or documentary footage of China, especially rural China, and [he] sees what [he] recognizes as home" (Rodriguez 4). Due to the fact that he lives in a Chinese area and he associates himself with Chinese people, he considers himself Chinese. Even though he has no Chinese blood in him, outside forces have caused him to seriously start to identify himself as Chinese primarily based on his location and his surroundings.

Even though both writers had different conclusions, they both could agree upon saying that outside of just your race and ethnicity, there are factors that influence your identity. My family is the main force behind shaping me to the kind of person I am today, and shaping my identity. I am a Roman Catholic that goes to church regularly, because my family does that. My family has many traditions that stem back to when my parents lived in Poland, that not only they keep with their family, but also I plan to keep with my future family. One of the main traditions is we have Wygilia on Christmas Eve. It is a very big dinner and a very big celebration with a lot of food, which is all meat free. These are some little things that my family has influenced me on and has had some serious influence on how I have shaped myself as a person.

In Poland my parents never celebrated thanksgiving, and being born and raised in Canada, which has a different day for thanksgiving than the United States, it was also not a huge deal when I moved here. Over the years, however, teachers asking how my thanksgiving was and asking my younger brothers to write down all that they had to eat, my parents realized that we had to start making it a bigger deal than we do. Now, having my brother in the Marines and me in college, thanksgiving is a time where the whole family comes together and we have a big meal together. We value every bit of family time we have because we do not have it often. People such as our mentors and peers have a huge influence on the things that's we do and ultimately the things that we end up valuing.

These outside factors determine not only how I see myself but also how others see me. If you do not know me, you will base your conclusion about me completely on how I look. I believe I dress in nice clothing and I am white and I have brown hair, brown eyes, and many people would see me as average. Even if they were to hear me talk, I speak English without an accent. However, little do many people know, English is my second language and I am fluent in Polish. I also speak French and was part of an English exchange program where I lived in France for two weeks. These things are huge factors that define me as a person. Unfortunately these things are oblivious to the human eye, and need further investigation into the person to know them.

My accomplishments in life include me moving from Toronto Ontario to Oakland Maine and then down here to Houston Texas. I have met a lot of people this way and not only have they shaped me but my experiences in all these places give me a different outlook on myself. This experience I had in my life of moving twice in one year, is quite unique. Many people cannot help define themselves by this factor. That is why identity is so unique for each person that having a huge standard such as White, or Black, or Asian, or Hispanic, or Indian is really just a joke.

Ethnicity and Race cannot be the only factors when looking at people's identity. It may be part of their culture, but there are so many other factors influencing people, that these cannot be the only ones. Because people are confused as to how they should identify themselves, we as people need to change our ways of identifying people based on race and ethnicity and come to a different way of thinking discussed in this essay. There are so many things that define my identity that I cannot simply put a single race to it. When I think about my identity I think about myself as a Roman Catholic, Canadian born, Polish, American, gun loving Texan, who is military oriented, keeps traditions alive, lives middle class, and is ESL. Simply put, so many factors influence my identity that assigning a single race or ethnicity is just not enough.

Works Cited

Ehrenreich, Barbara. "Cultural Baggage." *Rhetorically Arranged.* David Madden Ed. Boston: Thomson Wadsworth 2006. 155–158. Print.

Rodriguez, Richard. "Blaxicans and Other Reinvented Americans." *Chronicle of Higher Education* 50.3 (2006). B10. Web. 30 September 2009.

 For additional help with writing, reading, and research, go to
www.mycomplab.com

6

WRITING AN AUTOBIOGRAPHICAL NARRATIVE

This chapter focuses on the rhetorical aim "writing to express or share." Its writing projects ask you to write an autobiographical narrative about something significant in your own life. But rather than state the significance up front in a thesis, you let it unfold in storylike fashion. This narrative structure places autobiographical writing at the open end of the closed-to-open-form continuum, making it more like a nonfiction "short story" than a traditional academic essay. Consequently, many instructors pair this chapter with Chapter 11, which discusses in more detail the features of openform prose.

Autobiographical writing can help us explore, deepen, and complicate our perceptions of the world. In addition to telling stories to convey the complexity and significance of an event, we use stories to reveal something about ourselves. We also use others' stories, particularly during adolescence, to monitor our own growth. Many of us have read the stories of such people as Anne Frank, Maya Angelou, Helen Keller, Malcolm X, and Laura Ingalls Wilder in search of attitudes and behaviors to emulate. Reading their stories becomes a way of critiquing and understanding our own stories.

The writing projects for this chapter address two genres of narrative writing: (1) An **autobiographical narrative** on any significant event or moment in your life that uses the narrative strategies of plot, character, and setting to develop tension, move the story forward, and give it significance, and (2) a **literacy narrative** that uses the same narrative strategies but is centered on the writer's experience with language, reading, writing, school, teachers, or education. Both kinds of narratives draw on the sensibility that you bring to the ordinary as well as the unique events of your life. Good autobiographical narrative does not depend on having an exciting life with highly dramatic moments. On the contrary, some of the most memorable autobiographical and literacy narratives relate ordinary experiences in a vivid manner that shares the writer's humiliations, aspirations, self-discoveries, and revelations. All of us have experienced moments when our world became strange or new—perhaps a first day at a new school or job; a conflict with a parent, teacher, employer, lover, or friend; or an encounter in a lunchroom or on a street corner. Everyone enjoys hearing good writers describe how they coped with and understood these universal situations. It is precisely because readers have experienced these things that they can project themselves easily into the writer's world.

In this chapter, you will learn to:

- find and explore a significant moment in your life and
- write an autobiographical or literacy narrative using literary techniques

Exploring Autobiographical Narrative

One of the premises of this book is that good writing is rooted in the writer's perception of a problem. Problems are at the center not only of thesis-based writing but also of narrative writing. In effective narration, the problem usually takes the form of a *contrary*, two or more things in opposition—ideas, characters, expectations, forces, worldviews, or whatever. Three kinds of contraries that frequently form the plots of autobiographical narratives are the following:

1. *Old self versus new self.* The writer perceives changes in himself or herself as a result of some transforming or breakthrough moment or event.
2. *Old view of person X versus new view of person X.* The writer's perception of a person (favorite uncle, childhood hero, scary teacher) changes as a result of some revealing moment; the change in the narrator's perception of person X also indicates growth in the narrator's self-perception.
3. *Old values versus new values that threaten, challenge, or otherwise disrupt the old values.* The writer confronts an outsider (or a new, unfamiliar situation such as a class or a learning task) that challenges his or her worldview, or the writer undergoes a crisis that creates a conflict in values.

Prior to class discussion, freewrite for ten minutes about episodes in your own life that fit one or more of these typical plots. Then, working in small groups or as a whole class, share your discoveries. Your goal is to begin seeing that each person's life is a rich source of stories.

In considering experiences for a narrative, think of *significant* not as "unusual" or "exciting" but as "revealing" or "conveying an unexpected meaning or insight." Thought of in this way, a significant moment in a story might be a gesture, a remark, a smile, a way of walking or tying a shoe, the wearing of a certain piece of clothing, or the carrying of a certain object in a purse or pocket. Invent a short scene in which a gesture, smile, or brief action reverses one character's feelings about, or understanding of, another character.

1. You thought that Maria had led a sheltered life until _____.
2. You thought Mr. Watson was a racist until _____.
3. Marco (Jillian) seemed the perfect date until _____.

In each case, think of specific details about one revealing moment that reverse your understanding. Here is an example of a scene:

> My dad seemed unforgivingly angry at me until he suddenly smiled, turned my baseball cap backward on my head, and held up his open palm for a high five. "Girl, if you don't change your ways, you're going to be as big a high school screw-up as your old man was."

Understanding Autobiographical Writing

Autobiographical writing may include descriptions of places and people and depictions of events that are more entertaining than enlightening. However, the spine of most autobiographical writing is a key moment or event, or a series of key moments or events, that shapes or reveals the author's emerging character or growth in understanding.

Autobiographical Tension: The Opposition of Contraries

Key events in autobiography are characterized by a clash of opposing values or points of view. These oppositions are typically embodied in conflicts between characters or in divided feelings within the narrator. The contraries in a story can often be summed up in statements such as these:

> My best friend from the eighth grade was suddenly an embarrassment in high school.
>
> My parents thought I was too young to drive to the movies when in fact I was ready to ride off with Iggy's Motorcycle Maniacs.
>
> The school I had dreamed of attending turned into a nightmarish prison.
>
> The subject I had hated most in middle school—science—became my passion in high school.
>
> The job that bored me and made all my muscles ache rescued me from a hopeless summer.

Consider the differences between "No Cats in America?" and "The Stolen Watch."

An autobiographical piece without tension is like an academic piece without a problem or a surprising thesis. No writing is more tedious than a pointless "So what?" narrative that rambles on without tension. (You can read such a narrative in our discussion of the difference between a "story" and an "*and then* chronology" in Chapter 11. It is a good example of what *not* to do for this assignment.)

Like the risky thesis statement in closed-form writing, contrariety, or opposition, creates purpose and focus for open-form writing. It functions as an organizing principle, helping the writer determine what to include or omit. It also sets a direction for the writer. When a story is tightly wound and all the details contribute to the story line, the tension moves the plot forward as a mainspring moves the hands of a watch. The tension is typically resolved when the narrator experiences a moment of recognition or insight, vanquishes or is vanquished by a foe, or changes status.

How Literary Elements Work in Autobiographical Narratives

The basic elements of a literary narrative that work together to create a story are plot, character, setting, and theme.

The Importance of Plot By *plot* we mean the basic action of the story, including the selection and sequencing of scenes and events. Often stories don't open with the earliest chronological moment; they may start *in medias res* ("in the middle of things") at a moment of crisis and then flash backward to fill in earlier details that explain the origins of the crisis. What you choose to include in your story and where you place it are concerns of plot. The amount of detail you choose to devote to each scene is also a function of plot. How a writer varies the amount of detail in each scene is referred to as a plot's *pacing.*

Plots typically unfold in the following stages: (a) an arresting opening scene; (b) the introduction of characters and the filling in of background;

(c) the building of tension or conflict through oppositions embedded in a series of events or scenes; (d) the climax or pivotal moment when the tension or conflict comes to a head; and (e) reflection on the events of the plot and their meaning.

To help you recognize story-worthy events in your own life, consider the following list of pivotal moments that have figured in numerous autobiographical narratives:

- Moments of enlightenment or coming to knowledge
- Passages from one realm to the next: from innocence to experience, from outsider to insider or vice versa, from novice to expert, from what you once were to what you now are
- Confrontation with the unknown
- Moments of crisis or critical choice
- Problems maintaining relationships without compromising your own growth or denying your own needs
- Problems accepting limitations and necessities
- Contrasts between common wisdom and your own unique knowledge or experience:

The Importance of Character Which characters from your life will you choose to include in your autobiography? The answer to that question depends on the nature of the tension that moves your story forward. Characters who contribute significantly to that tension or who represent some aspect of that tension with special clarity belong in your story. Whatever the source of tension in a story, a writer typically chooses characters who exemplify the narrator's fears and desires or who forward or frustrate the narrator's growth in a significant way.

Sometimes writers develop characters not through description and sensory detail but through dialogue. Particularly if a story involves conflict between people, dialogue is a powerful means of letting the reader experience that conflict directly. The following piece of dialogue, taken from African-American writer Richard Wright's classic autobiography *Black Boy*, demonstrates how a skilled writer can let dialogue tell the story, without resorting to analysis and abstraction. In the following scene, young Wright approaches a librarian in an attempt to get a book by Baltimore author and journalist H. L. Mencken from a whites-only public library. He has forged a note and borrowed a library card from a sympathetic white coworker and is pretending to borrow the book in his coworker's name.

> "What do you want, boy?"
> As though I did not possess the power of speech, I stepped forward and simply handed her the forged note, not parting my lips.
> "What books by Mencken does he want?" she asked.
> "I don't know ma'am," I said avoiding her eyes.
> "Who gave you this card?"
> "Mr. Falk," I said.
> "Where is he?"

"He's at work, at the M— Optical Company," I said. "I've been in here for him before."

"I remember," the woman said. "But he never wrote notes like this."

Oh, God, she's suspicious. Perhaps she would not let me have the books? If she had turned her back at that moment, I would have ducked out the door and never gone back. Then I thought of a bold idea.

"You can call him up, ma'am," I said, my heart pounding.

"You're not using these books are you?" she asked pointedly.

"Oh no ma'am. I can't read."

"I don't know what he wants by Mencken," she said under her breath.

I knew I had won; she was thinking of other things and the race question had gone out of her mind.

—Richard Wright, *Black Boy*

It's one thing to hear *about* racial prejudice and discrimination; it's another thing to *hear* it directly through dialogue such as this. In just one hundred or so words of conversation, Wright communicates the anguish and humiliation of being a "black boy" in the United States in the 1920s.

Another way to develop a character is to present a sequence of moments or scenes that reveal a variety of behaviors and moods. Imagine taking ten photographs of your character to represent his or her complexity and variety and then arranging them in a collage.

The Importance of Setting Elements of setting are selected as characters are selected, according to how much they help readers understand the conflict or tension that drives the story. When you write about yourself, what you notice in the external world often reflects your inner world. In some moods you are apt to notice the expansive lawn, beautiful flowers, and swimming ducks in the city park; in other moods you might note the litter of paper cups, the blight on the roses, and the scum on the duck pond. The setting typically relates thematically to the other elements of a story. In "No Cats in America?" (pp. 160–161), for example, the author contrasts his parents' parties in the Philippines, replete with music and dancing, firecrackers, a mahjong gambling room, and exotic food and drink such as homemade mango juice and coconut milk, with the American school lunchroom where he opened his Tupperware lunchbox filled with fish and bagoong. The contrast of these settings, especially when the author's American classmates laugh at his lunch, embodies the story's tension.

FOR WRITING AND DISCUSSION

Capturing a Setting

In writing an autobiographical narrative, one of the challenges is to use words to capture scenes so vividly that readers can see in their own minds what you are describing and can share in your experience vicariously. The four photos in Figures 6.1 through 6.4 depict four common scenes: a wooded stream, a city street, an elementary school classroom, and an amusement ride at a fair. For this

FIGURE 6.1 A Wooded Stream

FIGURE 6.2 A City Street

FIGURE 6.3 An Elementary School Classroom

FIGURE 6.4 Amusement Ride at a Fair

exercise, choose one of these photos, and imagine a scene from your own life that might have taken place there.

Your goal in this exercise is to freewrite a vivid description of a setting, imagining that you are there. Describe the setting fully. What do you see? Hear? Smell? Once you have described the setting, imagine several characters entering this location and what conflict might play out. Try writing a short scene that portrays some tension. Then share your descriptions with your classmates, discussing how your settings might be used in an autobiographical narrative.

The Importance of Theme The word *theme* is difficult to define. Themes, like thesis statements, organize the other elements of the essay. But a theme is seldom stated explicitly and is never proved with reasons and factual evidence. Readers ponder—even argue about—themes, and often different readers are affected very differently by the same theme. Some literary critics view theme as simply a different way of thinking about plot. To use a phrase from critic Northrop Frye, a plot is "what happened" in a story, whereas the theme is "what happens" over and over again in this story and others like it. To illustrate this distinction, we summarize student writer Patrick José's autobiographical narrative "No Cats in America?", one of the essays in the Readings section of this chapter, from a plot perspective and from a theme perspective:

José's essay is on pp. 160–161.

> **Plot Perspective** It's the story of a Filipino boy who emigrates with his family from the Philippines to the United States when he is in the eighth grade. On the first day of school, he is humiliated when classmates snicker at the lunch his mother packed for him. Feeling more and more alienated each day, he eventually proclaims, "I hate being Filipino!"
>
> **Theme Perspective** It's the story of how personal identity is threatened when people are suddenly removed from their own cultures and immersed into new ones that don't understand or respect difference. The story reveals the psychic damage of cultural dislocation.

As you can see, the thematic summary goes beyond the events of the story to point toward the larger significance of those events. Although you may choose not to state your theme directly for your readers, you need to understand that theme to organize your story. This understanding usually precedes and guides your decisions about what events and characters to include, what details and dialogue to use, and what elements of setting to describe. But sometimes you need to reverse the process and start out with events and characters that, for whatever reason, force themselves on you, and then figure out your theme after you've written for a while. In other words, theme may be something you discover as you write.

WRITING PROJECT

Autobiographical Narrative

Write a narrative essay about something significant in your life using the literary strategies of plot, character, and setting. Develop your story through the use of contraries, creating tension that moves the story forward and gives it significance. You can discuss the significance of your story explicitly, perhaps as a revelation, or you can imply it. (The readings at the end of this chapter illustrate different options.) Use specific details and develop contraries that create tension.

This assignment calls for a story. In Chapter 11, we argue that narrative qualifies as a story only when it depicts a series of connected events that create for the reader a sense of tension or conflict that is resolved through a new understanding or change in status. Your goal for this assignment is to write a story about your life that fulfills these criteria. The suggestions that follow will help you.

Generating and Exploring Ideas

Choosing a Plot

For some of you, identifying a plot—a significant moment or insight arising out of contrariety—will present little problem; perhaps you have already settled on an idea that you generated in one of the class discussion exercises earlier in this chapter. However, if you are still searching for a plot idea, you may find the following list helpful:

- A time when you took some sort of test that conferred new status on you (Red Cross lifesaving exam, driver's test, SAT, important school- or work-related test, entrance exam, team tryout). If you failed, what did you learn from it or how did it shape you? If you succeeded, did the new status turn out to be as important as you had expected it to be?
- A situation in which your normal assumptions about life were challenged (an encounter with a foreign culture, a time when a person you'd stereotyped surprised you).
- A situation in which you didn't fit or fulfill others' expectations of you, or a situation in which you were acknowledged as a leader or exceeded others' expectations of you (call to jury duty, assignment to a new committee, being placed in charge of an unfamiliar project).
- A time when a person who mattered to you (parent, spouse, romantic interest, authority figure) rejected you or let you down, or a time when you rejected or let down someone who cared for you.
- A time when you were irresponsible or violated a principle or law and thereby caused others pain (you shoplifted or drank when underage and were caught, you failed to look after someone entrusted to your care).
- A time when you were criticized unjustly or given a punishment you didn't deserve (you were accused of plagiarizing a paper that you'd written, you were blamed unjustly for a problem at work).

Shaping and Drafting Your Narrative

Once you've identified an event about which you'd like to write, you need to develop ways to show readers what makes that event particularly story-worthy. In thinking about the event, consider the following questions:

HOW TO START

- What are the major contraries or tensions in this story?
- What events and scenes portraying these contraries might you include in your narrative?

- What insights or meaning do you think your story suggests? How would you articulate for yourself the theme of your narrative?
- How might you begin your narrative?

HOW TO THINK ABOUT AND DEVELOP CHARACTERS AND SETTING

- What characters are important in this story?
- How will you portray them—through description, action, dialogue?
- What settings or scenes can you re-create for readers?
- What particulars or physical details will make the setting, characters, and conflicts vivid and memorable?

HOW TO THINK ABOUT AND DEVELOP THE PLOT OF YOUR NARRATIVE

- How might you arrange the scenes in your story?
- What would be the climax, the pivotal moment of decision or insight?

HOW TO CONCLUDE YOUR NARRATIVE

- What resolution can you bring to the tensions and conflicts in your story?
- How can you convey the significance of your story? What will make it something readers can relate to?
- How can the ending of your narrative leave readers thinking about larger human issues and concerns?

When stuck, writers often work their way into a narrative by describing in detail a vividly recalled scene, person, or object. You may not be able to include all the descriptive material, but in the act of writing exhaustively about this one element, the rest of the story may begin to unfold for you, and forgotten items and incidents may resurface. In the course of describing scenes and characters, you will probably also begin reflecting on the significance of what you are saying. Try freewriting answers to such questions as "Why is this important?" and "What am I trying to do here?" Then continue with your rough draft. Remember that it is the storyteller's job to put readers into the story by providing enough detail and context for the readers to see why the event is significant.

Revising

Testing your narrative out on other readers can give you valuable feedback about your effectiveness in grabbing and holding their interest and conveying an insight. Plan to write several drafts of your narrative.

Questions for Peer Review

In addition to the generic peer review questions explained in Skill 9.4, ask your peer reviewers to address these questions:

OPENING AND PLOT

1. How could the title and opening paragraphs more effectively hook readers' interest and prepare them for the story to follow?
2. How might the writer improve the tension, structure, or pacing of the scenes?
3. How could the writer improve the connections between scenes or use a different organization such as a collage of scenes or flashbacks to enhance the clarity or drama of the narrative?

CHARACTERIZATION

4. Where might the writer provide more information about characters or describe them more fully?
5. Where might the writer use dialogue more effectively to reveal character?

SETTING, THEME, AND LANGUAGE

6. How might the writer make the setting more vivid and connected to the action and significance of the story?
7. What insight or revelation do you get from this story? How could the narrative's thematic significance be made more memorable or powerful?
8. Where do you find examples of specific language? Where could the writer use more concrete language?

Literacy Narrative

**WRITING
PROJECT**

Write an autobiographical narrative that focuses on your experiences with language, reading, writing, or education. You could explore positive or negative experiences in learning to read or write, breakthrough moments in your development as a literate person, or some educational experiences that have shaped your identity as a person or student. Incorporate the literary elements of plot, character, setting, theme, and descriptive language in the telling of your story. Think of your task as finding new significance for yourself in these experiences and sharing your discoveries with your readers in ways that hold their interest and bring them new understanding.

What Is a Literacy Narrative?

A literacy narrative uses the elements of a story to recount a writer's personal experience with language in all its forms—reading and writing, acquiring a second language, being an insider or outsider based on literacy level and cultural context—or with learning how to learn in general through experiences inside and outside of school. The academic and public fascination with literacy narratives has grown out of—and contributed to—contemporary discussions about cultural diversity in the United States and the connections between literacy and cultural power.

Literacy narratives are a frequently encountered and important genre. For example, one of the most famous literacy narratives is by Frederick Douglass, the ex-slave and abolitionist leader who describes learning to read and write as the key to his liberation from slavery. Another well-known literacy narrative is by Zitkala-Ša (Gertrude Bonnin), a Native American woman who exposes the forceful assimilation tactics employed by missionary schools to separate Native American children from their tribes in the late nineteenth and early twentieth centuries. Perhaps the most famous literacy narrative is by Helen Keller, who recounts the moments when an understanding of language broke through the isolation created by her blindness and deafness. More recently, literacy narratives by immigrants from many cultures have explored the role of education in thwarting or encouraging their integration into American society.

Writing a literacy narrative in college classes can help students explore their adjustment to college, link their earlier learning experiences to the literacy demands of college courses, and take ownership of their own education. Thinking about your own literacy experiences compels you to ponder your educational path and your own ideas of the purpose of education. In contemplating the way that ethnic, economic, gender, class, and regional considerations have shaped your own learning to read and write, you will experience the pleasure of self-discovery and cultural insight.

Typical Features of a Literacy Narrative

Literacy narratives resemble other autobiographical narratives in their open-form structure and their inclusion of some or all of these literary features: a plot built on some tensions and presented as well-sequenced scenes, vivid descriptions of settings, well-drawn characters, dialogue, and theme. Like other autobiographical narratives, literacy narratives rely on vivid, concrete language to make settings and dramatic moments come alive for readers. While literacy narratives share many elements with other autobiographical narratives, they differ in their attention to the following features:

DISTINCTIVE FEATURES OF LITERACY NARRATIVES

- A focus on a writer's experience with language, reading, writing, schooling, teachers, or some other important aspect of education.
- A focus on bringing an insight about the significance of learning, language, reading, or writing to readers through an implied theme (although this theme might be explicitly stated, most likely at the end of the narrative).
- A focus on engaging readers and connecting them to an understanding of the writer's educational/learning experience, prompting them to think about their own educational experiences and larger questions about the purpose and value of education.

Analyzing Features of Literacy Narratives

Read the following passages that depict key moments in two students' literacy experiences, and answer the questions about them that direct your attention to specific features.

EXCERPT FROM MEGAN LACY'S LITERACY NARRATIVE

... I was placed in the remedial reading group. Our books had red plastic covers while the other kids had books with yellow covers that looked gold to me. When it was reading time, the rest of the red group and I congregated around a rectangular wood table where Mrs. Hinckley would direct each of us to read a passage from the story aloud. The first time this happened, my stomach dropped. Even the remedial kids were sounding out the words, but I had no idea what those symbols on the page meant.

When my turn came, I muttered meekly, "I can't. ... "

"Don't say 'can't' in my classroom!" Mrs. Hinckley snapped. Then, more gently, she said, "Just sound it out. ... "

I did as she recommended and could hardly believe what was happening. I was reading. I felt superhuman with such a power. After that moment, I read to my mom every night. ...

EXCERPT FROM JEFFREY CAIN'S LITERACY NARRATIVE

In the Walla Walla Public Library, I remember the tomato soup colored carpet, the bad oil paintings of pioneers fording the Columbia River, the musty smell, the oak card catalog with brass knobs, the position of the clock when I first read Jerzi Kosinski's *The Painted Bird*.

"Just read it," my sister-in-law said. "I know you don't read much fiction, but just read this one," she pleaded

Reluctantly, at first, I turned the pages. But each word covertly seduced me; slowly the odyssey of the dark-skinned gypsy affected my spirit like an exotic opiate, until Lehki's painted bird lay pecked to death on the ground. The image haunted my conscience for days. During some of my more restless nights, I was chased like the characters by Nazis through the Black Forest.

Who was this Kosinski? Why did his book affect me this way? How and why did he write like this? Did all writers write like Kosinski?

The novel incited a series of questions that forced me to begin writing notes and summarizing my thoughts. I began a reading journal and my development as a writer shadowed my habits as a reader. ...

1. What literacy experiences have Megan and Jeffrey chosen to focus on?
2. How do Megan and Jeffrey use the narrative elements of plot, setting, and concrete, specific language to involve their readers in their experiences?
3. Based on these excerpts, how would you articulate the theme of each piece?
4. What educational memories of your own are triggered by these excerpts?

Generating and Exploring Ideas

Many of the questions for generating and exploring ideas for the autobiographical narrative (pp. 139–140) apply equally to literacy narratives. To discover ideas that you could fruitfully explore in your literacy narrative, try asking yourself the following questions:

- *Questions about your experiences with reading and writing* (obstacles you encountered and perhaps overcame; particularly vivid memories; role of literacy in your self-identity; ways you have changed or grown)
- *Questions about adjusting to college or educational challenges* (unexpected problems with reading and writing encountered in college, or earlier in middle school or high school; discovery of holes or weaknesses in your education; educational issues related to your "difference"—ethnic, class, physical/mental, sexual orientation—from the norm)
- *Questions about your experiences with language* (issues arising from learning a second language; from being bilingual; from speaking a nonstandard dialect; from having a speech or hearing impairment or a learning disability; from preferring math or art or athletics or video games rather than reading and writing)
- *Questions about influential (or inhibiting) teachers or mentors* (influence of people who have helped or hindered your literacy development; people who have changed your view of yourself as a reader or writer)
- *Questions about literacy and social status or citizenship* (issues connected to literacy and cultural power or economic success; role of education in preparing you for local, national, or global citizenship).

FOR WRITING AND DISCUSSION

Discovering Experiences with Literacy

Using one or more of the preceding question areas to trigger ideas, freewrite about some of your literacy experiences. Try to identify moments in your life—in the form of scenes that you could describe using the story elements of plot, dialogue, and setting—that might engage readers. What themes about literacy might these scenes uncover? What is at stake?

Shaping and Drafting Your Literacy Narrative

The following questions, which apply the contraries listed on page 145 (old self versus new self, old view of a person versus new view of person, and old values versus new, threatening, or challenging values), can help you shape your narrative in terms of tensions, scenes, and unfolding story.

- Can you portray your literacy experience in terms of a breakthrough or transforming moment that created a new sense of yourself as a reader, writer, or learner?
- Can you depict your literacy experience in terms of your relationship to a teacher or mentor who helped you or hindered you and led to a new view of this person?

- Can you depict your literacy experience as a conflict of values or as a process of change from one way of regarding literacy to another way? What will your readers understand, in terms of what you most value, by reading your literacy narrative?

While some literacy narratives will follow a clear chronological pattern or a tightly connected scene sequence, others may assume the pattern of a collage or a series of snapshots of key moments in your development. Your challenge is to find what pattern best fits the story you want to tell. Note how in her literacy narrative on pages 162–164, student writer Stephanie Whipple builds her literacy narrative around two contrasting scenes.

Revising

In writing about experiences that are very close to you, it is particularly important to get responses from readers. Your readers can help you determine how effectively you are capturing and holding their attention and conveying the significance behind your experiences.

Questions for Peer Review

The peer review questions for the autobiographical narrative (pp. 152–153) apply equally well to the literacy narrative. In addition, you can ask your peer reviewers the following questions, which focus specifically on the literacy narrative:

- What insight, revelation, or new understanding about the importance of reading, writing, or education does this narrative offer you?
- How can the narrative's thematic point about literacy be made more memorable or powerful?

Our first reading is by Kris Saknussemm, a poet and fiction writer. He is the author of the dystopian, futuristic novel Zanesville (2005), and his poems and short stories have appeared in literary magazines around the country, including *The Boston Review, New Letters, The Antioch Review,* and *ZYZZYVA*. This selection is taken from his autobiographical work in progress.

Kris Saknussemm
Phantom Limb Pain

1   When I was thirteen my sole purpose was to shed my baby fat and become the star halfback on our football team. That meant beating out Miller King, the best athlete at my school. He was my neighbor and that mythic kid we all know—the one who's forever better than we are—the person we want to be.

2   Football practice started in September and all summer long I worked out. I ordered a set of barbells that came with complimentary brochures with titles like "How to Develop a He-Man Voice." Every morning before sunrise I lumbered around our neighborhood wearing ankle weights loaded with sand. I taught myself how to do Marine push-ups and carried my football everywhere so I'd learn not to fumble. But that wasn't enough. I performed a ceremony. During a full moon, I burned my favorite NFL trading cards and an Aurora model of the great quarterback Johnny Unitas in the walnut orchard behind our house, where Miller and I'd gotten into a fight when we were seven and I'd burst into tears before he even hit me.

3   Two days after my ceremony, Miller snuck out on his older brother's Suzuki and was struck by a car. He lost his right arm, just below the elbow. I went to see him the day after football practice started—after he'd come back from the hospital. He looked pale and surprised, but he didn't cry. It was hard to look at the stump of limb where his arm had been, so I kept glancing around his room. We only lived about 200 feet away, and yet I'd never been inside his house before. It had never occurred to me that he would also have on his wall a poster of Raquel Welch from *One Million Years* B.C.

4   I went on to break all his records that year. Miller watched the home games from the bench, wearing his jersey with the sleeve pinned shut. We went 10–1 and I was named MVP, but I was haunted by crazy dreams in which I was somehow responsible for the accident—that I'd found the mangled limb when it could've been sewn back on—and kept it in an aquarium full of vodka under my bed.

5   One afternoon several months later, toward the end of basketball season, I was crossing the field to go home and I saw Miller stuck going over the Cyclone fence—which wasn't hard to climb if you had both arms. I guess he'd gotten tired of walking around and hoped no one was looking. Or maybe it was a matter of pride. I'm sure I was the last person in the world he wanted to see—to have to accept assistance from. But even that challenge he accepted. I helped ease him down the fence, one diamond-shaped hole at a time. When we were finally safe on the other side, he said to me, "You know, I didn't tell you this during the season, but you did all right. Thanks for filling in for me."

6   We walked home together, not saying much. But together. Back to our houses 200 feet apart. His words freed me from my bad dreams. I thought to myself, how many things I hadn't told him. How even without an arm he was more of a leader. Damaged but not diminished, he was still ahead of me. I was right to have admired him. I grew bigger and a little more real from that day on.

THINKING CRITICALLY
about "Phantom Limb Pain"

Perhaps the first thing the reader realizes about Saknussemm's narrative is that the climactic event—one boy helping another climb down a Cyclone fence—is a small action; however, it has a big psychological and emotional meaning for the narrator. The events leading to this moment have prepared us to understand the writer's revelation of his new relationship to his rival. Saknussemm's last paragraph comments on the preceding narrative, making connections and pulling out threads of meaning.

1. Saknussemm chooses to leave a lot unsaid, depending on his readers to fill in the gaps. Why do you suppose that he had never been inside Miller King's house before? Why does he feel "somehow responsible for the accident"? What details does Saknussemm use to sketch in Miller's admirable traits?

2. What examples can you find in this narrative of revelatory words, memory-soaked words, and other concrete words low on the ladder of abstraction? Where does Saknussemm use words that *show* what is happening in the narrative instead of simply telling readers?

3. In closed-form prose, writers seldom use sentence fragments. In open-form prose, however, writers frequently use fragments for special effects. Note the two fragments in Saknussemm's final paragraph: "But together. Back to our houses 200 feet apart." Why does Saknussemm use these fragments? What is their rhetorical effect?

4. Part of Saknussemm's style in this narrative is to use understatement and minimalistic language while also using words that resonate with multiple meanings. For example, he lets readers imagine what Miller would look like trying to climb the Cyclone fence with one arm. However, some phrases and words are figurative and symbolic. What does Saknussemm mean by the phrases "grew bigger" and "a little more real" in his final sentence? How do the ideas of size and of reality versus illusion play a role in this narrative and relate to the theme?

See Skill 11.2 for a discussion of concrete language including revelatory words and memory-soaked words. See Chapter 4, Concept 11, for a discussion of *show* words and *tell* words.

For a different approach to narrative, consider student writer Patrick José's "No Cats in America?" Unlike Saknussemm's narrative, José's includes plentiful description. Note also how José creates tension through contrasts in his narrative: between an ideal image of America and a factual image, between life in the Philippines and life in California.

Patrick José (student)
No Cats in America?

1   "There are no cats in America." I remember growing up watching *An American Tail* with my sisters and cousins. Ever since I first saw that movie, I had always wanted to move to America. That one song, "There Are No Cats in America," in which the Mousekewitz family is singing with other immigrating mice, had the most profound effect on me. These were Russian mice going to America to find a better life—a life without cats. At first, I thought America really had no cats. Later, I learned that they meant that America was without any problems at all. I was taught about the American Dream with its promise of happiness and equality. If you wanted a better life, then you better pack up all your belongings and move to America.

2   However, I loved living in the Philippines. My family used to throw the best parties in Angeles City. For a great party, you need some delicious food. Of course there would be lechon, adobo, pancit, sinigang, lumpia, and rice. We eat rice for breakfast, lunch, and dinner, and rice even makes some of the best desserts. (My mom's bibingka and puto are perfect!) And you mustn't forget the drinks. San Miguel and Coke are usually sufficient. But we also had homemade mango juice and coconut milk. And a party wouldn't be a party without entertainment, right? So in one room, we had the gambling room. It's usually outside the house. Everybody would be smoking and drinking while playing mahjong. And sometimes, others would play pepito or pusoy dos. Music and dancing is always a must. And when there are firecrackers, better watch out because the children would go crazy with them.

3   Then one day, a mixed feeling came over me. My dad told us that he had gotten a job … in California. In the span of two months, we had moved to America, found a small apartment, and located a small private Catholic school for the kids. We did not know many people in California that first summer. We only had ourselves to depend on. We would go on car trips, go to the beach, cook, play games. In August, I thought we were living the American Dream.

4   But at the end of summer, school began. I was in the eighth grade. I had my book bag on one shoulder, stuffed with notebooks, folder paper, calculators, a ruler, a pencil box, and my lunch. I still can remember what I had for lunch on the first day of school—rice and tilapia and, in a small container, a mixture of vinegar, tomatoes, and bagoong. My mom placed everything in a big Tupperware box, knowing I eat a lot.

5   When I walked into the classroom, everyone became quiet and looked at me. I was the only Filipino in that room. Everyone was white. We began the day by introducing ourselves. When it got to my turn, I was really nervous. English was one of the courses that I took in the Philippines, and I thought I was pretty proficient at it. But when I first opened my mouth, everyone began to laugh. The teacher told everyone to hush. I sat down, smiling faintly not understanding what was so funny. I knew English, and yet I was laughed at. But it had nothing to do with the language. It was my accent.

6   Some students tried to be nice, especially during lunch. But it didn't last long. I was so hungry for my lunch. I followed a group of students to the cafeteria and sat down at an empty table. Some girls joined me. I didn't really talk to them, but they asked if they could join me. As I opened my Tupperware, I saw their heads turn away. They didn't like the smell of fish and bagoong. The girls left and moved to another table of girls. From the corner of my eye I saw them looking and laughing at me. I tried to ignore it, concentrating on eating my lunch as I heard them laugh. In the Philippines, the only way to eat fish and rice is with your hands. But that was in the Philippines. My manners were primitive here in America. I was embarrassed at the smell, was embarrassed at the way I ate, was embarrassed to be me.

7   When I got home, I lied to my parents. I told them school was great and that I was excited to go back. But deep down, I wanted to go back to the Philippines. When lunch came the next day, I was hungry. In my hand was my lunch. Five feet away was the trash. I stood up, taking my lunch in my hands. Slowly, I walked my way towards the trashcan, opened the lid, and watched as my lunch filled the trashcan. Again, I told my parents I enjoyed school.

8   When my grades began to suffer, the teacher called my parents and scheduled an appointment. The next day, my parents came to the classroom, and when they started talking to the teacher I heard laughter in the background. It humiliated me to have my classmates hear my parents talk.

9   That night, my parents and I had a private discussion. They asked why I lied to them. I told them everything, including my humiliation. They told me not to worry about it, but I pleaded for us to return to the Philippines. My parents said no. "Living here will provide a better future for you and your sisters," they said. Then the unexpected came. I didn't know what I was thinking. I yelled to them with so much anger, "I hate being Filipino!" Silence filled the room. Teardrops rolled down my cheeks. My parents were shocked, and so was I.

10   I went to my room and cried. I didn't mean what I said. But I was tired of the humiliation. Lying on my bed, with my eyes closed, my mind began to wander. I found myself in the boat with the Mousekewitz family singing, "There are no cats in America." If only they knew how wrong they were.

THINKING CRITICALLY
about "No Cats in America?"

Patrick José lets the reader infer his essay's significance from the details of the narrative and from their connection to the framing story of the fictional mice and cats.

1. How do the settings help you understand José's theme at different points in the narrative?

2. What would you say is the narrative's climax or pivotal moment?

3. José's title, first paragraph, and last paragraph are about a children's movie that features the Mousekewitz's song proclaiming that there are no cats in America. How does the "no cats" image function both as part of the underlying tension

of this narrative and as a symbolic vehicle for conveying the theme of José's essay? What is the insight that José has achieved at the end?

4. During a rough draft workshop, José asked his peer reviewers whether he should retain his description of parties in the Philippines, which he thought was perhaps unconnected to the rest of the narrative. His classmates urged him to keep those details. Do you agree with their advice? Why?

See Skill 11.2 for a discussion of the power of memory-soaked words.

5. For Filipinos and Filipinas, the specific names of foods and party games would be rich examples of memory-soaked words. For other readers, however, these names are foreign and strange. Do you agree with José's decision to use these specific ethnic names? Why?

Our final reading, a literacy narrative, is by student writer Stephanie Whipple.

Stephanie Whipple (student)
One Great Book

1   When first asked to remember my earliest experiences with reading, I thought of my favorite books as a young teen, and I was excited to explore how they shaped the person that I am today. However, upon trying to remember the very first books that I ever read as a child, some quite negative and frankly painful memories were brought to the surface.

2   When I was a little girl living in Memphis, Tennessee, I was a well-behaved bright child who never had trouble learning at a good pace or working with other children. In what I am guessing was my first grade class I remember being so excited when I found out that that year I was going to learn to read. My entire life, my mother and both of my older sisters have all loved reading. I was so excited to be able to read with them and join the big girls' conversations about the books that they were reading.

3   My very first vivid memory of reading was in the playroom of our house in Memphis. I was sitting with my father reading *The Poky Little Puppy* with him, and my younger brother, who had just started kindergarten, was playing with his Nerf gun.

4   "Okay, Steph. Start with this word." My dad points to the first word on the page.

5   "Ff ... i ... fi—"

6   "Five!" My little brother pops his little freckled face over my shoulder.

7   "Stevie, Steph and I are reading this first. You can read it after her" says my father turning to me. "Go ahead Steph."

8   "Five ... li ... lit—"

9   "Little puppies!" yells Stevie from right behind me.

10   I turn away from the book, discouraged.

11   "Stephen!" says our father sternly. "Let Stephanie read. She knows the words; she just has to think about it for a little while. Go play over there and we will read a book when she is done." My Dad turns to me and smiles.

12   "Five little puppies ... d ... dug ... a ... h ... h—"

13   "A hole under the fence!" My brother is behind me again, and I cannot believe that he is smarter than I am. He is only in kindergarten. You're not even supposed to start learning words until the first grade! I drop *The Poky Little Puppy* and run to my mommy, telling myself that reading is stupid, and I don't want to learn how anymore. Drawing and doing other arts and crafts are much more fun anyway, and Stevie can't even draw a bunny!

14   I was by no means a slow learner; Steve was just an exceptionally fast learner when it came to reading. He knew how to read whole chapter books before any of his peers could even read *The Poky Little Puppy.* However, the fact that my little brother could read better than I could made me feel stupid and I lost all of my previous enthusiasm about books.

15   Both of my parents desperately tried to get me to like reading. They were always sure to separate my brother and me when they were helping me with my reading, but I had shut down. My rnom always tried to read to me before bed, but I told her that I hated books. Instead I wanted her to make up stories and tell them to me, or tell me stories about when she was a little girl. I had made up my mind that I hated reading. If I didn't like it, I wouldn't have to be good at it. So, I did just as much reading as my teacher and my parents forced me to do, but that was it. When my brother was reading every word of *Calvin and Hobbes* comics and needing no help from my father, I was coloring Calvin's hair pink and turning Hobbes into a purple tiger with big black sunglasses on.

16   I continued to dislike reading for years. As I got older, I never finished any of the chapter books that I was required to read for school, and I certainly never read the other books that my mother was constantly trying to get me to read. I remember her telling me, "If you just find one book that you really love, you will love reading forever. I promise." My response was always, "Mom, reading is boring. I'm not a nerd." I wanted to spend my spare time playing with my friends and making friendship bracelets, not reading *A Wrinkle in Time* like my dorky little brother.

17   My parents have since told me that my not liking to read broke their hearts. My dad felt like it was his fault for reading with me around my brother. They did not know what to do, and they were convinced that I would go through my entire life without ever enjoying a good book.

18   One rainy summer day when I was about fourteen years old, however, all of this changed. My family and I were at our mountain house in the Poconos and the weather was too bad to go out on the boat or play outside, so I was bored. I approached my mom to ask her to play a game with me while she was sitting on our screened-in porch reading. She told me that she bought me a book that she loved when she was my age, and suggested that she read some of it to me just to see if I might like it. I don't know if it was out of utter boredom, being worn down by my mom constantly nagging me to read, or just out of really wanting to spend time with my mother, but I agreed. The book was about a little girl named Francie who was extremely poor and lived in a city that I was completely unfamiliar with, but I still related to her. I loved Francie, and after my mom finished reading the first chapter to me and left to go to the store, I continued reading the book and didn't put it down

until it was time for dinner. I loved reading! When I was not reading, I was thinking about Francie and hoping that everything would turn out all right for her. The book had opened up a whole new world for me in which a family could be so poor and have almost none of the things that I was accustomed to, but still be happy and full of love and warmth and hope. I spent the whole week reading my book and discussing it with my mom and sisters.

19   I do not remember the next good book or even the next five good books that my mother gave me and I enthusiastically poured myself into. However, to this day whenever anyone mentions *A Tree Grows in Brooklyn*, or I see the movie on TV, or I read about another character named Frances or Francie, I get a warm feeling in my heart, and I thank God for my mother and her persistence. Without my mom, and without that one great book, I might not be the person and the reader that I am today. If anyone ever tells me that they do not like reading, I smile and tell them, "If you just find one book that you really love, you will love reading forever. I promise."

THINKING CRITICALLY
about "One Great Book"

1. In this literacy narrative, how does Stephanie Whipple create tension and establish the main conflicts?

2. In her desire to engage readers with her characters and setting, Stephanie chooses to use the present tense rather than the past tense for her early scene about reading. Do you find this choice effective? (It violates the normal rules about needless shifting of tense.) How else does she try to engage readers in her characters and setting?

3. This piece leads up to a moment of breakthrough and new insight about the significance of reading. How does Stephanie use story elements rather than straight exposition to convey her transformation in her attitude toward literature?

4. In much of this narrative, Stephanie includes words that are specific and descriptive—that is, low on the ladder of abstraction. What passages are vivid and memorable?

5. This piece is fairly straightforward, yet it points to some deeper themes about learning. What new understanding about children and reading does Stephanie want readers to grasp?

 For additional help with writing, reading, and research, go to **www.mycomplab.com**

WRITING AN INFORMATIVE (AND SURPRISING) ESSAY OR REPORT

7

As a reader, you regularly encounter writing with an informative aim, ranging from the instruction booklet for a smart phone to a newspaper feature story on the South African AIDS crisis. Informative documents include encyclopedias, cookbooks, voters' pamphlets, and various kinds of reports, as well as informative Web sites and magazine articles. In some informative prose, visual representations of information such as diagrams, photographs, maps, tables, and graphs can be as important as the prose itself.

A useful way to begin thinking about informative writing is to classify it according to the reader's motivation for reading. From this perspective, we can place informative prose in two categories.

In the first category, readers are motivated by an immediate need for information (setting the clock on a new microwave) or by curiosity about a subject (the impressionist movement in painting or new developments in rooftop solar panels). Informative writing in this category does not necessarily contain a contestable thesis. Documents are organized effectively, of course, but they often follow a chronological, step-by-step organization (as in a set of instructions) or an "all-about" topic-by-topic organization (as in an encyclopedia article on, say, Pakistan, divided into "Geography," "Climate," "Population," "History," and so forth). The writer provides factual information about a subject without necessarily shaping the information specifically to support a thesis.

In contrast, the second category of informative writing *is* thesis-based and is therefore aligned with other kinds of thesis-based prose. The thesis brings new or surprising information to readers who may not be initially motivated by a need-to-know occasion or by their own curiosity. In fact, readers might not be initially interested in the writer's topic at all, so the writer's first task is to hook readers' interest and motivate their desire to learn something new or surprising about a topic. An excellent strategy for creating this motivation is the technique of "surprising reversal," which we explain later.

In this chapter, you will learn to:

- write an informative report for a targeted audience
- write an informative essay using the surprising-reversal strategy

Exploring Informative (and Surprising) Writing

Let's say that you have just watched an old James Bond movie featuring a tarantula in Bond's bathroom. Curious about tarantulas, you do a quick Web search and retrieve the following short informative pieces. Read each one, and then proceed to the questions that follow.

Our first mini-article comes from the Web site EnchantedLearning.com, a commercial site aimed at providing interesting, fact-filled learning lessons for children.

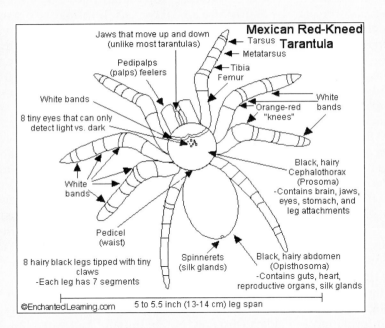

1   Tarantulas are large hairy spiders that live in warm areas around the world, including South America, southern North America, southern Europe, Africa, southern Asia, and Australia. The greatest concentration of tarantulas is in South America. There are about 300 species of tarantulas. The biggest tarantula is *Pseudotherathosa apophysis*, which has a leg span of about 13 inches (33 cm). These arachnids have a very long life span; some species can live over 30 years.

2   **Habitat:** Some tarantulas live in underground burrows; some live on the ground, and others live in trees. They live in rain forests, deserts, and other habitats.

3   **Diet:** Tarantulas are carnivores (meat-eaters). They eat insects (like grasshoppers and beetles), other arachnids, small reptiles (like lizards and snakes), amphibians (like frogs), and some even eat small birds. Tarantulas kill their prey using venomous fangs; they also inject a chemical into the prey that dissolves the flesh. Tarantulas can crush their prey using powerful mouthparts. No person has ever died of a tarantula bite.

4   **Anatomy:** Tarantulas have a hairy two-part body and very strong jaws (with venomous fangs). They have eight hairy legs; each leg has 2 tiny claws at the end and a cushioning pad behind the claws. The hairs on the body and legs are sensitive to touch, temperature, and smell. Tarantulas have a hard exoskeleton and not an internal skeleton. © Copyright EnchantedLearning.com. Used by permission.

The second mini-article comes from the Web site of the University of Washington's Burke Museum. The author of this piece is the curator of arachnids at the Burke Museum.

Rod Crawford
Myths about "Dangerous" Spiders

1   **Myth:** Tarantulas are dangerous or deadly to humans.

2   **Fact:** Outside of southern Europe (where the name is used for a wolf spider, famous in medieval superstition as the alleged cause of "tarantella" dancing), the word tarantula is most often used for the very large, furry spiders of the family Theraphosidae.

3   Hollywood is squarely to blame for these spiders' toxic-to-humans reputation. Tarantulas are large, photogenic and easily handled, and therefore have been very widely used in horror and action-adventure movies. When some "venomous" creature is needed to menace James Bond or Indiana Jones, to invade a small town in enormous numbers, or to grow to gigantic size and prowl the Arizona desert for human prey, the special-effects team calls out the tarantulas!

4   In reality, the venom of these largest-of-all-spiders generally has **very low toxicity to humans**. I myself was once bitten by a Texan species and hardly even felt it. None of the North American species or those commonly kept as pets are considered to pose even a mild bite hazard. There are some reports that a few tropical species may have venom more toxic to vertebrates, but human bite cases haven't been reported, so we can't know for sure.

5   The only health hazard posed by keeping pet tarantulas comes from the irritating chemicals on the hairs of the abdomen, which can cause skin rashes or inflammation of eyes and nasal passages. To prevent such problems, simply keep tarantulas away from your face and wash your hands after handling one.

6   Compared to common pets such as dogs, tarantulas are not dangerous at all. (For more information see the American Tarantula Society.)

European tarantula
Lycosa Tarentula
Southern Europe; body length 2–3 cm
(photo courtesy of Manuel J. Cabrero)
Click image to enlarge

Pink toe tarantula
Avicularia avicularia
Brazil to Trinidad; body length 6–7 cm
(photo courtesy of Ron Taylor)
Click image to enlarge

Both the *European wolf spiders* (**left**) originally called tarantulas, and the *theraphosid spiders* (**right**), often kept as pets and called tarantulas now, have been reputed dangerous to humans. They aren't.

THINKING CRITICALLY
about "Tarantulas" and "Myths about 'Dangerous' Spiders"

1. Why do you think the reading from EnchantedLearning.com uses a diagram of a tarantula while the Burke Museum Web site uses photographs? How is each choice connected to the piece's targeted audience and purpose?

2. How would you describe the difference in organizational strategies for each of the readings?

3. One might suppose that informational writing would be unaffected by the writer's angle of vision—that facts would simply be facts and that informational pieces on the same topic would contain the same basic information. Yet these two short pieces give somewhat different impressions of the tarantula. For example, how do these readings differ in the way they portray the bite of the tarantula? How else do they differ in overall effect?

Understanding Informative Writing

In informative writing, the writer is assumed to have more expertise than the reader on a given subject. The writer's aim is to enlarge the reader's view of the subject by bringing the reader new information. The writer's information can come from a variety of sources:

- From the writer's preexisting expertise in a subject
- From the writer's own personal experiences
- From field research such as observations, interviews, questionnaires, and so forth
- From library or Internet research

We turn now to a closer look at two commonly assigned genres with an informative aim.

Informative Reports

Although the term *report* can have numerous meanings, we will define a **report** as any document that presents the results of a fact-finding or data-gathering investigation. Sometimes report writers limit themselves to presenting newly discovered information, while at other times they go further by analyzing or interpreting the information to explain its implications and significance or to uncover patterns of cause and effect.

Reports of various kinds are among the most common genres that you will read and write as a workplace professional. Often managers have to prepare periodic reports to supervisors on sales, operations, expenses, or team productivity. Equally important are solicited reports, usually assigned by supervisors to individuals or task forces, requesting individuals to investigate a problem, gather crucial information, and report the results.

Characteristics of a Report The text of a report should be concise, with a tightly closed-form structure often broken into sections marked by headings. Individual points might be bulleted. Numeric data are usually displayed in graphs or tables. Long reports usually include a cover page and a table of contents and often begin with an "executive summary" that condenses the main findings into a paragraph.

The Introduction to a Report How you write the introduction to a report depends on the audience you are addressing. In some cases a report is aimed at general readers and published in, say, a popular magazine. In such cases, you must arouse your readers' interest and provide necessary background, just as you would do in most closed-form introductions. Kerri Ann Matsumoto's "How Much Does It Cost to Go Organic?" (p. 183) is a student example of an informative report written for a magazine audience. (Note how Matsumoto "desktop-published" her essay in two-column format to look like a magazine article.)

In other cases, the report is solicited (say, by a supervisor); it is aimed at a specific reader who is already interested in the information and is waiting for you to provide it. In this case, the report is often written as a memorandum. Instead of a title, short reports usually have an informative "subject line" that identifies the report's topic and purpose. The introduction typically creates a brief context for the report, states its purpose, and maps its structure. Here is an example of an introduction:

PROTOTYPE INTRODUCTION FOR A SOLICITED REPORT

To: Ms. Polly Carpenter, Business Manager
From: Ralph Hiner
Subject: Projected costs for the new seed catalog

As you requested, I have researched the projected costs for the new seed catalog. This memo provides background on the marketing plan, itemizes projected expenses, and presents an overall figure for budget planning.

For an example of a short informative report written for a general audience, see "Muslim Americans: Middle Class and Mostly Mainstream" on pages 180–181.

The following exercise will give you a taste of workplace report writing. Suppose that you are a marketing researcher for a company that designs and produces new video games. One day you receive the following memo from your manager:

To: You
From: Big Boss
Subject: Information about gender differences in video game playing

The marketing team wants to investigate differences in the amount of time male and female college students spend playing video games and in the kinds of video games that each gender enjoys. I want you to conduct appropriate research at local colleges using questionnaires, interviews, and focus groups. Specifically, the marketing team wants to know approximately how many minutes per week an average college male versus a college female spends playing video games. Also investigate whether there is any difference in the kinds of games they enjoy. We need your report by the end of the month.

FOR WRITING AND DISCUSSION

Producing a Solicited Report

1. Assume that your classroom is a "focus group" for your investigation. As a class, create an informal questionnaire to gather the information that you will need for your report.
2. Give the questionnaire to the class and tabulate results.
3. Working individually or in small groups, prepare a memo to Big Boss reporting your results.

Informative Essay Using the Surprising-Reversal Strategy

Another commonly encountered genre is an informative article with surprising information, often found in magazines or newspapers. In this section, we focus on a specific version of this kind of essay—a thesis-based informative article aimed at general audiences. Because readers are assumed to be browsing through the pages of a magazine, the writer's rhetorical challenge is to arouse the reader's curiosity and then to keep the reader reading by providing interesting new information. The writer's first task is to hook the reader on a question and then to provide a surprising thesis that gives shape and purpose to the information. A good way to focus and sharpen the thesis, as we will show, is to use the "surprising-reversal" strategy.

"All-About" Versus "Thesis-Governed" Informative Prose Let's begin by revisiting the difference between an encyclopedic (or "all-about") informative piece and a thesis-based piece. To appreciate this distinction, consider again the difference between the EnchantedLearning.com Web site on tarantulas (pp. 166–167) and the Burke Museum piece "Myths about 'Dangerous' Spiders" (pp. 167–168). The EnchantedLearning.com piece is a short "all-about" report organized under the topic headings "Habitat," "Diet," and "Anatomy." The Web writer may simply have adapted an encyclopedia article on tarantulas into a format for children. In contrast, the Burke Museum piece by Rod Crawford is thesis-based. Crawford wishes to refute the myth that "[t]arantulas are dangerous or deadly to humans." He does so by providing information on the low toxicity of tarantula venom to humans and the relative painlessness of tarantula bites. All of Crawford's data focus on the danger potential of tarantulas. There are no data about habitat, diet, or other aspects of tarantula life—material that would be included if this were an all-about report. Because the piece also includes data about misconceptions of tarantulas, it follows the basic pattern of surprising reversal: "Many people believe that tarantulas are toxic to humans, but I will show that tarantulas are not dangerous at all."

Surprising-Reversal Pattern **Surprising reversal**, as we explained in Chapter 2, Concept 5, is our term for a strategy in which the writer's thesis pushes sharply against a counterthesis. This structure automatically creates a thesis with tension focused on a question or problem. Because of its power to hook and sustain readers, surprising-reversal essays can be found in many publications, ranging from easy-reading magazines to scholarly journals. Here, for example, is an abstract of an article from *Atlantic Monthly*.

"REEFER MADNESS" BY ERIC SCHLOSSER

Marijuana has been pushed so far out of the public imagination by other drugs, and its use is so casually taken for granted in some quarters of society, that one might assume it had been effectively decriminalized. In truth, the government has never been tougher on marijuana offenders than it is today. In an era when violent criminals frequently walk free or receive modest jail terms, tens of thousands of people are serving long sentences for breaking marijuana laws.

This article asserts a surprising, new position ("the government has never been tougher on marijuana offenders than it is today") that counters a commonly held view (marijuana laws are no longer enforced). Here are additional examples of the surprising-reversal pattern:

Commonly Held, Narrow, or Inaccurate View	New, Surprising Information
Native Americans used to live in simple harmony with the earth.	Many American Indians used to "control" nature by setting fire to forests to make farming easier or to improve hunting.
Having fathers present in the delivery room helps the mother relax and have an easier birth.	Having fathers present in delivery rooms may reduce the amount of oxytocin produced by the mother and lead to more caesarian sections.

A similar pattern is often found in scholarly academic writing, which typically has the following underlying shape:

> Whereas some scholars say X, I am going to argue Y.

Because the purpose of academic research is to advance knowledge, an academic article almost always shows the writer's new view against a background of prevailing views (what other scholars have said). This kind of tension is what often makes thesis-based writing memorable and provocative.

The writer's surprising information can come from personal experience, field research, or library/Internet research. If a college writer bases an informative piece on research sources and documents them according to academic conventions, the magazine genre doubles as an effective college research paper by combining academic citations with a tone and style suitable for general readers. Shannon King's article on hydrogen cars (p. 184) is an example of a student research paper written in magazine article style.

"Surprise" as a Relative Term When using the surprising-reversal strategy, keep in mind that *surprise* is a relative term based on the relationship between you and your intended audience. You don't have to surprise everyone in the world, just those who hold a mistaken or narrow view of your topic. The key is to imagine an audience less informed about your topic than you are. Suppose, as an illustration, that you have just completed an introductory economics course. You are less informed about economics than your professor, but more informed about economics than persons who have never had an econ class. You might therefore bring surprising information to the less informed audience:

> The average airplane traveler thinks that the widely varying ticket pricing for the same flight is chaotic and silly, but I can show how this pricing scheme makes perfect sense economically. [written to the "average airplane traveler," who hasn't taken an economics course]

This paper would be surprising to your intended audience, but not to the economics professor. From a different perspective, however, you could also write about economics to your professor because you might know more than your professor about, say, how students struggle with some concepts:

> Many economics professors assume that students can easily learn the concept of "elasticity of demand," but I can show why this concept was particularly confusing

for me and my classmates. [written to economics professors who aren't aware of student difficulties with particular concepts]

Additionally, your surprising view doesn't necessarily have to be diametrically opposed to the common view. Perhaps you think the common view is *incomplete* or *insufficient* rather than *dead wrong*. Instead of saying, "View X is wrong, whereas my view, Y, is correct," you can say, "View X is correct and good as far as it goes, but my view, Y, adds a new perspective." In other words, you can also create surprise by going a step beyond the common view to show readers something new.

Informative Report

WRITING PROJECT

Write a short informative report based on data you have gathered from observations, interviews, questionnaires, or library/Internet research. Your report should respond to one of the following scenarios or to a scenario provided by your instructor:

- Your boss runs a chain of health food stores that sell high-nutrition smoothies. Because sales have been flat, she wants to create an advertising campaign to attract more customers to her smoothie bars. She has heard that the boutique coffee drinks sold at coffee shops such as Starbucks are actually high in calories and fat. She has asked you to research the nutritional information on coffee drinks. She would also like you to compare the fat/calorie content of various coffee drinks to that of cheeseburgers, fries, and milkshakes sold at fast-food restaurants. She's hoping that the information you provide will help her launch a campaign to lure customers from coffee shops to her smoothie bars. Write your report in the form of a memorandum to your boss, providing the requested information in a closed-form, crisply presented style.

- You are doing a service-learning project for a health maintenance organization. Your manager is worried about hearing loss in young people, possibly caused by listening to loud music through earbuds plugged into iPods or MP3 players. Your manager asks you to write a short informative article, suitable for publication in the HMO's newsletter, that reports on research on hearing loss due to earbuds. Write your report for a general audience who read the HMO newsletter for helpful health information.

Generating and Exploring Ideas

Your initial goal is to use effective research strategies to find the requested information. If your report draws on library/Internet research, consult Part 4 of

FIGURE 7.1 Framework for an Informative Report

Title	• For a report addressed to a general audience, an interest-grabbing title • For a solicited report, an informative subject line
Introduction (one to several paragraphs)	• For general audiences, provides background and context and arouses interest • For a solicited report, refers to the request, explains the purpose of the report, and maps its structure
Body section 1 (brief)	• Explains your research process and the sources of your data
Body section 2 (major)	• Provides the information in a logical sequence • Uses closed-form organizational strategies • Displays numeric data in graphs or tables referenced in the text
Conclusion	• Suggests the significance of the information provided

this textbook. For displaying numerical information in graphs or tables, consult Skill 10.9.

Shaping and Drafting

Although there is no one correct way to organize an informative report, such reports typically have the structure shown in Figure 7.1. Kerri Ann Matsumoto's essay on the cost of organic food (p. 183), aimed at general audiences, exhibits this typical structure. Her title and introduction announce her research question and engage her readers' interest (how much does it cost to buy organic food versus non-organic food?). The body of the paper then explains her process (she did comparison pricing for a chicken stir-fry for a family of four at an organic and a non-organic store); presents her findings in both words and graphics (organic foods cost more); and suggests the significance of her research (helps readers sort out the advantages of organic foods versus the advantages of spending the extra money in other ways).

Revising

As you revise, make sure that your graphics (if you used them) and your words tell the same story and reinforce each other. As you edit, try to achieve a clear, concise style that allows your intended audience to read quickly. For workplace reports, show your respect for the busy business environment that places many simultaneous demands on managers. When you have a near-final draft, exchange it with a classmate for a peer review.

Questions for Peer Review

In addition to the generic peer review questions explained in Skill 9.4, ask your peer reviewers to address these questions:

1. If the report is solicited, does the document have a professional appearance (memo format, pleasing use of white space, appropriate use of headings)? Do the subject line and opening overview passage effectively explain the report's occasion, purpose, and structure?
2. If the report is aimed at a general audience, does it follow the manuscript style and document design specified by the instructor? Do the title and introduction provide context and motivate reader interest?
3. Does the writer explain how the research was conducted?
4. Is the report clear, concise, and well organized? How might the presentation of the information be improved?
5. If the report uses graphics, are the graphics referenced in the text? Are they clear, with appropriate titles and labels? How might they be improved?

Informative Essay Using the Surprising-Reversal Strategy

WRITING PROJECT

Using personal experience, field research, or library/Internet research, write an informative magazine article using a surprising-reversal strategy in a tone and style suitable for general readers. Your task is to arouse your readers' curiosity by posing an interesting question, summarizing a common or expected answer to the question, and then providing new, surprising information that counters or "reverses" the common view. You imagine readers who hold a mistaken or overly narrow view of your topic; your purpose is to give them a new, surprising view.

Depending on the wishes of your instructor, this assignment can draw either on personal experience or on research. Shannon King's "How Clean and Green Are Hydrogen Fuel-Cell Cars?" (pp. 184–186) is an example of a researched essay that enlarges the targeted audience's view of a subject in a surprising way. Although it is an example of a short academic research article, it is written in a relaxed style suitable for magazine publication.

For this assignment, try to avoid issues calling for persuasive rather than informative writing. With persuasive prose, you imagine a resistant reader who may argue back. With informative prose, you imagine a more trusting reader, one willing to learn from your experience or research. Although you hope to enlarge your reader's view of a topic, you aren't necessarily saying that your audience's original view is wrong, nor are you initiating a debate. For example, suppose a writer wanted to develop the following claim: "Many of my friends think that having an alcoholic mother would be the worst thing that could happen to you, but I will show that my mother's disease forced our family closer together." In this case the writer isn't arguing that alcoholic mothers are good or that everyone should have an alcoholic mother. Rather, the writer is simply offering readers a new, unexpected, and expanded view of what it might be like to have an alcoholic mother.

Generating and Exploring Ideas

If you do field research or library/Internet research for your article, start by posing a research question. As you begin doing initial research on your topic area, you will soon know more about your topic than most members of the general public. Ask yourself, "What has surprised me about my research so far? What have I learned that I didn't know before?" Your answers to these questions can suggest possible approaches to your paper. For example, Shannon King began her research believing that fuel-cell technology produced totally pollution-free energy. She didn't realize that one needs to burn fossil fuels in order to produce the hydrogen. This initial surprise shaped her paper. She decided that if this information surprised her, it should surprise others also.

What follows are two exercises you can try to generate ideas for your paper.

Individual Task to Generate Ideas

Here is a template that can help you generate ideas by asking you to think specifically about differences in knowledge levels between you and various audiences.

> I know more about X [topic area] than [specific person or persons].

For example, you might say, "I know more about [computer games/gospel music/the energy crisis] than [my roommate/my high school friends/my parents]." This exercise helps you discover subjects about which you already have expertise compared to other audiences. Likewise, you can identify a subject that interests you, do a couple of hours of research on it, and then say: "Based on just this little amount of research, I know more about X than my roommate." Thinking in this way, you might be able to create an intriguing question that you could answer through your research.

Small-Group Task to Generate Ideas

Form small groups. Assign a group recorder to make a two-column list, with the left column titled "Mistaken or Narrow View of X" and the right column titled "Groupmate's Surprising View." Using the surprising-reversal strategy, brainstorm ideas for article topics until every group member has generated at least one entry for the right-hand column. Here are several examples:

Mistaken or Narrow View of X	Groupmate's Surprising View
Being an offensive lineman in football is a no-brain, repetitive job requiring size and strength, but only enough intelligence and athletic ability to push people out of the way.	Jeff can show that being an offensive lineman is a complex job that requires mental smarts as well as size, strength, and athletic ability.
Pawnshops are disreputable places.	Samantha's uncle owns a pawnshop that is a wholesome family business that serves an important social function.
To most straight people, *Frankenstein* is a monster movie about science gone amuck.	Cody can show how to the gay community, *Frankenstein* holds a special and quite different meaning.

To help stimulate ideas, you might consider topic areas such as the following:

- **People:** computer programmers, homeless people, cheerleaders, skateboarders, gang members, priests or rabbis, reality show stars, feminists, mentally ill or developmentally disabled persons.
- **Activities:** washing dishes, climbing mountains, wrestling, modeling, gardening, living with a chronic disease or disability, owning a certain breed of dog, riding a subway at night, posting status updates on Facebook, entering a dangerous part of a city.
- **Places:** particular neighborhoods, specific buildings or parts of buildings, local attractions, junkyards, college campuses, places of entertainment, summer camps.
- **Other similar categories:** groups, events, animals and plants, gadgets, and so forth; the list is endless.

Next, go around the room, sharing with the entire class the topics you have generated. Remember that you are not yet committed to writing about any of these topics.

Shaping, Drafting, and Revising

A surprising-reversal informative essay has the features and organization shown in Figure 7.2.

To create the "surprising-reversal" feel, it's important to delay your thesis until after you have explained your audience's common, expected answer to your opening question. This delay in presenting the thesis creates an open-form feel that readers often find engaging. Shannon King's research paper on hydrogen cars (pp. 182–184) has this surprising-reversal shape.

As a way of helping you generate ideas, we offer the following five questions. Following each question, we speculate about what King might have written if she had used the same questions to help her get started on her essay.

FIGURE 7.2 Framework for an Informative Essay Using the Surprising-Reversal Strategy

Introduction (one to several paragraphs)	• Engages readers' interest in the writer's question • Provides background and context
Body section 1 (brief)	• Explains the common or popular answer to the writer's question
Body section 2 (major)	• Provides a delayed thesis—the writer's surprising answer to the question • Supports the thesis with information from personal experience or research • Displays numeric data in graphs or tables referenced in the text
Conclusion	• Suggests the significance of the writer's new perspective on the question

1. ***What question does your essay address?*** (King might have asked, "Will hydrogen fuel-cell automobiles solve our nation's energy and pollution crises?")
2. ***What is the common, expected, or popular answer to this question held by your imagined audience?*** (King might have said, "Most people believe that hydrogen fuel-cell cars will solve our country's pollution and energy crises.")
3. ***What examples and details support your audience's view?*** Expand on these views by developing them with supporting examples and details. (King might have noted her research examples praising fuel-cell technology such as the Bush/Cheney National Energy Report or California Governor Arnold Schwarzenegger's desire to build hydrogen fuel stations across the state.)
4. ***What is your own surprising view?*** (King might have said, "Although hydrogen fuel-cell cars are pollution free, getting the hydrogen in the first place requires burning fossil fuels.")
5. ***What examples and details support this view? Why do you hold this view? Why should a reader believe you?*** Writing rapidly, spell out the evidence that supports your point. (King would have done a freewrite about her research discoveries that hydrogen has to be recovered from carbon-based fossils or from electrolysis of water—all of which means continued use of pollution-causing fossil fuels.)

After you finish exploring your responses to these five trigger questions, you will be well on your way to composing a first draft of your article. Now finish writing your draft fairly rapidly without worrying about perfection.

Once you have your first draft on paper, the goal is to make it work better, first for yourself and then for your readers. If you discovered ideas as you wrote, you may need to do some major restructuring. Check to see that the question you are addressing is clear. If you are using the surprising-reversal strategy, make sure that you distinguish between your audience's common view and your own surprising view. Apply the strategies for global revision explained in Chapter 9.

Questions for Peer Review

In addition to the generic peer review questions explained in Skill 9.4, ask your peer reviewers to address these questions:

1. What is the question the paper addresses? How effective is the paper at hooking the reader's interest in the question?
2. Where does the writer explain the common or popular view of the topic? Do you agree that this is the common view? How does the writer develop or support this view? What additional supporting examples, illustrations, or details might make the common view more vivid or compelling?
3. What is the writer's surprising view? Were you surprised? What details does the writer use to develop the surprising view? What additional supporting examples, illustrations, or details might help make the surprising view more vivid and compelling?
4. Is the draft clear and easy to follow? Is the draft interesting? How might the writer improve the style, clarity, or interest level of the draft?
5. If the draft includes graphics, are they effective? Do the words and the visuals tell the same story? Are the visuals properly titled and labeled? How might the use of visuals be improved?

Our first reading, "Muslim Americans: Middle Class and Mostly Mainstream," published in May 2007, illustrates an informative report. Based on field and research data compiled by the Pew Research Center for the People and the Press, this reading is the widely disseminated summary of the Center's longer, more detailed report. The complete report can be read on the Pew Research Center's Web site. This report summary has many features of a workplace document except that it is addressed to a general audience rather than a specific workplace audience.

The Pew Research Center for the People and the Press
Muslim Americans: Middle Class and Mostly Mainstream

1   The first-ever, nationwide, random sample survey of Muslim Americans finds them to be largely assimilated, happy with their lives, and moderate with respect to many of the issues that have divided Muslims and Westerners around the world.

2   The Pew Research Center conducted more than 55,000 interviews to obtain a national sample of 1,050 Muslims living in the United States. Interviews were conducted in English, Arabic, Farsi and Urdu. The resulting study, which draws on Pew's survey research among Muslims around the world, finds that Muslim Americans are a highly diverse population, one largely composed of immigrants. Nonetheless, they are decidedly American in their outlook, values and attitudes. This belief is reflected in Muslim American income and education levels, which generally mirror those of the public.

3   Key findings include:

- Overall, Muslim Americans have a generally positive view of the larger society. Most say their communities are excellent or good places to live.
- A large majority of Muslim Americans believe that hard work pays off in this society. Fully 71% agree that most people who want to get ahead in the U.S. can make it if they are willing to work hard.
- The survey shows that although many Muslims are relative newcomers to the U.S., they are highly assimilated into American society. On balance, they believe that Muslims coming to the U.S. should try and adopt American customs, rather than trying to remain distinct from the larger society. And by nearly two-to-one (63%–32%) Muslim Americans do not see a conflict between being a devout Muslim and living in a modern society.

Muslim Americans: Who Are They?

	Total
Proportion who are ...	%
Foreign-born Muslims	**65**
Arab region	24
Pakistan	8
Other South Asia	10
Iran	8
Europe	5
Other Africa	4
Other	6
Native-born Muslims	**35**
African American	20
Other	15
	100
Foreign-born Muslims	**65**
Year immigrated:	
2000–2007	18
1990–1999	21
1980–1989	15
Before 1980	11
Native-born Muslims	**35**
Percent who are ...	
Converts to Islam	21
Born Muslim	14

- Roughly two-thirds (65%) of adult Muslims in the U.S. were born elsewhere. A relatively large proportion of Muslim immigrants are from Arab countries, but many also come from Pakistan and other South Asian countries. Among native-born Muslims, roughly half are African American (20% of U.S. Muslims overall), many of whom are converts to Islam.
- Based on data from this survey, along with available Census Bureau data on immigrants' nativity and nationality, the Pew Research Center estimates the total population of Muslims in the United States at 2.35 million.
- Muslim Americans reject Islamic extremism by larger margins than do Muslim minorities in Western European countries. However, there is somewhat more acceptance of Islamic extremism in some segments of the U.S. Muslim public than others. Fewer native-born African American Muslims than others completely condemn al Qaeda. In addition, younger Muslims in the U.S. are much more likely than older Muslim Americans to say that suicide bombing in the defense of Islam can be at least sometimes justified. Nonetheless, absolute levels of support for Islamic extremism among Muslim Americans are quite low, especially when compared with Muslims around the world.
- A majority of Muslim Americans (53%) say it has become more difficult to be a Muslim in the U.S. since the Sept. 11 terrorist attacks. Most also believe that the government "singles out" Muslims for increased surveillance and monitoring.
- Relatively few Muslim Americans believe the U.S.-led war on terror is a sincere effort to reduce terrorism, and many doubt that Arabs were responsible for the 9/11 attacks. Just 40% of Muslim Americans say groups of Arabs carried out those attacks.

U.S. Muslims More Mainstream

Percent low-income compared with general public

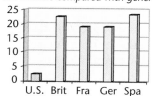

Think of self as Muslim first, not American/British/French/German/Spanish

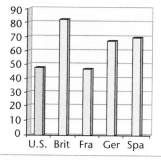

Life is better for women here than in Muslim countries

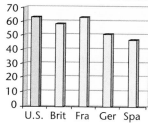

Very concerned about Islamic extremism in the world these days

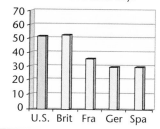

THINKING CRITICALLY
about "Muslim Americans: Middle Class and Mostly Mainstream"

1. Note how this document includes the typical features, with some modifications, of a typical informative report (see Figure 7.1). Where does the document include the following:
   a. An overview sentence that orients readers to the purpose and content of the document?
   b. An explanation of the writer's research process?
   c. Presentation of the writer's findings using both verbal text and graphics?

2. Typically, informative writing is valuable to the extent that it brings something needed, new, or surprising to the audience and therefore enlarges their view of the topic. What did you find new, surprising, or otherwise worthwhile in this informative report?

Our second reading, by student writer Kerri Ann Matsumoto (p. 195), is formatted to look like a popular magazine article.

THINKING CRITICALLY
about "How Much Does It Cost to Go Organic?"

1. In our teaching, we have discovered that students appreciate the concept of genre more fully if they occasionally "desktop-publish" a manuscript to look like a magazine article, a poster, or a brochure rather than a standard double-spaced academic paper. If Kerri Ann had been an actual freelance writer, she would have submitted this article double-spaced with attached figures, and the magazine publisher would have done the formatting. How does document design itself help signal the document's genre? To what extent has Kerri Ann made this article *sound* like a popular magazine article as well as look like one?

2. Do you think Kerri Ann used graphics effectively in her essay? How might she have revised the graphics or the wording to make the paper more effective?

3. Do you think it is worth the extra money to go organic? How would you make your case in an argument paper with a persuasive aim?

HOW MUCH DOES IT COST TO GO ORGANIC?

Kerri Ann Matsumoto

Organic foods, grown without pesticides, weed killers, or hormone additives, are gaining popularity from small privately owned organic food stores to large corporate markets. With the cost of living rising, how much can a family of four afford to pay for organically grown food before it becomes too expensive?

To find out more information about the cost of organic foods, I went to the Rainbow Market, which is a privately owned organic food store, and to a nearby Safeway. I decided to see what it would cost to create a stir-fry for a family of four. I estimated that the cost of organic vegetables for the stir-fry would cost $3.97. Non-organic vegetables for the same stir-fry, purchased at Safeway, would cost $2.37. If we imagined our family eating the same stir fry every night for a year, it would cost $1,499 for organic and $865 for non-organic for a difference of $584.

After pricing vegetables, I wanted to find out how much it would cost to add to the stir-fry free-range chicken fed only organic feeds, as opposed to non-organic factory farmed chicken. For good quality chicken breasts, the organic chicken was $6.99 per pound and the non-organic was $3.58 per pound. Projected out over a year, the organic chicken would cost $5,103 compared to $2,613 for non-organic chicken.

My research shows that over the course of one year it will cost $6,552 per year to feed our family organic stir-fry and $3,478 for non-organic for a difference of $3,074. If a family chose to eat not only organic dinner, but also all organic meals, the cost of food would sharply increase.

Before going to the Rainbow Market I knew that the price of organic foods was slightly higher than non-organic. However, I did not expect the difference to be so great. Of course, if you did comparison shopping at other stores, you might be able to find cheaper organic chicken and vegetables. But my introductory research suggests that going organic isn't cheap.

Cost of Feeding a Family of Four for One Year: Organic Versus Non-Organic Stir-Fry

Comparative Cost of Ingredients in an Organic Versus Non-Organic Stir-Fry				
	Vegetables per day	Chicken per day	Total per day	Total per year
Organic	$3.97	$13.98	$17.95	$6552
Non-Organic	$2.37	$7.16	$9.53	$3478

If we add the cost of chicken and vegetables together (see the table and the graph), we can compute how much more it would cost to feed our family of four organic versus non-organic chicken stir-fry for a year.

Is it worth it? Many people today have strong concerns for the safety of the foods that they feed to their family. If you consider that organic vegetables have no pesticides and that the organic chicken has no growth hormone additives, the extra cost may be worth it. Also if you are concerned about cruelty to animals, free-range chickens have a better life than caged chickens. But many families might want to spend the $3,074 difference in other ways. If you put that money toward a college fund, within ten years you could save over $30,000. So how much are you willing to pay for organic foods?

The next reading, by student writer Shannon King, is a short academic research paper using the surprising-reversal strategy. Shannon's paper uses research information to enlarge her readers' understanding of hydrogen fuel-cell vehicles by showing that hydrogen fuel is not as pollution-free as the general public believes.

Shannon King (student)
How Clean and Green Are Hydrogen Fuel-Cell Cars?

1   The United States is embroiled in a controversy over energy and pollution. We are rapidly using up the earth's total supply of fossil fuels, and many experts think that children being born today will experience the end of affordable oil. One energy expert, Paul Roberts, believes that serious oil shortages will start ccurring by 2015 when the world's demand for oil will outstrip the world's capacity for further oil production. An equally serious problem is that the burning of fossil fuels spews carbon dioxide into the atmosphere, which increases the rate of global warming.

2   One hopeful way of addressing these problems is to develop hydrogen fuel cell cars. According to Karim Nice, the author of the fuel cell pages on the *HowStuffWorks* Web site, a fuel cell is "an electrochemical energy conversion device that converts hydrogen and oxygen into water, producing electricity and heat in the process." A hydrogen-fueled car is therefore an electric car, powered by an electric motor. The car's electricity is generated by a stack of fuel cells that act like a battery. In the hydrogen fuel cell, the chemicals that produce the electricity are hydrogen from the car's pressurized fuel tank, oxygen from the air, and special catalysts inside the fuel cell. The fuel cell releases no pollutants or greenhouse gases. The only waste product is pure water.

3   To what extent will these pollution-free fuel cells be our energy salvation? Are they really clean and green?

4   Many people think so. The development of hydrogen fuel cells has caused much excitement. I know people who say we don't need to worry about running out of oil because cars of the future will run on water. One recent *New York Times* advertisement produced by General Motors has as its headline, "Who's driving the hydrogen economy?" The text of the ad begins by saying "The hydrogen economy isn't a pipe dream.... The hydrogen economy is the endgame of a multifaceted strategy General Motors set in motion years ago, with steps that are real, progressive, and well-underway" (General Motors). The Web site for the Hydrogen Fuel Cell Institute includes a picture of a crystal clear blue sky landscape with a large letter headline proclaiming "At long last, a technology too long overlooked promises to transform society." At the bottom of the picture are the words, "Offering clean & abundant power, hydrogen-based fuel cells could soon end our reliance on oil and minimize emissions of pollution and global-warming gases." According to CNN News, the Bush administration proposed devoting 1.7 billion dollars of federal funds to developing hydrogen fuel cells (CNN). The biggest nationally known proponent of hydrogen fuel cells is California Governor Arnold Schwarzenegger, who signed an Executive Order that California's "21 interstate freeways shall be designated as the 'California Hydrogen Highway Network.'" (California). In this executive order, Schwarzenegger envisioned

a network of hydrogen fueling stations along these roadways and in the urban centers that they connect, so that by 2010, every Californian will have access to hydrogen fuel, with a significant and increasing percentage produced from clean, renewable sources. (2)

Schwarzenegger's optimism about the hydrogen highway sums up the common view that hydrogen is a clean alternative energy source that is abundant throughout nature. All we have to do is bottle it up, compress it, and transport it to a network of new "gas stations" where the gas being pumped is hydrogen.

5   But what I discovered in my research is that hydrogen is not as green as most people think. Although hydrogen fuel cells appear to be an environmentally friendly alternative to fossil fuels, the processes for producing hydrogen actually require the use of fossil fuels. The problem is that pure hydrogen doesn't occur naturally on earth. It has to be separated out from chemical compounds containing hydrogen, and that process requires other forms of energy. What I discovered is that there are only two major ways to produce hydrogen. The first is to produce it from fossil fuels by unlocking the hydrogen that is bonded to the carbon in coal, oil, or natural gas. The second is to produce it from water through electrolysis, but the power required for electrolysis would also come mainly from burning fossil fuels. These problems make hydrogen fuel cell cars look less clean and green than they first appear.

6   One approach to creating hydrogen from fossil fuels is to use natural gas. According to Matthew L. Wald, writing in a *New York Times* article, natural gas is converted to hydrogen in a process called "steam reforming." Natural gas (made of hydrogen and carbon atoms) is mixed with steam (which contains hydrogen and oxygen atoms) to cause a chemical reaction that produces pure hydrogen. But it also produces carbon dioxide, which contributes to global warming. According to Wald, if fuel cell cars used hydrogen from steam reforming, they would emit 145 grams of global warming gases per mile compared to 374 grams an ordinary gas-powered car would emit. The good news is that using hydrogen power would cut carbon emissions by more than half. The bad news is that these cars would still contribute to global warming and consume natural gas. Moreover, Wald suggests that the natural gas supply is limited and that natural gas has many better, more efficient uses than converting it to hydrogen.

7   Another method for producing hydrogen would come from coal, which is the cheapest and most abundant source of energy. However, the current method of generating electricity by burning coal is the leading source of carbon dioxide emission. At Ohio University, engineers state we still have enough coal to last us two hundred and fifty years and that we should find some better uses for coal. The engineers have received a 4 million dollar federal grant to investigate the production of hydrogen from coal. They plan on mixing coal with steam, air, and oxygen under high temperatures and pressure to produce hydrogen and carbon monoxide ("Ohio University"). But this too would generate greenhouse gases and is a long way off from producing results.

8   The next likely source of hydrogen is to produce it directly from water using an electrolyzer. Wald explains that the electrolyzer uses an electrical current to break down water molecules into hydrogen and oxygen atoms. Creating hydrogen through electrolysis sounds like a good idea because its only waste product is oxygen. But the

hazardous environmental impact is not in the electrolysis reaction, but in the need to generate electricity to run the electrolyzer. Wald claims that if the electricity to run the electrolyzer came from a typical coal-fired electrical plant, the carbon dioxide emissions for a fuel cell car would be 17 percent worse than for today's gasoline powered cars. One solution would be to run the electrolyzer with wind-generated or nuclear-powered electricity. But wind power would be able to produce only a small fraction of what would be needed, and nuclear power brings with it a whole new set of problems including disposal of nuclear waste.

9   Although there seem to be various methods of producing hydrogen, the current sources being considered do not fulfill the claim that hydrogen fuel cell technology will end the use of fossil fuels or eliminate greenhouse gases. The problem is not with the fuel cells themselves but with the processes needed to produce hydrogen fuel. I am not arguing that research and development should be abandoned, and I hope some day that the hydrogen economy will take off. But what I have discovered in my research is that hydrogen power is not as clean and green as I thought.

Works Cited

California. Executive Dept. "Executive Order S-7-04." 20 Apr. 2004. Web. 24 May 2004.

CNN. "The Issues/George Bush." *CNN.com*. Cable News Network, 2004. Web. 23 May 2004.

General Motors. Advertisement. *New York Times* 28 July 2004: A19. Print.

Hydrogen Fuel Cell Institute. Wilder Foundation, 2001. Web. 27 May 2004.

Nice, Karim, and Jonathan Strickland. "How Fuel Cells Work." *HowStuffWorks.com*. HowStuffWorks, 18 Sept. 2000. Web. 27 May 2004.

"Ohio University Aims to Use Coal to Power Fuel Cells." *Fuel Cell Today*. N.p., 24 Nov. 2003. Web. 3 June 2004.

Roberts, Paul. "Running Out of Oil—and Time." *Los Angeles Times*. Common Dreams News Center, 6 Mar. 2004. Web. 23 Mar. 2004.

Wald, Matthew L. "Will Hydrogen Clear the Air? Maybe Not, Some Say." *New York Times* 12 Nov. 2003: C1. Print.

THINKING CRITICALLY
about "How Clean and Green Are Hydrogen Fuel-Cell Cars?"

1. Explain Shannon King's use of the surprising-reversal strategy. What question does she pose? What is the common answer? What is her surprising answer? How effectively does she use research data to support her surprising answer?

2. The line between information and persuasion is often blurred. Some might argue that Shannon's essay has a persuasive aim that argues against hydrogen fuel-cell cars rather than an informative aim that simply presents surprising information about hydrogen production. To what extent do you agree with our classification of Shannon's aim as primarily informative rather than persuasive? Can it be both?

Our final essay, by syndicated columnist Eugene Robinson, illustrates how an informative article for the general public can be based on data from a major research study—in this case a statistical report by the federal Bureau of Justice. At first glance, the study seems to indicate that no racial profiling occurs at the rate at which white, African-American, and Hispanic drivers are pulled over by police. But in this op-ed piece Robinson pushes deeper into the statistics and presents information showing that "driving while black" is "unsafe at any speed."

Eugene Robinson
You Have the Right to Remain a Target of Racial Profiling

1   Washington—This just in: Driving while black is still unsafe at any speed, even zero miles per hour. The same goes for driving while brown.

2   The federal Bureau of Justice Statistics released a report Sunday showing that white, African-American and Hispanic drivers are equally likely to be pulled over by police for an alleged traffic offense. In 2005, the year covered by the study, black drivers were actually less likely—by a tiny margin—to be stopped by police than drivers belonging to the other groups. You might be tempted to conclude that the constitutional imperative of equal protection had finally been extended to America's streets and highways.

3   But you would be wrong. The study reports that African-American and Hispanic drivers who are stopped by police are more than twice as likely as whites to be subjected to a search. Specifically, police searched only 3.6 percent of white drivers pulled over in a traffic stop, while they searched 9.5 percent of African-Americans who obeyed the flashing lights and 8.8 percent of Hispanics.

4   The report says the "apparent disparities" between racial groups "do not constitute proof that police treat people differently along demographic lines," since there could be "countless other factors and circumstances" that go into the decision of whom to spread-eagle on the hood.

5   All right, those figures alone might not constitute "proof" of bias that would convince a jury beyond a reasonable doubt. They are pretty compelling, though, especially when you also consider that black and Hispanic drivers are much more likely to experience "police use of force" than whites.

6   And besides, the following paragraph in the report pretty effectively demolishes that "move along, folks, nothing to see here" disclaimer about bias:

7   "Police actions taken during a traffic stop were not uniform across racial and ethnic categories. Black drivers (4.5 percent) were twice as likely as white drivers (2.1 percent) to be arrested during a traffic stop, while Hispanic drivers (65 percent) were more likely than white (56.2 percent) or black (55.8 percent) drivers to receive a ticket.

8   "In addition, whites (9.7 percent) were more likely than Hispanics (5.9 percent) to receive a written warning, while whites (18.6 percent) were more likely than blacks (13.7 percent) to be verbally warned by police."

9   African Americans have been putting up with the "driving while black" thing for so long that we've become somewhat cynical. For example, nearly three-quarters of whites and Hispanics who were pulled over for allegedly running a red light or a stop sign were willing to concede that they had been caught dead to rights, while nearly half of African Americans in that situation believed they had committed no infraction. About 90 percent of white drivers detained for some sort of vehicle defect, such as a busted tail-light, thought the stop was legitimate, as opposed to 67 percent of black drivers.

10   Think that's just paranoia? Then try to reconcile the counterintuitive fact that while blacks are much more likely than whites to be arrested in a traffic stop, they are also more likely to be released with no enforcement action, not even a warning. This looks to me like powerful evidence that racial profiling is alive and well. It suggests there was no good reason to stop those people.

11   "About one in 10 searches during a traffic stop uncovered evidence of a possible crime," the report says. What could be wrong with that? Isn't that what police should be doing—enforcing the nation's laws, capturing criminals, making law-abiding Americans that much safer?

12   Of course that's what we pay our police officers to do, but not selectively. Whites, too, drive around with drugs, illegal weapons, open containers of alcohol or other contraband in their cars. The numbers in the report suggest that if white drivers stopped by police were searched at the same rate as blacks or Hispanics, police would uncover evidence of tens of thousands of additional crimes each year, doubtless putting thousands of dangerous people behind bars.

13   But, of course, we don't want a society in which everybody is being patted down by police officers all the time. We don't want a society in which people have to stand by the side of the road, fuming, while police arbitrarily rummage through the stuff in their cars—shopping bags, children's toys, McDonald's wrappers—on the off chance of finding something illegal.

14   If you're black or brown, though, may I see your license and registration, please?

THINKING CRITICALLY
about "You Have the Right to Remain a Target of Racial Profiling"

1. Nationally syndicated African-American columnist Eugene Robinson high-lights statistical data to support his thesis about subtle but pervasive racial discrimination. In doing so, he gives his report a "surprising-reversal struc-ture." What is the common view, seemingly supported by the report, that Robinson believes is mistaken? What is his surprising view? How does he use report data to support his surprising view?

2. What pieces of information from the report do you find most compelling in supporting Robinson's thesis?

3. Analyze this piece from the perspectives of *logos*, *ethos*, and *pathos*.

 For support in learning this chapter's content, follow this path in **MyCompLab**: Resources ⇒ Writing ⇒ Writing Purposes ⇒ Writing to Inform.

ANALYZING AND SYNTHESIZING IDEAS

8

In many college courses, you'll be asked to explore connections and contradictions among groups of texts. Distilling main points from more than one text, seeing connections among texts, commenting on meaningful relationships, and showing how the texts have influenced your own thinking on a question are all part of the thinking and writing involved in synthesis.

Synthesis, which is a way of seeing and coming to terms with complexities, is a counterpart to **analysis**. When you analyze something, you break it down into its parts to see the relationships among them. When you synthesize, you take one more step, putting parts together in some new fashion. The cognitive researcher Benjamin Bloom schematized "synthesis" as the fifth of six levels of thinking processes, ranked in order of complexity and challenge: knowledge, comprehension, application, analysis, *synthesis*, and evaluation. Bloom defined synthesis in these terms: "putting together of constituent elements or parts to form a whole requiring original creative thinking."* Synthesis drives those light-bulb moments when you exclaim, "Ah! Now I see how these ideas are related!"

A second useful way to think of synthesis is as a dialectical thinking process. Throughout this text, we have explained that college writing involves posing a significant question that often forces you to encounter clashing or contradictory ideas. Such conflicts intrigued the German philosopher Hegel, who posited that thinking proceeds dialectically when a thesis clashes against an antithesis, leading the thinker to formulate a synthesis encompassing dimensions of both the original thesis and the antithesis. When you write to synthesize ideas, your thinking exemplifies this dialectical process.

Synthesis is an especially important component of academic research writing, where you use synthesis to carve out your own thinking space on a question while sifting through the writings of others. Synthesis, then, is the skill of wrestling with ideas from different texts or sources, trying to forge a new whole out of potentially confusing parts. It is the principal way you enter into a conversation on a social, civic, or scholarly issue.

This chapter introduces you to an important academic genre, the synthesis essay. By writing a synthesis essay, you will learn to:

- interact with a group of texts
- explore their alternative perspectives on an issue
- present a new, enlarged perspective of your own

---

*Benjamin Bloom, *Taxonomy of Educational Objectives: Handbook I: Cognitive Domain* (New York: David McKay, 1956).

Exploring the Analysis and Synthesis of Ideas

To introduce you to some of the essential thinking moves involved in analyzing and synthesizing, we offer this exercise, which asks you to read two articles on the question, "What effect are cell phones having on our lives as American citizens?" The first reading, "Mobile Phone Tracking Scrutinized" by Nikki Swartz, was published in the *Information Management Journal* for March/April 2006. This journal bills itself as "the leading source of information on topics and issues central to the management of records and information worldwide." The second reading, "Reach Out and Track Someone" by Terry J. Allen, appeared in the May 2006 edition of *In These Times*, a publication "dedicated to informing and analyzing popular movements for social, environmental and economic justice." Read these pieces carefully and then do the exercises that follow.

Nikki Swartz
Mobile Phone Tracking Scrutinized

1   Nearly 200 million Americans have cell phones, but many of them are not aware that wireless technology companies, as well as the U.S. government, track their movements through signals emitted by their handsets.

2   Cellular providers, including Verizon Wireless and Cingular Wireless, know, within about 300 yards, the location of their subscribers whenever a phone is turned on. Even if the phone is not in use, it still communicates with cell tower sites, and the wireless provider keeps track of the phone's position as it travels. These companies are marketing services that turn handsets into even more precise global positioning devices for driving or allowing parents to track the whereabouts of their children.

3   In recent years, law enforcement officials have used cellular technology as a tool for easily and secretly monitoring the movements of suspects. But this kind of surveillance, which investigators have been able to conduct with easily obtained court orders, has now come under tougher legal scrutiny.

4   The *New York Times* reports that, in the last four months of 2005, three federal judges denied prosecutors the right to get cell phone tracking information from wireless companies without first showing "probable cause" that a crime has been or is being committed—the same standard applied to requests for search warrants.

5   The rulings, issued by magistrate judges in New York, Texas, and Maryland, underscore the growing debate over privacy rights and government surveillance in the digital age. Wireless providers keep cell phone location records for varying lengths of time, from several months to years, and have said that they turn over cell location information when presented with a court order to do so.

6   Prosecutors argue that having such data is crucial to finding suspects, corroborating their whereabouts with witness accounts, or helping build a case for a wiretap on the phone. The government has routinely used records of cell phone calls and caller locations to show where a suspect was at a particular time, with access to those records obtainable under a lower legal standard.

7   But it is unclear how often prosecutors have asked courts for the right to obtain cell-tracking data as a suspect is moving. And the government is not required to report publicly when it makes such requests.

8   Prosecutors, while acknowledging that they must get a court order before obtaining real-time cell-site data, argue that a 1994 amendment to the 1986 Stored Communications Act—a standard that calls for the government to show "specific and articulable facts" that demonstrate that the records sought are "relevant and material to an ongoing investigation"—is actually lower than the probable-cause hurdle. In the cell-tracking cases, some legal experts say that the Stored Communications Act refers only to records of where a person has been—historical location data—but does not address live tracking.

9   Prosecutors in the recent cases also unsuccessfully argued that the expanded police powers under the USA PATRIOT Act could be read as allowing cell phone tracking.

10   The magistrate judges, however, ruled that surveillance by cell phone because it acts like an electronic tracking device that can follow people into homes and other personal spaces must meet the same high legal standard required to obtain a search warrant to enter private places.

11   "The distinction between cell site data and information gathered by a tracking device has practically vanished," wrote Stephen W. Smith, a magistrate in Federal District Court in the Southern District of Texas, in his ruling. He added that when a phone is monitored, the process is usually "unknown to the phone users, who may not even be on the phone."

12   In a digital era, the stream of data that carries a telephone conversation or an e-mail message contains a great deal of information, including when and where the communications originated. And that makes it harder for courts to determine whether a certain digital surveillance method invokes Fourth Amendment protections against unreasonable searches.

Terry J. Allen
Reach Out and Track Someone

1   If you are one of the more than 200 million Americans with a cell phone nestled in your pocket, authorities may be able to find you any time day or night—even if you never make or receive a call.

2   You know the Verizon ad where a lockstep crowd personifies the network that accompanies its customer everywhere? Well, within that seemingly friendly horde, a hightech Big Brother is lurking.

3   Most people know that when they make a mobile call—during a 911 emergency, for example—authorities can access phone company technology to pin down their location, sometimes to within a few feet.

4   A lesser-known fact: Cell phone companies can locate you any time you are in range of a tower and your phone is on. Cell phones are designed to work either with

global positioning satellites or through "pings" that allow towers to triangulate and pinpoint signals. Any time your phone "sees" a tower, it pings it.

5   That is what happened last month when a New York City murder highlighted the existence of the built-in capability of phones to locate people even when they aren't making calls.

6   The case of Imette St. Guillen captivated the New York City media as only the murder of a young, attractive, middle-class, white female can. One piece of evidence leading to the arrest of Darryl Littlejohn, the bouncer at the club where St. Guillen was last seen, was what police called "cell phone records." In fact, it was not an actual call that placed Littlejohn at the crime scene. Instead, according to the *New York Daily News*, police traced Littlejohn's route the day of the murder by tracking the "pings" of his cell phone, which were "stored" in a tower and "later retrieved from T-Mobile by cops."

7   Telecom companies and government are not eager to advertise that tracking capability. Nor will companies admit whether they are archiving the breadcrumb trail of pings from a cell phone so that they—or authorities—can trace back, after the fact, where the customer had been at a particular time. "Of course, there is that capability," says Bruce Schneier, chief technical officer with Counterpane Internet Security. "Verizon and the other companies have access to that information and the odds are zero that they wouldn't sell it if it is legal and profitable. This is capitalism after all."

8   But legality can be so tricky to pin down, especially when national security and corporate profits are involved. Communications companies and government have been repeatedly caught collaborating in highly questionable practices. Warrantless wiretapping, now sparking cries for Bush's impeachment, was implemented by the NSA* accessing the "gateway" switches that route calls around the globe. Most of these switches are controlled by AT&T, MCI and Sprint.

9   Recently, the Electronic Frontier Foundation (EFF) said it had internal AT&T documents and a sworn statement by retired AT&T technician Mark Klein showing that the company's use of a "dragnet surveillance" was "diverting Internet traffic into the hands of the NSA wholesale."

10   It is likely that authorities are also accessing cell phone call records and conducting real-time tracing of hapless Palestinians who donated to clinics and liberal activists who dared march for peace. And if the administration's record is a guide, it is interpreting privacy protection laws relating to cell phones in ways that bend and perhaps batter the Constitution.

11   "I think there's a substantial worry that location information about cell phone users is being released without a court order," EFF Staff attorney Kevin Bankston told CNN.

12   Echoing the Bush administration's rationale for warrantless wiretapping, the Justice Department argues that time lost justifying a search warrant can mean dangerous delays. Several judges around the country have disagreed. Citing officials' failure to show probable cause, they have denied government requests for cell phone tracking. According to EFF, a New York magistrate revealed that "the Justice Department had routinely been using a baseless legal argument to get secret authorizations from a number of courts, probably for many years."

*National Security Agency

13   "Justice Department officials countered that courts around the country have granted many such orders in the past without requiring probable cause," the Oct. 28 *Washington Post* reported.

14   Real-time tracking technology also opens disturbing entrepreneurial opportunities. Anyone who provides their kids, spouse or employees with a software-readied cell phone can secretly monitor them on the web. Wherify.com "locates loved ones within feet/meters in about a minute," and allows subscribers to "view location on both street and aerial mapping, to include date/time stamp, lat/long and block address" and "set breadcrumb schedule for periodic locates." Another Internet business promises to sell you the calling records for any phone number you provide. (Note to readers: If you have Karl Rove's number, I'll cough up the $100 fee to get a look.)

15   But as far as invasiveness goes, the ability of the government to secretly track and find you anywhere, anytime, ranks right up with a pelvic exam in Times Square.

INDIVIDUAL TASKS

1. How would you describe each writer's perspective or angle of vision on cell phones? In one or two sentences, summarize each writer's main points in these passages.
2. List ideas that these pieces have in common.
3. List any contradictions or differences you see in these pieces.
4. Freewrite your own response to these readings for five minutes, exploring what questions they raise for you or personal experiences that they might remind you of.

GROUP OR WHOLE-CLASS TASKS

1. Working in small groups or as a whole class, try to reach consensus answers to questions 1, 2, and 3.
2. Share your individual responses to question 4. What are the major questions and issues raised by your group or the whole class? What different views of cell phones in particular and technology in general emerged?

Understanding Analysis and Synthesis

Posing a Synthesis Question

As we have shown throughout this text, most academic and professional writing begins with the posing of a problem. Writing a synthesis essay follows the same principle. The need to synthesize ideas usually begins when you pose a problematic question that sends you off on an intellectual journey through a group of texts. The synthesis or focusing question directs you to look for ways that a group of texts are connected and ways that they differ in their approaches to a particular problem or issue. A synthesis question helps you zero in on a problem that these texts address or that you are trying to solve through exploring these texts. Your goal is to achieve your own informed view on that question, a view that reflects your intellectual wrestling with the ideas in your sources and in some way integrates ideas from these sources with your own independent thinking.

Although synthesis writing appears in college courses across the curriculum, how these assignments are set up varies widely. Sometimes instructors will specify the texts and the questions that you are to explore whereas at other times you will be asked to choose your texts and articulate your own synthesis questions. The following examples show typical synthesis assignments that you might encounter in different disciplines, with both the texts and synthesis questions provided in each case.

Environmental Politics Course

Texts to Be Analyzed	Synthesis Questions
Garrett Hardin's essay on overpopulation, "The Tragedy of the Commons," from *Science* (1968)	Are there any common assumptions about the world's environment in these readings?
Kenneth E. Boulding's essay "Economics of the Coming Spaceship Earth" (1966)	What problems and solutions appear in these readings?
A chapter from Ron Bailey's *The True State of the Planet* (1995)	What direction would you take in proposing a solution?
A chapter from Al Gore's *An Inconvenient Truth* (2006)	

American Literature Survey Course

Texts to Be Analyzed	Synthesis Questions
Selections from the *Lowell Offering*, a publication produced in Lowell, Massachusetts, in the 1840s, featuring the writings of young female factory workers	What common questions about changes in women's social roles in the 1800s emerge in these texts?
Historian Gerda Lerner's essay "The Lady and the Mill Girl: Changes in the Status of Women in the Age of Jackson 1800–1840" (1969)	Which text gives you the clearest understanding of the problems with women's changing roles and why?
Herman Melville's short story "The Paradise of Bachelors and the Tartarus of Maids" (1835)	

Synthesis Writing as an Extension of Summary/ Strong Response Writing

In Chapter 5, we introduced you to writing summaries of texts and responding strongly to them through critique of their rhetorical strategies and ideas. It is helpful to think of synthesis writing as an extension of those skills. In writing a synthesis essay, you use both with-the-grain and against-the-grain thinking. You listen carefully to texts as you summarize them to determine their main points. You also conduct—at least informally in your exploratory stages—a critique of both the rhetorical features and the ideas of these texts. This analysis builds the platform from which you create a synthesis of ideas—that is, from which you begin your own independent thinking based on the synthesis question that ties your texts together.

A synthesis essay differs from a summary/strong response essay in that a synthesis extends the process to more texts with the aim of bringing them into conversation with each other. A synthesis essay shows how you have taken apart, made sense of, assessed, and recombined the ideas of these texts. A synthesis essay most likely incorporates the following features:

TYPICAL FEATURES OF A SYNTHESIS ESSAY

- A statement of the synthesis question that shows your interest in the texts and presents this question as problematic and significant
- Short summaries of these texts to give your readers a sense of the readings you are working with
- A thesis that indicates how you have analyzed and synthesized the readings to arrive at a new perspective
- Your analysis of key points in these texts, determined in part by the synthesis question
- Your new view, which combines ideas gathered from readings with your own independent ideas

To review summary/strong response writing, see Chapter 5.

Student Example of a Synthesis Essay

Before we move to the writing project for this chapter—and to the idea-generating strategies of student writers who are analyzing and synthesizing texts—we show you a student example of a synthesis essay. This example, by student writer Kate MacAulay, was written for the writing project for this chapter and addresses the assigned question, "What effect is technology having on humanity and the quality of life in the twenty-first century?" The texts she was asked to analyze and synthesize are these two:

- George Ritzer, "The Irrationality of Rationality: Traffic Jams on Those 'Happy Trails.'" This is a chapter from Ritzer's widely discussed book *The McDonaldization of Society*. New Century Edition (Thousand Oaks, CA: Pine Forge Press, 2000).
- Sherry Turkle, "Who Am We?" published in the magazine *Wired* 4.1 (January 1996): 148–52, 194–99.

We have not reprinted these two lengthy texts; however, later in this chapter, we include students' summaries of both articles and the informal and analytical exploratory pieces of another student writer, Kara Watterson, in order to show you helpful steps in writing synthesis essays.

Kate MacAulay (student)

Technology's Peril and Potential

Introduces focusing questions and context

Recently in English class, we have been focusing on the question, What effect is technology having on humanity and the quality of life in the twenty-first century? We have had heated discussions about the use of cell phones, palm pilots, beepers, e-mail,

Introduces the texts to be analyzed

chat rooms, texting, and the Web. As part of my investigation of this question, I read two texts: a chapter from George Ritzer's book *The McDonaldization of Society*, entitled "The Irrationality of Rationality: Traffic Jams on Those 'Happy Trails,'" and an article published in the magazine *Wired* entitled "Who Am We?", by Sherry Turkle. In his

Brief summary of Ritzer's text

chapter, Ritzer, a sociology professor, explains how technology has rationalized businesses and many facets of society following the McDonald's model. He argues that modern technology is causing loss of quality products, time, and relationships. In the McDonaldized system, where everything is designed logically for economy and convenience, things have become more artificial, and our relationships have become more

Brief summary of Turkle's text

superficial. In her article "Who Am We?", Sherry Turkle, a psychology professor at MIT, shows how computers and the Internet are transforming our views of ourselves and the way we interact socially. Focusing on computers' capacities for simulation and promoting interaction, Turkle has explored MUDs (multiuser domains), which allow people to create virtual identities. MUDs, Turkle believes, contribute to the formation of postmodern multiple selves and raise new questions about personal iden-

Thesis statement with analytical points and synthesis points

tity and morality. Although both Turkle and Ritzer identify problems in technology's influence and in society's responses to it, Turkle sees more potential and gain where Ritzer sees mostly peril and loss. Both articles made me question how we define our values and morality in this postmodern, technologically advanced world and persuaded me of the need for caution in embracing technology.

Analytical point: compares and contrasts Ritzer's and Turkle's ideas

Although Ritzer and Turkle both see technology as having some negative effects on human relations and the quality of life, they disagree about exactly where the most interesting and serious problems lie. Ritzer believes that the problems caused by technology are not problems within the individual, but problems imposed on the individual by McDonaldized systems. For example, Ritzer claims that fast-food restaurants encourage us to eat unhealthy food quickly and also contribute to "the disintegration of the family" (141) by taking away family time. He also believes that rationalized systems create illusions of fun, reality, and friendliness. He talks about the "scripted

Analyzes and elaborates on Ritzer's ideas

interactions" (138) that employees are supposed to have with customers, where they are told exactly what to say to every customer, making interactions less real. Further, rationalized systems are dehumanizing in the kinds of jobs they create that "don't offer much in the way of satisfaction or stability" (137), benefiting only stockholders, owners, and employers.

Analyzes, contrasts, and elaborates on Turkle's ideas

In contrast, Turkle responds to technology's threat by focusing inward on technology's effect on the self and on relationships. While she is clearly intrigued by such Internet capabilities as multiuser domains, she acknowledges that this potential for multiple simultaneous identities threatens the wholeness of individuals, possibly damaging our emotional and psychological selves. Her concern is that people become addicted to these games because in the virtual world it is easy to create better "selves," to be what you wish you were. Turkle shows that people can lose themselves between the real world and the virtual world and be "imprisoned by the screens" (199). Although the virtual world is exciting and fun, she notes that "[o]ur experiences there are serious play" (199). She also examines cases of virtual characters who get into relationships with other characters, including cyber-sex relationships. She ponders the issue of cyber-sex immorality and adultery.

Analytical point: compares and contrasts Ritzer's and Turkle's ideas

Despite Turkle and Ritzer's agreement that technology can damage us as a society, they disagree on their overall outlook and on our power to respond positively to technology's influence. I find Ritzer's views almost entirely negative. He believes that we are irreversibly damaged by technological advances because we are completely caught up in the McDonaldized system, with few parts of society left unchanged. Almost all of the family-owned neighborhood restaurants or mom-and-pop grocery stores have been taken over by franchises like Red Robin or Safeway. The costs of these rationalized systems, he says, are "inefficiency, illusions of various types, disenchantment, dehumanization, and homogenization" (124). In this chapter of his book, Ritzer doesn't mention any ways that our lives could be improved by these systems; he gives only examples of the way we are misled and damaged by them.

Analyzes and elaborates on Ritzer's ideas

Presents writer's independent thinking

Turkle's approach strikes me as much more positive and balanced than Ritzer's. Optimistically, she explains that MUDs can give people self-knowledge that they can apply to real life: "[t]he anonymity of MUDs gives people the chance to express multiple and often unexplored aspects of the self, to play with their identity and to try out new ones" (152). Turkle sees an opportunity for us to grow as individuals and to learn to use technology in a positive way: "If we can cultivate awareness of what stands behind our screen personae, we are more likely to succeed in using virtual experience for personal transformation" (199). I think Turkle's views are more complex than Ritzer's. She believes that we have to take responsibility for our own habits and psychological responses to technology. She encourages us to be aware of how we interact with technology and believes that we can grow as individuals using this technology.

Analyzes, contrasts, and elaborates on Turkle's ideas

Presents writer's independent thinking

After reading these articles, I have realized how the continuing advancement of technology raises new moral questions. In a McDonaldized system, where everything is designed for convenience, there seem to be many places for morals to be left out of the picture. For example, is it okay for us to exchange real human interaction for convenience and saving time? Is there something wrong with our ethics when interesting and fulfilling jobs are eliminated by machines or replaced by dead-end, low-paying Mcjobs? Turkle too shows us how virtual worlds pose new moral questions for us. In MUDs, people can form virtual relationships, even cyber-sex relationships. The people behind the characters are real people, even if they are acting as someone else. If a married person has a cyber-sex relationship on a MUD, is he or she cheating? If a person commits a virtual assault or other crime that has no real-world, physical effects, should he or she feel guilty or sinful for the intention? Ritzer and Turkle have made me see how important these questions are.

Transition to writer's synthesis. Synthesis point discusses writer's own view

Elaborates on the connections the writer is making

Reading the articles made me strongly believe that we must use this technology in moderation in order to preserve individual qualities and our relationships. From our class discussions, I remember what Scott said about the way that the Internet connects people. He said that people like his uncle, who was severely injured on the job, use the

Synthesis point discusses writer's own view

Internet as a way of "getting out" to meet people and socialize. He pointed out how the Microsoft Gaming Zone has brought his uncle into an ongoing backgammon tournament through which he has made friends. Meanwhile his aunt has gotten a lot of pleasure out of playing and problem solving in the world of MUDs.

Synthesis point discusses writer's own view

But my own experience has left me concerned about the danger we face as emotional, social beings in the face of technology. The other night at a family gathering, one of my cousins, after discussing car buying with some of the relatives, got the urge to research new car prices. He left the room, logged onto the Internet, and spent the rest of the evening looking at cars and prices. We saw him only once the whole evening when he came out to get a slice of pie. My cousin's withdrawal from the conversation made me think about Ritzer's and Turkle's concerns that technology decreases real interactions among people.

Transition and final connections

Conclusion

Ritzer and Turkle offer us a warning that technology can be damaging if we don't recognize and overcome its dangers. I would encourage us not to let ourselves become dominated by technology, not to let it take our full attention just because it is there, and not to overlook the complex moral questions that technology poses. The convenience that technology offers—our e-mail, cell phones, and debit cards—should help us save time that can be spent in nurturing our relationships with other people. The real challenge is to find ways to become even better people because of technology.

Complete citation of articles in MLA format

Works Cited

Ritzer, George. *The McDonaldization of Society*. Thousand Oaks, CA: Pine Forge, 2000. Print.
Turkle, Sherry. "Who Am We?" *Wired* Jan. 1996: 148+. Print.

WRITING PROJECT

A Synthesis Essay

Write a synthesis essay that meets the following criteria:

- Addresses a synthesis question that your instructor provides or that you formulate for yourself
- Summarizes and analyzes the views of at least two writers on this question
- Shows how you have wrestled with different perspectives on the question and have synthesized these ideas to arrive at your own new view of the question.

Ideas for Synthesis Questions and Readings

The writing project for this chapter draws on the kinds of texts you will typically be asked to synthesize in your college courses. This text provides a number of options from which your instructor can choose. Some instructors may assign both the readings and the synthesis questions. Others may assign the readings but invite students to pose their own questions. Still others may leave both the questions and the readings up to the students. The following list of questions and readings found in this text gives you options for subject matter and focus for synthesis essays.

Reading Options for This Assignment

Synthesis Questions	Possible Readings
How have cell phones affected the lives of American citizens?	• Nikki Swartz, "Mobile Phone Tracking Scrutinized," pp. 190–191 • Terry J. Allen, "Reach Out and Track Someone," pp. 191–193
What are the biggest obstacles in managing the problem of undocumented immigrants? What should the United States do to make progress in solving this problem?	Two or more of the excerpts from blogs collected in the Readings section of this chapter, pp. 212–218
What should be our attitude toward outsourcing of American jobs? What is the most reasonable approach to solving problems caused by outsourcing?	• Thomas L. Friedman, "30 Little Turtles," pp. 130–131 • David Horsey, "Today's Economic Indicator" (editorial cartoon) p. 134 • Mike Lane, "Labor Day Blues" (editorial cartoon), p. 135 • Froma Harrop, "New Threat to Skilled U.S. Workers," pp. 136–137
Should the United States increase its production of electricity by building more nuclear power plants or by pursuing some other form of energy?	• David Rockwood, "A Letter to the Editor," pp. 6–7

Using Learning Logs

In our view, a productive way to generate ideas for your synthesis essay is to break your process into a series of incremental thinking steps that take you gradually from summaries of your chosen texts to an analysis of them and finally to a synthesis of their ideas with your own. The five learning log tasks in the sections that follow will guide you through this process. On several occasions you will have an opportunity to share your learning log explorations with classmates and to use these logs to generate further discussion of ideas. Your instructor will specify whether completion of these learning log tasks will be a requirement for this assignment. In our view, the learning log tasks work best if you keep your writing informal and exploratory with an emphasis on idea generation rather than on corrections and polish.

Exploring Your Texts through Summary Writing

Learning Log Task 1: Write a 200–250-word summary of each of the main texts you will use in your final paper.

As a starting point for grappling with a writer's ideas, writing careful summaries prompts you to read texts with the grain, adopting each text's perspective and walking in each author's shoes. When you summarize a text, you try to achieve an accurate, thorough understanding of it by stating its main ideas in a tightly distilled format.

What follows are student Kara Watterson's summary of the book chapter by Ritzer and student Kate MacAulay's summary of Turkle's article—the two readings they will use in their synthesis essays. Notice how they use attributive tags to show that they are representing Ritzer's and Turkle's ideas as objectively as they can and that these ideas belong to Ritzer or Turkle, not to them.

Instructions on how to write a summary are found on pp. 105–108.

Instructions on how to use attributive tags are found in Skill 12.3.

KARA'S SUMMARY OF RITZER'S CHAPTER

In "The Irrationality of Rationality," the seventh chapter in *The McDonaldization of Society*, sociologist George Ritzer identifies a major sociological and economic problem: in an effort to find the most efficient way to run a business (what Ritzer calls "rationalizing"), more and more companies are following the franchise model pioneered by McDonald's. Although McDonaldization is efficient and economical for the companies, Ritzer argues it can be irrational, inconvenient, inefficient, and costly for consumers who often stand in long lines at fast-food restaurants and supermarkets. Ritzer also claims that McDonaldized systems cause people to forfeit real fun for manufactured fun and illusion. He cites the example of fake international villages at amusement parks and the fake friendliness of the "scripted interactions" (138) that employees are supposed to have with customers. Ritzer explains that our McDonaldized society has begun focusing more on quantity than quality. He believes that McDonaldized systems are dehumanizing: jobs "don't offer much in the way of satisfaction or stability" (137) and families hardly ever eat together any more, a situation that is contributing to the "disintegration of the family" (141). Ritzer also argues that by franchising everywhere, we are losing cultural distinctions. Whether you are in Japan or the United States, products are beginning to look the same. Finally, Ritzer shows that when companies become rationalized, they limit the possibility of connection between human beings. Citing examples from fast-food restaurants to hospitals, he states that there are many serious drawbacks to "our fast-paced and impersonal society" (140).

KATE'S SUMMARY OF TURKLE'S ARTICLE

In her *Wired* article "Who Am We?" psychologist and MIT professor Sherry Turkle explores how computers and the Internet are transforming our views of ourselves and the way we interact socially. Turkle believes that the Internet is moving us toward a "decentered" (149) sense of the self. She says that computers used to be thought of as "calculating machines" (149), but they are increasingly now seen as intelligent objects capable of interaction and simulation. She uses children's interactive computer games to illustrate how some people now think of computers as having personalities and psyches, which make them "fitting partners for dialog and relationship" (150). In the second half of her article, she argues that virtual life raises new moral issues. She uses the example of MUDs (multiuser domains), which allow people to create multiple and often simultaneous virtual identities by playing different characters. She presents examples of the relationships of cyber characters—often cyber-sex—that raise the question of whether cyber-sex is an act of real-life infidelity or adultery. Turkle concludes that it is easy for people to lose themselves between the real world and these virtual worlds. Because we have the ability to create better "selves" in the virtual world, it is possible to become addicted to virtual life and be "imprisoned by the screens" (199). According to Turkle, we are moving toward a "postmodernist culture of simulation" (149), and she cautions that it is more important than ever that we are very self-aware.

FOR WRITING AND DISCUSSION

Summarizing Your Texts

Working in small groups or as a whole class, share your summaries of your two chosen or assigned readings. What important main ideas does your group agree must be included in a summary of each text? What points are secondary and can be left out?

Exploring Your Texts' Rhetorical Strategies

Learning Log Task 2: Analyze the rhetorical strategies used in each of your texts (for example, the way your texts handle purpose; audience; genre; angle of vision; appeals to *logos*, *ethos*, and *pathos*, and use of evidence).

Explanations of these terms and concepts are found in Concepts 3, 8, and 9.

In order to analyze a text and synthesize its ideas, you need to consider the text rhetorically. To whom is the author writing and why? Do you see how the genre of each text influences some of the author's choices about language and structure? What angle of vision shapes each text and accounts for what is included and excluded? Do you share the values of the author or of his or her intended audience?

In the next sections, we show examples of Kara's exploratory thinking. Here is Kara's learning log entry exploring the rhetorical contexts of the Ritzer and Turkle texts:

Instructions on how to write a rhetorical critique of a text are found in Chapter 5 on pp. 110–112.

KARA'S RESPONSE TO LEARNING LOG TASK 2

Although both George Ritzer and Sherry Turkle are scholars, their texts are not really written for scholarly audiences. Both would fall in the category of nonfiction books (articles) written for general audiences and both are written to raise audience awareness of sociological/cultural problems—in this case, the way that technological advances and the fast-food model of business are affecting the quality of life and the way that the Internet is affecting our sense of ourselves and our relationships.

Both Ritzer and Turkle have chosen to write in accessible language so that their ideas can easily be understood by a general audience, and both use many examples to build credibility. Still, because I had no previous personal background with multiuser domains, I found it challenging to imagine some of Turkle's descriptions of the virtual world of MUDs, but I did have previous experience with all of Ritzer's examples so I never felt in over my head while reading his chapters.

From Ritzer's angle of vision, McDonaldization has had a damaging and irreversible effect on the quality of contemporary life, and he is trying to prompt people to slow down this destructive process. His approach is quite one-sided, though. He does admit that "we undoubtedly have gained much from the rationalization of society in general" (132), but he does not develop this idea any further. He refuses to make any further concessions to the rationalization he is fighting. Instead of acknowledging contradicting ideas, Ritzer hammers his point strongly with example after example. By the end of the chapter, the reader is left with a glazed-over feeling, not really taking in the information.

Turkle's angle of vision seems to include curiosity and exploration as well as concern about the way computers are transforming society. She seems to analyze more than argue. She is trying to get across her notion that the Internet lets people adopt many different characters and have multiple selves, for example when they play in MUDs and simulation games. So maybe, in claiming that computers are no longer calculating machines, Turkle, like Ritzer, is only presenting one limited view of her subject, the view that interests her as a psychologist who has written many books and articles on computers, and our changing sense of identity and community.

> Kara defines "rationalization" in the opening sentences of her summary of Ritzer, p. 200.

FOR WRITING AND DISCUSSION

Examining the Rhetorical Strategies of Your Texts

Working in small groups or as a whole class, share what each of you discovered in Learning Log Task 2. Try to reach consensus on the most important rhetorical features of each of the texts you are using for your synthesis essay.

Exploring Main Themes and Similarities and Differences in Your Texts' Ideas

Learning Log Task 3: Identify main issues or themes in your assigned or chosen texts. Then explore the similarities and differences in their ideas.

This learning log task asks you to identify main issues, ideas, or themes that surface in your texts as preparation for looking for similarities and differences among your texts. This process of thinking—comparison and contrast—will help you clarify your understanding of each reading and promote analysis of the underlying values, assumptions, and ideas of each author. Here are some questions that can guide your learning log writing at this stage of your thinking:

QUESTIONS TO HELP YOU GRAPPLE WITH SIMILARITIES AND DIFFERENCES IN YOUR TEXTS

- What main ideas or themes related to your synthesis question do you see in each text?
- What similarities and differences do you see in the way the authors choose to frame the issues they are writing about? How do their theses (either implied or stated) differ?

- What are the main similarities and differences in their angles of vision?
- What commonalities and intersections related to your synthesis question do you see in their ideas? What contradictions and clashes do you see in their ideas?
- What similarities and differences do you see in the authors' underlying values and assumptions?
- What overlap, if any, is there in these authors' examples and uses of terms?
- On the subject of your synthesis question, how would Author A respond to Author B?

Here is an excerpt from Kara's learning log, showing her exploratory analyses of Ritzer's and Turkle's texts. Note how she begins to organize comparisons by points, to make analytical connections among them, and to push herself to think out exactly where these authors agree and differ.

EXCERPT FROM KARA'S RESPONSE TO LEARNING LOG TASK 3

Both Ritzer and Turkle make strong comments about health problems that may be caused by the particular type of technology they are dealing with. For Ritzer, the dangers that arise from McDonaldization can most easily be seen in fast-food restaurants and their fatty, unhealthy foods: "such meals are the last things many Americans need, suffering as they do from obesity, high cholesterol levels, high blood pressure, and perhaps diabetes" (133). He also considers the high level of stress created by our high-speed society that can cause heart attacks, panic attacks, maybe nervous breakdowns. Turkle, too, is concerned about the effects of technology on people's health, but her focus is people's psyches and minds. One person in her research study who creates different identities on the Internet thinks that "MUDding has ultimately made him feel worse about himself" (196). For Turkle, the Internet can be dangerous for what it can do to a person's psyche.

Both authors agree that technological advances are causing a loss of real human connection. McDonaldization fosters fake contact; employees are given guidelines about how to interact with customers and are programmed with what to say and what not to say: "rule Number 17 for Burger King workers is 'Smiles at all times'" (Ritzer 130). Quick sales, not real customer relations, are the main concern. For Turkle too, this loss of human contact is a dilemma. MUDs are not places where you truly get to know a person; they are places where people are acting out characters. These are not real friends that can aid you when you are feeling ill or down. Also, people are spending vast quantities of time logging on, spending time with a computer screen instead of family and friends. . . .

Generating Points about Themes, Shared Ideas, and Differences

Working as a whole class or in small groups, share your analyses of similarities and differences in your chosen or assigned texts. Pay close attention to these two overarching questions: How are the texts similar and different? How do each author's assumptions, beliefs, purposes, and values account for these similarities and differences?

FOR WRITING AND DISCUSSION

Generating Ideas of Your Own

> **Learning Log Task 4:** In light of what you have read and thought about so far, explore your own views on the original synthesis question that has guided your probing of the texts.

One of your biggest challenges in writing a synthesis essay is to move beyond analysis to synthesis. A successful synthesis essay incorporates ideas from your texts and yet represents your own independent thinking, showing evidence of the dialectic process. You need to think about how the differing perspectives of Texts A and B have led you to new realizations that will let you enter the conversation of these texts. As you begin to formulate your synthesis views, you will also need to reassert your personal/intellectual investment in the conversation of the texts. You will need to take ownership of the ideas and to emerge with a clearer sense of your own views. You may also want to consider which text—in your mind—makes the most significant contribution to the question you are exploring. You may want to evaluate the texts to determine which has influenced your thinking the most and why. The following questions should help you use Learning Log Task 4 to generate ideas of your own.

QUESTIONS TO HELP YOU DEVELOP YOUR OWN VIEWS

- What do I agree with and disagree with in the texts I have analyzed?
- How have these texts changed my perception and understanding of an issue, question, or problem? (You might want to use these prompts: "I used to think _____, but now I think _____." "Although these texts have persuaded me that _____, I still have doubts about _____.")
- Related to my synthesis question, what new, significant questions do these texts raise for me?
- What do I now see as the main controversies?
- What is my current view on the focusing question that connects my texts and that all my texts explore?
- How would I position myself in the conversation of the texts?
- If I find one author's perspective more valid, accurate, interesting, or useful than another's, why is that?

To illustrate this learning log task, we show you an excerpt from Kara's exploration.

EXCERPT FROM KARA'S RESPONSE TO LEARNING LOG TASK 4

When I was in Puerto Rico one spring break, I remember how excited my friend and I were to go to a burger place for dinner one night. It was so nice to have American food after days of eating fajitas and enchiladas. At the time, I did not think about how this American restaurant got to Puerto Rico; I was just glad it was there. However, after reading "The Irrationality of Rationality" by George Ritzer, I began to take a closer look at this experience. Both this article and "Who Am We?" have caused me to take a closer look at our society. ... What is it that causes people to surf the Internet for hours on end, to chat with people they have never met? What is this doing to our culture? Are we losing the distinctions evident when you travel from one region to the next, from one country to another? ...

Taking Your Position in the Conversation: Your Synthesis

Learning Log Task 5: Reread your first four learning logs and consider how your own views on the synthesis question have evolved and emerged. Think about the risky, surprising, or new views that you can bring to your readers. In light of your reading and thinking, explore what you want to say in your own voice to show the connections you have made and the new insights you now have.

After you have discovered what you think about the texts you have analyzed—what ideas you accept and reject, what new questions you have formulated, how your ideas have been modified and transformed through your reading experience—you need to find a way to pull your ideas together. Your synthesis view should be the fruit of your intellectual work, a perspective that you have come to after reading the ideas of other writers, pondering them reflectively and keenly. Here are some questions that can help you articulate the points that you want to develop in your essay:

QUESTIONS TO HELP YOU FORMULATE AND DEVELOP YOUR SYNTHESIS VIEWS

- What discoveries have I made after much thought?
- What are the most important insights I have gotten from these readings?
- What is my intellectual or personal investment with the synthesis question at this point?
- Where can I step out on my own, even take a risk, in my thinking about the ideas discussed in these texts?
- What new perspective do I want to share with my readers?

What follows is an excerpt from Kara's learning log. Note how she is beginning to find her stance on the synthesis question of whether technology enriches or dehumanizes our lives.

EXCERPT FROM KARA'S RESPONSE TO LEARNING LOG TASK 5

What is technology doing to our relationships with one another? Both Ritzer and Turkle seem to be urging us away from dependency on technology, and these authors have made me aware of my complacence in accepting technology, but still I see value in technology that these writers don't discuss. ...

I find myself questioning these writers' views. Ritzer seems to believe that families go to McDonald's rather than eat family meals together. He doesn't consider that it is when people are on the road or out already that these restaurants are visited, not when they are sitting at home deciding what is for dinner. Turkle also speaks of the loss of connection that can arise from people constantly at their computers. She raises some very important questions about what technology is doing to our relationships and self-image, but I think she focuses too much on MUDs. How many people actually are doing this MUDding? Also, there are some valid things that come out of relationships on the Internet. I know of several examples of people who have met their future spouses through chat rooms and Online Social Networks. When I left for college, I was not sure whom I would stay in touch with, but because of the Internet, I am able to stay connected to people I would have drifted away from otherwise.

Also, while we note the dangers of technology, I think we need to remember the benefits as well. I agree that cell phones are overused, but how often have cell phones saved people in emergencies or aided people stranded on the road with car problems? I hope to be a doctor. I have great appreciation for the way that cameras can see inside a patient as surgeons are operating and thus reduce the risk of many surgeries. . . .

FOR WRITING AND DISCUSSION

Generating Your Synthesis Points

Prior to the start of this task, work individually to write two or three main points that you want to make in the synthesis portion of your final essay. Working in small groups or as a whole class, share your short list of main points. Briefly explain to your group or to the whole class why these points interest you. Take notes on group ideas.

At this point, you might want to reread Kate MacAulay's synthesis essay (pp. 196–198), which shows evidence of the ideas discovered in the exploratory thinking she did in her learning logs. You can see how she selected, organized, and developed particular points that probably appeared as kernels in her exploratory writing, just as Kara's learning logs show her emerging ideas.

Shaping and Drafting

Your main project in shaping and drafting your synthesis essay is to move from the kernels of good ideas that you generated in your learning logs to a focused, fully developed, and logically organized discussion of these ideas. Focusing and organizing your ideas for a synthesis essay are both challenging writing tasks. We offer some suggestions for developing the analysis and synthesis sections of your essay and then for formulating a thesis that will direct and hold together your essay.

For the analysis part of your essay, identify the points in Learning Log Tasks 2 and 3 that strike you as the most interesting, lively, profound, or significant. The following strategies will help you focus and develop these ideas.

Strategies for Shaping the Analytical Section of Your Essay

What to Consider in Planning the Analysis Section of Your Essay	Questions and Decisions
• Your analysis section lays the foundation for your synthesis. • The analysis section usually forms about one-half to two-thirds of your essay. • This section discusses several ways that your texts relate to your synthesis question.	• How many analytical points do you want to develop? • What are these points?
• Your analysis section should show that you have wallowed in the complexity of your texts. • It may include points about the rhetorical features of your texts (as in a rhetorical critique), and it may include points about the ideas (as in an ideas critique). • It should map out and explain a number of important similarities and differences in your texts.	Consider developing answers to these questions: • How do your texts frame the problem? How do they present different angles of vision? Where do they intersect in their perspectives and approaches? How do they argue and support their views with evidence? • How rhetorically effective are these texts? • What do the authors do to make their readers think?

For the synthesis part of your essay, use the following strategies to develop points that emerged for you from Learning Log Tasks 4 and 5.

Strategies for Shaping the Synthesis Section of Your Essay

What to Consider in Planning the Synthesis Section of Your Essay	Questions and Decisions
• Your essay should build to your synthesis section. • Typically your synthesis ideas form at least one-third of your essay.	• How can you best show where the texts and their authors promote your own independent thinking? • What synthesis points do you want to explore and discuss?
• The synthesis section of your essay should show your informed, independent thinking. • It should show how you have worked your way to a new understanding.	• What new insights have you developed through studying these texts? • What new perspectives have you gained through the contrast and/or clash of different ideas? • How much or how little have these texts changed your views and why?

Writing a Thesis for a Synthesis Essay

In a synthesis essay, your thesis statement is particularly important and challenging to write. It sets up your readers' expectations, promising an illuminating view of the texts you have worked with. It should reflect earnest intellectual work, promise insights achieved through serious reflection, be your own original connection of ideas, and contain some element of risk and newness. Avoid bland, noncontestable thesis statements such as "These articles have both good and bad points."

You will probably want to work back and forth between formulating your thesis statement and drafting the analysis and synthesis sections of your essay. We recommend that you map out a rough thesis, draft your essay, and then revise and sharpen your thesis. For a synthesis essay, it is sometimes difficult to write a one-sentence, high-level thesis statement that encompasses both your analysis and your synthesis points. In such cases, you can write two lower-level, more specific thesis statements—one for your analysis section and one for your synthesis section—and simply join them together. What is important is that your thesis forecasts your main analysis and synthesis points and creates a map for your reader. The following examples illustrate these different options.

For a full explanation of thesis statements, purpose statements, and mapping statements, see Skill 10.2.

See Chapter 2, Concept 5, for a discussion of how to avoid unsurprising, noncontestable thesis statements.

LOW-LEVEL, TWO-SENTENCE THESIS

Lower-level thesis for analysis

Lower-level thesis for synthesis

Whereas Ritzer focuses on the way high-tech society makes us homogeneous and superficial, Turkle focuses on how the Internet unsettles traditional views of the self. Although I agree with Ritzer's argument that McDonaldization is dehumanizing, I think that role-playing in MUDs is actually a healthy way to oppose McDonaldization and expresses human desire to be creative, to develop the self, and to make human connections.

HIGH-LEVEL, ONE-SENTENCE THESIS

Writer chooses high-level, one-sentence thesis rather than two lower-level theses

Ritzer's attack on technological society and Turkle's more optimistic belief that it offers opportunity for growth and discovery have together forced me to consider the superficiality and vulnerability of human relationships in our high-tech society.

Organizing a Synthesis Essay

The biggest organizational decision you have to make in writing a synthesis essay is how much to summarize your texts and how to incorporate these summaries into your essay. Your decision should be guided by your audience's familiarity with the texts you are discussing and the complexity of the points you are making. Two ways of organizing a synthesis essay are shown in Figure 8.1.

Revising

As you revise your synthesis essay, make sure that you have set up the synthesis question effectively. Then work on clarifying and developing your analytical points while striving for an engaging style. Also consider how to make your synthesis views more clearly reflect your own wrestling with the texts' ideas. Think about finding the most interesting ways to show how these texts have enlarged and deepened your own views.

FIGURE 8.1 Two Frameworks for a Synthesis Essay

Framework 1

Introduction and summary of both texts (several paragraphs)	• Presents the synthesis question and hooks readers • Summarizes the texts (unless your instructor posits that readers have already read the texts, in which case you can omit the summaries or reduce them to one or two sentences each) • Presents your thesis, which maps out your main analytical and synthesis points (Your thesis might come at the end of the paragraphs with your summaries or in a mini-paragraph of its own.)
Analytical section	• Includes paragraphs discussing and developing your analytical points
Synthesis section	• Includes paragraphs discussing and developing your synthesis points
Concluding paragraph	• Reiterates the values and limitations of the texts you have analyzed • Pulls together your new insights • Leaves readers thinking about your views

Framework 2

Introduction	• Presents the synthesis question and hooks readers • Presents your thesis, which maps out your main analytical and synthesis points
Summary/analysis of first text	• Summarizes the first text • Analyzes the first text
Summary/analysis of second text	• Summarizes the second text • Analyzes the second text
Synthesis section	• Develops several main synthesis points
Concluding paragraph	• Reiterates values and limitations of the texts you have analyzed • Pulls together your new insights • Leaves readers thinking about your views

Questions for Peer Review

In addition to the generic peer review questions explained in skill 9.4, ask your peer reviewers to address these questions:

INTRODUCTION, SUMMARIES OF THE TEXT, AND THESIS

1. What works well about the writer's presentation of the synthesis question that connects the texts under examination? How could the writer better show this question's significance and problematic nature?

2. Where could the writer's summaries of the texts be expanded, condensed, or clarified? Where would the summaries be better located in the essay to help readers?
3. How could the thesis be made more focused, risky, and clear in setting up the writer's analytical and synthesis points?

ANALYTICAL SECTION OF THE ESSAY

1. How could the analytical points more clearly compare and contrast the authors' values, assumptions, angles of vision, or rhetorical strategies in addressing the synthesis question?
2. What further textual evidence could the writer add to develop these analytical points and make them more interesting or comprehensive?

SYNTHESIS SECTION OF THE ESSAY

1. How could the writer's synthesis points more clearly demonstrate the writer's thoughtful interaction with these texts?
2. What examples or other specifics could the writer include to develop these synthesis points more effectively?
3. How could the writer conclude this essay more effectively to leave readers with a new perspective on the texts and on the underlying question?

The readings in this chapter immerse you in a network of issues about illegal immigration and immigration reform, which continue to be volatile and contested. These issues cut across political parties and continue to perplex citizens, policymakers, and immigrants. Experts estimate that eleven to twelve million people have illegally crossed the border between the United States and Mexico and are currently living and working in the United States. What caused these persons to risk the dangers of border crossing in order to work in the United States? What questions about human rights and domestic security does this problem raise? What forces are interfering with effective policy discussions and decision making to solve these problems?

For this chapter's readings, we present five blogs on these issues. ("Blog" is an abbreviation for "Web log.") Blogging has become a popular arena for political discourse worldwide as well as for discourse on any subject ranging from hobbies to sports to conspiracy theories. The blogosphere constitutes a new and rapidly evolving rhetorical context open to anyone who desires to create a blogsite or respond to postings on someone else's site. Persons often blog under online pseudonyms. Because a blogger tends to attract persons with similar interests and views, a blogsite serves as a "virtual café" for like-minded people to exchange views. Consequently, blogs often have an uncomfortable "insider feel" for persons trying to enter a blog conversation for the first time. They are also often characterized by informal, colloquial, and occasionally obscene language that wouldn't be encountered in print media. Some widely known and highly influential sites—such as the Daily Kos on the left or MichelleMalkin or Little Green Footballs on the right—are major players in United States political debate. Many people now think that skilled and knowledgeable bloggers play a more important "free press" investigative role in our democracy than do major newspapers dominated by corporate interests.

To avoid influencing your own analysis of these readings, we omit the discussion questions that typically follow in other chapters. However, as you read each blog, consider the particular blogsite that is hosting this piece (mentioned in the headnote) and also think about these general questions: How does the writer frame the issue? What is the writer's main argument? What types of evidence are included? What is distinctive about the way the writer expresses his or her ideas?

Our first blog is by a Mexican-American woman who identifies herself only as "Dee." According to her blogsite, Dee is a United States citizen with a Hispanic ethnicity. She holds a mid-level management position in a large corporation. Upset by the divisive discourse over immigration, Dee started her own blogsite called "Immigration Talk with a Mexican American: Truth, Honesty, and the American Way." In the blog reprinted below (posted on August 7, 2007), she sums up her placement of blogosphere views of immigration in two categories: the PROs (those who support comprehensive immigration reform) and the ANTIs (those who oppose it). She places herself firmly among the PROs. In this brief blog, her reference to the 12M stands for the estimated twelve million undocumented workers currently in the United States. Her use of abbreviations suggests the insider audience characteristic of blog discourse.

Dee

Comprehensive Immigration Reform: PROs and ANTIs

http://immigrationmexicanamerican.blogspot.com/2007/08/
comprehensive-immigration-reform-pros.html

1   Our country is divided on how to resolve our Immigration issues in our country. Comprehensive Immigration Reform (CIR) is needed. Who is for CIR? PROs. Who is against CIR? ANTIs. What are their perspectives?

2   Pro Profile: There are many, many PRO groups. Each group has a different motivation and they rarely rally together. The largest group is Hispanic Americans. The ethnicities vary and include: Mexican, Central and South American, Cuban, Puerto Rican and more. The majority of PROs who post on the internet are from this group. Other Minority groups include Asian, Southern European, Middle Eastern, African. I only see their posts when I search the international sites. Other PRO groups who also rarely post include: Churches and Humanitarian groups, Businesses that prosper from sales to the 12M (e.g. Banks, Insurance Companies, Retail, etc.), Businesses experiencing Labor Shortages that hire the 12M (e.g. Farming, IT, Construction, Contractors, Retail, etc), Politicians with reasons to support the 12M (e.g. enhance Globalization, running for office, etc). And, of course, the illegal immigrants themselves. The majority of PROs who do post tend to have the following views: They advocate secure borders, sanctioning employers and comprehensive immigration reform (because the current program is broken). The biggest difference between the ANTIs and the PROs is, the PROs advocate a path to citizenship for the 12M, particularly since most of the 12M have worked and contributed to this country for + 5–20 years.

3   ANTI Profile: American. The majority are Anglos. (Anglos = white, Northern European ethnicity). Viewpoint: The majority advocate Deportation (mass or self) of the illegal immigrants in this country. Anything short of Deportation is termed Amnesty by the ANTIs. Many call for a 2000 mile southern border fence. They advocate for restrictive Official English laws even though English is already the National Language. They advocate for changing the 14th amendment and birthright citizenship, hoping to end, what they term "Anchor Babies." There are a few legal immigrants and minorities within their groups, but not many. There are a few politicians that support them, not many. There are hundreds of ANTI websites across the internet. There are hundreds of ANTI radio shows across the country. ANTIs tend to be very angry. They try their darndest to get African Americans to join forces with them citing their uncorroborated claim [that] the 12M drag down the minimum wage. The ANTIs tend to forget the deep alliances between the two ethnic groups which were forged over the previous four decades when they marched together for civil rights. Some of the Worst Terms the ANTIs use: 3rd World Country, Mexifornia, return to American Values.

Our next reading is a blog by Byron Williams, an African-American syndicated columnist. According to his online biography, the Reverend Byron Williams is "a writer, theologian, and activist [who] fuses theology with public policy to bring a fresh social justice perspective to the public arena." He serves as pastor of the Resurrection Community Church in Oakland, California. This blog was posted on The Huffington Post on May 9, 2006.

Byron Williams
Immigration Frenzy Points Out Need for Policy Debate

http://www.huffingtonpost.com/byron-williams/
immigration-frenzy-points_b_20717.html

1   As a child I recall Thanksgiving with mixed emotions. I enjoyed the big family feast with relatives I had not seen since the previous Thanksgiving, but I dreaded the days after. It was turkey ad nauseam. By the sixth day my father would make what he called "Turkey a la King," which was turkey remnants along with whatever else he could find to put in the pot.

2   As emotions flare on both sides of the immigration debate it has morphed into "Immigration a la King." But unlike my father's mysterious concoction, the ingredients are well known. It consists of one part legitimate public policy, one part ethnocentrism, and one part political pandering.

3   There is no doubting we need a legitimate public policy conversation around illegal immigration. The porous nature of America's borders coupled with the post 9/11 climate does warrant national concern.

4   If, however, we remove the legitimate public policy aspect, what's left? What's left is ugly, reactionary fear-based hatred symbolizing America at its worst.

5   With 9/11 approaching its 5th anniversary, why are we just getting around to dealing with immigration? Like a wounded, cornered animal, the Republican-led Congress and the president conveniently fan the flames of one of America's greatest tragedies, resurfacing fear, in order to gain short-term political points.

6   It is hard to embrace the concept that at this late date the administration and Congress are worried about Al Qaeda members coming across the border in man made tunnels or in the back of trucks when you consider the 9/11 attackers entered the country legally.

7   They have successfully created a climate where vigilantes known as the Minutemen—who do a disservice to the brave individuals who fought during the Revolutionary War by embracing the name—are viewed as patriotic by taking the law into their own hands allegedly protecting America's borders.

8   How many poor white southerners willingly accepted a death sentence by fighting for the Confederacy to protect a "southern way of life" in which they did not participate? They were seductively lured, in part, by the notion that all hell would break loose if emancipated African slaves were elevated to their same impoverished status.

9   The ethnocentrism and political pandering has sadly infected parts of the African American community. If one removes the veil of objecting to the comparisons between the civil rights movement and Hispanic immigration demonstrations, which a number of African Americans hide behind, they would discover the same fear that plagues the dominant culture.

10   This does not dismiss the obvious concerns about the plight of low-skilled African Americans who find themselves competing with immigrants for certain entry-level employment. But again, this is part of the much needed public policy debate that is submerged under the current political frenzy.

11   Freely throwing around words such [as] "illegal" and "Al Qaeda" opens the door to dehumanization. And once an individual has been dehumanized that individual can be taken advantage of.

12   Even those who compassionately advocate for a guest worker program, forget that the last such program that existed on a large scale in this country was struck down by Abraham Lincoln on September 22, 1863.

13   There are legitimate concerns on both sides of this issue. But history has shown us there is something wrong when marginalized groups are systematically pitted against each other.

14   For all of the cries to protect the borders and the loss of job opportunities for low-skilled Americans, I doubt there would be 11 million undocumented individuals in the country if no one was hiring. There can be no legitimate immigration debate that does not hold the business community equally accountable for hiring undocumented individuals while paying less than a living wage.

15   Each individual must come to his or her decision as to how they feel about immigration. But the only way to have an authentic policy is to have an authentic policy debate—one that does not include the unnecessary ingredients that ultimately lead to dehumanization.

Our third reading, by Victor Davis Hanson, is a posting to Roundup: Historians' Take, a spot for "historians writing about the news," on the History News Network site. Victor Davis Hanson, a former professor of classics and now a Senior Fellow at the Hoover Institution, is known as a military historian, a political essayist, and a regular conservative columnist for the *National Review* and Tribune Media Services. He has published numerous books and his writing has appeared frequently in such well-known newspapers and journals as the *New York Times*, the *Wall Street Journal*, and the *American Spectator*. He also blogs regularly at Pajamas Media. This posting appeared on Wednesday, June 6, 2007.

Victor Davis Hanson
The Global Immigration Problem

http://hnn.us/roundup/entries/39776.html

1   Thousands of aliens crossing our 2,000-mile border from an impoverished Mexico reflect a much larger global one-way traffic problem.

2   In Germany, Turkish workers—both legal and illegal—are desperate to find either permanent residence or citizenship.

3   "Londonstan" is slang for a new London of thousands of unassimilated Pakistani nationals.

4   In France, there were riots in 2005 because many children of North African immigrants are unemployed—and unhappy.

5   Albanians flock to Greece to do farm work, and then are regularly deported for doing so illegally.

6   The list could go on.

7   So why do millions of these border-crossers head to Europe, the United States or elsewhere in the West?

8   Easy. Stable democracies and free markets ensure economic growth, rising standards of living and, thus, lots of jobs, while these countries' birth rates and native populations fall.

9   Employers may console themselves that they pay better than what the immigrants earned back at home. This might be true, but the wages are never enough to allow such newcomers to achieve parity with their hosts.

10   Naturally, immigrants soon get angry. And rather than showing thanks for a ticket out of the slums of Mexico City or Tunis, blatant hypocrisy can follow: the once thankful, but now exhausted, alien may wave the flag of the country he would never return to while shunning the culture of the host county he would never leave.

11   In the second generation—as we see from riots in France or gangs in Los Angeles—things can get even worse.

12   The moment illegal immigrants arrive, a sort of race begins: can these newcomers become legal, speak the host language and get educated before they age, get hurt or lose their job? If so, then they assimilate and their children are held up as models of diversity. If not, the end of the story can be welfare or jail.

13   Hypocrisy abounds on all sides. Free-marketers claim they must have cheap workers to stay competitive. Yet they also count on public subsidies to take care of their former employees when old, sick or in trouble.

14   Governments in countries such as Mexico and Morocco usually care far more about their emigrants once they are long gone. Then these poor are no longer volatile proof of their own failures, but victims of some wealthy foreign government's indifference. And these pawns usually send cash home.

15   The lower middle classes complain most about massive immigration, but then they have to compete with aliens for jobs, often live among them and don't use their services. The wealthier, who hire immigrants for low wages and see them only at work, often think mass immigration, even if illegal, is wonderful.

16   The lasting solution is not the status quo—or even walls, fines, deportation, amnesty or guest-worker programs. Instead, failed societies in Latin America, Africa and much of the Middle East must encourage family planning and get smarter about using their plentiful natural wealth to keep more of their own people home.

17   The remedy for the richer West?

18   It is past time to remember that paying our own poorer laborers more, doing some occasional physical work and obeying the laws—the immigration ones especially—are not icky or a bummer. Rather, this is the more ethical and, in the long run, cheaper approach.

19   There is a final irony. The more Western elites ignore their own laws, allow unassimilated ethnic ghettos and profit from an exploitive labor market, the more their own nations will begin to resemble the very places immigrants fled from.

Our final two pieces focus on disagreements over the "temporary guest worker" program that was part of an immigration reform bill considered (and ultimately rejected) by Congress in 2007. One provision of the bill would have allowed currently illegal immigrants to stay in the United States legally for up to six years as guest workers. In this excerpt from a posting on The Hill Blog, Republican Senator Mike Crapo from Idaho explains why he supported the guest worker provision of the bill, although he eventually voted against the bill for other reasons.

Senator Mike Crapo

Excerpt from "Immigration Policy Must Help Economy While Preserving Ideals"

http://blog.thehill.com/2007/07/07/
immigration-policy-must-help-economy-while-preserving-ideals-sen-mike-crapo/

A robust economy hinges on having a temporary guest worker program to fill jobs that are not filled by American citizens. U.S.-based businesses need economic incentives to keep operations stateside. If they have a dependable labor pool at all skill levels, incentives to move operations overseas are greatly decreased. We appreciate consumer goods and agriculture products "Made in America." We can keep things that way by approaching immigration rationally and sensibly. Whatever the skill level, any temporary guest worker system must be enforceable and reliable for the worker and employer. Once Americans have been given "first right" to jobs, employers such as the agriculture industry must have access to a system that's cost-effective, not bureaucratic, and doesn't carry the risk of prosecution while employers are trying to comply with the law. Congress understands the urgency of reaching a workable solution and is moving in the right direction.

Our last piece is an excerpt from "The Progressive Case Against the Immigration Bill," which appeared in the liberal blog The Daily Kos on June 25, 2007. It gives a different view of the temporary guest worker program than that expressed by Senator Mike Crapo. The author of this piece is "Trapper John," the online identity for Jake McIntyre, who is a contributing editor for The Daily Kos.

Trapper John

Excerpt from "The Progressive Case Against the Immigration Bill"

http://www.dailykos.com/story/2007/6/25/73229/6647

1   This immigration bill is an historically bad bill, one that will undermine wage markets and which will permanently cripple skills training in vital sectors of the

economy. ... [T]he fatal flaw in this bill isn't "amnesty"—it's the euphemistically termed "temporary worker program."

2   The temporary worker program has nothing to do with immigration policy. To the contrary—it is a guaranteed cheap labor program grafted on to an immigration bill. When most people think of "immigration" to the US, they think of people coming to America to build a new life for themselves and their families, just as their ancestors did. But the temporary worker program has nothing to do with building American families and American dreams. Under the program, *400,000–600,000 guest workers would enter the country every year* on two-year visas. Although the visas can be renewed twice, recipients would be denied any path to permanent residency or citizenship. In fact, the guest workers would be precluded from even applying for permanent residency while here on temporary visas.

3   In short, the "temporary workers" will be just that—"temporary," and "workers." Not "immigrants." And they can never be "Americans." Instead, we will have created a permanent caste of non-citizens with no hope of ever becoming citizens. A class of over half-a-million workers without a voice in the political process, here at the sole sufferance of their employers. And those employers won't have to pay their new indentured servants any more than the minimum wage. See, unlike the existing H-2B visa—the visa that governs most "unskilled" temporary workers in the US today—the proposed temporary worker program contains no requirements that employers pay their temporary help the federally determined "prevailing wage" for their occupation and the geographic area. Today, if a contractor can't find a qualified electrician to work on a project in Chicago, the contractor can apply for an H-2B visa. But the contractor is required to pay any foreign electrician entering the US on the H-2B no less than $53.57 per hour, including benefits. That's the prevailing wage for an electrician in Chicago, according to the Department of Labor. And by requiring H-2B sponsors to pay their foreign help the prevailing wage, the H-2B program limits the ability of employers to use guest workers as a tool to undermine wage markets. The proposed temporary worker plan changes all that.

4   Under the proposed plan, there is no wage floor. If the Chicago contractor can't find an electrician in the US to work on his project for $20 per hour, he can import a temporary worker who will. The result will be a swift collapse of wage markets in many industries populated by skilled non-professional workers, like construction. And all of a sudden, we'll be hearing that the work of an electrician is one of those "jobs Americans won't do," like fruit picking. The truth, of course, is that there is no job that an American won't do for the right price. But by creating a steady flow of temporary workers with no ability to stay in the country for more than a couple years, and no practical ability to fight for better wages, the number of jobs that "Americans won't do" will grow dramatically. And they include a host of the jobs that sustain and nourish the middle class. The construction trades. Cosmetology. Culinary arts. These are jobs that take years to master, and consequently pay quite well, because not just anybody can do them. But by busting open the labor markets for these jobs, and opening them with no restrictions to folks from countries with much lower costs of living, we will strangle the middle class lives of the millions of Americans who have proudly earned their paychecks with their skills. ...

5   There's no question that we need immigration reform in this country. We need to find a way to bring the millions of immigrants laboring in the shadows into the light, and into our American family. And to the extent that we have bona fide labor shortages in this country, we need to address them through an expansion of legal immigration. But the price of immigration reform cannot be a temporary worker program that exploits foreign workers, limits real immigration, and guts wages for American workers.

PEARSON **mycomplab** | For support in learning this chapter's content, follow this path in **MyCompLab**: Resources ⇒ Writing ⇒ Writing Purposes ⇒ Writing to Analyze. Review the Instruction and Multimedia resources, then complete the Exercises and click on Gradebook to measure your progress.

A GUIDE TO COMPOSING AND REVISING

This ad for the United States Army, which first appeared in a general news commentary magazine, highlights qualities traditionally associated with patriotic military service to the country: respect, honor, and courage. Note that this poster does not depict soldiers in uniform on a battlefield or in the midst of a drill. Consider the way the images of the father and daughter and the words in this ad connect character-building, family relationships, the Army, and success. Think about how gender functions in this ad by focusing on the young woman's long hair, tasteful makeup, and earnest manner.

YOU TAUGHT HER ABOUT RESPECT, HONOR AND COURAGE.
IS IT ANY SURPRISE THAT NOW SHE WANTS TO USE THEM?

She'll experience the most challenging training, use the latest technology and get the strongest support. Every drill and every mission will reinforce in her that character always leads to success. Encourage her to consider becoming a Soldier — AN ARMY OF ONE.®

AN ARMY OF ONE

GOARMY.COM U.S.ARMY

PART 3   A GUIDE TO COMPOSING AND REVISING

Part 3 addresses the following outcomes for first-year composition from the Council of Writing Program Administrators.

RHETORICAL KNOWLEDGE	<ul><li>Focus on a purpose (Ch. 10, 11)</li><li>Respond to the needs of different audiences (Skills 10.1, 11.3)</li><li>Respond appropriately to different kinds of rhetorical situations (Ch. 10, 11)</li><li>Use conventions of format and structure appropriate to the rhetorical situation (Ch. 10, 11)</li><li>Adopt appropriate voice, tone, and level of formality (Skills 11.5, 11.6)</li><li>Understand how genres shape reading and writing (Ch. 10, 11)</li></ul>
PROCESSES	<ul><li>Be aware that it usually takes multiple drafts to create and complete a successful text (Skill 9.1)</li><li>Develop flexible strategies for generating, revising, editing, and proof-reading (Skills 9.2 and 9.33)</li><li>Understand writing as an open process that permits writers to use later invention and re-thinking to revise their work (Skills 9.2 and 9.3)</li><li>Understand the collaborative and social aspects of writing processes (Skill 9.4)</li><li>Learn to critique their own and others' works (Skill 9.4)</li><li>Learn to balance the advantages of relying on others with the responsibility of doing their part (Skill 9.3)</li></ul>
KNOWLEDGE OF CONVENTIONS	<ul><li>Learn common formats for different kinds of texts (Ch. 10, 11)</li><li>Develop knowledge of genre conventions ranging from structure and paragraphing to tone and mechanics (Ch. 10, 11)</li></ul>
COMPOSING IN ELECTRONIC ENVIRONMENTS	<ul><li>Understand and exploit the differences in the rhetorical strategies and in the affordances available for both print and electronic composing processes and texts (Skill 9.1)</li></ul>

WRITING AS A PROBLEM-SOLVING PROCESS

9

I rewrite as I write. It is hard to tell what is a first draft because it is not determined by time. In one draft, I might cross out three pages, write two, cross out a fourth, rewrite it, and call it a draft. I am constantly writing and rewriting. I can only conceptualize so much in my first draft—only so much information can be held in my head at one time; my rewriting efforts are a reflection of how much information I can encompass at one time. There are levels and agenda which I have to attend to in each draft.*

—*Description of Revision by an Experienced Writer*

I read what I have written and I cross out a word and put another word in; a more decent word or a better word. Then if there is somewhere to use a sentence that I have crossed out, I will put it there.*

—*Description of Revision by an Inexperienced Writer*

Blot out, correct, insert, refine,
Enlarge, diminish, interline;
Be mindful, when invention fails,
To scratch your head, and bite your nails.

—*Jonathan Swift*

Throughout this text, we have emphasized writing as a critical thinking process requiring writers to "wallow in complexity." This opening chapter of Part 3 explains how experienced writers use multiple drafts to manage the complexities of writing.

In this chapter, you will learn to improve your own writing processes:

- SKILL 9.1 Follow the experts' practice of using multiple drafts.
- SKILL 9.2 Revise globally as well as locally.
- SKILL 9.3 Develop ten expert habits to improve your writing processes.
- SKILL 9.4 Use peer reviews to help you think like an expert.

*From Nancy Sommers, "Revision Strategies of Student Writers and Experienced Adult Writers," *College Composition and Communication* 31 (October 1980): 291–300.

SKILL 9.1 **Follow the experts' practice of using multiple drafts.**

We begin this chapter with a close look at why expert writers use multiple drafts to move from an initial exploration of ideas to a finished product. As composition theorist Peter Elbow has asserted about the writing process, "meaning is not what you start out with" but "what you end up with." In the early stages of writing, experienced writers typically discover, deepen, and complicate their ideas before they can clarify them and arrange them effectively. Only in the last drafts will expert writers be in sufficient control of their ideas to shape them elegantly for readers.

What most distinguishes expert from novice writers is the experts' willingness to keep revising their work until they feel it is ready to go public. They typically work much harder at drafting and revising than do novice writers, taking more runs at their subject. Expert writers also make more substantial alterations in their drafts during revision—what we call "global" rather than "local" revision. This difference between expert and novice writers might seem counterintuitive. One might think that novices would need to revise more than experts. But decades of research on the writing process of experts reveals how extensively experts revise. Compare the first two quotations that open this chapter—one from an experienced and one from an inexperienced writer. The experienced writer crosses out pages and starts over while the inexperienced writer crosses out a word or two. The experienced writer feels cognitive overload while drafting, having to attend to many different "levels and agendas" at once. In contrast, the inexperienced writer seems to think only of replacing words or adding an occasional transition. Learning to revise extensively is thus a hallmark of a maturing writer.

Figure 9.1 shows how a first-year college student demonstrates expert writing behavior when she makes a substantial revision of an early draft. Note that she crosses out several sentences at the end of one paragraph, creates a new topic sentence for the next paragraph, and moves a detail sentence so that it follows the topic sentence.

Why Expert Writers Revise So Extensively

Our emphasis on experts' substantial revision might have surprised you. If the experts are such good writers, why do they need multiple drafts? Why don't they get it right the first time? Our answer is simply this: Expert writers use multiple drafts to break a complex task into manageable subtasks. Let's look more closely at some of the functions that drafting and revising can perform for writers.

- ***Multiple drafts help writers overcome the limits of short-term memory.*** Cognitive psychologists have shown that working memory—often called short-term memory—has remarkably little storage space. You can picture short-term memory as a small tabletop surrounded by filing cabinets (long-term memory). As you write, you can place on your tabletop (working memory) only a few chunks of material at any given moment—a few sentences of a draft or several ideas in an outline. The remaining portions of your draft-in-progress

First Draft with Revisions

sticks of our favorite flavors in the bottom of the bag. ~~That discovery was, by far, the best discovery that could ever be made, week after week. So, as you can probably guess, my opinion of farmer's markets has always been very high as they were what fulfilled my sugar fix.~~

~~However, another important point can come out of that story. That point being about~~ the man who sold us our precious honey sticks. He was kind, patient, and genuinely happy to have our business. ~~Not quite the same vibe that one would expect to get from~~ *In contrast to*

the supermarket employee who doesn't ~~even really~~ know what isle you need in order to *often*

find the peanut butter. ~~A~~ *Another* huge selling point of farmer's markets, for me, is that you can go and talk to people who know about the food they are selling. It is so refreshing to go

Revised Draft

sticks of our favorite flavors in the bottom of the bag.

Another huge selling point of farmer's markets, for me, is that you can go and talk to people who know about the food they are selling. The man who sold us our *precious* honey sticks was kind, patient, and genuinely happy to have our business, in contrast to the supermarket employee who doesn't ~~even really~~ know what aisle you need in order to find the peanut *often*

butter.

FIGURE 9.1 A First-Year Student's Substantial Revisions

fall off the table without getting stored in long-term memory. (Think of your horror when your computer eats your draft—proof that you can't rely on long-term memory to restore what you wrote.) Writing a draft captures and stores your ideas as your working memory develops them. When you reread these stored ideas, you can then see your evolving ideas whole, note problem areas, develop more ideas, see material that doesn't fit, recall additional information, and begin extending or improving the draft.

- *Multiple drafts help accommodate shifts and changes in the writer's ideas.* Early in the writing process, expert writers often are unsure of where their ideas are leading; they find that their ideas shift and evolve as their drafts progress. An expert writer's finished product often is radically different from the first draft—not simply in form and style but also in actual content.
- *Multiple drafts help writers clarify audience and purpose.* While thinking about their subject matter, experienced writers also ask questions

about audience and purpose: What do my readers already know and believe about my subject? How am I trying to change their views? In the process of drafting and revising, the answers to these questions may evolve so that each new draft reflects a deeper or clearer understanding of audience and purpose.

- ***Multiple drafts help writers improve structure and coherence for readers.*** Whereas the ideas in early drafts often follow the order in which writers conceived them, later drafts are often restructured—sometimes radically—to meet readers' needs. Writing teachers sometimes call this transformation a movement from writer-based to reader-based prose.* The composing and revising skills taught in Chapter 10 will help you learn how to revise your drafts from a reader's perspective.
- ***Multiple drafts let writers postpone worrying about correctness.*** Late in the revision process, experienced writers turn their energy toward fixing errors and revising sentences for increased cohesion, conciseness, and clarity. Focusing on correctness too soon can shut down the creative process.

An Expert's Writing Processes Are Recursive

Given this background on why expert writers revise, we can see that for experts, the writing process is recursive rather than linear. Writers continually cycle back to earlier stages as their thinking evolves. Sometimes writers develop a thesis statement early in the writing process. But just as frequently, they formulate a thesis during an "aha!" moment of discovery later in the process, perhaps after several drafts. ("So *this* is my point! Here is my argument in a nutshell!") Even very late in the process, while checking usage and punctuation, experienced writers are apt to think of new ideas, thus triggering more revision.

SKILL 9.2 **Revise globally as well as locally.**

To think like an expert writer, you need to appreciate the difference between "global" and "local" revision. You revise **locally** whenever you make changes to a text that affect only the one or two sentences that you are currently working on. In contrast, you revise **globally** when a change in one part of your draft drives changes in other parts of the draft. Global revision focuses on the big-picture concerns of ideas, structure, purpose, audience, and genre. It often involves substantial rewriting, even starting over in places with a newly conceived plan. For example, your revising part of the middle of your essay might cause you to rewrite the whole introduction or to change the tone or point of view throughout the essay.

*The terms "writer-based" and "reader-based" prose come from Linda Flower, "Writer-Based Prose: A Cognitive Basis for Problems in Writing." College English, 1979, 41.1, 19–37.

What follows are some on-the-page strategies that you can adopt to practice the global and local revision strategies of experts:*

On-the-Page Strategies for Doing Global and Local Revision	
Strategies to Use on the Page	**Reasons**
Throw out the whole draft and start again.	• Original draft helped writer discover ideas and see the whole territory. • New draft needs to be substantially refocused and restructured.
Cross out large chunks and rewrite from scratch.	• Original passage was unfocused; ideas have changed. • New sense of purpose or point meant that the whole passage needed reshaping. • Original passage was too confused or jumbled for mere editing.
Cut and paste; move parts around; (then write new transitions, mapping statements, and topic sentences).	• Parts didn't follow in logical order. • Parts occurred in the order writer thought of them rather than the order needed by readers. • Conclusion was clearer than introduction; part of conclusion had to be moved to introduction. • Revised thesis statement required different order for parts.
Add/revise topic sentences of paragraphs; insert transitions.	• Reader needs signposts to see how parts connect to previous parts and to whole. • Revision of topic sentences often requires global revision of paragraph.
Make insertions; add new material.	• Supporting particulars needed to be added: examples, facts, illustrations, statistics, other evidence (usually added to bodies of paragraphs). • New section was needed or more explanation was needed for a point. • Gaps in argument needed to be filled in.
Delete material.	• Material is no longer needed or is irrelevant. • Deleted material may have been good but went off on a tangent.

(continued)

*We have chosen to say "on the page" rather than "on the screen" because global revision is often facilitated by a writer's working off double-spaced hard copy rather than a computer screen. See pages 229–230 for our advice on using hard copy for revision.

Strategies to Use on the Page	Reasons
Recast sentences (cross out and rewrite portions; combine sentences; rephrase sentences; start sentences with a different grammatical structure).	• Passage violated old/new contract (see Skill 10.7). • Passage was wordy/choppy or lacked rhythm or voice. • Grammar was tangled, diction odd, or meaning confused. • Passage lost focus of topic sentence of paragraph.
Edit sentences to correct mistakes.	• Writer found comma splices, fragments, dangling modifiers, nonparallel constructions, or other problems of grammar and usage. • Writer found spelling errors, typos, repeated or omitted words.

FOR WRITING AND DISCUSSION

Revising a Paragraph Globally

Choose an important paragraph in the body of a draft you are currently working on. Then write your answers to these questions about that paragraph.

1. Why is this an important paragraph?
2. What is its main point?
3. Where is that main point stated?

Now—as an exercise only—write the main point at the top of a blank sheet of paper, put away your original draft, and, without looking at the original, write a new paragraph with the sole purpose of developing the point you wrote at the top of the page.

When you are finished, compare your new paragraph to the original. What have you learned that might help you revise your original?

Here are some typical responses of writers who have tried this exercise:

I recognized that my original paragraph was unfocused. I couldn't find a main point.

I recognized that my original paragraph was underdeveloped. I had a main point but not enough particulars supporting it.

I began to see that my draft was scattered and that I had too many short paragraphs.

I recognized that I was making a couple of different points in my original paragraph and that I needed to break it into separate paragraphs.

I recognized that I hadn't stated my main point (or that I had buried it in the middle of the paragraph).

I recognized that there was a big difference in style between my two versions and that I had to choose which version I liked best. (It's not always the "new" version!)

SKILL 9.3 Develop ten expert habits to improve your writing processes.

Now that you understand why experts revise more extensively than novices and what they do on the page, we describe in Skill 9.3 the habitual ways of thinking and acting that experts use when they write. Our hope is that this description will help you develop these same habits for yourself. Because one of the best ways to improve your writing process is to do what the experts do, we offer you the following ten habits of experienced writers, expressed as advice:

1. ***Use exploratory writing and talking to discover and clarify ideas.*** Don't let your first draft be the first occasion when you put your ideas into writing. Use exploratory strategies such as freewriting and idea mapping to generate ideas (see Chapter 2, Concept 4). Also seek out opportunities to talk about your ideas with classmates or friends in order to clarify your own thinking and appreciate alternative points of view.

2. ***Schedule your time.*** Don't begin your paper the night before it is due. Plan sufficient time for exploration, drafting, revision, and editing. Recognize that your ideas will shift, branch out, and even turn around as you write. Allow some time off between writing the first draft and beginning revision. For many writers, revision takes considerably longer than writing the first draft. If your institution has a writing center, consider scheduling a visit.

3. ***Discover what methods of drafting work best for you.*** Some people compose rough drafts directly on the computer; others write longhand. Some make outlines first; others plunge directly into drafting and make outlines later. Some revise extensively on the computer as they are drafting; others plough ahead until they have a complete draft before they start revising. Some people sit at their desk for hours at a time; others need to get up and walk around every couple of minutes. Some people need a quiet room; others work best in a coffee shop. Discover the methods that work best for you.

4. ***Think about audience and purpose from the start.*** Early on, think about the effect you want your writing to have on readers. In formulating a thesis, look to change your readers' view of your subject. ("Before reading my paper, my readers will think X. But after reading my paper, my readers will think Y.")

5. ***For the first draft, reduce your expectations.*** Many novice writers get blocked by trying to make their first draft perfect. In contrast, expert writers expect the first draft to be an unreadable mess. (They often call it a "zero draft" or a "garbage draft" because they don't expect it to be good.) They use the first draft merely to get their ideas flowing, knowing they will revise later. If you get blocked, just keep writing. Get some ideas on paper.

6. ***Revise on double- or triple-spaced hard copy.*** Although many experienced writers revise on the screen without going through paper drafts, there are powerful advantages in printing occasional paper drafts. Research suggests that writers are more apt to make global changes in a draft if they work from hard copy because they can see more easily how the parts connect to the whole. They can refer quickly to page two while revising page six without having to scroll back and forth. We suggest that you occasionally print out a double- or triple-spaced hard copy of your draft and then mark it up aggressively. (See again Figure 9.1, which shows how a first-year student learned the benefits of revising off hard copy.) When your draft gets too messy, keyboard your changes into your computer and begin another round of revision.

7. ***As you revise, think increasingly about the needs of your readers.*** Experts use first drafts to help them clarify their ideas for themselves but not necessarily for readers. In many respects, writers of first drafts are talking to

themselves. Through global revision, however, writers gradually convert "writer-based prose" to "reader-based prose." Writers begin to employ consciously the skills of reader-expectation theory that we explain in detail in Chapter 10.

8. ***Exchange drafts with others.*** Get other people's reactions to your work in exchange for your reactions to theirs. Experienced writers regularly seek critiques of their drafts from trusted readers. Later in this chapter we explain procedures for peer review of drafts.

9. ***Save correctness for last.*** To revise productively, concentrate first on the big questions: Do I have good ideas in this draft? Am I responding appropriately to the assignment? Are my ideas adequately organized and developed? Save questions about exact wording, grammar, mechanics, and documentation style for later. These concerns are important, but they cannot be efficiently attended to until after higher-order concerns are met. Your first goal is to create a thoughtful, richly developed draft.

10. ***To meet deadlines and bring the process to a close, learn how to satisfice.*** Our description of the writing process may seem formidable. Technically, it seems, you could go on revising forever. How can you ever know when to stop? There is no ready answer to that question, which is more a psychological than a technical problem. Expert writers have generally learned how to **satisfice**, a term coined by influential social scientist Herbert Simon from two root words, *suffice* and *satisfy*. It means to do the best job you can under the circumstances considering your time constraints, the pressures of other demands on you, and the difficulty of the task. Expert writers begin the writing process early and get as far as they can before their deadline looms. Then they let the deadline give them the energy for intensive revision. From lawyers preparing briefs for court to engineers developing design proposals, writers have used deadlines to help them put aside doubts and anxieties and to conclude their work, as every writer must. "Okay, it's not perfect, but it's the best I can do for now."

FOR WRITING AND DISCUSSION

Analyzing Your Own Writing Process

When you write, do you follow a process resembling the one we just described? Have you ever

- had a writing project grow out of your engagement with a problem or question?
- explored ideas by talking with others or by doing exploratory writing?
- made major changes to a draft because you changed your mind or otherwise discovered new ideas?
- revised a draft from a reader's perspective by consciously trying to imagine and respond to a reader's questions, confusions, and other reactions?
- road tested a draft by trying it out on readers and then revising it as a result of what they told you?

Working in groups or as a whole class, share stories about previous writing experiences that match or do not match the description of experienced writers' processes. To the extent that your present process differs, what strategies of experienced writers might you like to try?

SKILL 9.4 **Use peer reviews to help you think like an expert.**

One of the best ways to become a better reviser is to see your draft from a *reader*'s rather than a *writer*'s perspective. As a writer, you know what you mean; you are already inside your own head. But you need to see what your draft looks like to readers—that is, to people who are not inside your head.

A good way to learn this skill is to practice reading your classmates' drafts and have them read yours. In this section we offer advice on how to respond candidly to your classmates' drafts and how to participate in peer reviews.

Becoming a Helpful Reader of Classmates' Drafts

When you respond to a writer's draft, learn to make *readerly* rather than *writerly* comments. For example, instead of saying, "Your draft is disorganized," say, "I got lost when . . . . " Instead of saying, "This paragraph needs a topic sentence," say, "I had trouble seeing the point of this paragraph." In other words, describe your mental experience in trying to understand the draft rather than use technical terms to point out problem areas or to identify errors.

When you help a writer with a draft, your goal is both to point out where the draft needs more work and to brainstorm with the writer possible ways to improve the draft. Begin by reading the draft all the way through at a normal reading speed. As you read, make mental notes to help focus your feedback. We recommend that you also mark passages that you find confusing. Write "G!" for "Good" next to parts that you like. Write "?" next to places where you want to ask questions.

After you have read the draft, use the following strategies for making helpful responses, either in writing or in direct conversation with the writer.

Strategies for Responding Helpfully to a Classmate's Draft	
Kinds of Problems Noted	**Helpful Responses**
If the ideas in the draft seem thin or undeveloped, or if the draft is too short	<ul><li>Help the writer brainstorm for more ideas.</li><li>Help the writer add more examples, better details, more supporting data or arguments.</li></ul>
If you get confused or lost in some parts of the draft	<ul><li>Show the writer where you got confused or miscued in reading the draft ("I started getting lost here because I couldn't see why you were giving me this information" or "I thought you were going to say X, but then you said Y").</li><li>Have the writer talk through ideas to clear up confusing spots.</li></ul>

(continued)

Kinds of Problems Noted	Helpful Responses

If you get confused or lost at the "big-picture" level	• Help the writer sharpen the thesis: suggest that the writer view the thesis as the answer to a controversial or problematic question; ask the writer to articulate the question that the thesis answers.
	• Help the writer create an outline, tree diagram, or flowchart (see Skill 10.3).
	• Help the writer clarify the focus by asking him or her to complete these statements about purpose:
	  • The purpose of this paper is _____.
	  • The purpose of this section (paragraph) is _____.
	  • Before reading my paper, my reader will think X. But after reading my paper, my reader will think Y.

If you can understand the sentences but can't see the point	• Help the writer articulate the meaning by asking "So what?" questions, making the writer bring the point to the surface. ("I can understand what you are saying here but I don't quite understand why you are saying it. What do these details have to do with the topic sentence of the paragraph? Or what does this paragraph have to do with your thesis?") • Help the writer create transitions, new topic sentences, or other means of making points clear.
If you disagree with the ideas or think the writer has avoided alternative points of view	• Play devil's advocate to help the writer deepen and complicate ideas. • Show the writer specific places where you had queries or doubts.

Using a Generic Peer Review Guide

When participating in peer reviews, writers and reviewers often appreciate a list of guiding questions or checkpoints. What follows is a list of generic questions that can be used for peer-reviewing many different kinds of drafts. In each assignment chapter for Part 2 of this text, we have created additional peer review questions tailored specifically to that chapter's rhetorical aim and genres. For any given peer review session, your instructor may specify which generic or assignment-specific questions you are to use for the peer review.

Generic Peer Review Guide

For the writer

Prepare two or three questions you would like your peer reviewer to address while responding to your draft. The questions can focus on some aspect of your draft that you are uncertain about, on one or more sections where you particularly seek help or advice, on some feature that you particularly like about your draft, or on some part you especially wrestled with. Write out your questions and give them to your peer reviewer along with your draft.

For the reviewer

Basic overview: Read the draft at a normal reading speed from beginning to end. As you read do the following:

- Mark a "?" next to any passages that you find confusing, that somehow slow down your reading, or that raise questions in your mind.
- Mark a "G" next to any passages where you think the writing is particularly good, strong, or interesting.

Going into more depth: Prior to discussion with the writer, complete the following tasks:

- Identify at least one specific place in the draft where you got confused. Make notes for why you got confused, using readerly rather than writerly comments.
- Identify one place in the draft where you think the ideas are thin or need more development. Make discussion notes.
- Identify one place where you might write "So what?" after the passage. These are places where you don't understand the significance or importance of the writer's points. These are also places where you can't see how certain sentences connect to a topic sentence or how certain paragraphs or sections connect to the thesis statement.
- Identify at least one place where you could play devil's advocate or otherwise object to the writer's ideas. Make notes on the objections or alternative views that you will raise with the writer.

Evaluating the writer's argument: Look at the draft's effectiveness from the perspective of the classical rhetorical appeals:

- *Logos:* How effectively does the writer use reasons and evidence to support his or her claim? How effectively does the writer use details, particulars, examples, and other means as evidence to support points? How logical are the points and how clearly are they connected?
- *Ethos:* What kind of image does the writer project? How effective is the tone? How trustworthy, reliable, knowledgeable, and fair does this writer seem?
- *Pathos:* How effectively does the writer engage the audience's interest? How effectively does the writer tie into the audience's beliefs and values? To what extent does the writer make the reader care about the topic?

Noting problems of grammar and editing: Mark the draft wherever you notice problems in grammar, spelling, punctuation, documentation form, or other issues of mechanics.

Summing up: Create a consolidated summary of your review:
- Sum up the strengths of the draft.
- Identify two or three main weaknesses or problem areas.
- Make two or three suggestions for revision.

**FOR
WRITING
AND
DISCUSSION**

Practicing a Peer Review

Background: In the following exercise, we invite you to practice a peer review by responding to a student's draft ("Should the University Carpet the Dorm Rooms?" below) or to another draft provided by your instructor. The "Carpets" assignment asked students to take a stand on a local campus issue. Imagine that you have exchanged drafts with this student and that your task is to help this student improve the draft through both global and local revision.

Individual task: Read the draft carefully following the instructions in the "Generic Peer Review Guide." Write out your responses to the bulleted items under "Going into more depth," "Evaluating the writer's argument," and "Summing up."

Small group or whole class: Share your responses. Then turn to the following additional tasks:

1. With the instructor serving as a guide, practice explaining to the writer where or how you got confused while reading the draft. Readers often have difficulty explaining their reading experience to a writer. Let several class members role-play being the reader. Practice using language such as "I like the way this draft started because . . . ." "I got confused when . . . ." "I had to back up and reread when . . . ." "I saw your point here, but then I got lost again because . . . ." Writing theorist Peter Elbow calls such language a "movie of your mind."
2. Have several class members role-play being devil's advocates by arguing against the writer's thesis. Where are the ideas thin or weak?

SHOULD THE UNIVERSITY CARPET THE DORM ROOMS?

Tricia, a university student, came home exhausted from her work-study job. She took a blueberry pie from the refrigerator to satisfy her hunger and a tall glass of milk to quench her thirst. While trying to get comfortable on her bed, she tipped her snack over onto the floor. She cleaned the mess, but the blueberry and milk stains on her brand-new carpet could not be removed.

Tricia didn't realize how hard it was to clean up stains on a carpet. Luckily this was her own carpet.

A lot of students don't want carpets. Students constantly change rooms. The next person may not want carpet.

Some students say that since they pay to live on campus, the rooms should reflect a comfortable home atmosphere. Carpets will make the dorm more comfortable. The carpet will act as insulation and as a soundproofing system.

Paint stains cannot be removed from carpets. If the university carpets the rooms, the students will lose the privilege they have of painting their rooms any color. This would limit students' self-expression.

The carpets would be an institutional brown or gray. This would be ugly. With tile floors, the students can choose and purchase their own carpets to match their taste. You can't be an individual if you can't decorate your room to fit your personality.

According to Rachel Jones, Assistant Director of Housing Services, the cost will be $300 per room for the carpet and installation. Also the university will have to buy more vacuum cleaners. But will vacuum cleaners be all that is necessary to keep the carpets clean? We'll need shampoo machines too.

What about those stains that won't come off even with a shampoo machine? That's where the student will have to pay damage deposit costs.

There will be many stains on the carpet due to shaving cream fights, food fights, beverage parties, and smoking, all of which can damage the carpets.

Students don't take care of the dorms now. They don't follow the rules of maintaining their rooms. They drill holes into the walls, break mirrors, beds, and closet doors, and leave their food trays all over the floor.

If the university buys carpets our room rates will skyrocket. In conclusion, it is a bad idea for the university to buy carpets.

Participating in Peer Review Workshops

If you are willing to respond candidly to a classmate's draft—in a readerly rather than a writerly way—you will be a valuable participant in peer review workshops. In a typical workshop, classmates work in groups of two to six to respond to each other's rough drafts and offer suggestions for revisions. These workshops are most helpful when group members have developed sufficient levels of professionalism and trust to exchange candid responses. A frequent problem in peer review workshops is that classmates try so hard to avoid hurting each other's feelings that they provide vague, meaningless feedback. Saying, "Your paper's great. I really liked it. Maybe you could make it flow a little better" is much less helpful than saying, "Your issue about environmental pollution in the Antarctic is well defined in the first paragraph, but I got lost in the second paragraph when you began discussing penguin coloration."

Responsibilities of Peer Reviewers and Writers Learning to respond conscientiously and carefully to others' work may be the single most important thing you can do to improve your own writing. When you review a classmate's draft, you are not acting as a teacher, but simply as a fresh reader. You can help the writer appreciate what it's like to encounter his or her text for the first time. Your primary responsibility is to articulate your understanding of what the writer's words say to you and to identify places where you get confused, where you need more details, where you have doubts or queries, and so on.

When you play the role of writer during a workshop session, your responsibilities parallel those of your peer reviewers. You need to provide a legible rough draft, preferably typed and double-spaced, that doesn't baffle the reader with hard-to-follow corrections and confusing pagination. Your instructor may ask you to bring copies of your draft for all group members. During the workshop, your primary responsibility is to *listen*, taking in how others respond to your draft without becoming defensive. Many instructors also ask writers to formulate two or three specific questions about their drafts—questions they particularly want their reviewers to address. These questions might focus on something writers particularly like about their drafts or on specific problem areas or concerns.

Responding to Peer Reviews

After you and your classmates have gone over each other's papers and walked each other through the responses, everyone should identify two or three things about his or her draft that particularly need work. Before you leave the session, you should have some notion about how you want to revise your paper.

You may get mixed or contradictory responses from different reviewers. One reviewer may praise a passage that another finds confusing or illogical. Conflicting advice is a frustrating fact of life for all writers, whether students or professionals. Such disagreements reveal how readers cocreate a text with a writer: Each brings to the text a different background, set of values, and way of reading.

It is important to remember that you are in charge of your own writing. If several readers offer the same critique of a passage, then no matter how much you love that passage, you probably need to follow their advice. But when readers disagree, you have to make your own best judgment about whom to heed.

Once you have received advice from others, reread your draft again slowly and then develop a revision plan, allowing yourself time to make sweeping, global changes if needed. You also need to remember that you can never make your draft perfect. Plan when you will bring the process to a close so that you can turn in a finished product on time and get on with your other classes and your life.

 For support in learning this chapter's content, follow this path in MyCompLab: Resources ⇒ Writing ⇒ Writing Process ⇒ Drafting and Revising. Review the Instruction and Multimedia resources about drafting and revising, and then complete the Exercises and click on Gradebook to measure your progress.

COMPOSING AND REVISING CLOSED-FORM PROSE

10

Form is an arousing and fulfillment of desires. A work has form insofar as one part of it leads a reader to anticipate another part, to be gratified by the sequence.

—*Kenneth Burke, Rhetorician*

hapter 9 presents strategies for improving your revising process. In Chapter 10 we focus specifically on strategies for composing and revising closed-form prose. To help you avoid information overload, we recommend that you don't try to read this whole chapter in one sitting. The skills taught in this chapter are presented in ten self-contained lessons that can be read comfortably in half an hour or less. You will benefit most from these lessons if you focus on one skill at a time and then return to the lessons periodically as you progress through the term. Each lesson's advice will become increasingly meaningful and relevant as you gain experience as a writer. The first lesson (Skill 10.1) is intended as a theoretical overview to the rest of the chapter. The remaining lessons can then be assigned and read in any order your instructor desires.

In this chapter, you will learn how these skills can improve your writing:

- **SKILL 10.1**   Understand reader expectations.
- **SKILL 10.2**   Convert loose structures into thesis/support structures.
- **SKILL 10.3**   Plan and visualize your structure.
- **SKILL 10.4**   Set up reader expectations through effective titles and introductions.
- **SKILLS 10.5–10.7** Keep readers on track through the use of topic sentences, transitions, and the old/new contract.
- **SKILL 10.8**   Learn four expert moves for organizing and developing ideas.
- **SKILL 10.9**   Use effective tables, graphs, and charts to present numeric data.
- **SKILL 10.10**   Write effective conclusions.

Together these lessons will teach you strategies for making your closed-form prose reader-friendly, well structured, clear, and persuasive.

SKILL 10.1 **Understand reader expectations.**

In this opening lesson, we show you how to think like a reader. Imagine for a moment that your readers have only so much *reader energy*, which they can use either to follow your ideas or to puzzle over confusing passages.* In order to follow your ideas, skilled readers continually make predictions about where a text is heading based on cues provided by the writer. When readers get lost, the writer has often either failed to provide cues or has given misleading cues. "Whoa, you lost me on the turn," a reader might say. "How does this passage relate to what you just said?" In this lesson we explain what readers of closed-form prose expect from writers in order to predict where a text is heading. Specifically we show you that readers expect three things in a closed-form text:

- They expect unity and coherence.
- They expect old information before new information.
- They expect forecasting and fulfillment.

  Let's look at each in turn.

Unity and Coherence

Together the terms *unity* and *coherence* are defining characteristics of closed-form prose:

- **Unity** refers to the relationship between each part of an essay and the larger whole.
- **Coherence** refers to the relationship between adjacent sentences, paragraphs, and parts.

The following thought exercise will explore your own expectations for unity and coherence:

THOUGHT EXERCISE 1

Read the following two passages and try to explain why each fails to satisfy your expectations as a reader:

A. Recent research has given us much deeper—and more surprising—insights into the father's role in childrearing. My family is typical of the east side in that we never had much money. Their tongues became black and hung out of their mouths. The back-to-basics movement got a lot of press, fueled as it was by fears of growing illiteracy and cultural demise.

B. Recent research has given us much deeper—and more surprising—insights into the father's role in childrearing. Childrearing is a complex process that is frequently investigated by psychologists. Psychologists have also investigated sleep patterns and dreams. When we are dreaming, psychologists have shown, we are often reviewing recent events in our lives.

*For the useful term *reader energy*, we are indebted to George Gopen and Judith Swan, "The Science of Scientific Writing," *American Scientist* 78 (1990): 550–559. In addition, much of our discussion of writing in this chapter is indebted to the work of Joseph Williams, George Gopen, and Gregory Colomb. See especially Gregory G. Colomb and Joseph M. Williams, "Perceiving Structure in Professional Prose: A Multiply Determined Experience," in Lee Odell and Dixie Goswamie (eds.), *Writing in Nonacademic Settings* (New York: The Guilford Press, 1985), pp. 87–128.

If you are like most readers, Passage A comically frustrates your expectations because it is a string of random sentences. Because the sentences don't relate to each other or to a larger point, Passage A is neither unified nor coherent.

Passage B frustrates expectations in a subtler way. If you aren't paying attention, Passage B may seem to make sense because each sentence is linked to the one before it. But the individual sentences don't develop a larger whole: The topics switch from a father's role in childrearing to psychology to sleep patterns to the function of dreams. This passage has coherence without unity.

To fulfill a reader's expectations, then, a closed-form passage must be both unified and coherent:

> C. (*Unified and coherent*) Recent research has given us much deeper—and more surprising—insights into the father's role in childrearing. It shows that in almost all of their interactions with children, fathers do things a little differently from mothers. What fathers do—their special parenting style—is not only highly complementary to what mothers do but is by all indications important in its own right. [The passage continues by showing the special ways that fathers contribute to childrearing.]

This passage makes a unified point—that fathers have an important role in childrearing. Because all the parts relate to that whole (unity) and because the connections from sentence to sentence are clear (coherence), the passage satisfies our expectations: It makes sense.

Because achieving unity and coherence is a major goal in revising closed-form prose, we'll refer frequently to these concepts in later lessons.

Old before New

One dominant way that readers process information and register ideas is by moving from already known (old) information to new information. In a nutshell, this concept means that new material is meaningful to a reader only if it is linked to old material that is already meaningful. To illustrate this concept, consider the arrangement of names and numbers in a telephone directory. Because we read from left to right, we want people's names in the left column and the telephone numbers in the right column. A person's name is the old, familiar information we already know and the number is the new, unknown information that we seek. If the numbers were in the left column and the names in the right, we would have to read backward.

You can see the same old-before-new principle at work in the following thought exercise:

THOUGHT EXERCISE 2

You are a passenger on an airplane flight into Chicago and need to transfer to Flight 16 to Memphis. As you descend into Chicago, the flight attendant announces transfer gates. Which of the following formats is easier for you to process? Why?

Option A		Option B	
To Atlanta on Flight 29	Gate C12	Gate C12	Flight 29 to Atlanta
To Dallas on Flight 35	Gate C25	Gate C25	Flight 35 to Dallas
To Memphis on Flight 16	Gate B20	Gate B20	Flight 16 to Memphis

If you are like most readers, you prefer Option A, which puts old information before new. In this case, the old/known information is our destination (cities arranged alphabetically) and perhaps our flight number (To Memphis on Flight 16). The new/unknown information is Gate B20. Option B causes us to expend more energy than does Option A because it forces us to hold the number of each gate in memory until we hear its corresponding city and flight number. Whereas Option A allows us to relax until we hear the word "Memphis," Option B forces us to concentrate intensely on each gate number until we find the meaningful one.

Old before New at the Essay Level The principle of old before new has great explanatory power for writers. At the level of the whole essay, this principle helps writers establish the main structural frame and ordering principle of their argument. An argument's frame derives from the writer's purpose to change some aspect of the reader's view of the topic. The reader's original view of the topic—what we might call the common, expected, or ordinary view—constitutes old/known/familiar material. The writer's surprising view constitutes the new/unknown/unfamiliar material. The writer's hope is to move readers from their original view to the writer's new and different view. By understanding what constitutes old/familiar information to readers, the writer can determine how much background to provide, how to anticipate readers' objections, and how to structure material by moving from the old to the new. We treat these matters in more depth in Skill 10.4, on writing effective titles and introductions.

Old before New at the Sentence Level At the sentence level, the principle of old before new also helps writers create coherence between adjacent parts and sentences. Most sentences in an essay should contain both an old element and a new element. To create coherence, the writer begins with the old material, which links back to something earlier, and then puts the new material at the end of the sentence. (See the discussion of the old/new contract in Skill 10.7.)

Forecasting and Fulfillment

Finally, readers of closed-form prose expect writers to forecast what is coming and then to fulfill those forecasts. To appreciate what we mean by forecasting and fulfillment, try one more thought exercise:

THOUGHT EXERCISE 3

Although the following paragraph describes a simple procedure in easy-to-follow sentences, most readers still scratch their heads in bewilderment. Why? What makes the passage difficult to understand?

The procedure is actually quite simple. First, you arrange things into different groups. Of course, one pile may be sufficient depending on how much there is to do. If you have to go somewhere else due to lack of facilities, that is the next step; otherwise, you are pretty well set. Next you operate the machines according to the instructions. After the procedure is completed, one arranges the materials into different groups again. Then they can be put in their appropriate places. Eventually, they will be used once more and the whole cycle will have to be repeated. However, that is part of life.

Most readers report being puzzled about the paragraph's topic. Because the opening sentence doesn't provide enough context to tell them what to expect, the paragraph makes no forecast that can be fulfilled. Now try rereading the paragraph, but this time substitute the following opening sentence:

> The procedure for washing clothes is actually quite simple.

With the addition of "for washing clothes," the sentence provides a context that allows you to predict and understand what's coming. In the language of cognitive psychologists, this new opening sentence provides a schema for interpretation. A *schema* is the reader's mental picture of a structure for upcoming material. The new opening sentence allows you as reader to say mentally, "This paragraph will describe a procedure for washing clothes and argue that it is simple." When the schema proves accurate, you experience the pleasure of prediction and fulfillment. In the language of rhetorician Kenneth Burke, the reader's experience of form is "an arousing and fulfillment of desires."

What readers expect from a closed-form text, then, is an ability to predict what is coming as well as regular fulfillment of those predictions. Writers forecast what is coming in a variety of ways:

- by writing effective titles
- by writing effective introductions with forecasting cues
- by placing topic sentences near the beginning of paragraphs
- by creating effective transitions and mapping statements
- by using effective headings and subheadings if appropriate for the genre.

To meet their readers' needs for predictions and fulfillment, closed-form writers start and end with the big picture. They tell readers where they are going before they start the journey, they refer to this big picture at key transition points, and they refocus on the big picture in their conclusion.

SKILL 10.2 **Convert loose structures into thesis/support structures.**

In Skill 10.1 we described readers' expectations for unity and coherence, old information before new, and forecasting and fulfillment. In academic contexts, readers also expect closed-form prose to have a thesis/support structure. As we explained in Chapter 2, most closed-form academic writing—especially writing with the aim of analysis or persuasion—is governed by a contestable or risky thesis statement. Because developing and supporting a thesis is complex work requiring much critical thought, writers sometimes retreat into loose structures that are easier to compose than a thesis-based argument with points and particulars.

In this lesson we help you better understand thesis-based writing by contrasting it with prose that looks like thesis-based writing but isn't. We show you three common ways in which inexperienced writers give the appearance of writing thesis-based prose while actually retreating from the rigors of making and developing an argument. Avoiding the pitfalls of these loose structures can go a long way toward improving your performance on most college writing assignments.

Avoiding *And Then* Writing, or Chronological Structure

Chronological structure, often called "narrative," is the most common organizing principle of open-form prose. It may also be used selectively in closed-form prose to support a point. But sometimes the writer begins recounting the details of a story and chronological order takes over, driving out the thesis-based structure of points and particulars.

To a large degree, chronological order is the default mode we fall into when we aren't sure how to organize material. For example, if you were asked to analyze a fictional character, you might slip into a plot summary instead. In much the same way, you might substitute historical chronology ("First A happened, then B happened ...") for historical analysis ("B happened because A happened ..."); or you might give a chronological recounting of your research ("First I discovered A, then I discovered B ...") instead of organizing your material into an argument ("I question A's account of this phenomenon on the grounds of my recent discovery of B ...").

The tendency toward loose chronological structure is revealed in the following example from a student's essay on Shakespeare's *The Tempest*. This excerpt is from the introduction of the student's first draft:

> #### PLOT SUMMARY— *AND THEN* WRITING
>
> Prospero cares deeply for his daughter. In the middle of the play Prospero acts like a gruff father and makes Ferdinand carry logs in order to test his love for Miranda and Miranda's love for him. In the end, though, Prospero is a loving father who rejoices in his daughter's marriage to a good man.

Here the student seems simply to retell the play's plot without any apparent thesis. (The body of her rough draft primarily retold the same story in more detail.) However, during an office conference, the instructor discovered that the student regarded her sentence about Prospero's being a loving father as her thesis. In fact, the student had gotten in an argument with a classmate over whether Prospero was a good person or an evil one. The instructor helped her convert her draft into a thesis/support structure:

> #### REVISED INTRODUCTION—THESIS/SUPPORT STRUCTURE
>
> Many persons believe that Prospero is an evil person in the play. They claim that Prospero exhibits a harsh, destructive control over Miranda and also, like Faust, seeks superhuman knowledge through his magic. However, I contend that Prospero is a kind and loving father.

Chapter 2, Concept 5, discusses this principle in depth: "A strong thesis statement surprises readers with something new or challenging."

This revised version implies a problem (What kind of father is Prospero?), presents a view that the writer wishes to change (Prospero is harsh and hateful), and asserts a contestable thesis (Prospero is a loving father). The body of her paper can now be converted from plot summary to an argument with reasons and evidence supporting her claim that Prospero is loving.

This student's revision from an *and then* to a thesis/support structure is typical of many writers' experience. Because recounting events chronologically is a natural way to organize, many writers—even very experienced ones—lapse into long stretches of *and then* writing in their rough drafts. However, experienced writers have learned to recognize these *and then* sections in their drafts and to rework this material into a closed-form, thesis-based structure.

Avoiding *All About* Writing, or Encyclopedic Structure

Whereas *and then* writing turns essays into stories by organizing details chronologically, *all about* writing turns essays into encyclopedia articles by piling up details in heaps. When *all about* writing organizes these heaps into categories, it can appear to be well organized: "Having told you everything I learned about educational opportunities in Cleveland, I will now tell you everything I learned about the Rock and Roll Hall of Fame." But the categories do not function as points and particulars in support of a thesis. Rather, like the shelving system in a library, they are simply ways of arranging information for convenient retrieval, not a means of building a hierarchical structure.

An Example of "All About" Structure To illustrate the differences between *all about* writing and thesis-based writing, consider the case of two students choosing to write term papers on the subject of female police officers. One student is asked simply to write "all about" the topic; the other is asked to pose and investigate some problem related to female police officers and to support a thesis addressing that problem. In all likelihood, the first student would produce an initial outline with headings such as the following:

I. History of women in police roles
   A. Female police or soldiers in ancient times
   B. 19th century (Calamity Jane)
   C. 1900s–1960
   D. 1960–present
II. How female police officers are selected and trained
III. A typical day in the life of a female police officer
IV. Achievements and acts of heroism of female police officers
V. What the future holds for female police officers

Such a paper is a data dump that places into categories all the information the writer has uncovered. It is riskless, and, except for occasional new information, surpriseless. In contrast, when a student focuses on a significant question—one that grows out of the writer's own interests and demands engagement—the writing can be quite compelling.

Conversion to Problem-Thesis Structure Consider the case of a student, Lynnea, who wrote a research paper entitled "Women Police Officers: Should Size and Strength Be Criteria for Patrol Duty?" Her essay begins with a group of male police officers complaining about being assigned to patrol duty with a new female officer, Connie Jones (not her real name), who is four feet ten inches tall and weighs ninety pounds. Here is the rest of the introduction to Lynnea's essay.

FROM LYNNEA'S INTRODUCTION

Connie Jones has just completed police academy training and has been assigned to patrol duty in _____. Because she is so small, she has to have a booster seat in her patrol car and has been given a special gun, since she can barely manage to pull the trigger of a standard police-issue .38 revolver. Although she passed the physical requirements at the academy, which involved speed and endurance running, situps, and monkey bar tests, most of the officers in her department doubt her ability to perform competently as a patrol officer. But nevertheless she is on patrol because men and women receive equal assignments in most of today's police forces. But is this a good policy? Can a person who is significantly smaller and weaker than her peers make an effective patrol officer?

Lynnea examined all the evidence she could find—through library and field research (interviewing police officers)—and arrived at the following thesis: "Because concern for public safety overrides all other concerns, police departments should set stringent size and strength requirements for patrol officers, even if these criteria exclude many women." This thesis has plenty of tension because it sets limits on equal rights for women. Because Lynnea considers herself a feminist, it caused her considerable distress to advocate setting these limits and placing public safety ahead of gender equity. The resulting essay was engaging precisely because of the tension it creates and the controversy it engenders.

Avoiding *Engfish* Writing, or Structure without Surprise

Unlike the chronological story and the *all about* paper, the **engfish** essay has a thesis.* But the thesis is a riskless truism supported with predictable reasons—often structured as the three body paragraphs in a traditional five-paragraph theme. It is fill-in-the-blank writing: "The food service is bad for three reasons. First, it is bad because the food is not tasty. Blah, blah, blah about tasteless food. Second, it is bad because it is too expensive. Blah, blah, blah about the expense." And so on. The writer is on autopilot and is not contributing to a real conversation about a real question. In some situations, writers use *engfish* intentionally: bureaucrats and politicians may want to avoid saying something risky; students may want to avoid writing about complex matters that they fear they do not fully understand. In the end, using *engfish* is bad not because what you say is *wrong*, but because what you say couldn't *possibly be* wrong. To avoid *engfish*, stay focused on the need to surprise your reader.

---

*The term *engfish* was coined by the textbook writer Ken Macrorie to describe a fishy kind of canned prose that bright but bored students mechanically produce to please their teachers. See Ken Macrorie, *Telling Writing* (Rochelle Park, NJ: Hayden Press, 1970).

**FOR
WRITING
AND
DISCUSSION**

Developing a Thesis/Support Structure

As a class, choose a topic from popular culture such as reality TV shows, Twitter, rap, fad diets, legalizing marijuana, or a topic similar to these.

1. Working as a whole class or in small groups, give examples of how you might write about this topic in an *and then* way, an *all about* way, and an *engfish* way.
2. Then develop one or more questions about the topic that could lead to thesis/support writing. What contestable theses can your class create?

SKILL 10.3 **Plan and visualize your structure.**

As we explained in Skill 10.2, closed-form writing supports a contestable thesis through a hierarchical network of points and particulars. One way to visualize this structure is to outline its skeleton, an exercise that makes visually clear that not all points are on equal levels. The highest-level point is an essay's thesis statement, which is usually supported by several main points that are in turn supported by subpoints and sub-subpoints, all of which are supported by their own particulars. In this lesson we show you how to create such a hierarchical structure for your own papers and how to visualize this structure through an outline, tree diagram, or flowchart.

At the outset, we want to emphasize that structural diagrams are not rigid molds, but flexible planning devices that evolve as your thinking shifts and changes. The structure of your final draft may be substantially different from your initial scratch outline. In fact, we want to show you how your evolving outlines or diagrams can help you generate more ideas and reshape your structure.

With this background, we now proceed to a sequence of steps you can take to plan and visualize a structure.

Making Lists of "Chunks" and a Scratch Outline Early in the Writing Process

Early in the writing process, before you know how to organize your material, you know that you have certain ideas, sections, parts, or "chunks" that you want to include somewhere. Just making a list of these chunks will help you get started. Here is a list of chunks by student writer James Gardiner early in his process of writing a researched argument on online social networks:

> We first introduced James's research problem in Chapter 2, p. 30; James's final paper is shown in Chapter 13, pp. 340–348.

CHUNKS THAT I WANT TO INCLUDE SOMEWHERE IN MY PAPER

- Section on the popularity of online social networks (OSNs)
- Tamyra Pierce article that OSNs can lead to bad grades
- Examples of athletes embarrassing team by putting drinking pictures on Facebook
- One of my research article's argument about OSNs and narcissism
- Danah Boyd's argument that OSNs are positive and provide a place to experiment with identity

- Story of college student who posted a revealing picture of herself as Catwoman and was later embarrassed
- The term "Facebook trance"

Once you make a list of chunks, you can begin thinking about which of them are high-level points and which are details in support of a point. Before writing a rough draft, many writers like to make a brief scratch outline to help with planning. Here is James's initial scratch outline.

JAMES'S INITIAL SCRATCH OUTLINE

- Attention-grabber (maybe story of my watching friends use Facebook or some kind of statistic)
- Evidence of popularity of OSNs
- Show the good side of OSNs (Boyd's argument, statements from my friends)
- Then move to bad side (use term "Facebook trance")
  - Narcissism
  - Embarrassing cases (Catwoman, athletes)
  - Lower grades

"Nutshelling" Your Argument as an Aid to Finding a Structure

As you begin drafting, you will find your ideas gradually becoming clearer and more structured. You can accelerate this process through the following short exercise that will help you "nutshell" your argument. The six prompts in this exercise invite you to look at your argument from different perspectives. We recommend that you write your responses to each prompt as a preliminary step in helping you visualize your structure.

EXERCISE FOR NUTSHELLING YOUR ARGUMENT

1. What puzzle or problem initiated your thinking about X?
2. *Template: Many people think X, but I am going to argue Y.*

   Before reading my paper, my readers will think X: [specify what you imagine your readers initially think about your topic] _____.

   But after reading my paper, my readers will think Y: [specify the new or different way readers will think after finishing your paper] _____.
3. The purpose of my paper is _____.
4. My paper addresses the following question: _____.
5. My one-sentence summary answer to this question is this: _____.
6. A tentative title for my paper is this: _____.

   Here are James Gardiner's responses to these prompts:

1. I was initially puzzled why so many students used online social networks. I didn't have a profile on Facebook or MySpace and wondered what the advantages and disadvantages of OSNs might be.
2. Before reading my paper, my readers will believe that OSNs have few detrimental consequences. After reading my paper, my readers will appreciate the potential dangers of OSNs.

3. The purpose of this paper is to point out potential negative consequences of OSNs.
4. What are the possible negative consequences of OSNs?
5. Overuse of OSNs can contribute to a decline in grades, to a superficial view of relationships, to an increase in narcissism, and to possible future embarrassment.
6. Some Dangers of Online Social Networks

Articulating a Working Thesis with Main Points

Once you have nutshelled your argument, you are ready to create a working thesis statement that includes main supporting points. These supporting points help you visualize an emerging structure. Here is James Gardiner's working thesis statement.

> Despite the benefits of online social networks such as MySpace or Facebook, these networks can have negative consequences such as a decline in grades, a superficial view of relationships, an increase in narcissism, and possible future embarrassment.

Chapter 2, Concept 5, explains in detail how a thesis statement needs to surprise readers with something new or challenging.

Using Complete Sentences in Outlines to Convey Meanings

An effective working outline helps you organize *meanings*, not topics. Note that in the outline, tree diagram, and flowchart that follow, James Gardiner uses *complete sentences* rather than phrases in the high-level slots. Because sentences have both subjects and verbs, they can make a point, which asserts a meaning, unlike a phrase, which identifies a topic but doesn't make an assertion about it. Here are examples:

> **Phrase:** Lower grades
> **Sentence:** OSNs can have a negative effect on grades.
>
> **Phrase:** OSNs and narcissism
> **Sentence:** OSNs may contribute to a rise in narcissism among today's young people.

Any point—whether a thesis, a main point, or a subpoint—is a contestable assertion that requires its own particulars for support. By using complete sentences rather than phrases in an outline, the writer is forced to articulate the point of each section of the emerging argument.

Sketching Your Structure Using an Outline, Tree Diagram, or Flowchart

Once you have created a working thesis statement, you can sketch your structure to show how points, subpoints, and particulars can be arranged to support your thesis. We offer you three different ways to visualize your argument: outlines, tree diagrams, and flowcharts. Use whichever strategy best fits your way of thinking and perceiving.

Outlines The most common way of visualizing structure is the traditional outline, which uses letters and numerals to indicate levels of points, subpoints, and particulars. If you prefer outlines, we recommend that you use the outlining feature of your word processing program, which allows you to move and insert material and change heading levels with great flexibility.

Figure 10.1 shows the first half of James Gardiner's detailed outline for his argument. Note that, except in the introduction, James uses complete sentences rather than phrases for each level.

FIGURE 10.1 James Gardiner's Outline for First Half of Paper

Thesis: Despite the benefits of online social networks like MySpace or Facebook, these networks can have negative consequences such as a decline in grades, a superficial view of relationships, an increase in narcissism, and possible future embarrassment.

I Introduction
   A Attenion-grabber about walking into any computer lab
   B Media evidence shows a large increase in the popularity of OSNs among young people.
   C The term "Facebook Trance" indicates possible harms of OSNs.
   D Thesis paragraph

II Admittedly, OSNs have positive benefits.
   A They provide a way to stay in close contact with friends and family.
   B Researcher Danah Boyd says that OSNs give young people a place to experiment with identities and voices.
   C They provide a way to get quick additional information about someone you've met in class or at a party.

III Despite these benefits, OSNs have potential negative consequences.
   A They can have a negative effect on grades.
      1 Researcher Tamyra Pierce found that high school students with MySpace accounts were more likely to report a decline in grades than those without accounts.
      2 Her data show heavy use of OSNs among as many as 59 percent of students, taking time away from school, work, and sleep.
      3 Other writers apply the high school study to college.
   B OSNs have a tendency to promote superficial relationships.
      1 A study by Chou, Condron, and Belland shows that for some users, online relationships can result in problems with real-life interpersonal relationships.
      2 Another researcher, Matsuba, found that online relationships might hinder some people from developing an adult identity.
      3 A possible contributing factor to the superficiality of online relationships might be the absence of nonverbal communication.
   C OSNs might also contribute to a rise in narci

Tree Diagrams A tree diagram displays a hierarchical structure visually, using horizontal and vertical space instead of letters and numbers. Figure 10.2 shows James's argument as a tree diagram. His thesis is at the top of the tree. His main reasons, written as point sentences, appear as branches beneath his claim. Supporting evidence and arguments are subbranches beneath each reason.

Unlike outlines, tree diagrams allow us to *see* the hierarchical relationship of points and particulars. When you develop a point with subpoints or particulars, you move down the tree. When you switch to a new point, you move across the tree to make a new branch. Our own teaching experience suggests that for many writers, this visual/spatial technique produces fuller, more detailed, and more logical arguments than does a traditional outline.

Flowcharts A flowchart presents the sequence of sections as separate boxes, inside which (or next to which) the writer notes the material needed to fill each box. A flowchart of James's essay is shown in Figure 10.3.

FIGURE 10.2 James's Tree Diagram

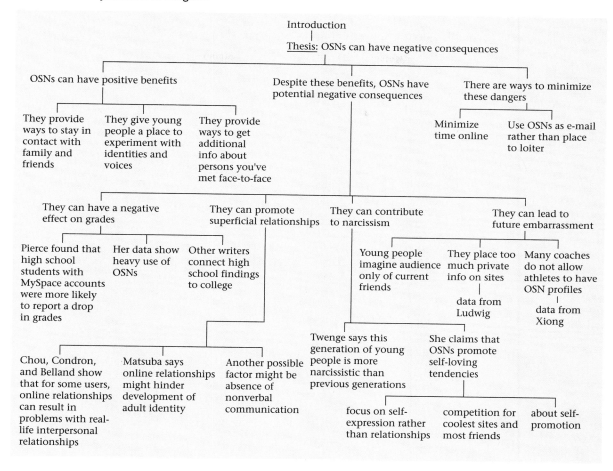

Letting the Structure Evolve

Once you have sketched out an initial structural diagram, use it to generate ideas. Tree diagrams are particularly helpful because they invite you to place question marks on branches to "hold open" spots for new points or supporting particulars. If you have only two main points, for example, you could draw a third main branch and place a question mark under it to encourage you to think of another supporting idea. Likewise, if a branch has few supporting particulars, add question marks beneath it. The trick is to think of your structural diagrams as evolving sketches rather than rigid blueprints. As your ideas grow and change, revise your structural diagram, adding or removing points, consolidating and refocusing sections, moving parts around, or filling in details.

FIGURE 10.3 James's Flowchart

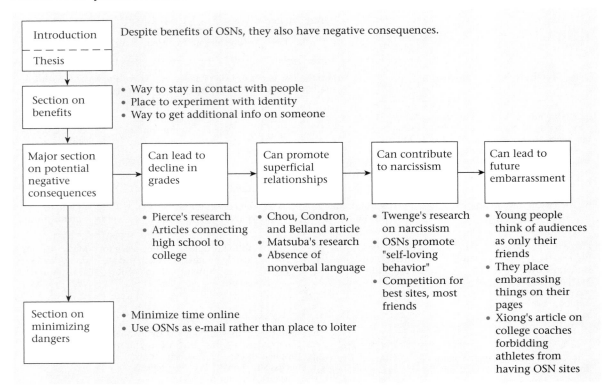

Making Outlines, Tree Diagrams, or Flowcharts

Working individually, complete the outline or the tree diagram for James Gardiner's researched argument. Use complete sentences in the outline. Then convene in small groups to compare your outlines. Finally, share points of view on which method of representing structure—outlines, tree diagrams, or flowcharts—works best for different members of the class.

SKILL 10.4 Set up reader expectations through effective titles and introductions.

Because effective titles and introductions give readers a big-picture overview of a paper's argument, writers often can't compose them until they have finished one or more drafts. But as soon as you know your essay's big picture, you'll find that writing titles and introductions follows some general principles that are easy to learn.

Avoiding the "Topic Title" and the "Funnel Introduction"

Some students have been taught an opening strategy, sometimes called the "funnel," that encourages students to start with broad generalizations and then narrow down to their topics. This strategy often leads to a "topic title" (which names the topic area but doesn't forecast the problem being addressed or the surprise the writer will bring to readers) and vapid generalizations in the opening of the introduction, as the following example shows:

B. F. SKINNER

Since time immemorial people have pondered the question of freedom. The great philosophers of Greece and Rome asked what it means to be free, and the question has echoed through the ages up until the present day. One modern psychologist who asked this question was B. F. Skinner, who wanted to study whether humans had free will or were programmed by their environment to act the way they did. . . .

Here the writer eventually gets to his subject, B. F. Skinner, but so far presents no sense of what the point of the essay will be or why the reader should be interested. A better approach is to hook your readers immediately with an effective title and a problem-posing introduction.

Hooking Your Reader with an Effective Title

Good titles follow the principle of old before new information that we introduced in Skill 10.1. A good title needs to have something old (a word or phrase that hooks into a reader's existing interests) and something new (a word or phrase that forecasts the writer's problematic question, thesis, or purpose). Here are examples of effective titles from two student essays in this textbook:

"Why Facebook Might Not Be Good for You"
"Paintball: Promoter of Violence or Healthy Fun?"

The old information in these titles ("Facebook" and "Paintball") ties into readers' preexisting knowledge or interests. But the titles also indicate each essay's direction or purpose—the new information that promises to expand or challenge the readers' views. The first writer will argue that Facebook might be harmful in some way; the second writer will explore the problem of violence versus fun in paintball.

As these examples show, your title should provide a brief overview of what your paper is about. Academic titles are typically longer and more detailed than are titles in popular magazines. There are three basic approaches that academic writers take, as shown in the following strategies chart.

Strategies for Writing Titles of Academic Papers

What to Do	Examples
State or imply the question that your essay addresses.	Will Patriarchal Management Survive Beyond the Decade?
	The Impact of Cell Phones on Motor Vehicle Fatalities [Implied question: What is the impact . . . ?]

(continued)

What to Do	Examples
State or imply, often in abbreviated form, your essay's thesis.	The Writer's Audience Is Always a Fiction How Foreign Aid Can Foster Democratization in Authoritarian Regimes
Use a two-part title separated by a colon: • On the left, present key words from your essay's issue or problem or a "mystery phrase" that arouses interest. • On the right, place the essay's question, thesis, or summary of purpose.	Deep Play: Notes on a Balinese Cockfight Coping with Hurricane Katrina: Psychological Stress and Resilience among African-American Evacuees

Such titles might seem overly formal to you, but they indicate how much an academic writer wishes to preview an article's big picture. Although the titles in popular magazines may be more informal, they often use these same strategies. Here are some titles from popular magazines such as *Redbook* and *Forbes*:

"Is the Coffee Bar Trend About to Peak?" (question)
"A Man *Can* Take Maternity Leave—And Love It" (abbreviated thesis)
"Feed Your Face: Why Your Complexion Needs Vitamins" (two parts linked by colon)

Composing a title for your essay can help you find your focus when you get bogged down in the middle of a draft. Thinking about your title forces you to *nutshell* your ideas by seeing your project's big picture. It causes you to reconsider your purpose and to think about what's old and what's new for your audience.

From Old to New: The General Principle of Closed-Form Introductions

In this section, we elaborate on the rhetorical concept introduced in Chapter 2, Concept 6: "In closed-form prose, an introduction starts with the problem, not the thesis."

Just as effective titles present something old and something new, so do dynamic and powerful introductions. Old information is something your readers already know and find interesting before they start reading your essay. New information is the surprise of your argument, the unfamiliar material that you add to your readers' understanding.

Because the writer's thesis statement forecasts the new information the paper will present, a thesis statement for a closed-form essay typically comes *at the end of the introduction*. What precedes the thesis is typically the problem or question that the thesis addresses—the old information that the reader needs in order to understand the conversation that the thesis joins. A typical closed-form introduction has the following shape:

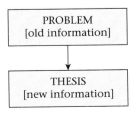

The length and complexity of your introduction is a function of how much your reader already knows and cares about the question or problem your paper addresses. The function of an introduction is to capture the reader's interest in the first few sentences, to identify and explain the question or problem that the essay addresses, to provide any needed background information, and to present the thesis. You can leave out any of the first three elements if the reader is already hooked on your topic and already knows the question you are addressing. For example, in an essay exam you can usually start with your thesis statement because you can assume the instructor already knows the question and finds it interesting.

To illustrate how an effective closed-form introduction takes the reader from the question to the thesis, consider how the following student writer revised his introduction to a paper on Napster.com:

ORIGINAL INTRODUCTION (CONFUSING)

Napster is all about sharing, not stealing, as record companies and some *[Thesis statement]* musicians would like us to think. Napster is an online program that was released in October of '99. Napster lets users easily search for and trade mp3s—compressed, high-quality music files that can be produced from a CD. Napster is the leading file *[Background on Napster]* sharing community; it allows users to locate and share music. It also provides instant messaging, chat rooms, an outlet for fans to identify new artists, and a forum to communicate their interests.

Most readers find this introduction confusing. The writer begins with his thesis statement before the reader is introduced to the question that the thesis addresses. He seems to assume that his reader is already a part of the Napster conversation, and yet in the next sentences, he gives background on Napster. If the reader needs background on Napster, then the reader also needs background on the Napster controversy. In rethinking his assumptions about old-versus-new information for his audience, this writer decided he wants to reach general newspaper readers who may have heard about a lawsuit against Napster and are interested in the issue but aren't sure of what Napster is or how it works. Here is his revised introduction:

REVISED INTRODUCTION (CLEARER)

Several months ago the rock band Metallica filed a lawsuit against Napster.com, *[Triggers readers' memory of lawsuit]* an online program that lets users easily search for and trade mp3s—compressed, high-quality music files that can be produced from a CD. Napster.com has been *[Background on Napster]* wildly popular among music lovers because it creates a virtual community where users can locate and share music. It also provides instant messaging, chat rooms, an *[Clarification of problem (Implied question: Should Napster be shut down?)]* outlet for fans to identify new artists, and a forum to communicate their interests. But big-name bands like Metallica, alarmed at what they see as lost revenues, claim that Napster.com is stealing their royalties. However, Napster is all about sharing, not stealing, as some musicians would like us to think. *[Thesis]*

This revised introduction fills in the old information the reader needs in order to recall and understand the problem; then it presents the thesis.

Typical Elements of a Closed-Form Introduction

Now that you understand the general principle of closed-form introductions, let's look more closely at its four typical features or elements:

1. ***An opening attention-grabber.*** If you aren't sure that your reader is already interested in your problem, you can begin with an attention-grabber (what journalists call the "hook" or "lead"), which is typically a dramatic vignette, a startling fact or statistic, an arresting quotation, an interesting scene, or something else that taps into your reader's interests. Attention-grabbers are uncommon in academic prose (where you assume your reader will be initially engaged by the problem itself) but frequently used in popular prose.

2. ***Explanation of the question to be investigated.*** If your reader already knows about the problem and cares about it, then you need merely to summarize it. This problem or question is the starting point of your argument. If you aren't sure whether your audience fully understands the question or fully cares about it, then you need to explain it in more detail, showing why it is both problematic and significant.

3. ***Background information.*** In order to understand the conversation you are joining, readers sometimes need background information such as a definition of key terms, a summary of events leading up to the problem, factual details needed for explaining the context of the problem, and so forth. In academic papers, this background often includes a review of what other scholars have said about the problem.

4. ***A preview of where your paper is heading.*** The final element of a closed-form introduction sketches the big picture of your essay by previewing the kind of surprise or challenge readers can expect and giving them a sense of the whole. This preview is initially new information for your readers (this is why it comes at the end of the introduction). Once stated, however, it becomes old information that readers will use to locate their position in their journey through your argument. By predicting what's coming, this preview initiates the pleasurable process of forecasting/fulfillment that we discussed in Skill 10.1. Writers typically forecast the whole by stating their thesis, but they can also use a purpose statement or a blueprint statement to accomplish the same end. These strategies are the subject of the next section.

Forecasting the Whole with a Thesis Statement, Purpose Statement, or Blueprint Statement

The most succinct way to forecast the whole is to state your thesis directly. Student writers often ask how detailed their thesis statements should be and whether it is permissible, sometimes, to delay revealing the thesis until the conclusion—an open-form move that gives papers a more exploratory, mystery-novel feel. It is useful, then, to outline briefly some of your choices as a writer. To illustrate a writer's options for forecasting the whole, we use James Gardiner's research paper on online social networks.

To see the choices James Gardiner actually made, see his complete essay on pp. 340–348.

Strategies for Forecasting the Whole Paper

Options	What to Do	Examples
Short thesis	State claim without summarizing your supporting argument or forecasting your structure.	Online social networks can have negative consequences.
Detailed thesis	Summarize whole argument; may begin with an *although* clause that summarizes the view you are trying to change.	Despite the benefits of online social networks like MySpace or Facebook, these networks can have negative consequences such as a decline in grades, a superficial view of relationships, an increase in narcissism, and possible future embarrassment.
Purpose statement	State your purpose or intention without summarizing the argument. A purpose statement typically begins with a phrase such as "My purpose is to ..." or "In the following paragraphs I wish to ..."	My purpose in this essay is to show the potential negative consequences of online social networks.
Blueprint or mapping statement	Describe the structure of your essay by announcing the number of main parts and describing the function or purpose of each one.	After discussing briefly the positive benefits of online social networks, I will describe four potential negative consequences. Finally I will suggest ways to avoid these consequences by using OSNs wisely.
Combination of elements	Include two or more of these elements. In long essays, academic writers sometimes have a purpose statement followed by a detailed thesis and blueprint statement.	[James's essay is not long enough nor complex enough to need an extensive multisentence overview.]
Thesis question only *[Implies a reflective or exploratory paper rather than an argument]*	State the question only, without initially implying your answer. This open-form strategy invites the reader to join the writer in a mutual search.	Although online social networks are widely popular, something about them makes me feel uncomfortable. I am wondering if there are unappreciated risks as well as benefits associated with OSNs.

Which of these options should a writer choose? There are no firm rules to help you answer this question. How much you forecast in the introduction and where you reveal your thesis is a function of your purpose, audience, and genre. The more you forecast, the clearer your argument is and the easier it is to read quickly. You minimize the demands on readers' time by giving them the gist of your argument in the introduction, making it easier to skim your essay if they don't have time for a thorough reading. The less you forecast, the more demands you make on readers' time: You invite them, in effect, to accompany you through the twists and turns of your own thinking process, and you risk losing them if they become confused, lost, or bored. For these reasons, academic writing is generally closed form and aims at maximum clarity. In many rhetorical contexts, however, more open forms are appropriate.

Chapter 1, Concept 1, gives more advice on when to choose closed or open forms.

If you choose a closed-form structure, we can offer some advice on how much to forecast. Readers sometimes feel insulted by too much forecasting, so include only what is needed for clarity. For short papers, readers usually don't need to have the complete supporting argument forecast in the introduction. In longer papers, however, or in especially complex ones, readers appreciate having the whole argument forecast at the outset. Academic writing in particular tends to favor explicit and often detailed forecasting.

FOR WRITING AND DISCUSSION

Revising a Title and Introduction

Individual task: Choose an essay you are currently working on or have recently completed and examine your title and introduction. Ask yourself these questions:

- What audience am I imagining? What do I assume are my readers' initial interests that will lead them to read my essay (the old information I must hook into)? What is new in my essay?
- Do I have an attention-grabber? Why or why not?
- Where do I state or imply the question or problem that my essay addresses?
- Do I explain why the question is problematic and significant? Why or why not?
- For my audience to understand the problem, do I provide too much background information, not enough, or just the right amount?
- What strategies do I use to forecast the whole?

Based on your analysis of your present title and introduction, revise as appropriate.

Group task: Working with a partner or in small groups, share the changes you made in your title or introduction and explain why you made the changes.

SKILL 10.5 Create effective topic sentences for paragraphs.

In our lesson on outlining (Skill 10.3) we suggested that you write complete sentences rather than phrases for the high-level slots of the outline in order to articulate the *meaning* or *point* of each section of your argument. In this lesson we show you how to place these points where readers expect them: near the beginning of the sections or paragraphs they govern.

When you place points before particulars, you follow the same principle illustrated in our old-before-new exercise (Skill 10.1) with the flight attendant announcing the name of the city before the departure gate (the city is the old information, the departure gate the new information). When you first state the point, it is the new information that the next paragraph or section will develop. Once you have stated it, it becomes old information that helps readers understand the meaning of the particulars that follow. If you withhold the point until later, the reader has to keep all the particulars in short-term memory until you finally reveal the point that the particulars are supposed to support or develop.

Placing Topic Sentences at the Beginning of Paragraphs

Readers of closed-form prose need to have point sentences (usually called "topic sentences") at the beginnings of paragraphs. However, writers of rough drafts often don't fulfill this need because, as we explained in Chapter 16, drafting is an exploratory process in which writers are often still searching for their points as they compose. Consequently, in their rough drafts writers often omit topic sentences entirely or place them at the ends of paragraphs, or they write topic sentences that misrepresent what the paragraphs actually say. During revision, then, you should check your body paragraphs carefully to be sure you have placed accurate topic sentences near the beginning.

What follow are examples of the kinds of revisions writers typically make. We have annotated the examples to explain the changes the writer has made to make the paragraphs unified and clear to readers. The first example is from a later draft of the essay on the dorm room carpets from Chapter 9 (pp. 234–235).

Revision–Topic Sentence First

Another reason for the university not to buy carpets is the cost.
∧ According to Rachel Jones, Assistant Director of Housing Services, the

Topic sentence placed first

initial purchase and installation of carpeting would cost $300 per room. Considering the number of rooms in the three residence halls, carpeting amounts to a substantial investment. Additionally, once the carpets are installed, the university would need to maintain them through the purchase of more vacuum cleaners and shampoo machines. This money would be better spent on other dorm improvements that would benefit more residents, such as expanded kitchen facilities and improved recreational space. ~~Thus carpets would be too expensive.~~

In the original draft, the writer states the point at the end of the paragraph. In his revision he states the point in an opening topic sentence that links back to the thesis statement, which promises "several reasons" that the university should not buy carpets for the dorms. The words "Another reason" thus link the topic sentence to the argument's big picture.

Revising Paragraphs for Unity

In addition to placing topic sentences at the heads of paragraphs, writers often need to revise topic sentences to better match what the paragraph actually says, or revise the paragraph to better match the topic sentence. Paragraphs have unity when all their sentences develop the point stated in the topic sentence. Paragraphs in rough drafts are often not unified because they reflect the writer's shifting, evolving, thinking-while-writing process. Consider the following paragraph from an early draft of an argument against euthanasia by student writer Dao Do. Her peer reviewer labeled it "confusing." What makes it confusing?

We look at more examples from Dao's essay later in this chapter.

Early Draft–Confusing

First, euthanasia is wrong because no one has the right to take the life of another person. Some people say that euthanasia or suicide will end suffering and pain. But what proofs do they have for such a claim? Death is still mysterious to us; therefore, we do not know whether death will end suffering and pain or not. What seems to be the real claim is that death to those with illnesses will end *our* pain. Such pain involves worrying over them, paying their medical bills, and giving up so much of our time. Their deaths end our pain rather than theirs. And for that reason, euthanasia is a selfish act, for the outcome of euthanasia benefits us, the nonsufferers, more. Once the sufferers pass away, we can go back to our normal lives.

The paragraph opens with an apparent topic sentence: "Euthanasia is wrong because no one has the right to take the life of another person." But the rest of the paragraph doesn't focus on that point. Instead, it focuses on how euthanasia benefits the survivors more than the sick person. Dao had two choices: to revise the paragraph to fit the topic sentence or to revise the topic sentence to fit the paragraph. Here is her revision, which includes a different topic sentence and an additional sentence midparagraph to keep particulars focused on the opening point. Dao unifies this paragraph by keeping all its parts focused on her main point: "Euthanasia ... benefits the survivors more than the sick person."

Revision for Unity

Revised topic sentence better forecasts focus of paragraph

Keeps focus on "sick person"

First, euthanasia is wrong because it benefits the survivors more than the sick person.
~~First, euthanasia is wrong because no one has the right to take the life of~~ → *the sick person's*

~~another person.~~ Some people say that euthanasia or suicide will end ˄suffering

and pain. But what proofs do they have for such a claim? Death is still mysterious to us; therefore, we do not know whether death will end suffering and *Moreover, modern pain killers can relieve most of the pain a sick person has to endure.* ◄——— pain or not.ₐWhat seems to be the real claim is that death to those with illnesses will end *our* pain. Such pain involves worrying over them, paying their medical bills, and giving up so much of our time. Their deaths end our pain rather than theirs. And for that reason, euthanasia is a selfish act, for the outcome of euthanasia benefits us, the nonsufferers, more. Once the sufferers pass away, we can go back to our normal lives.

Concludes subpoint about sick person

Supports subpoint about how euthanasia benefits survivors

A paragraph may lack unity for a variety of reasons. It may shift to a new direction in the middle, or one or two sentences may simply be irrelevant to the point. The key is to make sure that all the sentences in the paragraph fulfill the reader's expectations based on the topic sentence.

Adding Particulars to Support Points

Just as writers of rough drafts often omit point sentences from paragraphs, they also sometimes leave out the particulars needed to support a point. In such cases, the writer needs to add particulars such as facts, statistics, quotations, research summaries, examples, or further subpoints. Consider how adding additional particulars to the following draft paragraph strengthens a student writer's argument opposing the logging of old-growth forests.

DRAFT PARAGRAPH: PARTICULARS MISSING

One reason that it is not necessary to log old-growth forests is that the timber industry can supply the world's lumber needs without doing so. For example, we have plenty of new-growth forest from which timber can be taken (Sagoff 89). We could also reduce the amount of trees used for paper products by using other materials besides wood for paper pulp. In light of the fact that we have plenty of trees and ways of reducing our wood demands, there is no need to harvest old-growth forests.

REVISED PARAGRAPH: PARTICULARS ADDED

One reason that it is not necessary to log old-growth forests is that the timber industry can supply the world's lumber needs without doing so. For example, we have plenty of new-growth forest from which timber can be taken as a result of major reforestation efforts all over the United States (Sagoff 89). In the Northwest, for instance, Oregon law requires every acre of timber harvested to be replanted. According to Robert Sedjo, a forestry expert, the world's demand for industrial wood could be met by a widely implemented tree farming system (Sagoff 90). We could also reduce the amount of trees used for paper products by using a promising new innovation called Kenaf, a fast-growing annual herb which is fifteen feet tall and is native to Africa. It has been used for making rope for many years, but recently it was found to work just as well for paper pulp. In light of the fact that we have plenty of trees and ways of reducing our wood demands, there is no need to harvest old-growth forests.

Added particulars support subpoint that we have plenty of new-growth forest

Added particulars support second subpoint that wood alternatives are available

Revising Paragraphs for Points-First Structure

Individual task: Bring to class a draft-in-progress for a closed-form essay. Pick out several paragraphs in the body of your essay and analyze them for "points-first" structure. For each paragraph, ask the following questions:

- Does my paragraph have a topic sentence near the beginning?
- If so, does my topic sentence accurately forecast what the paragraph says?
- Does my topic sentence link to my thesis statement or to a higher-order point that my paragraph develops?
- Does my paragraph have enough particulars to develop and support my topic sentence?

Group task: Then exchange your draft with a partner and do a similar analysis of your partner's selected paragraphs. Discuss your analyses of each other's paragraphs and then help each other plan appropriate revision strategies. If time permits, revise your paragraphs and show your results to your partner. [Note: Sometimes you can revise simply by adding a topic sentence to a paragraph, rewording a topic sentence, or making other kinds of local revisions. At other times, you may need to cross out whole paragraphs and start over, rewriting from scratch after you rethink your ideas.]

SKILL 10.6 Guide your reader with transitions and other signposts.

As we have explained, when readers read closed-form prose, they expect each new sentence, paragraph, and section to link clearly to what they have already read. They need a well-marked trail with signposts signaling the twists and turns along the way. They also need resting spots at major junctions where they can review where they've been and survey what's coming. In this lesson, we show you how transition words as well as summary and forecasting passages can keep your readers securely on the trail.

Using Common Transition Words to Signal Relationships

Transitions are like signposts that signal where the road is turning and limit the possible directions that an unfolding argument might take. Consider how the use of "therefore" and "nevertheless" limits the range of possibilities in the following examples:

> While on vacation, Suzie caught the chicken pox. Therefore, _____.
> While on vacation, Suzie caught the chicken pox. Nevertheless, _____.

"Therefore" signals to the reader that what follows is a consequence. Most readers will imagine a sentence similar to this one:

> Therefore, she spent her vacation lying in bed itchy, feverish, and miserable.

In contrast, "nevertheless" signals an unexpected or denied consequence, so the reader might anticipate a sentence such as this:

> Nevertheless, she enjoyed her two weeks off, thanks to a couple of bottles of calamine lotion, some good books, and a big easy chair overlooking the ocean.

Here is a list of the most common transition words and phrases and what they signal to the reader:*

Words or Phrases	What They Signal
first, second, third, next, finally, earlier, later, meanwhile, afterward	*sequence*—First we went to dinner; then we went to the movies.
that is, in other words, to put it another way, — (dash), : (colon)	*restatement*—He's so hypocritical that you can't trust a word he says. To put it another way, he's a complete phony.
rather, instead	*replacement*—We shouldn't use the money to buy opera tickets; rather, we should use it for a nice gift.
for example, for instance, a case in point	*example*—Mr. Carlyle is very generous. For example, he gave the janitors a special holiday gift.
because, since, for	*reason*—Taxes on cigarettes are unfair because they place a higher tax burden on the working class.
therefore, hence, so, consequently, thus, then, as a result, accordingly, as a consequence	*consequence*—I failed to turn in the essay; therefore I flunked the course.
still, nevertheless	*denied consequence*—The teacher always seemed grumpy in class; nevertheless, I really enjoyed the course.
although, even though, granted that (*with* still)	*concession*—Even though the teacher was always grumpy, I still enjoyed the course.
in comparison, likewise, similarly	*similarity*—Teaching engineering takes a lot of patience. Likewise, so does teaching accounting.
however, in contrast, conversely, on the other hand, but	*contrast*—I disliked my old backpack immensely; however, I really like this new one.
in addition, also, too, moreover, furthermore	*addition*—Today's cars are much safer than those of ten years ago. In addition, they get better gas mileage.
in brief, in sum, in conclusion, finally, to sum up, to conclude	*conclusion or summary*—In sum, the plan presented by Mary is the best choice.

Using Transitions

FOR WRITING AND DISCUSSION

This exercise is designed to show you how transition words govern relationships between ideas. Working in groups or on your own, finish each of the following statements using ideas of your own invention. Make sure what you add fits the logic of the transition word.

1. Writing is difficult; therefore _____.
2. Writing is difficult; however, _____.

(continued)

*Although all the words on the list serve as transitions or connectives, grammatically they are not all equivalent, nor are they all punctuated the same way.

3. Writing is difficult because _____.
4. Writing is difficult. For example, _____.
5. Writing is difficult. To put it another way, _____.
6. Writing is difficult. Likewise, _____.
7. Although writing is difficult, _____.

In the following paragraph, various kinds of linking devices have been omitted. Fill in the blanks with words or phrases that would make the paragraph coherent. Clues are provided in brackets.

> Writing an essay is a difficult process for most people. _____ [contrast] the process can be made easier if you learn to practice three simple techniques. _____ [sequence] learn the technique of nonstop writing. When you are first trying to think of ideas for an essay, put your pen to your paper and write nonstop for ten or fifteen minutes without letting your pen leave the paper. Stay loose and free. Let your pen follow the waves of thought. Don't worry about grammar or spelling. _____ [concession] this technique won't work for everyone, it helps many people get a good cache of ideas to draw on. A _____ [sequence] technique is to write your rough draft rapidly without worrying about being perfect. Too many writers try to get their drafts right the first time. _____ [contrast] by learning to live with imperfection, you will save yourself headaches and a wastepaper basket full of crumpled paper. Think of your first rough draft as a path hacked out of the jungle—as part of an exploration, not as a completed highway. As a _____ [sequence] technique, try printing out a triple-spaced copy to allow space for revision. Many beginning writers don't leave enough space to revise. _____ [consequence] these writers never get in the habit of crossing out chunks of their rough draft and writing revisions in the blank spaces. After you have revised your rough draft until it is too messy to work from anymore, you can _____ [sequence] enter your changes into your word processor and print out a fresh draft, again setting your text on triple-space. The resulting blank space invites you to revise.

Writing Major Transitions between Parts

In long closed-form pieces, writers often put *resting places* between major parts—transitional passages that allow readers to shift their attention momentarily away from the matter at hand to get a sense of where they've been and where they're going. Often such passages sum up the preceding major section, refer back to the essay's thesis statement or opening blueprint plan, and then preview the next major section. Here are three typical examples:

> So far I have looked at a number of techniques that can help people identify debilitating assumptions that block their self-growth. In the next section, I examine ways to question and overcome these assumptions.

> Now that the difficulty of the problem is fully apparent, our next step is to examine some of the solutions that have been proposed.

> These, then, are the major theories explaining why Hamlet delays. But let's see what happens to Hamlet if we ask the question in a slightly different way. In this next section, we shift our critical focus, looking not at Hamlet's actions, but at his language.

Signaling Major Transitions with Headings

In many genres, particularly scientific and technical reports, government documents, business proposals, textbooks, and long articles in magazines or scholarly journals, writers conventionally break up long stretches of text with headings and subheadings. Headings are often set in different type sizes and fonts and mark transition points between major parts and subparts of the argument.

SKILL 10.7 **Bind sentences together by placing old information before new information.**

The previous skill focused on marking the reader's trail with transitions. This skill will enable you to build a smooth trail without potholes or washed-out bridges.

The Old/New Contract in Sentences

A powerful way to prevent gaps is to follow the old/new contract—a writing strategy derived from the principle of old before new that we explained and illustrated in Skill 10.1. Simply put, the old/new contract asks writers to begin sentences with something old—something that links to what has gone before—and then to end sentences with new information.

To understand the old/new contract more fully, try the following thought exercise. We'll show you two passages, both of which explain the old/new contract. One of them, however, follows the principle it describes; the other violates it.

THOUGHT EXERCISE

Which of these passages follows the old/new contract?

VERSION 1

The old/new contract is another principle for writing clear closed-form prose. Beginning your sentences with something old—something that links to what has gone before—and then ending your sentences with new information that advances the argument is what the old/new contract asks writers to do. An effect called *coherence*, which is closely related to *unity*, is created by following this principle. Whereas the clear relationship between the topic sentence and the body of the paragraph and between the parts and the whole is what *unity* refers to, the clear relationship between one sentence and the next is what *coherence* relates to.

VERSION 2

Another principle for writing clear closed-form prose is the old/new contract. The old/new contract asks writers to begin sentences with something old—something that links to what has gone before—and then to end sentences with new information that advances the argument. Following this principle creates an effect called *coherence*, which is closely related to unity. Whereas *unity* refers to the clear relationship between the body of a paragraph and its topic sentence and between the parts and the whole, *coherence* refers to the clear relationship between one sentence and the next, between part and part.

If you are like most readers, you have to concentrate much harder to understand Version 1 than Version 2 because Version 1 violates the old-before-new way that our minds normally process information. When a writer doesn't begin a sentence with old material, readers have to hold the new material in suspension until they have figured out how it connects to what has gone before. They can stay on the trail, but they have to keep jumping over the potholes between sentences.

To follow the old/new contract, place old information near the beginning of sentences in what we call the **topic position** and place new information that advances the argument in the predicate or **stress position** at the end of the sentence. We associate topics with the beginnings of sentences simply because in the standard English sentence, the topic (or subject) comes before the predicate— hence the notion of a "contract" by which we agree not to fool or frustrate our readers by breaking with the "normal" order of things. The contract says that the old, backward-linking material comes at the beginning of the sentence and that the new, argument-advancing material comes at the end.

FOR WRITING AND DISCUSSION

Practicing the Old/New Contract

Here are two more passages, one of which obeys the old/new contract while the other violates it. Working in small groups or as a whole class, reach consensus on which of these passages follows the old/new contract. Explain your reasoning by showing how the beginning of each sentence links to something old.

PASSAGE A

Play is an often-overlooked dimension of fathering. From the time a child is born until its adolescence, fathers emphasize caretaking less than play. Egalitarian feminists may be troubled by this, and spending more time in caretaking may be wise for fathers. There seems to be unusual significance in the father's style of play. Physical excitement and stimulation are likely to be part of it. With older children more physical games and teamwork that require the competitive testing of physical and mental skills are also what it involves. Resemblance to an apprenticeship or teaching relationship is also a characteristic of fathers' play: Come on, let me show you how.

PASSAGE B

An often-overlooked dimension of fathering is play. From their children's birth through adolescence, fathers tend to emphasize play more than caretaking. This emphasis may be troubling to egalitarian feminists, and it would indeed be wise for most fathers to spend more time in caretaking. Yet the fathers' style of play seems to have unusual significance. It is likely to be both physically stimulating and exciting. With older children it involves more physical games and teamwork that require the competitive testing of physical and mental skills. It frequently resembles an apprenticeship or teaching relationship: Come on, let me show you how.

How to Make Links to the "Old"

To understand how to link to "old information," you need to understand more fully what we mean by "old" or "familiar." In the context of sentence-level coherence, we mean everything in the text that the reader has read so far. Any upcoming sentence is new information, but once the reader has read it, it becomes old information. For example, when a reader is halfway through a text, everything previously read—the title, the introduction, half the body—is old information to which you can link to meet your readers' expectations for unity and coherence.

In making these backward links, writers have three targets:

1. They can link to a key word or concept in the immediately preceding sentence (creating coherence).
2. They can link to a key word or concept in a preceding point sentence (creating unity).
3. They can link to a preceding forecasting statement about structure (helping readers map their location in the text).

Writers have a number of textual strategies for making these links. In Figure 10.4 our annotations show how a professional writer links to old

FIGURE 10.4 How a Professional Writer Follows the Old/New Contract

Recent research has given us much deeper—and more surprising—insights into the father's role in childrearing. It shows that in almost all of their interactions with children, fathers do things a little differently from mothers. What fathers do—their special parenting style—is not only highly complementary to what mothers do but is by all indications important in its own right.

For example, an often-overlooked dimension of fathering is play. From their children's birth through adolescence, fathers tend to emphasize play more than caretaking. This may be troubling to egalitarian feminists, and it would indeed be wise for most fathers to spend more time in caretaking.

Yet the fathers' style of play seems to have unusual significance. It is likely to be both physically stimulating and exciting. With older children it involves more physical games and teamwork that require the competitive testing of physical and mental skills. It frequently resembles an apprenticeship or teaching relationship: Come on, let me show you how.

David Popenoe, "Where's Papa?" from *Life Without Father: Compelling New Evidence that Fatherhood and Marriage Are Indispensable for the Good of Children and Society.*

information within the first five or six words of each sentence. What follows is a compendium of these strategies:

Strategies for Linking to the "Old"	
What to Do	**Example Shown in Figure 10.4**
Repeat a key word from the preceding sentence or an earlier point sentence.	Note the number of sentences that open with "father," "father's," or "fathering." Note also the frequent repetitions of "play."
Use a pronoun to substitute for a key word.	In our example, the second sentence opens with the pronouns "It," referring to "research," and "their," referring to "fathers." The last three sentences open with the pronoun "It," referring to "father's style of play."
Summarize, rephrase, or restate earlier concepts.	In the second sentence, "interactions with children" restates the concept of childrearing. Similarly, the phrase "an often-overlooked dimension" sums up a concept implied in the preceding paragraph—that recent research reveals something significant and not widely known about a father's role in childrearing. Finally, note that the pronoun "This" in the second paragraph sums up the main concept of the previous two sentences. (But see our warning on p. 267 about the overuse of "this" as a pronoun.)
Use a transition word such as *first ...* , *second ...* , *third ...* , or *therefore* or *however* to cue the reader about the logical relationship between an upcoming sentence and the preceding ones.	Note how the second paragraph opens with "For example," indicating that the upcoming paragraph will illustrate the concept identified in the preceding paragraph.

These strategies give you a powerful way to check and revise your prose. Comb your drafts for gaps between sentences where you have violated the old/new contract. If the opening of a new sentence doesn't refer back to an earlier word, phrase, or concept, your readers could derail, so use what you have learned to repair the tracks.

FOR WRITING AND DISCUSSION

Applying the Old/New Contract to Your Own Draft

Individual task: Bring to class a draft-in-progress for a closed-form essay. On a selected page, examine the opening of each sentence. Place a vertical slash in front of any sentence that doesn't contain near the beginning some backward-looking element that links to old, familiar material. Then revise these sentences to follow the old/new contract.

Group task: Working with a partner, share the changes you each made on your drafts. Then on each other's pages, work together to identify the kinds of links made at the beginning of each sentence. (For example, does the opening of a sentence repeat a key word, use a pronoun to substitute for a key word, rephrase or restate an earlier concept, or use a transition word?)

As we discussed in Skill 10.1, the principle of old before new has great explanatory power in helping writers understand their choices when they compose. In this last section, we give you some further insights into the old/new contract.

Avoiding Ambiguous Use of "This" to Fulfill the Old/New Contract

Some writers try to fulfill the old/new contract by frequent use of the pronoun *this* to sum up a preceding concept. Occasionally such usage is effective, as in our example passage on fathers' style of play when the writer says: "*This* may be troubling to egalitarian feminists." But frequent use of *this* as a pronoun creates lazy and often ambiguous prose. Consider how our example passage might read if many of the explicit links were replaced by *this*:

LAZY USE OF *THIS* AS PRONOUN

Recent research has given us much deeper—and more surprising—insights into **this.** It shows that in doing **this,** fathers do things a little differently from mothers. **This** is not only highly complementary to what mothers do but is by all indications important in its own right.

For example, an often-overlooked dimension of **this** is play.

Perhaps this passage helps you see why we refer to *this* (used by itself as a pronoun) as "the lazy person's all-purpose noun-slot filler."*

SKILL 10.8 **Learn four expert moves for organizing and developing ideas.**

Writers of closed-form prose often employ a conventional set of moves to organize parts of an essay. In using the term *moves*, we are making an analogy with the "set moves" or "set plays" in such sports as basketball, volleyball, and soccer. For example, a common set move in basketball is the "pick," in which an offensive player without the ball stands motionless in order to block the path of a defensive player who is guarding the dribbler. Similarly, certain organizational patterns in writing occur frequently enough to act as set plays for writers. These patterns set

---

*It's acceptable to use *this* as an adjective, as in "this usage"; we refer here only to *this* used by itself as a pronoun.

up expectations in the reader's mind about the shape of an upcoming stretch of prose, anything from a few sentences to a paragraph to a large block of paragraphs. As you will see, these moves also stimulate the invention of ideas. Next, we describe four of the most powerful set plays.*

The *For Example* Move

Perhaps the most common set play occurs when a writer makes an assertion and then illustrates it with one or more examples, often signaling the move explicitly with transitions such as *for example, for instance*, or *a case in point is . . .* . Here is how student writer Dao Do used the *for example* move to support her third reason for opposing euthanasia:

FOR EXAMPLE MOVE

Topic sentence ————→   My third objection to euthanasia is that it fails to see the value in suffering.
Transition signaling the move   Suffering is a part of life. We see the value of suffering only if we look deeply within our suffering. For example, I never thought my crippled uncle from Vietnam was a blessing to my grandmother until I talked to her. My mother's little brother was born prematurely. As a result of oxygen and nutrition deficiency, he was born crippled. His tiny arms and legs were twisted around his body, preventing him from any normal movements such as walking, picking up things, and lying down. He could only sit. Therefore, his world was very limited, for it consisted of his own room and the garden viewed through his window. Because of his disabilities, my grandmother had to wash him, feed him, and watch him constantly. It was hard, but she managed to care for him for forty-three years. He passed away after the death of my grandfather in 1982. Bringing this situation out of Vietnam and into Western society shows the difference between Vietnamese and Western views. In the West, my uncle might have been euthanized as a baby. Supporters of euthanasia would have said he wouldn't have any quality of life and that he would have been a great burden. But he was not a burden on my grandmother. She enjoyed taking care of him, and he was always her company after her other children got married and moved away. Neither one of them saw his defect as meaningless suffering because it brought them closer together.

Extended example supporting point

This passage uses a single, extended example to support a point. You could also use several shorter examples or other kinds of illustrating evidence such as facts or statistics. In all cases the *for example* move creates a pattern of expectation and fulfillment. This pattern drives the invention of ideas in one of two ways: It urges the writer either to find examples to develop a generalization or to formulate a generalization that shows the point of an example.

---

*You might find it helpful to follow the set plays we used to write this section. This last sentence is the opening move of a play we call "division into parallel parts." It sets up the expectation that we will develop four set plays in order. Watch for the way we chunk them and signal transitions between them.

Practicing the *For Example* Move

Working individually or in groups, develop a plan for supporting one or more of the following generalizations using the *for example* move:

1. Another objection to state sales taxes is that they are so annoying.
2. Although assertiveness training has definite benefits, it can sometimes get you into real trouble.
3. Sometimes effective leaders are indecisive.

The *Summary/However* Move

This move occurs whenever a writer sums up another person's viewpoint in order to qualify or contradict it or to introduce an opposing view. Typically, writers use transition words such as *but, however, in contrast,* or *on the other hand* between the parts of this move. This move is particularly common in academic writing, which often contrasts the writer's new view with prevailing views. Here is how Dao uses a *summary/however* move in the introduction of her essay opposing euthanasia:

SUMMARY/HOWEVER MOVE

Should euthanasia be legalized? My classmate Martha and her family think it should be. Martha's aunt was blind from diabetes. For three years she was constantly in and out of the hospital, but then her kidneys shut down and she became a victim of life support. After three months of suffering, she finally gave up. Martha believes this three-month period was unnecessary, for her aunt didn't have to go through all of that suffering. If euthanasia were legalized, her family would have put her to sleep the minute her condition worsened. Then, she wouldn't have had to feel pain, and she would have died in peace and with dignity. However, despite Martha's strong argument for legalizing euthanasia, I find it wrong.

Issue over which there is disagreement

Summary of opposing viewpoint

Transition to writer's viewpoint

Statement of writer's view

The first sentence of this introduction poses the question that the essay addresses. The main body of the paragraph summarizes Martha's opposing view on euthanasia, and the final sentence, introduced by the transition "However," presents Dao's thesis.

Practicing the *Summary/However* Move

For this exercise, assume that you favor development of wind-generated electricity. Use the *summary/however* move to acknowledge the view of civil engineer David Rockwood, whose letter opposing wind-generated electricity you read in Chapter 1 (p. 6). Assume that you are writing the opening paragraph of your own essay. Follow the pattern of Dao's introduction: (a) begin with a one-sentence issue or question; (b) summarize Rockwood's view in approximately one hundred words; and (c) state your own view, using *however* or *in contrast* as a transition. Write out your paragraph on your own, or work in groups to write a consensus paragraph. Then share and critique your paragraphs.

The *Division-into-Parallel-Parts* Move

Among the most frequently encountered and powerful of the set plays is the *division-into-parallel-parts* move. To initiate the move, a writer begins with an umbrella sentence that forecasts the structure and creates a framework. (For example, "Freud's theory differs from Jung's in three essential ways" or "The decline of the U.S. space program can be attributed to several factors.") Typical overview sentences either specify the number of parts that follow by using phrases such as "two ways," "three differences," or "five kinds," or they leave the number unspecified, using words such as *several, a few*, or *many*. Alternatively, the writer may ask a rhetorical question that implies the framework: "What are some main differences, then, between Freud's theory and Jung's? One difference is. ... "

To signal transitions from one part to the next, writers use two kinds of signposts in tandem. The first is a series of transition words or bullets to introduce each of the parallel parts. Here are typical series of transition words:

> First ... Second ... Third ... Finally ...
> First ... Another ... Still another ... Finally ...
> One ... In addition ... Furthermore ... Also ...

The second kind of signpost, usually used in conjunction with transitions, is an echolike repetition of the same grammatical structure to begin each parallel part.

> I learned several things from this course. First, *I learned that* [development]. Second, *I learned that* [development]. Finally, *I learned that* [development].

The *division-into-parallel-parts* move can be used within a single paragraph, or it can control larger stretches of text in which a dozen or more paragraphs may work together to complete a parallel series of parts. (For example, you are currently in the third part of a parallel series introduced by the mapping sentence on p. 268: "Next, we describe four of the most powerful set plays.") Here is an example of a student paragraph organized by the *division-into-parallel-parts* move.

Mapping statement forecasts "move"

Transition to first parallel part

Transition to second parallel part

Transition to third parallel part

Final transition completes "move"

DIVISION-INTO-PARALLEL-PARTS MOVE

In this paper I will argue that political solutions to homelessness must take into account four categories of homeless people. A first category is persons who are out of work and seek new jobs. Persons in this category may have been recently laid off, unable to meet their rental payments, and forced temporarily to live out of a car or van. They might quickly leave the ranks of the homeless if they can find new jobs. A second category includes the physically disabled or mentally ill. Providing housing addresses only part of their problems since they also need medical care and medication. For many, finding or keeping a job might be impossible. A third category is the street alcoholic or drug addict. These persons need addiction treatment as well as clothing and shelter and will not become productive citizens until they become sober or drug free. The final category includes those who, like the old railroad "hobo," choose homelessness as a way of life.

Instead of transition words, writers can also use bullets followed by indented text:

USE OF BULLETS TO SIGNAL PARALLEL PARTS

The Wolf Recovery Program is rigidly opposed by a vociferous group of ranchers who pose three main objections to increasing wolf populations:

- They perceive wolves as a threat to livestock. [development]
- They fear the wolves will attack humans. [development]
- They believe ranchers will not be compensated by the government for their loss of profits. [development]

Practicing the *Division-into-Parallel-Parts* Move

FOR WRITING AND DISCUSSION

Working individually or in small groups, use the *division-into-parallel-parts* move to create, organize, and develop ideas to support one or more of the following point sentences.

1. To study for an exam effectively, a student should follow these [specify a number] steps.
2. Why do U.S. schoolchildren lag so far behind European and Asian children on standardized tests of mathematics and science? One possible cause is … [continue].
3. Constant dieting is unhealthy for several reasons.

The *Comparison/Contrast* Move

A common variation on the *division-into-parallel-parts* move is the *comparison/contrast* move. To compare or contrast two items, you must first decide on the points of comparison (or contrast). If you are contrasting the political views of two presidential candidates, you might choose to focus on four points of comparison: differences in their foreign policy, differences in economic policy, differences in social policy, and differences in judicial philosophy. You then have two choices for organizing the parts: the *side-by-side pattern,* in which you discuss all of candidate A's views and then all of candidate B's views; or the *back-and-forth pattern,* in which you discuss foreign policy, contrasting A's views with B's views, then move on to economic policy, then social policy, and then judicial philosophy. Figure 10.5 shows how these two patterns would appear on a tree diagram.

There are no cut-and-dried rules that dictate when to use the *side-by-side pattern* or the *back-and-forth pattern.* However, for lengthy comparisons, the *back-and-forth pattern* is often more effective because the reader doesn't have to store great amounts of information in memory. The *side-by-side pattern* requires readers to remember all the material about A when they get to B, and it is sometimes difficult to keep all the points of comparison clearly in mind.

FIGURE 10.5 Two Ways to Structure a Comparison or Contrast

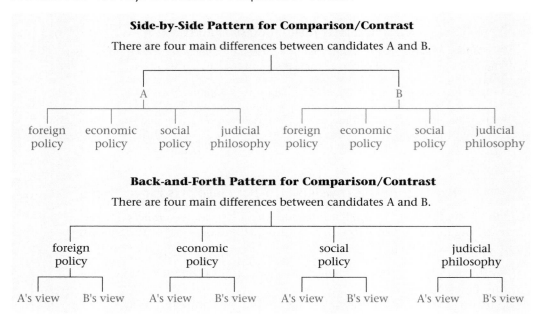

FOR WRITING AND DISCUSSION

Practicing the *Comparison/Contrast* Move

Working individually or in groups, create tree diagrams for stretches of text based on one or more of the following point sentences, all of which call for the *comparison/contrast* move. Make at least one diagram follow the *back-and-forth pattern* and at least one diagram follow the *side-by-side pattern*.

1. To understand U.S. politics, an outsider needs to appreciate some basic differences between Republicans and Democrats.
2. Although they are obviously different on the surface, there are many similarities between the Boy Scouts and a street gang.
3. There are several important differences between closed-form and open-form writing.

SKILL 10.9 Use effective tables, graphs, and charts to present numeric data.

In contemporary analyses and arguments, writers often draw on quantitative data to support their points. Writers can make numbers speak powerfully by means of reader-effective graphics including tables, graphs, and charts. Generally, quantitative data displayed in tables invite the reader to tease out many different stories that the numbers might tell. In contrast, line graphs, bar graphs, or pie charts focus vividly on one story.

How Tables Tell Many Stories

Data displayed in tables usually have their origins in raw numbers collected from surveys, questionnaires, observational studies, scientific experiments, and so forth. These numbers are then consolidated and arranged in tables where they can be analyzed for potentially meaningful patterns. Consider, for example, Table 10.1, produced by the National Center for Education Statistics. It shows the number of postsecondary degrees earned by men and women from 1960 to 2007.

Reading a Table Tables are read in two directions: from top to bottom and from left to right. To read a table efficiently, begin with the title, *which always includes elements from both the vertical and horizontal dimensions of the table.* Note how this rule applies to Table 10.1.

- The table's horizontal dimension is indicated in the first part of the title: "Earned Degrees Conferred by Level and Sex." Reading horizontally, we see the names of the degrees (associate's, bachelor's, and so forth) with subcategories indicating male and female.
- The table's vertical dimension is indicated in the second part of the title: "1960 to 2007." Reading vertically, we see selected years between 1960 and 2007.

Beneath the title are further instructions: Numbers represent thousands except for one column labeled "percent."

We are now prepared to read specific information from the table. In 1994, for example, colleges and universities in the United States conferred 2,206,000 degrees, of which 45.1 percent were earned by men. In that same year, 532,000 men and 637,000 women earned bachelors's degrees while 27,000 men and 17,000 women earned doctoral degrees.

Discovering Stories in the Data You need to peruse the table carefully before interesting patterns begin to emerge. Among the stories the table tells are these:

- The percent of women receiving postsecondary degrees rose substantially between 1960 and 2007 (with a corresponding fall for men).
- This increased percentage of degrees given to women is more dramatic for associate's and bachelor's degrees than it is for master's, first professional, or doctoral degrees.

As we show in the next section, these two stories, which must be teased out of this table, can be told more dramatically with graphs.

Using a Graphic to Tell a Story

Whereas tables can embed many stories and invite detailed examination of the numbers, a graph or chart makes one selected story immediately visible.

Line Graph A line graph converts numerical data to a series of points on a grid and connects them to create flat, rising, or falling lines. The result gives us a picture of the relationship between the variables represented on the horizontal and vertical axes.

TABLE 10.1 Earned Degrees Conferred by Level and Sex: 1960 to 2007

[In thousands (477 represents 477,000), except percent. Based on survey; see Appendix III]

Year ending	All degrees Total	All degrees Percent male	Associate's Male	Associate's Female	Bachelor's Male	Bachelor's Female	Master's Male	Master's Female	First professional Male	First professional Female	Doctoral Male	Doctoral Female
1960[1]	477	65.8	(NA)	(NA)	254	138	51	24	(NA)	(NA)	9	1
1970	1,271	59.2	117	89	451	341	126	83	33	2	26	4
1975	1,666	56.0	191	169	505	418	162	131	49	7	27	7
1980	1,731	51.1	184	217	474	456	151	147	53	17	23	10
1985	1,828	49.3	203	252	483	497	143	143	50	25	22	11
1990	1,940	46.6	191	264	492	560	154	171	44	27	24	14
1991	2,025	45.8	199	283	504	590	156	181	44	28	25	15
1992	2,108	45.6	207	297	521	616	162	191	45	29	26	15
1993	2,167	45.5	212	303	533	632	169	200	45	30	26	16
1994	2,206	45.1	215	315	532	637	176	211	45	31	27	17
1995	2,218	44.9	218	321	526	634	179	219	45	31	27	18
1996[2]	2,248	44.2	220	336	522	642	179	227	45	32	27	18
1997[2]	2,288	43.6	224	347	521	652	181	238	46	33	27	19
1998[2]	2,298	43.2	218	341	520	664	184	246	45	34	27	19
1999[2]	2,323	42.7	218	342	519	682	186	254	44	34	25	19
2000[2]	2,385	42.6	225	340	530	708	192	265	44	36	25	20
2001[2]	2,416	42.4	232	347	532	712	194	274	43	37	25	20
2002[2]	2,494	42.2	238	357	550	742	199	283	43	38	24	20
2003[2]	2,621	42.1	253	380	573	775	211	301	42	39	24	22
2004[2]	2,755	41.8	260	405	595	804	230	329	42	41	25	23
2005[2]	2,850	41.6	268	429	613	826	234	341	44	43	27	26
2006[2]	2,936	41.3	270	443	631	855	238	356	44	44	29	27
2007[2]	3,007	41.2	275	453	650	875	238	366	45	45	30	30

NA Not available.

[1] First-professional degrees are included with bachelor's degrees.

[2] Beginning 1996, data reflect the new classification of institutions.

Source: U.S. National Center for Education Statistics, Digest of Education Statistics, annual.

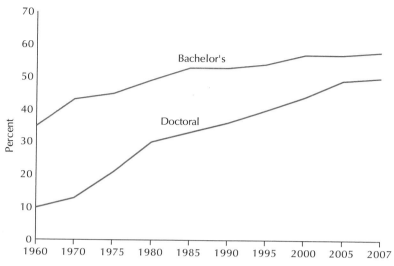

FIGURE 10.6 Percentage of Bachelor's and Doctoral Degrees Conferred on Females: 1960–2007

Suppose you wanted to tell the story of the increasing percentage of women receiving bachelor's and doctoral degrees from 1960 to 2007. Using Table 10.1 you can calculate these percentages yourself and display them in a line graph as shown in Figure 10.6. To determine what a graph tells you, you need to clarify what's represented on the two axes. By convention, the horizontal axis of a graph contains the predictable, known variable that has no surprises, such as time or some other sequence—in this case, the years 1960 to 2007 in predictable chronological order. The vertical axis contains the unpredictable variable that tells the graph's story—in this case, the percent of degrees conferred on women in each year on the graph. The ascending lines tell the stories at a glance.

Bar Graph Bar graphs use bars of varying lengths, extending either horizontally or vertically, to contrast two or more quantities. To make the story of women's progress in earning doctoral degrees particularly vivid (the same story told in the "doctoral" line in Figure 10.6), you could use a bar graph as shown in Figure 10.7. To read a bar graph, note carefully the title and the axes to see what is compared to what. Bars are typically distinguished from each other by use of different colors, shades, or patterns of cross-hatching. The special power of bar graphs is that they can help you make quick comparisons. Figure 10.7 tells you at a glance that in 1960, women received far fewer doctoral degrees than men but that in 2007 they received an equal percentage.

Pie Chart A pie chart, also called a circle graph, depicts the different percentages of a total (the pie) represented by variously sized slices. Suppose you wanted to know the most popular undergraduate majors in American colleges and universities. These statistics, which are available in table format from the National Center for Education Statistics, can be quickly converted into a pie chart as

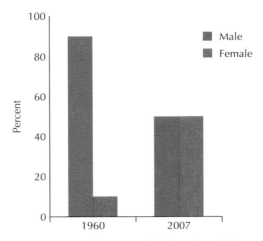

FIGURE 10.7 Percentage of Doctoral Degrees Conferred on Males and Females: 1960 and 2007

shown in Figure 10.8. As you can see, a pie chart shows at a glance how the whole of something is divided into segments. In 2007, for example, 7 percent of graduating seniors majored in education while 22 percent majored in business. The effectiveness of pie charts diminishes as you add more slices. In most cases, you begin to confuse readers if you include more than five or six slices.

Incorporating a Graphic into Your Essay

Today, most word processing programs, often integrated with a spreadsheet, easily allow you to create a graphic and insert it into your document. In some cases,

FIGURE 10.8 Distribution of Bachelor's Degrees by Majors, 2007

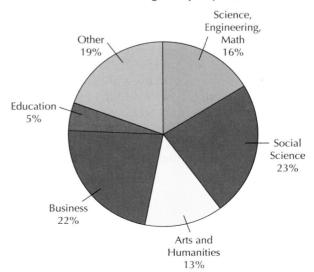

your instructor may give you permission to make a graphic with pen or pencil and paste it into your document.

Designing Your Graphic In academic manuscripts, graphics are designed conservatively without bells and whistles such as three-dimensional effects or special fonts and patterns. Keep the graphic as simple and uncluttered as possible. Also in academic manuscripts, do not wrap text around the graphic. In contrast, in popular published work, writers often use flashy fonts, three dimensions, text wrapping, and other effects that would undermine your *ethos* in an academic setting.

Numbering, Labeling, and Titling the Graphic In newspapers and popular magazines, writers often include graphics in boxes or sidebars without specifically referring to them in the text. However, in academic manuscripts or scholarly works, graphics are always labeled, numbered, titled, and referred to in the text. Tables are listed as "Tables," while line graphs, bar graphs, pie charts, or any other kinds of drawings or photographs are labeled as "Figures." By convention, the title for tables goes above the table, while the title for figures goes below.

Referencing the Graphic in Your Text Academic and professional writers follow a referencing convention called independent redundancy. The graphic should be understandable without the text; the text should be understandable without the graphic. In other words, the text should tell in words the same story that the graphic displays visually. An example is shown in Figure 10.9.

FIGURE 10.9 Example of a Student Text with a Referenced Graph

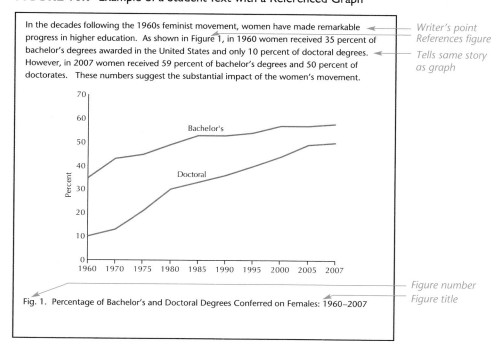

In the decades following the 1960s feminist movement, women have made remarkable progress in higher education. As shown in Figure 1, in 1960 women received 35 percent of bachelor's degrees awarded in the United States and only 10 percent of doctoral degrees. However, in 2007 women received 59 percent of bachelor's degrees and 50 percent of doctorates.   These numbers suggest the substantial impact of the women's movement.

— Writer's point
References figure

— *Tells same story as graph*

Figure number
Figure title

Fig. 1. Percentage of Bachelor's and Doctoral Degrees Conferred on Females: 1960–2007

SKILL 10.10 **Write effective conclusions.**

Conclusions can best be understood as complements to introductions. In both the introduction and the conclusion, writers are concerned with the essay as a whole more than with any given part. In a conclusion, the writer attempts to bring a sense of completeness and closure to the profusion of points and particulars laid out in the body of the essay. The writer is particularly concerned with helping the reader move from the parts back to the big picture and to understand the importance or significance of the essay.

Because many writers find conclusions challenging to write, we offer six possible strategies for ending an essay.

Strategies for Concluding an Essay		
Strategies	**What to Do**	**Comments**
***Simple summary* conclusion**	Recap what you have said.	This approach is useful in a long or complex essay or in an instructional text that focuses on concepts. However, in a short, easy-to-follow essay, a summary conclusion can be dull and even annoying to readers. A brief summary followed by a more artful concluding strategy can sometimes be effective.
***Larger significance* conclusion**	Draw the reader's attention to the importance or the applications of your argument.	The conclusion is a good place to elaborate on the significance of your problem by showing how your proposed solution to a question leads to understanding a larger, more significant question or brings practical benefits to individuals or society. If you posed a question about values or about the interpretation of a confusing text or phenomenon, you might show how your argument could be applied to related questions, texts, or phenomena.
***Proposal* conclusion**	Call for action.	Often used in analyses and arguments, a *proposal* conclusion states the action that needs to be taken and briefly

Strategies	What to Do	Comments
		explains its advantages over alternative actions or describes its beneficial consequences. If your paper analyzes the negative consequences of shifting from a graduated to a flat-rate income tax, your conclusion may recommend an action such as modifying or opposing the flat tax.
	Call for future study.	A *call-for-future-study* conclusion indicates what else needs to be known or resolved before a proposal can be offered. Such conclusions are especially common in scientific writing.
Scenic or *anecdotal* **conclusion**	Use a scene or brief story to illustrate the theme without stating it explicitly.	Often used in popular writing, a scene or anecdote can help the reader experience the emotional significance of the topic. For example, a paper favoring public housing for the homeless may end by describing an itinerant homeless person collecting bottles in a park.
Hook and return **conclusion**	Return to something mentioned at the beginning of the essay.	If the essay begins with a vivid illustration of a problem, the conclusion can return to the same scene or story but with some variation to indicate the significance of the essay.
Delayed-thesis **conclusion**	State the thesis for the first time at the end of the essay.	This strategy is effective when you are writing about complex or divisive issues and you don't want to take a stand until you have presented all sides. The introduction of the essay merely states the problem, giving the essay an exploratory feel.

FOR WRITING AND DISCUSSION

Writing Conclusions

Choose a paper you have just written and write an alternative conclusion using one of the strategies discussed in this lesson. Then share your original and revised conclusions in groups. Have group members discuss which one they consider most effective and why.

COMPOSING AND REVISING OPEN-FORM PROSE

11

Good writing is supposed to evoke sensation in the reader—not the fact that it's raining, but the feel of being rained upon.

—*E. L. Doctorow, Novelist*

lthough much of this book focuses on closed-form prose, there are many kinds of good writing, and we probably all share the desire at times to write in ways other than points-first, thesis-governed prose. In our epigraph, novelist E. L. Doctorow suggests another way to think of "good writing": Writing that evokes sensations, that triggers in the reader's imagination the very feel of the rain.

In this chapter, we shift our attention to open-form writing, which, because it uses literary strategies such as story, plot, characterization, setting, and theme, is often called *literary nonfiction*. Of course, it should be remembered that writing exists on a continuum from closed to open forms and that many features of open-form prose can appear in primarily closed-form texts. In fact, many of the example essays in this book combine elements of both open and closed styles. At the extremes of the continuum, closed- and open-form writing are markedly different, but the styles can be blended in pleasing combinations.

For more on plot, characterization, setting, and theme, see Chapter 6.

Our goal in this chapter is to give you some practical lessons on how to write effective open-form prose. But we need to acknowledge at the outset that, whereas closed-form prose is governed by a few widely accepted conventions, one of the main features of open-form prose is its freedom to play with conventions in a bewildering variety of ways. Consequently, our discussion of open-form writing seeks more to introduce you to guiding principles rather than to treat open-form writing exhaustively.

In this chapter, you will learn these skills for open-form writing:

- **SKILL 11.1** Make your narrative a story, not an *and then* chronology.
- **SKILL 11.2** Write low on the ladder of abstraction.
- **SKILL 11.3** Disrupt your reader's desire for direction and clarity.
- **SKILL 11.4** Tap the power of figurative language.
- **SKILL 11.5** Expand your repertoire of styles.
- **SKILL 11.6** Use open-form elements to create "voice" in closed-form prose.

Key Features of Open-Form Prose

As we have discussed throughout this text, writing at the closed end of the spectrum seeks to be efficient and reader-friendly. By forecasting what's coming, placing points first, and putting old information before new, closed-form writers try to convey complex ideas in as clear a way as possible, enabling readers to grasp ideas quickly. In contrast, open-form writers, by violating or simply stretching those same conventions, set up a different kind of relationship with readers. They often provide more pleasure in reading, but just as often demand more patience, more tolerance of ambiguity, and more openness to a range of meanings and nuance. They are likely to take readers backstage to share the process of their thinking. They often cast themselves in the role of narrators or characters reporting all the coincidences, disappointments, and confusion they experienced during their quest for understanding. In this process of sharing, they make readers codiscoverers of ideas and insights.

Open-form prose is also characterized by its emphasis on an aesthetic use of language—that is, language used to please and entertain. Without the benefit of a thesis or points appearing first to convey meaning, open-form prose depends on the very specificity of words—the ability of words to create mental pictures, to appeal to readers' senses and emotions, and to conjure up memories.

SKILL 11.1 Make your narrative a story, not an *and then* chronology.

We have said that open-form prose is narrative based and uses the strategies of a story. In this first section we want you to think more deeply about the concept of a story—particularly how a story differs from an *and then* chronology. Both a story and an *and then* chronology depict events happening in time. But there are important differences between them. In the following exercise, we'd like you to try your own hand at articulating the differences between a story and an *and then* chronology.

FOR WRITING AND DISCUSSION	*And Then* Chronology Versus Story

Individual task:

1. Read the student autobiographical narrative "No Cats in America?" by Patrick José in Chapter 6, pages 160–161.
2. Then read the following autobiographical narrative entitled "The Stolen Watch," which was submitted by a student as a draft for an assignment on narrative writing.

THE STOLEN WATCH

Last fall and winter I was living in Spokane with my brother, who during this time had a platonic girlfriend come over from Seattle and stay for a weekend. Her name was Karen, and we became interested in each other and I went over to see her at the first of the year. She then invited me to, supposedly, the biggest party of the year, called the Aristocrats' Ball. I said sure and made my way back to Seattle in February. It started out bad on Friday, the day my brother and I left Spokane. We left town an hour late, but what's new. Then my brother had to stop along the way and pick up some parts; we stayed there for an hour trying to find this guy. It all started out bad because we arrived in Seattle and I forgot to call Karen. We were staying at her brother's house and after we brought all our things in, we decided to go to a few bars. Later that night we ran into Karen in one of the bars, and needless to say she was not happy with me. When I got up the next morning I knew I should have stayed in Spokane, because I felt bad vibes. Karen made it over about an hour before the party. By the time we reached the party, which drove me crazy, she wound up with another guy, so her friends and I decided to go to a few bars. The next morning when I was packing, I could not find my watch and decided that someone had to have taken it. We decided that it had to have been the goon that Karen had wound up with the night before, because she was at her brother's house with him before she went home. So how was I going to get my watch back?

We decided the direct and honest approach to the problem would work out the best. We got in contact and confronted him. This turned out to be quite a chore. It turned out that he was visiting some of his family during that weekend and lived in Little Harbor, California. It turned out that Karen knew his half brother and got some information on him, which was not pretty. He had just been released by the army and was trained in a special forces unit, in the field of Martial Arts. He was a trained killer! This information did not help matters at all, but the next bit of information was just as bad if not worse. Believe it or not, he was up on charges of attempted murder and breaking and entering. In a way, it turned out lucky for me, because he was in enough trouble with the police and did not need any more. Karen got in contact with him and threatened him that I would bring him up on charges if he did not return the watch. His mother decided that he was in enough trouble and sent me the watch. I was astounded, it was still working and looked fine. The moral of the story is don't drive 400 miles to see a girl you hardly know, and whatever you do, don't leave your valuables out in the open.

Group task: Share your responses to the following questions:

1. How does your experience of reading "No Cats in America?" differ from your experience of reading "The Stolen Watch"? Try to articulate the different ways you reacted to the two pieces while in the process of reading them.
2. Based on the differences between these two pieces, how would you define a "story"? Begin by brainstorming all the ways that the two pieces differ. Then try to identify the essential differences that make one a "story" and the other an *and then* chronology.

Now that you have tried to define a story for yourselves, we would like to explain our own four criteria for a story: (1) depiction of events through time, (2) connectedness, (3) tension, and (4) resolution. If we combine these criteria into a sentence, it would read like this: A story depicts events that are connected causally or thematically to create a sense of tension that is resolved through action, insight, or understanding. These four criteria occurring together turn a chronology into a story.

Depiction of Events through Time

The essence of storytelling is the depiction of events through time. Whereas thesis-based writing descends from problem to thesis to supporting reasons and evidence, stories unfold linearly, temporally, from event to event. You may start in the middle of the action and then jump backward and forward, but you always encounter some sequence of events happening in time. This temporal focus creates a sense of "onceness." Things that happen at a point in time happen only once, as the classic fairy-tale opening "Once upon a time" suggests. When you compose and revise a narrative, you want to try to capture the "onceness" of that experience. As the essayist E. B. White once advised a young writer, "Don't write about Man but about a man."

Consider how Val Plumwood, a professor of women's studies and author of the book *Feminism and the Mastery of Nature*, depicts the events leading up to a disturbing encounter with a crocodile. (Later in the story, the reader sees how this encounter shapes her understanding of humans' place in the food chain and the need for a respectful, rather than a dominating, attitude toward other animals.)

In the early wet season, Kakadu's paper-bark wetlands are especially stunning, as the water lilies weave white, pink, and blue patterns of dreamlike beauty over the shining thunderclouds reflected in their still waters. Yesterday, the water lilies and the wonderful bird life had enticed me into a joyous afternoon's idyll as I ventured onto the East Alligator Lagoon for the first time in a canoe lent by the park service. "You can play about on the backwaters," the ranger had said, "but don't go onto the main river channel. The current's too swift, and if you get into trouble, there are the crocodiles. Lots of them along the river!" I followed his advice and glutted myself on the magical beauty and bird life of the lily lagoons, untroubled by crocodiles.

Today, I wanted to repeat the experience despite the drizzle beginning to fall as I neared the canoe launch site. I set off on a day trip in search of an Aboriginal rock art site across the lagoon and up a side channel. The drizzle turned to a warm rain within a few hours, and the magic was lost. The birds were invisible, the water lilies were sparser, and the lagoon seemed even a little menacing. I noticed now how low the 14-foot canoe sat in the water, just a few inches of fiberglass between me and the great saurian, close relatives of the ancient dinosaurs. ...

After hours of searching the maze of shallow channels in the swamp, I had not found the clear channel leading to the rock art site, as shown on the ranger's sketch map. When I pulled my canoe over in driving rain to a rock outcrop for a hasty, sodden lunch, I experienced the unfamiliar sensation of being watched. Having never been one for timidity, in philosophy or in life, I decided, rather than return defeated to my sticky trailer, to explore a clear, deep channel closer to the river I had traveled the previous day.

The rain and wind grew more severe, and several times I pulled over to tip water from the canoe. The channel soon developed steep mud banks and snags. Farther on, the channel opened up and was eventually blocked by a large sandy bar. I pushed the canoe toward the bank, looking around carefully before getting out of the shallow and pulling the canoe up. I would be safe from crocodiles in the canoe—I had been told—but swimming and standing or wading at the water's edge were dangerous. Edges are one of the crocodile's favorite food-capturing places. I saw nothing, but the feeling of unease that had been with me all day intensified.

In this example of literary nonfiction, Plumwood persuades readers to appreciate the beauties of the exotic Australian rain forest as well as its dangers. Note how her method includes the depicting of events that happen once in time—her wondrous first day of exploration, the ranger's warning to stay away from the main river, her second day's unsuccessful search by canoe for a site of Aboriginal rock art, and then her emerging discovery that in the increasing intensity of the rainstorm, she had reached the junction with the main river. Plumwood's powerful narrative becomes the basis for a profound concluding reflection on what she calls humans' "ecological identity."

Connectedness

The events of a story must also be connected, not merely spatially or sequentially, but causally or thematically. When discussing "The Stolen Watch" in the previous exercise, you might have asked yourselves, "What does all that stuff about forgetting to call Karen and stopping for parts, etc., have to do with the stolen watch? Is this story about the watch or about confronting a potential killer?" If so, you instinctively understood the concept of connectedness. Stories are more than just chronicles of events. Novelist E. M. Forster offered the simplest definition of a story when he rejected "The king dies and then the queen died," but accepted "The king died and then the queen died ... of grief." The words "of grief" connect the two events to each other in a causal relationship, converting a series of events into a patterned, meaningfully related sequence of events. Now examine this passage to see the connections the writer establishes between the scenes.

THEMATIC AND CAUSAL CONNECTEDNESS

I have been so totally erased from nature lately, like a blackboard before school starts, that yesterday when I was in the Japanese section of San Francisco, Japantown, I saw the sidewalk littered with chocolate wrappers.

There were hundreds of them. Who in the hell has been eating all these chocolates? I thought. A convention of Japanese chocolate eaters must have passed this way.

Then I noticed some plum trees on the street. Then I noticed that it was autumn. Then I noticed that the leaves were falling as they will and as they must every year. Where had I gone wrong?

—Richard Brautigan, "Leaves"

Brautigan's narrative becomes a story only when you realize that the "chocolate wrappers" are really plum leaves; the two images are connected by the writer's changed perception, which illuminates the thematic question raised at the beginning and end: Why has he become "so totally erased from nature"? As you write, connect the elements of your narrative causally and thematically.

Tension or Conflict

The third criterion for a story—tension or conflict—creates the anticipation and potential significance that keep the reader reading. In whodunit stories, the tension follows from attempts to identify the murderer or to prevent the murderer from doing in yet another victim. In many comic works, the tension is generated by confusion or misunderstanding that drives a wedge between people who would normally be close. Tension always involves contraries, such as those between one belief and another, between opposing values, between the individual and the environment or the social order, between where I am now and where I want to be or used to be. In the following passage, notice how the contraries create dramatic tension that engages readers.

DRAMATIC TENSIONS

Straddling the top of the world, one foot in China and the other in Nepal, I cleared the ice from my oxygen mask, hunched a shoulder against the wind, and stared absently down at the vastness of Tibet. I understood on some dim, detached level that the sweep of earth beneath my feet was a spectacular sight. I'd been fantasizing about this moment, and the release of emotion that would accompany it, for many months. But now that I was finally here, actually standing on the summit of Mount Everest, I just couldn't summon the energy to care.

It was early in the afternoon of May 10, 1996. I hadn't slept in fifty-seven hours. The only food I'd been able to force down over the preceding three days was a bowl of ramen soup and a handful of peanut M&M's. Weeks of violent coughing had left me with two separated ribs that made ordinary breathing an excruciating trial. At 29,028 feet up in the troposphere, so little oxygen was reaching my brain that my mental capacity was that of a slow child. Under the circumstances, I was incapable of feeling much of anything except cold and tired.

—Jon Krakauer, *Into Thin Air*

Notice how this passage presents several contraries or conflicts: the opposition between the narrator's expectation of what it would be like to stand on the top of Mount Everest and the actuality once he's there; and the opposition between the physical strength and stamina of the climber and the extreme danger of climbing this mountain. The reader wonders how Krakauer reached the summit with no sleep, almost no food, and a violent and agonizing cough; more important, the reader wonders why he kept on climbing. We can ask this important query of any narrative: What conflicts and tensions are prompting readers' ongoing questions and holding their interest?

Resolution, Recognition, or Retrospective Interpretation

The final criterion for a story is the resolution or retrospective interpretation of events. The resolution may be stated explicitly or implied. Fables typically sum up the story's significance with an explicit moral at the end. In contrast, the interpretation of events in poetry is almost always implicit. Note how the following haiku collapses events and resolution.

RESOLUTION

A strange old man
stops me,
Looking out of my deep mirror.

—Hitomaro, *One Hundred Poems from the Japanese*

In this tiny story, two things happen simultaneously. The narrator is stopped by a "strange old man" and the narrator looks into a mirror. The narrator's *recognition* is that he is that same old man. This recognition—"That's me in the mirror; when I wasn't looking, I grew old!"—in turn ties the singular event of the story back to more universal concerns and the reader's world.

The typical direction of a story, from singular event(s) to general conclusion, reverses the usual points-first direction of closed-form essays. Stories force readers to read inductively, gathering information and looking for a pattern that's confirmed or unconfirmed by the story's resolution. This resolution is the point *toward* which readers read. It often drives home the significance of the narrative. Typically, a reader's satisfaction or dissatisfaction with a story hinges on how well the resolution manages to explain or justify the events that precede it. Writers need to ask: How does my resolution grow out of my narrative and fit with the resolution the reader has been forming?

Identifying Criteria for "Story"

FOR WRITING AND DISCUSSION

1. Working as a whole class or in small groups, return to Patrick José's essay "No Cats in America?" and explain how it qualifies as a story rather than an *and then* chronology. How does it meet all four of the criteria: depiction of events through time, connectedness, tension, and resolution?

2. Consider again "The Stolen Watch." It seems to meet the criterion of "depiction of events through time," but it is weak in connectedness, tension, and resolution. How could the writer revise the chronology to make it a story? Brainstorm several different ways that this potentially exciting early draft could be rewritten.

3. If you are working on your own open-form narrative, exchange drafts with a classmate. Discuss each other's draft in light of this lesson's focus on story. To what extent do your drafts exhibit the features of a story rather than those of an *and then* chronology? Working together, develop revision plans that might increase the story elements in your narratives.

SKILL 11.2 **Write low on the ladder of abstraction.**

In Chapter 4 we introduced the concept of "ladder of abstraction," in which words can be arranged from the very abstract (living creatures, clothing) down to the very specific (our dog Charley with the floppy ears; my hippie Birkenstocks with the saltwater stains; see Chapter 4, Concept 11). In this lesson we show why and how open-form writers stay low on the ladder of abstraction through their use of concrete words, revelatory words, and memory-soaked words.

Concrete Words Evoke Images and Sensations

To appreciate the impact of specific, concrete language, look again at the opening sentence of Val Plumwood's narrative about her encounter with crocodiles (p. 284):

> In the early wet season, Kakadu's paper-bark wetlands are especially stunning, as the water lilies weave white, pink, and blue patterns of dreamlike beauty over the shining thunderclouds reflected in their still waters.

Here is how that same passage might sound if rewritten a level higher on the ladder of abstraction:

> In the early wet season the Kakadu landscape is especially stunning, as the water plants weave their colorful patterns of dreamlike beauty over the clouds reflected in the water's surface.

This is still quite a nice sentence. But something is lost when you say "landscape" rather than "paper-bark wetlands," "clouds" rather than "thunderclouds," or "colorful" rather than "white, pink, and blue." The lower you write on the ladder of abstraction, the more you tap into your readers' storehouse of particular memories and images.

The power of concrete words has been analyzed by writer John McPhee in a widely quoted and cited interview. When asked why he wrote the sentence "Old white oaks are rare because they had a tendency to become bowsprits, barrel staves, and queen-post trusses" instead of a more generic sentence such as, "Old white oaks are rare because they were used as lumber," he responded in a way that reveals his love of the particular:

> There isn't much life in [the alternative version of the sentence]. If you can find a specific, firm, and correct image, it's always going to be better than a generality, and hence I tend, for example, to put in trade names and company names and, in an instance like this, the names of wood products instead of a general term like "lumber." You'd say "Sony" instead of "tape recorder" if the context made it clear you meant to say tape recorder. It's not because you're on the take from Sony, it's because the image, at least to this writer or reader, strikes a clearer note.

Some readers might complain that the particulars "bowsprits, barrel staves, and queen-post trusses" don't help readers' understanding, as do particulars in closed-form prose, but instead give most readers a moment's pause. Today most barrel staves and bowsprits are made of metal, not oak, and few contemporary readers encounter them on a regular basis no matter what they're made of. Furthermore, few readers at any time could readily identify "queen-post trusses," a technical term from the building trade. Instead of smoothly completing the reader's understanding of a point, McPhee's particulars tend to arrest and even sidetrack, sending the reader in pursuit of a dictionary.

But if McPhee's examples momentarily puzzle, it's the sort of puzzlement that can lead to greater understanding. Precisely because they are exotic terms, these words arouse the reader's curiosity and imagination. "Exotic language is of value," says McPhee. "A queen-post truss is great just because of the sound of the words and what they call to mind. The 'queen,' the 'truss'—the ramifications in everything."

For McPhee, the fact that these words trip up the reader is a point in their favor. If McPhee had said that old white oaks are rare these days because they became parts of "ships, barrels, and roofs," no one would blink or notice. If you were to visualize the items, you'd probably call up some ready-made pictures that leave little trace in your mind. You also wouldn't hear the sounds of the words. (In this regard, notice McPhee's emphasis on images sounding "a clearer note.") Your forward progress toward the point would be unimpeded, but what would be lost? A new glimpse into a lost time when oak trees were used to make exotic items that today exist mostly in old books and memories.

Another quality also recommends words that readers trip over, words such as *bowsprit, barrel stave,* and *queen-post truss:* their power to persuade the reader to believe in the world being described. Tripping over things, whether they're made of steel or words, forces the reader to acknowledge their independence, the reality of a world outside the reader's own head. For this reason, writers of formula fiction—thrillers, westerns, romances, and the like—will load their texts with lots of little details and bits of technical information from the time and place they describe. Because their stories are otherwise implausible (e.g., the description of the Evil Empire's doomsday machine), they need all the help they can get from their details (the size of the toggle bolts used to keep the machine in place while it's blasting out intergalactic death rays) to convince readers that the story is real.

Using Revelatory Words and Memory-Soaked Words

As we have seen, concrete language, low on the ladder of abstraction, can evoke imaginative experiences for readers. Two particularly powerful kinds of concrete language are revelatory words and memory-soaked words. By *revelatory* words we mean specific details that reveal the social status, lifestyle, beliefs, and values of people. According to writer Tom Wolfe, carefully chosen details can reveal a person's *status life*—"the entire pattern of behavior and possessions through which people express their position in the world or what they think it is or hope it to be." Wolfe favors writing that records "everyday gestures, habits, manners, customs, styles of furniture, clothing, decoration, styles of traveling, eating, keeping house, modes of behaving toward children, servants, superiors, inferiors, peers, plus the various looks, glances, poses, styles of walking and other symbolic details that might exist within a scene." Thus subtle differences in a person's status life might be revealed in details about fast food (a Big Mac versus a Subway turkey wrap), body piercing (pierced ears versus pierced tongue), a watch (a Timex versus a Rolex), or music (Kenny Chesney versus Busta Rhymes).

Another way to create powerful concrete language is through *memory-soaked* words. Such words trigger a whole complex of ideas, emotions, and sensations in readers who share memories from a particular era. People who grew up in the 1950s, for example, might have deep associations with 45-rpm records, the *Ed Sullivan Show,* or the words "duck tail" or "tail fins." For Vietnam veterans, Nancy

Sinatra's "These Boots Were Made for Walking" or the whirr of helicopter blades might evoke strong memories. Persons growing up in the 1970s or 1980s might remember "Cookie Monster," "Pez guns," or 8-track tapes. In recent years, our students have come up with these memory-soaked words from their own childhoods: American Girl dolls, Power Rangers, Ghostbuster action figures, Super Nintendo, Pokeman, *American Idol,* and The Sims.

<table>
<tr><td>

**FOR
WRITING
AND
DISCUSSION**

</td><td>

Working Low on the Ladder of Abstraction

1. Working in small groups or as a whole class, try your own hand at using revelatory words to reveal status life. Create a list of specific details that you might associate with each of the following: middle school girls at a slumber party; friends at a tailgate party before a football game; the kitchen of an upscale urban apartment of a two-profession couple who subscribe to *Gourmet* magazine; the kitchen of a middle-class, middle America family with three kids and a collection of *Good Housekeeping* magazines; the kitchen of an apartment shared by college students. (If you are describing kitchens, for example, consider the different *status life* signaled by ketchup versus stone-ground mustard or by an iceberg lettuce salad with ranch dressing versus an almond mandarin salad.)
2. Also try your hand at finding memory-soaked words. Make a list of specific words and names associated with your childhood that you now rarely hear or see. Share your list with others in your group and identify the items that have the strongest associations.
3. If you are working on your own open-form narrative, exchange drafts with a classmate and, working together, find specific examples where each of you has successfully used concrete, revelatory, or memory-soaked words. Then find passages that could be profitably revised by moving down a rung on the ladder of abstraction or by adding concrete details that follow the advice in this lesson.

</td></tr>
</table>

SKILL 11.3 Disrupt your reader's desire for direction and clarity.

The epigraph to Chapter 10 by the philosopher Kenneth Burke speaks about form as "an arousing and fulfillment of desires." In closed-form prose, we can easily see this process at work: The writer previews what he or she is going to say, arousing the reader's desire to see the general outline fleshed out with specifics, and then fulfills that desire speedily through a presentation of pertinent points and particulars.

In more open-form prose, the fulfillment of desire follows a less straightforward path. Writers offer fewer overviews and clues, leaving readers less sure of where they're headed; or writers mention an idea and then put it aside for a while as they pursue some other point whose relevance may seem tenuous to the reader. Rather than establish the direction or point of their prose, writers suspend that direction, waiting until later in the prose to show how the ideas are meaningfully related. In other words, the period of arousal is longer and more drawn out; the fulfillment of desire is delayed until the end, when the reader finally sees how the pieces fit together.

Open-form prose gives you the opportunity to overlay your narrative core with other patterns of ideas—to move associatively from idea to idea, to weave a complex pattern of meaning in which the complete picture emerges later. Often the way you achieve these surprising twists and turns of structure and meaning is by playing with the conventions of closed-form prose. For example, in the autobiographical narrative "No Cats in America?", Patrick José breaks the cardinal closed-form rule that titles should forecast the essay's thesis: If José's essay were closed form, it should be about some kind of surprising decline of cats in America. However, José's title is metaphoric, and the reader doesn't completely comprehend its significance until the last lines of the essay. This delaying of meaning—requiring the reader to help cocreate the meaning—is typical of open-form prose. Here in this section we describe some of your open-form options for surprising your readers and delaying their fulfillment of desires.

Disrupting Predictions and Making Odd Juxtapositions

Open-form writers frequently violate the principle of forecasting and mapping that we stressed in Chapter 10. Consider the following introduction to an essay:

PASSAGE WITH DISRUPTED PREDICTIONS AND ODD JUXTAPOSITIONS

> I suppose their little bones have years ago been lost among the stones and winds of those high glacial pastures. I suppose their feathers blew eventually into the piles of tumbleweed beneath the straggling cattle fences and rotted there in the mountain snows, along with dead steers and all the other things that drift to an end in the corners of the wire. I do not quite know why I should be thinking of birds over the *New York Times* at breakfast, particularly the birds of my youth half a continent away. It is a funny thing what the brain will do with memories and how it will treasure them and finally bring them into odd juxtapositions with other things, as though it wanted to make a design, or get some meaning out of them, whether you want it or not, or even see it.

Whose bones? What feathers?

Birds? What birds?

What do birds have to do with how the brain works? Where is this writer going?

> —Loren Eisley, "The Bird and the Machine"

Note the sequence of ideas from bones to birds to breakfast over the *New York Times* to comments about the workings of the brain. In fact, in this essay it takes Eisley six full paragraphs in which he discusses mechanical inventions to return to the birds with the line: "... or those birds, I'll never forget those birds. ... "

Throughout these paragraphs, what drives the reader forward is curiosity to discover the connections between the parts and to understand the meaning of the essay's title, "The Bird and the Machine." Actually, Eisley's comment about the brain's "odd juxtapositions" of memories with "other things, as though it wanted to make a design, or get some meaning out of them" could be a description of this open-form technique we've called "disrupting predictions and making odd juxtapositions." Open-form writers can choose when "odd juxtapositions" are an appropriate strategy for inviting the reader to accompany the discovering, reflecting writer on a journey toward meaning.

Leaving Gaps

An important convention of closed-form prose is the old/new contract, which specifies that the opening of every sentence should link in some way to what has gone before. Open-form prose often violates this convention, leaving *gaps* in the text, forcing the reader to puzzle over the connection between one part and the next.

The following passage clearly violates the old/new contract. This example recounts the writer's thoughts after startling a weasel in the woods and exchanging glances with it.

PASSAGE WITH INTENTIONAL GAPS

Gap caused by unexplained or unpredicted shift from weasel to philosophic musing

What goes on in [a weasel's brain] the rest of the time? What does a weasel think about? He won't say. His journal is tracks in clay, a spray of feathers, mouse blood and bone: uncollected, unconnected, loose-leaf, and blown.

I would like to learn, or remember, how to live. I come to Hollins Pond not so much to learn how to live as, frankly, to forget about it.

—Annie Dillard, "Living Like Weasels"

Dillard suddenly switches, without transition, from musing about the mental life of a weasel to asserting that she would like to learn how to live. What is the connection between her encounter with the weasel and her own search for how to live? Dillard's open-form techniques leave these gaps for readers to ponder and fill in, inviting us to participate in the process of arriving at meaning. Just as open-form writers can deliberately avoid predicting or mapping statements, they also have the liberty to leave gaps in a text when it suits their purpose.

FOR WRITING AND DISCUSSION

Disrupting Reader Expectations

If you are currently working on an open-form narrative, exchange drafts with a classmate. Discuss in what way the strategies explained in this lesson might be appropriate for your purposes. Where might you currently "explain too much" and benefit by juxtaposing scenes without explanatory filler? Where might you use other strategies from this lesson?

SKILL II.4 **Tap the power of figurative language.**

Open-form writers often use figurative language in situations in which closed-form writers would use literal language. In this brief section, we show you some of the power of figurative language.

When journalist Nicholas Tomalin describes a captured Vietnamese prisoner as young and slight, the reader understands him in a literal way, but when, a moment later, he compares the prisoner to "a tiny, fine-boned wild animal," the reader understands him in a different way; the reader understands not only what the subject looks like—his general physical attributes—but how that particular boy appears in that moment to those around him—fierce, frightened, trapped.

Metaphors abound when literal words fail. When writers encounter eccentric people or are overwhelmed by the strangeness of their experiences, they use *figurative language*—imaginative comparisons—to explain their situation and their reactions to it. Figurative language—similes, metaphors, and personifications—enables the writer to describe an unfamiliar thing in terms of different, more familiar things. The surprise of yoking two very unlike things evokes from the reader a perception, insight, or emotional experience that could not otherwise be communicated. The originality and vividness of the imaginative comparison frequently resonates with meaning for readers and sticks in their minds long afterward.

In the following passage, Isak Dinesen describes an experience that most of us have not had—seeing iguanas in the jungle and shooting one. After reading this passage, however, we have a striking picture in our minds of what she saw and a strong understanding of what she felt and realized.

PASSAGE USING FIGURATIVE LANGUAGE

In the Reserve I have sometimes come upon the Iguana, the big lizards, as they were sunning themselves upon a flat stone in a riverbed. They are not pretty in shape, but nothing can be imagined more beautiful than their coloring. They shine like a heap of precious stones or like a pane cut out of an old church window. When, as you approach, they swish away, there is a flash of azure, green and purple over the stones, the color seems to be standing behind them in the air, like a comet's luminous tail.

Similes heaped up

Simile

Once I shot an Iguana. I thought that I should be able to make some pretty things from his skin. A strange thing happened then, that I have never afterwards forgotten. As I went up to him, where he was lying dead upon his stone, and actually while I was walking a few steps, he faded and grew pale, all color died out of him as in one long sigh, and by the time that I touched him he was gray and dull like a lump of concrete. It was the live impetuous blood pulsating within the animal, which had radiated out all that glow and splendor. Now that the flame was put out, and the soul had flown, the Iguana was as dead as a sandbag.

Metaphor of dying applied to color

Simile

Metaphor

Simile

—Isak Dinesen, "The Iguana"

The figurative language in this passage enables readers to share Dinesen's experience. It also compacts a large amount of information into sharp, memorable images.

Using Figurative Language

FOR
WRITING
AND
DISCUSSION

1. Figurative language can fall flat when it takes the form of clichés ("I stood transfixed like a bump on a log") or mixed metaphors ("Exposed like a caterpillar on a leaf, he wolfed down his lunch before taking flight"). But when used effectively, figurative language adds powerfully compressed and meaningful images to a passage. Working individually or in small groups, find examples of figurative language in one or more of the example

passages in this chapter or in Chapter 6 (pp. 144–164). See if you can reach consensus on what makes a particular instance of figurative language effective or ineffective.

2. If you are currently working on an open-form narrative, exchange drafts with a classmate. See if you can find instances of figurative language in your current drafts and analyze their effectiveness. Perhaps you can also discover places where figurative language could be profitably added to the text.

SKILL 11.5 **Expand your repertoire of styles.**

In Chapter 4, we introduced you to the concept of style, which is a combination of sentence structure, word choice, and rhythm that allows writers to vary their emphasis and tone in a variety of ways. In this section, we show you how to expand your repertoire of styles through a classic method of teaching in which you try to imitate other writers' styles. This rhetorical practice—called "creative imitation"—has a long history beginning with the rhetoricians of classical Greece and Rome. When you do creative imitation, you examine a passage from an expert stylist and try to emulate it. You substitute your own subject matter, but you try to imitate the exact grammatical structures, lengths and rhythms of the sentences, and the tones of the original passage. The long-range effect of creative imitation is to expand your stylistic choices; the more immediate effect is to increase your skill at analyzing a writer's style. Most practitioners find that creative imitation encourages surprising insights into their own subject matter (when seen through the lens of the original writer's style) as well as a new understanding of how a particular piece of writing creates its special effects.

See Chapter 4, Concept 11, for a discussion of style.

You begin a creative imitation by asking questions such as these: What is distinctive about the sentences in this passage of writing? How do choices about sentence length and complexity, kinds of words, figures of speech, and so forth create a writer's voice? After close examination of the passage, you then think of your own subject matter that could be appropriately adapted to this writer's style.

To help you understand creative imitation, we provide the following example. In this passage, the writer, Victoria Register-Freeman, is exploring how relations between young men and women today threaten to undo some of the twentieth century's progress toward gender equality. In the section of her article that precedes this passage, Register-Freeman explains how she, as a single mother, taught her boys to cook, sew, do laundry, and "carry their weight domestically." But then, as she explains in this passage, teenage girls undid her attempts at creating gender equality:

REGISTER-FREEMAN PASSAGE

Then came puberty and hunkhood. Over the last few years, the boys' domestic skills have atrophied because handmaidens have appeared en masse. The damsels have driven by, beeped, phoned and faxed. Some appeared so frequently outside the front door they began to remind me of the suction-footed Garfields spread-eagled on car windows. While the girls varied according to height, hair color and basic body type, they shared one characteristic. They were ever eager to help the guys out.

—Victoria Register-Freeman, "My Turn: Hunks and Handmaidens"

Register-Freeman's voice projects the image of a concerned mother and feminist social critic. Her tone includes a range of attitudes: serious, personal, factual, ironic, frustrated. Note how this passage begins and ends with short, clipped sentences. The second sentence states a problem that the next three sentences develop with various kinds of details. The third sentence includes a series of colorful verbs; the fourth uses a metaphor (the ever-present girls compared to Garfields on car windows). The fifth sentence builds to the point in the sixth sentence, which is delivered bluntly and simply.

Here is one writer's attempt at a creative imitation:

CREATIVE IMITATION OF REGISTER-FREEMAN

Then came prosperity and popularity. Over the last ten years, Seattle's special charms have faded because expansion has occurred too rapidly. Traffic has multiplied, thickened, amplified, and slowed. Traffic jams appeared so often on the freeways and arterials they began to remind me of ants swarming over spilled syrup. While the congestion varied according to time, seasons, and weather conditions, it had one dominant effect. It increasingly threatened to spoil the city's beauty.

Practicing Style through Creative Imitation

FOR WRITING AND DISCUSSION

1. Do your own creative imitation of the passage from Register-Freeman.
2. Choose one or both of the following passages for creative imitation. Begin by jotting down all the specific observations you can make about the stylistic features of the passage. Then choose a topic that matches the topic of the original in its degree of lightness or seriousness and its depth. Explore your topic by presenting it using the sentence structures and kinds of words used in the original. Try to imitate the original phrase by phrase and sentence by sentence. You may find it helpful to use a dictionary and thesaurus.

   a. Africa is mystic; it is wild; it is a sweltering inferno; it is a photographer's paradise, a hunter's Valhalla, an escapist's Utopia. It is what you will, and it withstands all interpretations. It is the last vestige of a dead world or the cradle of a shiny new one. To a lot of people, as to myself, it is just "home." It is all of these things but one thing—it is never dull.

   —Beryl Markham, "Flying Elsewhere," *West with the Night*

   b. The disease was bubonic plague, present in two forms: one that infected the bloodstream, causing the buboes and internal bleeding, and was spread by contact; and a second, more virulent pneumonic type that infected the lungs and was spread by respiratory infection. The presence of both at once caused the high mortality and speed of contagion. So lethal was the disease that cases were known of persons going to bed well and dying before they woke, of doctors catching the illness at bedside and dying before the patient.

   —Barbara Tuchman, "This Is the End of the World," *A Distant Mirror*

SKILL II.6 Use open-form elements to create "voice" in closed-form prose.

So far we have been talking about features of open-form prose in its purer forms. Sometimes, however, writers wish simply to loosen basically closed-form prose by combining it with some features of open-form prose. If, for example, an academic wanted to share new developments in a field with a popular audience, he or she would be well-advised to leaven his or her prose with some elements of open-form writing. In this final section, we offer several pieces of advice for loosening up closed-form prose.

Introducing Some Humor

Humor is rare in tightly closed prose because humor is nonfunctional—it doesn't *have* to be there for a writer to make a point—and closed-form prose values efficiency, saying what you have to say in the most economical fashion.

Humor is particularly valuable in that it can make imposing subjects more manageable for readers. Formal, abstract language can put readers off, estranging them from the subject; humor has the power to "de-strange" a subject, to allow the audience to look at it long enough to understand it. Many popular books on science and many of the best instructional books on car repair, cooking, money management, and others of life's drearier necessities use a humorous style to help their phobic readers get on with life.

To appreciate the effect of humor, consider the following passages from two different instructional books on how to operate the database program Paradox. The first passage, from *Windows in 21 Days*, uses a clear, humor-free, closed-form style.

> In this book, you learn by following detailed step-by-step exercises based on real-world problems in database application design. Every exercise leads you further into the power of "Paradox for Windows" as you develop the components of an automated application. This section does the following: explains the assumptions and conventions used in this book; lists the hardware and software requirements and setup needed to run Paradox for Windows and use this book efficiently; and offers some suggestions for strategies to get the most from this book. The step-by-step exercises make it easy.

Now note the different effect produced by the following passage from one of the hugely popular *For Dummies* books:

> Welcome to *Paradox for Windows for Dummies*, a book that's not afraid to ask the tough questions like "When's lunch?" and "Who finished the cookie dough ice cream?" If you're more interested in food (or Australian Wombats, for that matter) than you are in Paradox for Windows, this book is for you. If you're more interested in Paradox for Windows, please get some professional help before going out into society again.
>
> My goal is to help you get things done despite the fact that you're using Paradox. Whether you're at home, in your office, or at home in your office (or even if you just *feel* like you live at work) *Paradox for Windows for Dummies* is your all-in-one guidebook through the treacherous, frustrating, and appallingly technical world of the relational database.

Thinking about Humor

1. Which of these two instructional books would you prefer to read?
2. The second passage says that the world of relational databases is "treacherous, frustrating, and appallingly technical," whereas the first stresses that the "step-by-step exercises [in the book] make it easy." Why do you suppose the humorous passage stresses the difficulty of databases whereas the humorless passage stresses the ease of a step-by-step approach? Is it good strategy for the humorous writer to stress the difficulty of Paradox?
3. Under what rhetorical circumstances are humorous instructions better than strictly serious instructions? When is a strictly serious approach better?

Using Techniques from Popular Magazines

Writers who publish regularly for popular audiences develop a vigorous, easy-reading style that differs from the style of much academic writing. The effect of this difference is illustrated by the results of a famous research study conducted by Michael Graves and Wayne Slater at the University of Michigan. For this study, teams of writers revised passages from a high school history textbook.* One team consisted of linguists and technical writers trained in producing closed-form texts using the strategies discussed in Chapter 10 (forecasting structure, putting points first, following the old/new contract, using transitions). A second team consisted of two *Time-Life* book editors.

Whereas the linguists aimed at making the passages clearer, the *Time-Life* writers were more concerned with making them livelier. The result? One hundred eleventh-grade students found the *Time-Life* editors' version both more comprehensible and more memorable. The problem with the original textbook wasn't lack of clarity but rather dryness. According to the researchers, the *Time-Life* editors did not limit themselves

> to making the passages lucid, well-organized, coherent, and easy to read. Their revisions went beyond such matters and were intended to make the texts interesting, exciting, vivid, rich in human drama, and filled with colorful language.

To see how they achieved this effect, let's look at their revision. Here is a passage about the Vietnam War taken from the original history text:

ORIGINAL HISTORY TEXT

> The most serious threat to world peace developed in Southeast Asia. Communist guerrillas threatened the independence of the countries carved out of French Indo-China by the Geneva conference of 1954. In South Vietnam, Communist guerrillas (the Viet Cong) were aided by forces from Communist North Vietnam in a struggle to overthrow the American-supported government. . . .

*The study involved three teams, but for purposes of simplification we limit our discussion to two.

Shortly after the election of 1964, Communist gains prompted President Johnson to alter his policy concerning Vietnam. American military forces in Vietnam were increased from about 20,000 men in 1964 to more than 500,000 by 1968. Even so, North Vietnamese troops and supplies continued to pour into South Vietnam.

Here is the *Time-Life* editors' revision:

HISTORY PRESENTED IN POPULAR MAGAZINE STYLE

In the early 1960s the greatest threat to world peace was just a small splotch of color on Kennedy's map, one of the fledgling nations sculpted out of French Indo-China by the Geneva peacemakers of 1954. It was a country so tiny and remote that most Americans had never uttered its name: South Vietnam. ...

Aided by Communist North Vietnam, the Viet Cong guerrillas were eroding the ground beneath South Vietnam's American-backed government. Village by village, road by road, these jungle-wise rebels were waging a war of ambush and mining: They darted out of tunnels to head off patrols, buried exploding booby traps beneath the mud floors of huts, and hid razor-sharp bamboo sticks in holes. ...

No sooner had Johnson won the election than Communist gains prompted Johnson to go back on his campaign promise. The number of American soldiers in Vietnam skyrocketed from 20,000 in 1964 to more than 500,000 by 1968. But in spite of GI patrols, leech-infested jungles, swarms of buzzing insects, and flash floods that made men cling to trees to escape being washed away— North Vietnamese troops streamed southward without letup along the Ho Chi Minh Trail.

What can this revision teach you about invigorating closed-form prose? What specifically are the editors doing here?

First, notice how far the level of abstraction drops in the revision. The original is barren of sensory words; the revision is alive with them ("South Vietnam" becomes a "small splotch of color on Kennedy's map"; "a struggle to overthrow the American-supported government" becomes "[They] buried exploding booby traps beneath the mud floors of huts, and hid razor-sharp bamboo sticks in holes").

Second, notice how much more dramatic the revision is. Actual scenes, including a vision of men clinging to trees to escape being washed away by flash floods, replace a chronological account of the war's general progress. According to the editors, such scenes, or "nuggets"—vivid events that encapsulate complex processes or principles—are the lifeblood of *Time-Life* prose.

Finally, notice how the revision tends to delay critical information for dramatic effect, moving information you would normally expect to find early on into a later position. In the first paragraph, the *Time-Life* writers talk about "the greatest threat to world peace" in the early 1960s for four lines before revealing the identity of that threat—South Vietnam.

Enlivening Closed-Form Prose with Open-Form Elements

Here is a passage from a student argument opposing women's serving on submarines. Working individually or in small groups, enliven this passage by using some of the techniques of the *Time-Life* writers.

> Not only would it be very expensive to refit submarines for women personnel, but having women on submarines would hurt the morale of the sailors. In order for a crew to work effectively, they must have good morale or their discontent begins to show through in their performance. This is especially crucial on submarines, where if any problem occurs, it affects the safety of the whole ship. Women would hurt morale by creating sexual tension. Sexual tension can take many forms. One form is couples' working and living in a close space with all of the crew. When a problem occurs within the relationship, it could affect the morale of those directly involved and in the workplace. This would create an environment that is not conducive to good productivity. Tension would also occur if one of the women became pregnant or if there were complaints of sexual harassment. It would be easier to deal with these problems on a surface ship, but in the small confines of a submarine these problems would cause more trouble.

 For additional help with writing, go to
www.mycomplab.com.

A RHETORICAL GUIDE TO RESEARCH

This screen capture shows the home page of Women Against Gun Control (www.wagc.com), a grassroots organization dedicated to supporting women's right to defend themselves. This organization participates in pro-gun political activism, legislative research, media awareness, distribution of print resources, and gun-related education. The Web site itself uses color, images, other design features, and bold text to stake out its position in the complex controversy over women's role in the hotly contested, larger issue of gun control.

Ladies of High-Caliber

Protect Your Rights!

Join Now!

Click Here for the 10 Commandments of gun safety!

Home

WAGC Information

WAGC Features

WAGC Boycotts

WAGC Links

WAGC Site map

WAGC Contact

Get your pin in honor of WAGC!

Women Against Gun Control

"The Second Amendment IS the Equal

Click here to sign and read our new forum board!

WAGC sends amicus brief to the U.S. Supreme Court!
Click Here (Opens New Window)
Click here to read a press release regarding this hearing.

Click here for a special message from WAGC President, Janalee Tobias

Contact Us

Postal Address

- WAGC

  PO Box 95357
  South Jordan, UT
  84095

Telephone

- 801-328-9660

E-Mail

- info@wagc.com
- State and Local Chapters
- webmaster

It's a Fact:

RECENT RESEARCH INDICATES THAT GUNS ARE USED DEFENSIVELY 2.5 MILLION TIMES PER YEAR.

It's not surprising then, that more women than ever want to keep their rights to own and carry a gun.
The reason is simple: Women **are** concerned about becoming victims of crime. Guns give women a fighting chance against crime.

Join Women Against Gun Control.
Take the Women Against Gun Control Pledge and you qualify for a membership in Women Against Gun Control, a grass roots volunteer organization dedicated to preserving our gun rights.

Join thousands of women (and men) in sending a powerful message throughout the world.

"Guns **SAVE** Lives. We do **NOT** support gun control. Gun Control does **NOT** control crime!"

2nd Amendment
A well regulated Militia being necessary to the security of a free State, the right of the people to keep and bear Arms shall not be infringed.

"The Second Amendment IS Homeland Security."

Special Article
Have gun, will not fear it anymore

Rosie O'Donnel

Hillary Clinton

Janet Reno

Diane Feinstein

Want Americans to believe all women support gun control...

Let's BLOW HOLES in this MYTH!

If women are disarmed, a rapist will never hear...

"STOP OR I'LL SHOOT!"

Looking for Pro-Second Amendment and Pro-Freedom Books? Check Out These Book Reviews and Help Support This Site!

Support WAGC Efforts with the Utah GIRAFFE Society!

PART 4 A RHETORICAL GUIDE TO RESEARCH

Part 4 addresses the following outcomes for first-year composition from the Council of Writing Program Administrators.

RHETORICAL KNOWLEDGE	• Focus on purpose (Skill 12.1) • Use conventions of format and structure appropriate to the rhetorical situation (Skills 12.1-12.5, 13.1-13.4)
CRITICAL THINKING, READING, AND WRITING	• Integrate their own ideas with those of others (Skills 12.1-12.5)
PROCESSES	• Understand the collaborative and social aspects of writing processes (Skill 12.5) • Learn to balance the advantages of relying on others with the responsibility of doing their part (Skill 12.5)
KNOWLEDGE OF CONVENTIONS	• Learn common formats for different kinds of texts (Skills 12.2-12.4, 13.1-13.4) • Practice appropriate means of documenting their work (Skills 13.1-13.4)

INCORPORATING SOURCES INTO YOUR OWN WRITING

12

So far, we have covered strategies for finding and evaluating sources. Now we focus on the skills needed for incorporating sources into your own writing.

In this chapter, you will learn the following skills:

- **SKILL 12.1** Let your own argument determine your use of sources.
- **SKILL 12.2** Know when and how to use summary, paraphrase, and quotation.
- **SKILL 12.3** Use attributive tags to distinguish your ideas from a source's.
- **SKILL 12.4** Punctuate quotations correctly.
- **SKILL 12.5** Avoid plagiarism by following academic conventions for ethical use of sources.

Many of the examples in this chapter will be based on the following short article about violence in the Old West. This chapter will be most useful to you if you read the article first.

Roger D. McGrath
The Myth of Violence in the Old West*

1   It is commonly assumed that violence is part of our frontier heritage. But the historical record shows that frontier violence was very different from violence today. Robbery and burglary, two of our most common crimes, were of no great significance in the frontier towns of the Old West, and rape was seemingly nonexistent.

2   Bodie, one of the principal towns on the trans-Sierra frontier, illustrates the point. Nestled high in the mountains of eastern California, Bodie, which boomed in the late 1870s and early 1880s, ranked among the most notorious frontier towns of the Old West. It was, as one prospector put it, the last of the old-time mining camps.

*From Roger D. McGrath, "The Myth of Violence in the Old West," *Gunfighters, Highwaymen, and Vigilantes: Violence on the Frontier*. Regents of the University of California, 1984.

3   Like the trans-Sierra frontier in general, Bodie was indisputably violent and law-less, yet most people were not affected. Fistfights and gunfights among willing combatants—gamblers, miners, and the like—were regular events, and stagecoach holdups were not unusual. But the old, the young, the weak, and the female—so often the victims of crime today—were generally not harmed.

4   Robbery was more often aimed at stagecoaches than at individuals. Highwaymen usually took only the express box and left the passengers alone. There were eleven stagecoach robberies in Bodie between 1878 and 1882, and in only two instances were passengers robbed. (In one instance, the highwaymen later apologized for their conduct.)

5   There were only ten robberies and three attempted robberies of individuals in Bodie during its boom years, and in nearly every case the circumstances were the same: the victim had spent the evening in a gambling den, saloon, or brothel; he had revealed that he had on his person a significant sum of money; and he was staggering home drunk when the attack occurred.

6   Bodie's total of twenty-one robberies—eleven of stages and ten of individuals—over a five-year period converts to a rate of eighty-four robberies per 100,000 inhabi-tants per year. On this scale—the same scale used by the FBI to index crime—New York City's robbery rate in 1980 was 1,140, Miami's was 995, and Los Angeles's was 628. The rate for the United States as a whole was 243. Thus Bodie's robbery rate was significantly below the national average in 1980.

7   Perhaps the greatest deterrent to crime in Bodie was the fact that so many people were armed. Armed guards prevented bank robberies and holdups of stagecoaches carrying shipments of bullion, and armed homeowners and merchants discouraged burglary. Between 1878 and 1882, there were only thirty-two burglaries—seventeen of homes and fifteen of businesses—in Bodie. At least a half-dozen burglaries were thwarted by the presence of armed citizens. The newspapers regularly advocated shooting burglars on sight, and several burglars were, in fact, shot at.

8   Using the FBI scale, Bodie's burglary rate for those five years was 128. Miami's rate in 1980 was 3,282, New York's was 2,661, and Los Angeles's was 2,602. The rate of the United States as a whole was 1,668, thirteen times that of Bodie.

9   Bodie's law enforcement institutions were certainly not responsible for these low rates. Rarely were robbers or burglars arrested, and even less often were they con-victed. Moreover, many law enforcement officers operated on both sides of the law.

10   It was the armed citizens themselves who were the most potent—though not the only—deterrent to larcenous crime. Another was the threat of vigilantism. Highway-men, for example, understood that while they could take the express box from a stage-coach without arousing the citizens, they risked inciting the entire populace to action if they robbed the passengers.

11   There is considerable evidence that women in Bodie were rarely the victims of crime. Between 1878 and 1882 only one woman, a prostitute, was robbed, and there were no reported cases of rape. (There is no evidence that rapes occurred but were not reported.)

12   Finally, juvenile crime, which accounts for a significant portion of the violent crime in the United States today, was limited in Bodie to pranks and malicious mischief.

13   If robbery, burglary, crimes against women, and juvenile crime were relatively rare on the trans-Sierra frontier, homicide was not: thirty-one Bodieites were shot, stabbed, or beaten to death during the boom years, for a homicide rate of 116. No U.S. city today comes close to this rate. In 1980, Miami led the nation with a homicide rate of 32.7; Las Vegas was a distant second at 23.4. A half-dozen cities had rates of zero. The rate for the United States as a whole in that year was a mere 10.2.

14   Several factors contributed to Bodie's high homicide rate. A majority of the town's residents were young, adventurous, single males who adhered to a code of conduct that frequently required them to fight even if, or perhaps especially if, it could mean death. Courage was admired above all else. Alcohol also played a major role in fostering the settlement of disputes by violence.

15   If the men's code of conduct and their consumption of alcohol made fighting inevitable, their sidearms often made it fatal. While the carrying of guns probably reduced the incidence of robbery and burglary, it undoubtedly increased the number of homicides.

16   For the most part, the citizens of Bodie were not troubled by the great number of killings; nor were they troubled that only one man was ever convicted of murder. They accepted the killings and the lack of convictions because most of those killed had been willing combatants.

17   Thus the violence and lawlessness of the trans-Sierra frontier bear little relation to the violence and lawlessness that pervade American society today. If Bodie is at all representative of frontier towns, there is little justification for blaming contemporary American violence on our frontier heritage.

SKILL 12.1   **Let your own argument determine your use of sources.**

For effective college-level research, your own argument should govern your use of sources. How you incorporate a research source into your own paper—whether, for example, you summarize it fully or simply draw a few pieces of factual information from it—depends on your own purpose. As an illustration, consider how three hypothetical writers might use Roger D. McGrath's article "The Myth of Violence in the Old West." In each case, the writer's goal is not to reproduce McGrath's article but to use the article in support of the writer's own argument.

Writer 1: An Analytical Paper on Causes of Violence in Contemporary Society

The first writer is analyzing the causes of violence in contemporary U.S. society. She wants to reject one possible cause—that contemporary violence is a direct outgrowth of our violent past. To make this point, she summarizes McGrath's argument that the Old West was not as violent as most people think. This summary then becomes evidence for her own argument.

Identification of source

Summary of McGrath's argument

Page number of original material

Writer 1's own argument

Many people believe that our Wild West heritage is one of the causes of contemporary violence. But Roger McGrath, in his article "The Myth of Violence in the Old West," shows that today's violence is much different from frontier violence. He explains that in a typical frontier town, violence involved gunslingers who were "willing combatants," whereas today's typical victims—"the old, the young, the weak, and the female"—were unaffected by crime (304). Because the presence of an armed populace deterred robbery and burglary, theft was much less common in the Old West than today. On the other hand, McGrath explains, killings were fueled by guns, alcohol, and a code of conduct that invited fighting, so murders were much more frequent than in any U.S. city today (305). Thus, according to McGrath, there is little resemblance between violence on the frontier and violence in today's cities, so we cannot blame current violence on a tumultuous frontier past.

In this passage the author summarizes McGrath's argument in order to refute the violent frontier theory about the causes of contemporary violence. This author will proceed to other causes of violence and will not return to McGrath.

Writer 2: A Persuasive Paper Supporting Gun Control

In our next case, the writer uses McGrath's article to argue in favor of gun control. The writer wants to refute the popular pro-gun argument that law-abiding citizens need to be armed to protect themselves against criminals.

Identification of source

Data from McGrath's article

Page number in original

Writer 2's own analysis of the data and his argument

Opponents of gun control often argue that guns benefit society by providing protection against intruders. But such protection is deadly, as Roger McGrath shows in his study of violence in the frontier town of Bodie, California. Although guns reduced theft, as seen in the low rate of theft in the well-armed town of Bodie, the presence of guns also led to a homicide rate far above that of the most violent city in the U.S. today. The homicide rate in the frontier town of Bodie, California, for example, was 116 per 100,000, compared to the current national average of 10.2 per 100,000 (305). True, Bodie citizens reduced the theft rate by being heavily armed, but at a cost of a homicide rate more than ten times the current national average. To protect our consumer goods at the cost of so much human life is counter to the values of most Americans.

McGrath's article contains data (low rate of crimes against property, high homicide rate) that can be used on either side of the gun control debate. This writer acknowledges the evidence from Bodie showing that gun possession reduces theft and then works that potentially damaging information into an argument for gun control. How might you use the McGrath article to oppose gun control?

Writer 3: An Informative Paper Showing Shifting Definitions of Crime

The third writer summarizes part of McGrath's article to support her thesis that a community's definition of crime is constantly shifting.

Our notion of criminal activity shifts over time. For example, only a short time ago on the American frontier, murder was often ignored by law enforcement. Roger McGrath, in his discussion of violence in the frontier town of Bodie, California, during the 1870s and 1880s, showed that the townspeople accepted homicides as long as both the murderer and the victim were "willing combatants" who freely participated in gunfights (304). These young males who were the "willing combatants" in Bodie share many characteristics with modern gang members in that they were encouraged to fight by a "code of conduct." According to McGrath, "A majority of the town's residents were young, adventurous, single males who adhered to a code of conduct that frequently required them to fight even if ... it could mean death" (305). Today's gang members also follow a code of conduct that requires violence—often in the form of vengeance. Although joining a gang certainly makes youths "willing combatants," that status doesn't prevent prosecution in court. Today's "willing combatants" are criminals, but yesterday's "willing combatants" were not.

Identification of source

Partial summary of McGrath's article

Page number

Writer draws comparisons with modern criminals.

Quotation from McGrath's article

Writer extends her comparison.

This writer uses McGrath's article to make a point completely different from McGrath's. But by extending and applying information from McGrath's article to a new context, the writer gathers fuel for her own argument about shifting definitions of the word *criminal*.

Using Sources for a Purpose

FOR WRITING AND

Each of the hypothetical writers uses McGrath's article for a different purpose. Working individually or in groups, answer the following questions.

1. What are the differences in the ways the writers use the original article?
2. How are these differences related to differences in each writer's purpose?

SKILL 12.2 **Know when and how to use summary, paraphrase, and quotation.**

As a research writer, you need to incorporate sources gracefully into your own prose so that you stay focused on your own argument. Depending on your purpose, you might (1) summarize all or part of a source author's argument, (2) paraphrase a relevant portion of a source, or (3) quote small passages from the source directly. Whenever you use a source, you need to avoid plagiarism by referencing the source with an in-text citation, by putting paraphrases and summaries entirely in your own words, and by placing quotation marks around quoted passages. The following strategies chart gives you an overview of summary, paraphrase, and quotation as ways of incorporating sources into your own prose.

For an explanation of plagiarism in academic writing and a summary of how to avoid plagiarism, see Skill 12.5. For making in-text citations, see Chapter 13.

Strategies for Incorporating Sources into Your Own Prose

Strategies	What to Do	When to Use These Strategies
Summarize the source.	Condense a source writer's argument by keeping main ideas and omitting details (see Chapter 5, pp. 105–110).	• When the source writer's whole argument is relevant to your purpose • When the source writer presents an alternative or opposing view that you want to push against • When the source writer's argument can be used in support of your own
Paraphrase the source.	Reproduce an idea from a source writer but translate the idea entirely into your own words; a paraphrase should be approximately the same length as the original.	• When you want to incorporate factual information from a source or to use one specific idea from a source • When the source passage is overly complex or technical for your targeted audience • When you want to incorporate a source's point in your own voice without interrupting the flow of your argument

Strategies	What to Do	When to Use These Strategies
Quote short passages from the source using quotation marks.	Work brief quotations from the source smoothly into the grammar of your own sentences (see Skill 12.4 on the mechanics of quoting).	• When you need testimony from an authority (state the authority's credentials in an attributive tag—see Skill 12.3) • In summaries, when you want to reproduce a source's voice, particularly if the language is striking or memorable • In lieu of paraphrase when the source language is memorable
Quote long passages from the source using the block method.	Results in a page with noticeably lengthy block quotations (see Skill 12.4)	• When you intend to analyze or critique the quotation—the quotation is followed by your detailed analysis of its ideas or rhetorical features • When the flavor and language of testimonial evidence is important

With practice, you'll be able to use all these strategies smoothly and effectively.

Summarizing

Detailed instructions on how to write a summary of an article and incorporate it into your own prose are provided in Chapter 5, "Reading Rhetorically" (pp. 105–110). Summaries can be as short as a single sentence or as long as a paragraph. Make the summary as concise as possible so that you don't distract the reader from your own argument. Writer 1's summary of the McGrath article is a good example of a graceful summary used in support of the writer's own thesis.

Paraphrasing

Unlike a summary, which is a condensation of a source's whole argument, a **paraphrase** translates a short passage from a source's words into the writer's own words. Writers often choose to paraphrase when the details of a source passage are particularly important or when the source is overly technical and needs to be simplified for the intended audience. When you paraphrase, be careful to avoid reproducing the original writer's grammatical structure and syntax. If you mirror the original sentence structure while replacing occasional words with synonyms or small structural changes, you will be doing what composition specialists call

"patchwriting"—that is, patching some of your language into someone else's writing.* Patchwriting is a form of academic dishonesty because you aren't fully composing your own sentences and thus misrepresent both your own work and that of the source writer. An acceptable paraphrase needs to be entirely in your own words. To understand patchwriting more fully, track the differences between unacceptable patchwriting and acceptable paraphrase in the following example.

ORIGINAL

There is considerable evidence that women in Bodie were rarely the victims of crime. Between 1878 and 1882 only one woman, a prostitute, was robbed, and there were no reported cases of rape. (There is no evidence that rapes occurred but were not reported.)

Finally, juvenile crime, which accounts for a significant portion of the violent crime in the United States today, was limited in Bodie to pranks and malicious mischief.

UNACCEPTABLE PATCHWRITING

Note phrases taken word for word from original.

According to McGrath, much evidence exists that women in Bodie were rarely the victims of crime. Between 1878 and 1882 only one woman was robbed, and she was a prostitute. There were no reported cases of rape and no evidence that unreported rapes occurred. Also juvenile crime, which occurs frequently in the United States today, was limited in Bodie to pranks and mischief.

ACCEPTABLE PARAPHRASE

Only one word-for-word phrase

Quotation marks around exact phrase

Page number of original

Violence in Bodie was different from violence today. According to McGrath, women in Bodie seldom suffered at the hands of criminals. No reported rapes occurred in Bodie between 1878 and 1882, and the only female robbery victim was a prostitute. Another difference, as McGrath points out, is that juvenile crime was rare except for occasional "pranks and malicious mischief" (304).

Both the patchwriting example and the acceptable paraphrase reproduce the same ideas as the original in approximately the same number of words. But the writer of the paraphrase has been more careful to change the sentence structure substantially and to focus more clearly on his own argument (differences between Bodie and the present). In the acceptable paraphrase, one unquoted phrase still mirrors the original: "between 1878 and 1882." But this phrase is short and carries little of the passage's meaning. The longer mirrored phrase is quoted exactly. In contrast, the patchwritten version contains longer strings of borrowed language without quotation marks.

*We are indebted to the work of Rebecca Moore Howard and others who have led composition researchers to reexamine the use of sources and plagiarism from a cultural and rhetorical perspective. See especially Rebecca Moore Howard, *Standing in the Shadow of Giants: Plagiarists, Authors, Collaborators*. Stamford, CT: Ablex Pub., 1999.

Among novice writers, the use of Web sources can particularly lead to patch-writing. It is all too easy to copy and paste a Web-based passage into your own draft and then attempt to revise it by changing some of the words. In contrast, patchwriting almost never occurs if you are generating your own language—that is, if you are converting information from a source into your own words in order to make your own argument.

When you first practice paraphrasing, you might try paraphrasing a passage twice to avoid patchwriting and achieve an acceptable paraphrase.

- The first time, read the passage carefully and put it into your own words, looking at the source as little as possible.
- The second time, paraphrase your own paraphrase. Then recheck your final version against the original to make sure you have eliminated similar sentence structure and word-for-word strings.

We'll return to the problem of patchwriting in our discussion of plagiarism (Skill 12.5).

Quoting

Besides summary and paraphrase, writers often choose to quote directly in order to give the reader the flavor and style of the source author's prose or to make a memorable point in the source author's own voice. Our previous example of an acceptable paraphrase includes such a quotation in the last sentence. Be careful not to quote a passage that you don't fully understand. (Sometimes novice writers quote a passage because it sounds impressive.) When you quote, you must reproduce the source author's original words exactly, without any changes, unless you indicate changes with ellipses or brackets. Also be careful to represent the author's intentions and meaning fairly; don't change the author's meaning by taking quotations out of context. Because the mechanics of quoting offers its own difficulties, we devote a separate section to it later in this chapter (Skill 12.4).

SKILL 12.3   Use attributive tags to distinguish your ideas from a source's.

Whenever you use sources in your writing, you need to signal to your reader which words and ideas come from your source and which are your own. There are generally two ways of doing so:

- ***State source author's name in an attributive tag.*** You can identify the source by using a short phrase (called an **attributive tag** or sometimes a **signal phrase** or **signal tag**) such as "according to McGrath," "McGrath says," "in McGrath's view," and so on. In the humanities, the source author's full name is commonly used the first time the author is mentioned. If the tag refers to a specific passage or quotation in the source, then a page number is placed in parentheses at the end of the quotation (see Skill 13.2).

Attributive tag

According to Roger D. McGrath, violence was not as common in the Wild West as most people think.

Attributive tag

Page number of quotation.

McGrath explains that "frontier violence was very different from violence today" (303).

- ● **State source author's name in a parenthetical citation.** You can identify a source by placing the author's name in parentheses at the end of the material taken from the source (called a **parenthetical citation**).

Violence was not as common in the Wild West as most people think (McGrath).

Source identified in parentheses

Page number of quotation.

"Frontier violence was very different from violence today" (McGrath 303).

Of these two methods, attributive tags are generally preferred, especially when you are writing for general rather than specialist audiences. The attributive tag method has three advantages:

- ● It signals where borrowed material starts and ends.
- ● It avoids ambiguities about what is "fact" and what is filtered through a source's angle of vision.
- ● It allows the writer to frame the borrowed material rhetorically.

Let's look at each of these in turn.

Attributive Tags Mark Where Source Material Starts and Ends

The parenthetical method requires readers to wait until the end of the writer's use of source material before the source is identified. Attributive tags, in contrast, identify the source from the moment it is first used. Here are excerpts from Writer 1's summary of McGrath, in which we have highlighted the attributive tags. Note the frequency with which the writer informs the reader that this material comes from McGrath.

USE OF ATTRIBUTIVE TAGS IN WRITER 1'S SUMMARY

Many people believe that our Wild West heritage is one of the causes of contemporary violence. But Roger McGrath, in his article "The Myth of Violence in the Old West," shows that today's violence is much different from frontier violence. He explains that. ... On the other hand, McGrath explains, killings were fueled. ... Thus, according to McGrath, there is little resemblance between violence on the frontier and violence in today's cities. ...

Here the attributive tags signal the use of McGrath's ideas throughout the summary. The reader is never confused about which words and ideas come from McGrath.

Attributive Tags Avoid Ambiguities that Can Arise with the Parenthetical Citations

Not only does the parenthetical method fail to mark where the source material begins, it also tends to imply that the source material is a "fact" rather than the view of the source author. In contrast, attributive tags always call attention to the source's angle of vision. Note this ambiguity in the following passage, where parenthetical citations are used without attributive tags:

AMBIGUOUS ATTRIBUTION

There are many arguments in favor of preserving old-growth forests. First, it is simply unnecessary to log these forests to supply the world's lumber. We have plenty of new-growth forest from which lumber can be taken (Sagoff 89–90). Recently there have been major reforestation efforts all over the United States, and it is common practice now for loggers to replant every tree that is harvested. These new-growth forests, combined with extensive planting of tree farms, provide more than enough wood for the world's needs. Tree farms alone can supply the world's demand for industrial lumber (Sedjo 90).

When confronted with this passage, skeptical readers might ask, "Who are Sagoff and Sedjo? I've never heard of them." It is also difficult to tell how much of the passage is the writer's own argument and how much is borrowed from Sagoff and Sedjo. Is this whole passage a paraphrase? Finally, the writer tends to treat Sagoff's and Sedjo's assertions as uncontested facts rather than as professional opinions. Compare the preceding version with this one, in which attributive tags are added:

CLEAR ATTRIBUTION

There are many arguments in favor of preserving old-growth forests. First, it is simply unnecessary to log these forests to supply the world's lumber. According to environmentalist Carl Sagoff, we have plenty of new-growth forest from which lumber can be taken (89–90). Recently there have been major reforestation efforts all over the United States, and it is common practice now for loggers to replant every tree that is harvested. These new-growth forests, combined with extensive planting of tree farms, provide more than enough wood for the world's needs. According to forestry expert Robert Sedjo, tree farms alone can supply the world's demand for industrial lumber (90).

We can now see that most of the paragraph is the writer's own argument, into which she has inserted the expert testimony of Sagoff and Sedjo, whose views are treated not as indisputable facts but as the opinions of authorities in this field.

Attributive Tags Frame the Source Material Rhetorically

When you introduce a source for the first time, you can use the attributive tag not only to introduce the source but also to shape your readers' attitudes toward the source. In the previous example, the writer wants readers to respect Sagoff and Sedjo, so she identifies Sagoff as an "environmentalist" and Sedjo as a "forestry expert." If the writer favored logging old-growth forests and supported the logging industry's desire to create more jobs, she might have used different tags: "Carl Sagoff, an outspoken advocate for spotted owls over people," or "Robert Sedjo, a forester with limited knowledge of world lumber markets."

When you compose an initial tag, you can add to it any combination of the following kinds of information, depending on your purpose, your audience's values, and your sense of what the audience already knows or doesn't know about the source:

Strategies for Modifying Attributive Tags to Shape Reader Response	
Add to Attributive Tags	**Examples**
Author's credentials or relevant specialty (enhances credibility)	Civil engineer David Rockwood, a noted authority on stream flow in rivers
Author's lack of credentials (decreases credibility)	City Council member Dilbert Weasel, a local politician with no expertise in international affairs
Author's political or social views	Left-wing columnist Alexander Cockburn [has negative feeling]; Alexander Cockburn, a longtime champion of labor [has positive feeling]
Title of source if it provides context	In her book *Fasting Girls: The History of Anorexia Nervosa*, Joan Jacobs Brumberg shows that [establishes credentials for comments on eating disorders]
Publisher of source if it adds prestige or otherwise shapes audience response	Dr. Carl Patrona, in an article published in the prestigious *New England Journal of Medicine*
Historical or cultural information about a source that provides context or background	In his 1960s book popularizing the hippie movement, Charles Reich claims that
Indication of source's purpose or angle of vision	Feminist author Naomi Wolfe, writing a blistering attack on the beauty industry, argues that

Our point here is that you can use attributive tags rhetorically to help your readers understand the significance and context of a source when you first introduce it and to guide your readers' attitudes toward the source.

Evaluating Different Ways to Use and Cite a Source

FOR WRITING AND DISCUSSION

What follow are four different ways that a writer can use the same passage from a source to support a point about the greenhouse effect. Working in groups or as a whole class, rank the four methods from "most effective" to "least effective." Assume that you are writing a researched argument addressed to your college classmates.

1. ***Quotation with parenthetical citation***
   The greenhouse effect will have a devastating effect on the earth's environment: "Potential impacts include increased mortality and illness due to heat stress and worsened air pollution, as in the 1995 Chicago heat wave that killed hundreds of people. ... Infants, children and other vulnerable populations—especially in already-stressed regions of the world—would likely suffer disproportionately from these impacts" (Hall 19).

2. ***Quotation with attributive tag***
   The greenhouse effect will have a devastating effect on the earth's environment. David C. Hall, president of Physicians for Social Responsibility, claims the following: "Potential impacts include increased mortality and illness due to heat stress and worsened air pollution, as in the 1995 Chicago heat wave that killed hundreds of people. ... Infants, children and other vulnerable populations—especially in already-stressed regions of the world—would likely suffer disproportionately from these impacts" (19).

3. ***Paraphrase with parenthetical citation***
   The greenhouse effect will have a devastating effect on the earth's environment. One of the most frightening effects is the threat of diseases stemming from increased air pollution and heat stress. Infants and children would be most at risk (Hall 19).

4. ***Paraphrase with attributive tag***
   The greenhouse effect will have a devastating effect on the earth's environment. One of the most frightening effects, according to David C. Hall, president of Physicians for Social Responsibility, is the threat of diseases stemming from increased air pollution and heat stress. Infants and children would be most at risk (19).

SKILL 12.4 **Punctuate quotations correctly.**

In Skill 12.2, we explained your options for incorporating a source into your own paper—summary, paraphrase, and quotation. Whenever you quote, you must make nuts-and-bolts decisions about punctuation such as when and how to use quotation marks, commas, colons, brackets, and ellipses. When you learn these skills, you will know how to punctuate any quotation correctly, including how to make slight changes in the quotation to fit the grammar of your own sentence. This section answers the following mechanical question about quotations:

- How do I quote a complete sentence from my source?
- How do I insert quoted words and phrases into my own sentences?
- How do I indicate my own modifications to a quotation?
- How do I indicate that I have left something out of a quotation?
- How do I quote something that already has quotation marks in it?
- What if I want to use a long quotation?

These explanations will cover the big picture about the mechanics of quoting. Additional explanations covering variations and specific cases can be found in any good handbook.

Quoting a Complete Sentence

In some cases, you will want to quote a complete sentence from your source. Typically, you will include an attributive tag that tells the reader who is being quoted. At the end of the quotation, you usually indicate its page number in parentheses (see Skill 13.2).

ORIGINAL PASSAGE

It was the armed citizens themselves who were the most potent—though not the only—deterrent to larcenous crime. [found on p. 304 of source]

WRITER'S QUOTATION OF THIS PASSAGE

Because quotation is a complete sentence, it starts with capital letter.

According to McGrath, "It was the armed citizens themselves who were the most potent—though not the only—deterrent to larcenous

Final quotation mark goes before the parentheses.

crime" (304).

Page number from source

Period comes after the parentheses.

Inserting Quoted Words and Phrases into Your Own Sentences

Instead of quoting a complete sentence, you often want to quote only a few words or phrases from your source and insert them into your own sentence. In these cases, make sure that the grammatical structure of the quotation fits smoothly into the grammar of your own sentence.

ORIGINAL PASSAGE

But the old, the young, the weak, and the female—so often the victims of crime today—were generally not harmed. [found on p. 304 of source]

QUOTED PHRASE INSERTED INTO WRITER'S OWN SENTENCE

Quotation marks show where quotation starts and ends.

McGrath contrasts frontier violence to crime today, pointing out that today's typical crime victims are "the old, the young, the weak, and the female" and

Period comes after parentheses.

showing that these groups were not molested in Bodie (304).

Modifying a Quotation

Occasionally you may need to alter a quotation to make it fit your own context. Sometimes the grammar of a desired quotation doesn't match the grammar of your own sentence. At other times, the meaning of a quoted word is unclear because it is removed from its original context. In these cases, use brackets to modify the quotation's grammar or to add a clarifying explanation. Place your changes or additions in brackets to indicate that the bracketed material is not part of the original wording. You should also use brackets to show a change in capitalization.

ORIGINAL PASSAGES

The newspapers regularly advocated shooting burglars on sight, and several burglars were, in fact, shot at. [found on p. 304 of source]

Highwaymen, for example, understood that while they could take the express box from a stagecoach without arousing the citizens, they risked inciting the entire populace to action if they robbed the passengers. [found on p. 304 of source]

QUOTATIONS MODIFIED WITH BRACKETS

By "regularly advocat[ing] shooting burglars on sight," newspapers in Bodie helped an armed citizenry deter crime (McGrath 304).

Public sentiment influenced what laws were likely to be broken. According to McGrath, "[W]hile they [highwaymen] could take the express box from a stagecoach without arousing the citizens, they risked inciting the entire populace to action if they robbed the passengers" (304).

Brackets show change in quotation to fit grammar of writer's sentence.

Parenthetical method of identifying source

Attributive tag

Brackets show a lowercase letter changed to a capital letter.

Brackets show that writer has added a word to explain what "they" stands for.

Omitting Something from a Quoted Passage

Another way that writers modify quotations is to leave words out of the quoted passage. To indicate an omission, use three spaced periods called an **ellipsis** (. . .). Placement of the ellipsis depends on where the omission of material occurs. In the middle of a sentence, each of the periods should be preceded and followed by a space. When your ellipsis comes at the boundary between sentences, use an additional period to mark the end of the first sentence. When a parenthetical page number must follow the ellipsis, insert it before the final (fourth) period in the sequence.

ORIGINAL PASSAGES

Finally, juvenile crime, which accounts for a significant portion of the violent crime in the United States today, was limited in Bodie to pranks and malicious mischief. [found on p. 304 of source]

Bodie's law enforcement institutions were certainly not responsible for these low rates. Rarely were robbers or burglars arrested, and even less often were they convicted. Moreover, many law enforcement officers operated on both sides of the law. [found on p. 304 of source]

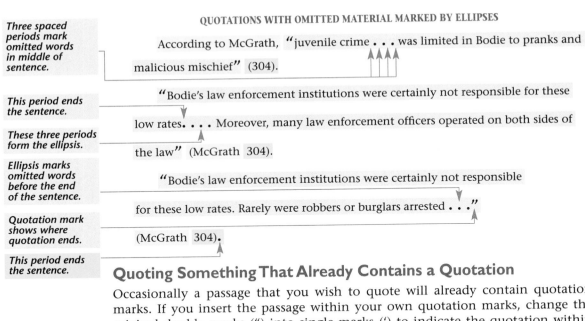

Three spaced periods mark omitted words in middle of sentence.

QUOTATIONS WITH OMITTED MATERIAL MARKED BY ELLIPSES

According to McGrath, "juvenile crime . . . was limited in Bodie to pranks and malicious mischief" (304).

This period ends the sentence.

These three periods form the ellipsis.

"Bodie's law enforcement institutions were certainly not responsible for these low rates. . . . Moreover, many law enforcement officers operated on both sides of the law" (McGrath 304).

Ellipsis marks omitted words before the end of the sentence.

Quotation mark shows where quotation ends.

This period ends the sentence.

"Bodie's law enforcement institutions were certainly not responsible for these low rates. Rarely were robbers or burglars arrested . . ."

(McGrath 304).

Quoting Something That Already Contains a Quotation

Occasionally a passage that you wish to quote will already contain quotation marks. If you insert the passage within your own quotation marks, change the original double marks (") into single marks (') to indicate the quotation within the quotation. The same procedure works whether the quotation marks are used for quoted words or for a title. Make sure that your attributive tag signals who is being quoted. Because the McGrath article contains no internal quotation marks, we will use a different example to illustrate quotations within quotations.

ORIGINAL PASSAGE

And finally, we tend to stereotype because it helps us make sense out of a highly confusing world, a world which William James once described as "one great, blooming, buzzing confusion." [Passage from an article by Robert Heilbroner, who here quotes William James]

Regular quotation marks indicate the material quoted from Heilbroner.

USE OF SINGLE QUOTATION MARKS TO IDENTIFY A QUOTATION WITHIN A QUOTATION

Robert Heilbroner explains that people create stereotypes "because it helps us

Heilbroner's own attributive tag notes William James.

make sense out of a highly confusing world, a world which William James once

described as 'one great, blooming, buzzing confusion'."

Single quotation marks indicate the material quoted from James.

Using a Block Quotation for a Long Passage

If your quoted passage uses more than four lines in your own paper, use the block indentation method rather than quotation marks. Block quotations are generally introduced with an attributive tag followed by a colon. The indented block of text, rather than quotation marks, signals that the material is a direct quotation. Block quotations occur rarely in scholarly writing and are used primarily in cases where the writer intends to analyze the text being quoted. If you overuse block quotations, you produce a "choo-choo train" paper that is simply a collage of other people's voices.

ORIGINAL PASSAGE

Fistfights and gunfights among willing combatants—gamblers, miners, and the like—were regular events, and stagecoach holdups were not unusual. But the old, the young, the weak, and the female—so often the victims of crime today—were generally not harmed.

BLOCK QUOTATION

McGrath describes the people most affected by violence in the frontier town of Bodie:

> Fistfights and gunfights among willing combatants—gamblers, miners, and the like—were regular events, and stagecoach holdups were not unusual. But the old, the young, the weak, and the female—so often the victims of crime today—were generally not harmed. (304)

Block quotation introduced with a colon

No quotation marks

Block indented 1 inch on left.

Period and mark end of sentence.

Page number in parentheses after the closing period and space.

SKILL 12.5   Avoid plagiarism by following academic conventions for ethical use of sources.

In the next chapter, we proceed to the nuts and bolts of citing and documenting sources—a skill that will enhance your *ethos* as a skilled researcher and as a person of integrity. Unethical use of sources—called **plagiarism**—is a major concern not only for writing teachers but for teachers in all disciplines. To combat plagiarism, many instructors across the curriculum use plagiarism-detection software like turnitin.com. Their purpose, of course, is to discourage students from cheating. But sometimes students who have no intention of cheating can fall into producing papers that look like cheating. That is, they produce papers that might be accused of plagiarism even though the students had no intention of deceiving their readers.* Our goal in this section is to explain the concept of plagiarism more fully and to sum up the strategies needed to avoid it.

Why Some Kinds of Plagiarism May Occur Unwittingly

To understand how unwitting plagiarism might occur, consider Table 12.1, where the middle column—"Misuse of Sources"—shows common mistakes of novice writers. Everyone agrees that the behaviors in the "Fraud" column constitute deliberate cheating and deserve appropriate punishment. Everyone also agrees that good scholarly work meets the criteria in the "Ethical Use of Sources" column. Novice researchers, however, may find themselves unwittingly in the middle column until they learn the academic community's conventions for using research sources.

---

*See Rebecca Moore Howard, *Standing in the Shadow of Giants: Plagiarists, Authors, Collaborators.* Stamford, CT: Ablex Pub., 1999.

TABLE 12.1   Plagiarism and the Ethical Use of Sources

Plagiarism		Ethical Use of Sources
Fraud	**Misuse of Sources** *(Common Mistakes Made by New Researchers)*	
The writer • buys paper from a paper mill • submits someone else's work as his own • copies chunks of text from sources with obvious intention of not being detected • fabricates data or makes up evidence • intends to deceive	The writer • copies passages directly from a source, references the source with an in-text citation, but fails to use quotation marks or block indentation • in attempting to paraphrase a source, makes some changes, but follows too closely the wording of the original ("patchwriting") • fails to indicate the sources of some ideas or data (often is unsure what needs to be cited or has lost track of sources through poor note taking) • in general, misunderstands the conventions for using sources in academic writing	The writer • writes paper entirely in her own words or uses exact quotations from sources • indicates all quotations with quotation marks or block indentation • indicates her use of all sources through attribution, in-text citation, and an end-of-paper list of works cited

You might appreciate these conventions more fully if you recognize how they have evolved from Western notions of intellectual property and patent law associated with the rise of modern science in the seventeenth and eighteenth centuries. A person not only could own a house or a horse, but also could own an idea and the words used to express that idea. You can see these cultural conventions at work—in the form of laws or professional codes of ethics—whenever a book author is disgraced for lifting words or ideas from another author or whenever an artist or entrepreneur is sued for stealing song lyrics, publishing another person's photographs without permission, or infringing on some inventor's patent.

This understanding of plagiarism may seem odd in some non-Western cultures where collectivism is valued more than individualism. In these cultures, words written or spoken by ancestors, elders, or other authority figures may be regarded with reverence and shared with others without attribution. Also in these cultures, it might be disrespectful to paraphrase certain passages or to document them in a way that would suggest the audience didn't recognize the ancient wisdom.

However, such collectivist conventions won't work in research communities committed to building new knowledge. In the academic world, the conventions separating ethical from unethical use of sources are essential if research findings are to win the community's confidence. Effective research can occur only within ethical and responsible research communities where people do not fabricate data and where current researchers respect and acknowledge the work of those who have gone before them.

Strategies for Avoiding Plagiarism

The following chart will help you review the strategies presented throughout Chapter 13 for using source material ethically and avoiding plagiarism.

Strategies for Avoiding Plagiarism or the Appearance of Plagiarism		
What to Do	**Why to Do It**	**Where to Find More Information**
At the beginning		
Read your college's policy on plagiarism as well as statements from your teachers in class or on course syllabi.	Understanding policies on plagiarism and academic integrity will help you research and write ethically.	
Pose a research question rather than a topic area.	Arguing your own thesis gives you a voice, establishes your *ethos,* and urges you to write ethically.	
At the note-taking stage		
Create a bibliographic entry for each source.	This action makes it easy to create an end-of-paper bibliography and encourages rhetorical reading	
When you copy a passage into your notes, copy word for word and enclose it with in quotation marks.	It is important to distinguish a source's words from your own words.	
When you enter summaries or paraphrases into your notes, avoid patchwriting.	If your notes contain any strings of a source's original wording, you might later assume that these words are your own.	Skill 12.2
Distinguish your informational notes from your personal exploratory notes	Keeping these kinds of notes separate will help you identify borrowed ideas when it's time to incorporate the source material into your paper.	

(continued)

What to Do	Why to Do It	Where to Find More Information
When writing your draft		
Except for exact quotations, write the paper entirely in your own words.	This strategy keeps you from patchwriting when you summarize or paraphrase.	Skill 12.2
Indicate all quotations with quotation marks or block indentation. Use ellipses or brackets to make changes to fit your own grammar.	Be careful to represent the author fairly; don't change meaning by taking quotations out of context.	Skills 12.2 and 12.4
When you summarize or paraphrase, avoid patchwriting.	Word-for-word strings from a source must either be avoided or placed in quotation marks. Also avoid mirroring the source's grammatical structure.	Skill 12.2
Never cut and paste a Web passage directly into your draft. Paste it into a separate note file and put quotation marks around it.	Pasted passages are direct invitations to patchwrite.	Skill 12.2
Inside your text, use attributive tags or parenthetical citations to identify all sources. List all sources alphabetically in a concluding works cited or references list.	This strategy makes it easy for readers to know when you are using a source and where to find it.	Skill 12.3 Skill 13.1
Cite with attributive tags or parenthetical citations all quotations, paraphrases, summaries, and any other references to specific sources.	These are the most common in-text citations in a research paper.	Skills 13.1 and 13.2
Use in-text citations to indicate sources for all visuals and media such as graphs, maps, photographs, films, videos, broadcasts, and recordings.	The rules for citing words and ideas apply equally to visuals and media cited in your paper.	Skill 13.1
Use in-text citations for all ideas and facts that are not common knowledge.	Although you don't need to cite widely accepted and noncontroversial facts and information, it is better to cite them if you are unsure.	Skill 13.1

Avoiding Plagiarism

Read the passage below. Unlike the ethical summary of McGrath's article produced by Writer 1 on page 306, the writer of the following passage would likely be accused of plagiarism.

SUMMARY OF McGRATH'S ARTICLE (AN EXAMPLE OF PLAGIARISM)

It is commonly assumed that violence is part of our Wild West heritage. But Roger McGrath, in his article "The Myth of Violence in the Old West," shows that frontier violence was very different from violence today. He explains that in a typical frontier town, violence involved gunslingers who were "willing combatants," whereas today's typical victims—the old, the young, the weak, and the female—were unaffected by crime (304). The greatest deterrent to crime in Bodie was the fact that so many people were armed. Armed guards prevented bank robberies and stagecoach holdups, and armed citizens stopped burglary. On the other hand, McGrath explains, Bodie had a high homicide rate. Most of the town's residents were young single males who adhered to a code of conduct that frequently required them to fight. Alcohol also played a major role. Therefore murders were much more frequent than in any U.S. city today (304). Thus, according to McGrath, there is little resemblance between violence on the frontier and violence in today's cities, so we cannot blame current violence on our tumultuous frontier past.

Working in small groups or as a whole class, respond to the following questions.

1. How does this passage cross the line into plagiarism? (You'll need to compare the passage to Writer 1's ethical summary on p. 306.)
2. The writer of this passage might say, "How can this be plagiarism? I cited my source and gave page numbers." How would you explain the problem to this writer?
3. Psychologically or cognitively, what may have caused this writer to misuse the source? How might this writer's note-taking process or composing process have differed from that of Writer 1 on page 306? In other words, what happened that got this writer into trouble?

PEARSON
mycomplab || For support in learning this chapter's content, follow this path in MyCompLab: Resources ⇒ Research ⇒ The Research Assignment ⇒ Integrating Sources. Review the Instruction and Multimedia resources about integrating sources, then complete the Exercises and click on Gradebook to measure your progress.

13 | CITING AND DOCUMENTING SOURCES

I n the previous chapter we explained how to incorporate sources into your writing; in this chapter we focus on the nuts and bolts of documenting those sources in a way appropriate to your purpose, audience, and genre, using the systems of the Modern Language Association (MLA) and the American Psychological Association (APA).* Accurate documentation not only helps other researchers locate your sources but also contributes substantially to your own *ethos* as a writer.

Specifically, in this chapter you will learn the following skills:

- **SKILL 13.1** Know what needs to be cited and what doesn't.
- **SKILL 13.2** Understand the connection between in-text citations and the end-of-paper list of cited works.
- **SKILL 13.3** Cite and document sources using MLA style.
- **SKILL 13.4** Cite and document sources using APA style.

SKILL 13.1 **Know what needs to be cited and what doesn't.**

Beginning researchers are often confused about what needs to be cited and what doesn't. Table 13.1 will help you make this determination. If you are in doubt, it is better to cite than not to cite.

It is often difficult to determine when a given piece of information falls into the "common knowledge" column of Table 13.1. The answer depends both on your target audience's background knowledge and on your own ability to speak as an authority. Consider the statement "Twitter and Facebook are forms of social networking." That information is noncontroversial and well known and so doesn't require citation. But if you added, "Twitter is more popular with middle-aged adults than with teenagers," you would need to cite your source (some newspaper article or poll?) unless you are a teenager speaking with authority from your own experience, in which case you would provide personal-experience examples. If you are uncertain, our best advice is this: When in doubt, cite.

*Our discussion of MLA style is based on the *MLA Handbook for Writers of Research Papers*, 7th ed. (2009). Our discussion of APA style is based on the *Publication Manual of the American Psychological Association*, 6th ed. (2010).

TABLE 13.1   **Determining What Needs to Be Cited**

What Needs to Be Cited	What Does Not Need to Be Cited
You must cite all references to your research sources as well as any information that is not commonly known by your targeted audience:	You do not need to cite commonly shared, widely known knowledge that will be considered factual and noncontroversial to your targeted audience:
<ul><li>Any quotation</li><li>Any passage that you paraphrase</li><li>Any passage or source that you summarize or otherwise refer to</li><li>Any image, photograph, map, drawing, graph, chart, or other visual that you download from the Web (or find elsewhere) and include in your paper</li><li>Any sound or video file that you use in a multimedia project</li><li>Any idea, fact, statistic, or other information that you find from a source and that is not commonly known by your targeted audience</li></ul>	<ul><li>Commonly known facts (Water freezes at 32 degrees Fahrenheit.)</li><li>Commonly known dates (Terrorists flew airplanes into New York's World Trade Center on September 11, 2001.)</li><li>Commonly known events (Barack Obama defeated John McCain for the presidency.)</li><li>Commonly known historical or cultural knowledge (Twitter and Facebook are forms of social networking.)</li></ul>

SKILL 13.2 **Understand the connection between in-text citations and the end-of-paper list of cited works.**

The most common forms of documentation use what are called in-text citations that match an end-of-paper list of cited works (as opposed to footnotes or end-notes). An ***in-text citation*** identifies a source in the body of the paper at the point where it is summarized, paraphrased, quoted, inserted, or otherwise referred to. At the end of your paper you include a list—alphabetized by author (or by title if there is no named author)—of all the works you cited. Both the Modern Language Association (MLA) system, used primarily in the humanities, and the American Psychological Association (APA) system, used primarily in the social sciences, follow this procedure. In MLA, your end-of-paper list is called **Works Cited.** In APA it is called **References.**

Whenever you place an in-text citation in the body of your paper, your reader knows to turn to the Works Cited or References list at the end of the paper to get the full bibliographic information. The key to the system's logic is this:

- Every source in Works Cited or References must be mentioned in the body of the paper.
- Conversely, every source mentioned in the body of the paper must be included in the end-of-paper list.
- The first word in each entry of the Works Cited or References list (usually an author's last name) must also appear in the in-text citation. In other words, there must be a one-to-one correspondence between the first word in each entry in the end-of-paper list and the name used to identify the source in the body of the paper.

Suppose a reader sees this phrase in your paper: "According to Debra Goldstein. ..." The reader should be able to turn to your Works Cited list and find an alphabetized entry beginning with "Goldstein, Debra." Similarly, suppose that in looking over your Works Cited list, your reader sees an article by "Guillen, Manuel." This means that the name "Guillen" has to appear in your paper in one of two ways:

For more on attributive tags, see Skill 12.3.

- As an attributive tag: Economics professor Manuel Guillen argues that....
- As a parenthetical citation, often following a quotation: "...changes in fiscal policy" (Guillen 49).

Because this one-to-one correspondence is so important, let's illustrate it with some complete examples using the MLA formatting style:

If the body of your paper has this:	Then the Works Cited list must have this:
According to linguist Deborah Tannen, political debate in America leaves out the complex middle ground where most solutions must be developed.	Tannen, Deborah. *The Argument Culture: Moving from Debate to Dialogue*. New York: Random, 1998. Print.
In the 1980s, cigarette advertising revealed a noticeable pattern of racial stereotyping (Pollay, Lee, and Carter-Whitney).	Pollay, Richard W., Jung S. Lee, and David Carter-Whitney. "Separate, but Not Equal: Racial Segmentation in Cigarette Advertising." *Journal of Advertising* 21.1 (1992): 45–57. Print.
On its Web site, the National Men's Resource Center offers advice to parents on how to talk with children about alcohol and drugs ("Talking").	"Talking with Kids about Alcohol and Drugs." *Menstuff*. National Men's Resource Center, 1 Mar. 2007. Web. 26 June 2007.

How to format an MLA in-text citation and a Works Cited list entry is the subject of the next section. The APA system is similar except that it emphasizes the date of publication in both the in-text citation and the References entry. APA formatting is the subject of Skill 13.4.

SKILL 13.3 Cite and document sources using MLA style.

An in-text citation and its corresponding Works Cited entry are linked in a chicken-and-egg system: You can't cite a source in the text without first knowing how the source's entry will be alphabetized in the Works Cited list. However, since most Works Cited entries are alphabetized by the first author's last name, for convenience we start with in-text citations.

In-Text Citations in MLA Style

A typical in-text citation contains two elements: (1) the last name of the author and (2) the page number of the quoted or paraphrased passage. However, in some cases a work is identified by something other than an author's last name, and sometimes no page number is required. Let's begin with the most common cases. Typically, an in-text citation uses one of these two methods:

- **Parenthetical method.** Place the author's last name and the page number in parentheses immediately after the material being cited.

> The Spanish tried to reduce the status of Filipina, women who had been able to
>
> do business, get divorced, and sometimes become village chiefs (Karnow 41).

- **Attributive tag method.** Place the author's name in an attributive tag at the beginning of the source material and the page number in parentheses at the end.

> According to Karnow, the Spanish tried to reduce the status of Filipina women,
>
> who had been able to do business, get divorced, and sometimes become village
>
> chiefs (41).

Once you have cited an author and it is clear that the same author's material is being used, you need cite only the page numbers in parentheses in subsequent citations. A reader who wishes to look up the source will find the bibliographic information in the Works Cited section by looking for the entry under "Karnow."

Let's now turn to the variations. Table 13.2 identifies the typical variations and shows again the one-to-one connection between the in-text citation and the Works Cited list.

TABLE 13.2   In-Text Citations in MLA Style

Type of Source	Works Cited Entry at End of Paper (Construct the entry while taking notes on each source.)	In-Text Citation in Body of Paper (*Use the first word of the Works Cited entry in parentheses or an attributive tag; add page number at end of quoted or paraphrased passage.*)
One author	Pollan, Michael. *The Omnivore's Dilemma: A Natural History of Four Meals.* New York: Penguin, 2006. Print.	…(Pollan 256). OR According to Pollan,…(256).
More than one author	Pollay, Richard W., Jung S. Lee, and David Carter-Whitney. "Separate, but Not Equal: Racial Segmentation in Cigarette Advertising." *Journal of Advertising* 21.1 (1992): 45–57. Print.	…race" (Pollay, Lee, and Carter-Whitney 52). OR Pollay, Lee, and Carter-Whitney have argued that "advertisers…race" (52). *For the in-text citation, cite the specific page number rather than the whole range of pages given in the Works Cited entry.*

(continued)

TABLE 13.2 *continued*

Type of Source	Works Cited Entry at End of Paper	In-Text Citation in Body of Paper (*Use the first word of the Works Cited entry in parentheses or an attributive tag; add page number at end of quoted or paraphrased passage.*)
Author has more than one work in Works Cited list	Dombrowski, Daniel A. *Babies and Beasts: The Argument from Marginal Cases.* Urbana: U of Illinois P, 1997. Print. ---. *The Philosophy of Vegetarianism.* Amherst: U of Massachusetts P, 1984. Print.	...(Dombrowski, *Babies* 207). ...(Dombrowski, *Philosophy* 328). OR According to Dombrowski,...(*Babies* 207). Dombrowski claims that... (*Philosophy* 328). *Because author has more than one work in Works Cited, include a short version of title to distinguish between entries.*
Corporate author	American Red Cross. *Standard First Aid.* St. Louis: Mosby Lifeline, 1993. Print.	...(American Red Cross 102). OR Snake bite instructions from the American Red Cross show that... (102).
No named author (Work is therefore alphabetized by title.)	"Ouch! Body Piercing." *Menstuff.* National Men's Resource Center, 1 Feb. 2001. Web. 17 July 2004.	...("Ouch!"). According to the National Men's Resource Center,...("Ouch!"). • *Add "Ouch!" in parentheses to show that work is alphabetized under "Ouch!" not "National."* • *No page numbers are shown because Web site pages aren't stable.*
Indirect citation of a source that you found in another source *Suppose you want to use a quotation from Peter Singer that you found in a book by Daniel Dombrowski. Include Dombrowski but not Singer in Works Cited.*	Dombrowski, Daniel A. *Babies and Beasts: The Argument from Marginal Cases.* Urbana: U of Illinois P, 1997. Print.	Animal rights activist Peter Singer argues that...(qtd. in Dombrowski 429). • *Singer is used for the attributive tag, but the in-text citation is to Dombrowski.* • *"qtd. in" stands for "quoted in."*

When to Use Page Numbers in In-Text Citations When the materials you are citing are available in print or in .pdf format, you can provide accurate page numbers for parenthetical citations. If you are working with Web sources or HTML files, however, do not use the page numbers obtained from a printout because they will not be consistent from printer to printer. If the item has numbered paragraphs, cite them with the abbreviation *par.* or *pars.*—for example,

"(Jones, pars. 22–24)." In the absence of reliable page numbers for the original material, MLA says to omit page references from the parenthetical citation. The following chart summarizes the use of page numbers in in-text citations.

Include a page number in the in-text citation:	Do not include a page number:
If the source has stable page numbers (print source or .pdf version of print source): • If you quote something • If you paraphrase a specific passage • If you refer to data or details from a specific page or range of pages in the source	• If you are referring to the argument of the whole source instead of a specific page or passage • If the source does not have stable page numbers (articles on Web sites, HTML text, and so forth)

Works Cited List in MLA Style

In the MLA system, you place a complete Works Cited list at the end of the paper. The list includes all the sources that you mention in your paper. However, it does *not* include works you read but did not use. Entries in the Works Cited list follow these general guidelines:

- Entries are arranged alphabetically by author, or by title if there is no author.
- Each entry includes the medium of publication of the source you consulted— for example, *Print, Web, DVD, Performance, Oil on canvas,* and so on.
- If there is more than one entry per author, the works are arranged alphabetically by title. For the second and all additional entries, type three hyphens and a period in place of the author's name.

> Dombrowski, Daniel A. *Babies and Beasts: The Argument from Marginal Cases.*
>   Urbana: U of Illinois P, 1997. Print.
>
> ---. *The Philosophy of Vegetarianism.* Amherst: U of Massachusetts P, 1984. Print.

You can see a complete, properly formatted Works Cited list on the last pages of James Gardiner's paper (pp. 347–348).

The remaining pages in this section show examples of MLA citation formats for different kinds of sources and provide explanations and illustrations as needed.

MLA Citation Models

Print Articles in Scholarly Journals

General Format for Print Article in Scholarly Journal

Author. "Article Title." *Journal Title* volume number.issue number (year): page
    numbers. Print.

Note that all scholarly journal entries include both volume number and issue number, regardless of how the journal is paginated. For articles published in a scholarly Web journal, see page 336. For scholarly journal articles retrieved from an online database, see page 333.

To see what citations look like when typed in a research paper, see James Gardiner's Works Cited list on pp. 347–348.

One author

Herrera-Sobek, Maria. "Border Aesthetics: The Politics of Mexican Immigration in Film
and Art." *Western Humanities Review* 60.2 (2006): 60–71. Print.

Two or three authors

Pollay, Richard W., Jung S. Lee, and David Carter-Whitney. "Separate, but Not Equal:
Racial Segmentation in Cigarette Advertising." *Journal of Advertising* 21.1 (1992):
45–57. Print.

Four or more authors

Either list all the authors in the order in which they appear, or use "et al." (meaning "and others") to replace all but the first author.

Buck, Gayle A., et al. "Examining the Cognitive Processes Used by Adolescent Girls and
Women Scientists in Identifying Science Role Models: A Feminist Approach."
Science Education 92.4 (2008): 688–707. Print.

Print Articles in Magazines and Newspapers

If no author is identified, begin the entry with the title or headline. Distinguish
between news stories and editorials by putting the word "Editorial" after the title.
If a magazine comes out weekly or biweekly, include the complete date ("27 Sept.
2010"). If it comes out monthly, then state the month only ("Sept. 2010").

General Format for Magazines and Newspapers

Author. "Article Title." *Magazine Title* day Month year: page numbers. Print.

Note: If the article continues in another part of the magazine or newspaper,
add "+" to the number of the first page to indicate the nonsequential pages.

Magazine article with named author

Snyder, Rachel L. "A Daughter of Cambodia Remembers: Loung Ung's Journey." *Ms.*
Aug.–Sept. 2001: 62–67. Print.

Magazine article without named author

"Daddy, Daddy." *New Republic* 30 July 2001: 2–13. Print.

Review of book, film, or performance

Schwarz, Benjamin. "A Bit of Bunting: A New History of the British Empire Elevates
Expediency to Principle." Rev. of *Ornamentalism: How the British Saw Their Empire,*
by David Cannadine. *Atlantic Monthly* Nov. 2001: 126–35. Print.

Kaufman, Stanley. "Polishing a Gem." Rev. of *The Blue Angel,* dir. Josef von Sternberg.
New Republic 30 July 2001: 28–29. Print.

Lahr, John. "Nobody's Darling: Fascism and the Drama of Human Connection in *Ashes to Ashes*." Rev. of *Ashes to Ashes*, by Harold Pinter. The Roundabout Theater Co. Gramercy Theater, New York. *New Yorker* 22 Feb. 1999: 182–83. Print.

Newspaper article

Henriques, Diana B. "Hero's Fall Teaches Wall Street a Lesson." *Seattle Times* 27 Sept. 1998: A1+. Print.

Page numbers in newspapers are typically indicated by a section letter or number as well as a page number. The "+" indicates that the article continues on one or more pages later in the newspaper.

Newspaper editorial

"Dr. Frankenstein on the Hill." Editorial. *New York Times* 18 May 2002, natl. ed.: A22. Print.

Letter to the editor of a magazine or newspaper

Tomsovic, Kevin. Letter. *New Yorker* 13 July 1998: 7. Print.

Print Books

General Format for Print Books

Author. *Title.* City of publication: Publisher, year of publication. Print.

One author

Pollan, Michael. *The Omnivore's Dilemma: A Natural History of Four Meals*. New York: Penguin, 2006. Print.

Two or more authors

Dombrowski, Daniel A., and Robert J. Deltete. *A Brief, Liberal, Catholic Defense of Abortion*. Urbana: U of Illinois P, 2000. Print.

Belenky, Mary, et al. *Women's Ways of Knowing: The Development of Self, Voice, and Mind*. New York: Basic, 1986. Print.

If there are four or more authors, you have the choice of listing all the authors in the order in which they appear on the title page or using "et al." (meaning "and others") to replace all but the first author. Your Works Cited entry and the parenthetical citation should match.

Second, later, or revised edition

Montagu, Ashley. *Touching: The Human Significance of the Skin*. 3rd ed. New York: Perennial, 1986. Print.

In place of "3rd ed.," you can include abbreviations for other kinds of editions: "Rev. ed." (for "Revised edition") or "Abr. ed." (for "Abridged edition").

MLA Style

Republished book (for example, a paperback published after the original hardback edition or a modern edition of an older work)

Hill, Christopher. *The World Turned Upside Down: Radical Ideas During the English Revolution.* 1972. London: Penguin, 1991. Print.

Wollstonecraft, Mary. *The Vindication of the Rights of Woman, with Strictures on Political and Moral Subjects.* 1792. Rutland: Tuttle, 1995. Print.

The date immediately following the title is the original publication date of the work.

Multivolume work

Churchill, Winston S. *A History of the English-Speaking Peoples.* 4 vols. New York: Dodd, 1956–58. Print.

Churchill, Winston S. *The Great Democracies.* New York: Dodd, 1957. Print. Vol. 4 of *A History of the English-Speaking Peoples.* 4 vols. 1956–58.

Use the first method when you cite the whole work; use the second method when you cite one individually titled volume of the work.

Article in familiar reference work

"Mau Mau." *The New Encyclopaedia Britannica.* 15th ed. 2002. Print.

Article in less familiar reference work

Ling, Trevor O. "Buddhism in Burma." *Dictionary of Comparative Religion.* Ed. S. G. F. Brandon. New York: Scribner's, 1970. Print.

Translation

De Beauvoir, Simone. *The Second Sex.* 1949. Trans. H. M. Parshley. New York: Bantam, 1961. Print.

Illustrated book

Jacques, Brian. *The Great Redwall Feast.* Illus. Christopher Denise. New York: Philomel, 1996. Print.

Graphic novel

Miyazaki, Hayao. *Nausicaa of the Valley of Wind.* 4 vols. San Francisco: Viz, 1995–97. Print.

Corporate author (a commission, committee, or other group)

American Red Cross. *Standard First Aid.* St. Louis: Mosby Lifeline, 1993. Print.

No author listed

The New Yorker Cartoon Album: 1975–1985. New York: Penguin, 1987. Print.

Whole anthology

O'Connell, David F., and Charles N. Alexander, eds. *Self Recovery: Treating Addictions Using Transcendental Meditation and Maharishi Ayur-Veda.* New York: Haworth, 1994. Print.

Anthology article

Royer, Ann. "The Role of the Transcendental Meditation Technique in Promoting
       Smoking Cessation: A Longitudinal Study." *Self Recovery: Treating Addictions*
       Using Transcendental Meditation and Maharishi Ayur-Veda. Ed. David F.
       O'Connell and Charles N. Alexander. New York: Haworth, 1994.
       221–39. Print.

When you cite an individual article, give the inclusive page numbers for the article at the end of the citation, before the medium of publication.

Articles or Books from an Online Database

General Format for Material from Online Databases

Author. "Title." *Periodical Name* Print publication data including date and volume/
       issue numbers: pagination. *Database*. Web. Date of access.

Journal article from online database

Matsuba, M. Kyle. "Searching for Self and Relationships Online." *CyberPsychology and*
       Behavior 9.3 (2006): 275–84. *Academic Search Complete*. Web. 14 Apr. 2007.

To see where each element in this citation was found, see Figure 13.1, which shows the online database screen from which the Matsuba article was accessed. For articles in databases, follow the formats for print newspapers, magazines, or scholarly journals, as relevant. When the database text provides only the starting page number of a multipage article, insert a plus sign after the number, before the period.

Broadcast transcript from online database

Conan, Neal. "Arab Media." *Talk of the Nation*. With Shibley Telhami. 4 May 2004.
       Transcript. *LexisNexis*. Web. 31 July 2004.

The label "Transcript" after the broadcast date indicates a text (not audio) version.

E-book from online database

Hanley, Wayne. *The Genesis of Napoleonic Propaganda, 1796–1799*. New York: Columbia
       UP, 2002. *Gutenberg-e*. Web. 31 July 2010.

Machiavelli, Niccolo. *Prince*. 1513. *Bibliomania*. Web. 31 July 2009.

Information about the original print version, including a translator if relevant and available, should be provided.

Other Internet Sources

General Format for Web Sources Since Web sources are often unstable, MLA recommends that you download or printout your Web sources. The goal in

FIGURE 13.1 Article Downloaded from an Online Database, with Elements Identified for an MLA-Style Citation

Matsuba, M. Kyle. "Searching for Self and Relationships Online." *CyberPsychology and Behavior* 9.3 (2006): 275–84. *Academic Search Complete*. Web. 14 Apr. 2007.

citing these sources is to enable readers to locate the material. To that end, use the basic citation model and adapt it as necessary.

Author, editor, director, narrator, performer, compiler, or producer of the work, if available. *Title of a long work, italicized.* OR "Title of page or document that is part of a larger work, in quotation marks. *Title of the overall site, usually taken from the home page, if this is different from the title of the work.* Publisher or sponsor of the site (if none, use N.p.), day Month year of publication online or last update of the site (if not available, use n.d.). Web. day Month year you accessed the site.

Saucedo, Robert. "A Bad Idea for a Movie." *theeagle.com.* Bryan College Station Eagle, 1 July 2010. Web. 7 July 2010.

To see where each element of the Saucedo citation comes from, see the Web article in Figure 13.2.

FIGURE 13.2 An Article Published on the Web, with Elements Identified for an MLA-Style Citation

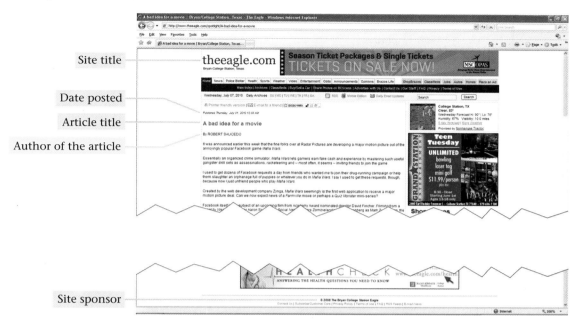

Site title
Date posted
Article title
Author of the article
Site sponsor

Saucedo, Robert. "A Bad Idea for a Movie." *theeagle.com*. Bryan College Station Eagle, 1 July 2010. Web. 7 July 2010.

MLA assumes that readers will use a search engine to locate a Web source, so do not include a URL *unless* the item would be hard to locate without it. If you do include a URL, it goes at the end of the citation, after the access date. Enclose it in angle brackets <> followed by a period. If you need to break the URL from one line to the next, divide it only after a slash. Do not hyphenate a URL. See the home page entries on page 336 for examples of citations with URLs.

Entire Web site

BlogPulse. Intelliseek, n.d. Web. 24 July 2010.

Padgett, John B., ed. *William Faulkner on the Web*. U of Mississippi, 26 Mar. 2007. Web. 25 June 2009.

Documents within a Web site

Marks, John. "Overview: Letter from the President." *Search for Common Ground*. Search for Common Ground, n.d. Web. 25 June 2007.

Gourlay, Alexander S. "Glossary." *The William Blake Archive*. Lib. of Cong., 2005. Web. 21 Jan. 2009.

"Ouch! Body Piercing." *Menstuff*. National Men's Resource Center, 1 Feb. 2001. Web. 17 July 2004. <http://www.menstuff.org/issues/byissue/fathersgeneral .html#bodypiercing>.

Article from a newspaper or newswire site

Bounds, Amy. "Thinking Like Scientists." *Daily Camera* [Boulder]. Scripps Interactive
Newspaper Group, 26 June 2007. Web. 26 June 2007.

"Great Lakes: Rwanda Backed Dissident Troops in DRC-UN Panel." *IRIN*. UN Office for
the Coordination of Humanitarian Affairs, 21 July 2004. Web. 31 July 2004.

Article from a scholarly e-journal

Welch, John R., and Ramon Riley. "Reclaiming Land and Spirit in the Western Apache
Homeland." *American Indian Quarterly* 25.4 (2001): 5–14. Web. 19 Dec. 2001.

Broadcast transcript from a Web site

Woodruff, Judy, Richard Garnett, and Walter Dellinger. "Experts Analyze Supreme
Court Free Speech Rulings." Transcript: background and discussion. *Online
NewsHour*. PBS, 25 June 2007. Web. 26 June 2007.

Blog posting

Dyer, Bob, and Ella Barnes. "The 'Greening' of the Arctic." *Greenversations*. U.S.
Environmental Protection Agency, 7 Oct. 2008. Web. 11 Oct. 2010.
<http://blog.epa.gov/blog/2008/10/07/the-greening-of-the-artic/>.

To see where each element of this citation comes from, refer to Figure 13.3.

Podcast

"The Long and Winding Road: DNA Evidence for Human Migration." *Science Talk*.
Scientific American, 7 July 2008. Web. 21 July 2010.

Web video

Beck, Roy. "Immigration Gumballs." *YouTube*. YouTube, 2 Nov. 2006. Web. 23 July 2009.

For films and DVDs, see page 338.

Home Pages

Agatucci, Cora. *Culture and Literature of Africa*. Course home page. Humanities Dept.,
Central Oregon Community College, Jan. 2007–May 2007. Web. 31 July 2007.
<http://web.cocc.edu/cagatucci/classes/hum211/>.

African Studies Program. Home page. School of Advanced International Study, Johns
Hopkins U, n.d. Web. 31 July 2007.

Sharpe, William F. Home page. May 2004. Web. 31 July 2004.
<http://www.stanford.edu/~wfsharpe/>.

E-mail

Daffinrud, Sue. "Scoring Guide for Class Participation." Message to the author. 12 Dec.
2001. E-mail.

Use the subject line as the title of the e-mail. Use "E-mail" as the medium of publication and omit your access date.

FIGURE 13.3 A Blog Posting from the Web, with Citation Elements Identified

Dyer, Bob, and Ella Barnes. "The 'Greening' of the Arctic." *Greenversations*. U.S. Environmental Protection Agency,

7 Oct. 2008. Web. 11 Oct. 2008. <http://blog.epa.gov/blog/2008/10/07/the-greening-of-the-arctic/>.

Miscellaneous Sources

Television or radio program

Begin with the episode name, if any, in quotation marks, followed by the program name, italicized. Use "Television" or "Radio" as the medium of publication.

"Lie Like a Rug." *NYPD Blue*. Dir. Steven Bochco and David Milch. ABC. KOMO, Seattle.

6 Nov. 2001. Television.

If you accessed a program on the Web, give the basic citation information without the original medium of publication; then include the Web publication information with an access date.

Ashbrook, Tom. "Turf Wars and the American Lawn." *On Point*. Natl. Public Radio,

22 July 2008. Web. 23 July 2009.

For podcasts, see page 336.

MLA Style

Film or video recording

Shakespeare in Love. Dir. John Madden. Perf. Joseph Fiennes and Gwyneth Paltrow.

Screenplay by Marc Norman and Tom Stoppard. Universal Miramax, 1998. Film.

Use "DVD" or "Videocassette" rather than "Film" as the medium of publication if that is the medium you consulted. If you accessed a film or video on the Web, omit the original medium of publication, include the Web site or database name (italicized), the sponsor and posting date, "Web" as medium of publication, and the date of access.

Shakespeare in Love. Dir. John Madden. Perf. Joseph Fiennes and Gwyneth Paltrow.

Screenplay by Marc Norman and Tom Stoppard. Universal Miramax, 1998.

Netflix. Netflix, n.d. Web. 9 Mar. 2010.

For videos published originally on the Web, see page 336.

Sound recording

Begin the entry with what your paper emphasizes—for example, the artist's, composer's, or conductor's name—and adjust the elements accordingly. List the medium—CD, LP, Audiocassette—last.

Dylan, Bob. "Rainy Day Women #12." *Blonde on Blonde*. Columbia, 1966. LP.

If you accessed the recording on the Web, drop the original medium of publication and include the Web site or database name (italicized), "Web" as the medium of publication, and the access date.

Dylan, Bob. "Rainy Day Women #12." *Blonde on Blonde*. Columbia, 1966. *Lala*. La La

Media, n.d. Web. 10 Mar. 2010.

Cartoon or advertisement

Trudeau, Garry. "Doonesbury." Comic strip. *Seattle Times* 19 Nov. 2001: B4. Print.

Banana Republic. Advertisement. *Details* Oct. 2001: 37. Print.

Interview

Castellucci, Marion. Personal interview. 7 Oct. 2010.

Lecture, speech, or conference presentation

Sharples, Mike. "Authors of the Future." Conference of European Teachers of Academic
    Writing. U of Groningen. Groningen, Neth. 20 June 2001. Lecture.

Government publications

In general, follow these guidelines:

- Usually cite as author the government agency that produced the document. Begin with the highest level and then branch down to the specific agency:

    United States. Dept. of Justice. FBI.

    Idaho. Dept. of Motor Vehicles.

- Follow this with the title of the document, italicized.
- If a specific person is clearly identified as the author, you may begin the citation with that person's name, or you may list the author (preceded by the word "By") after the title of the document.
- Follow standard procedures for citing publication information for print sources or Web sources.

> United States. Dept. of Justice. FBI. *The School Shooter: A Threat Assessment Perspective.* By Mary Ellen O'Toole. 2000. Web. 16 Aug. 2001.

James Gardiner (student), "Why *Facebook* Might Not Be Good for You" (MLA-Style Research Paper)

As an illustration of a student research paper written in MLA style, we present James Gardiner's paper on online social networks. James's process in producing this paper has been discussed in various places throughout the text.

Gardiner 1

James Gardiner

Professor Johnson

Writing Seminar: Inquiry and Argument

15 May 2007

Why *Facebook* Might Not Be Good for You:

Some Dangers of Online Social Networks

Walk into any computer lab located at any college campus across the country and you'll see dozens of students logged onto an online social network (OSN). In the last few years, the use of these networks has skyrocketed among Internet users, especially young adults. These new virtual communities are significantly influencing the way young people communicate and interact with one another. A report titled "E-Expectations: The Class of 2007" went so far as to label upcoming college freshmen "the Social-Networking Generation" (qtd. in Joly).

In late 2006, the Pew Internet Project, a nonpartisan, nonprofit research group that examines the social impact of the Internet, reported that 55 percent of online teens have created a personal profile on OSNs and that 48 percent of teens visit social networking Web sites daily, with 22 percent visiting several times a day (Lenhart and Madden 2). The two most popular OSNs are *MySpace* and *Facebook*. *MySpace* is a general networking site that allows anyone to join, develop a profile, and display personal information. In less than four years of existence, *MySpace* has exploded to become the third most visited Web site on the Internet behind only *Google* and *Yahoo* ("Top Sites") with more than 100 million members (Joly). *Facebook* is geared more toward college students (until recently it required that a person attend a university to join the network) and is the number-one site accessed by 18- to 24-year-olds. According to research studies cited in an article in the *Toronto Star*, 90 percent of all undergraduates log on to *Facebook* and

Include your last name and page number on each page.

Center title.

Indent paragraphs 5 spaces or 1/2 inch.

Double space all text.

Use 1-inch margins.

Italicize book and periodical titles and Web site names.

Gardiner 2

60 percent log on daily (George-Cosh W1). *Facebook* has also experienced unprecedented growth in its relatively short existence and now ranks as the seventh most visited site on the Internet ("Top Sites") and has a member base of more than 19 million (Joly).

With the use of OSNs increasing among young people, the term "Facebook trance" has emerged to describe a person who loses all track of time and stares at the screen for hours (Copeland). While "Facebook trance" might describe only an occasional and therefore harmless phenomenon, it gives rise to important questions: What are the possible negative consequences of OSNs? What should youthful users be watchful for and guard against? The purpose of this paper is to identify the possible harms of OSNs. I will suggest that overuse of OSNs can be a contributing factor to a decline in grades as well as to other problems such as a superficial view of relationships, an increase in narcissism, and possible future embarrassment.

I don't mean to deny that OSNs have positive consequences for young people. For one thing, they provide a "virtual hangout" that acts as a convenient and cost-effective way to stay in close contact with friends and family. According to the Pew survey, 91 percent of users use OSNs to keep in touch with their regularly seen friends, while 82 percent use the sites to stay in touch with distant friends (Lenhart and Madden). OSNs let young people regularly view their friends' profiles, leave short messages or comments, and share personal information. OSN researcher Danah Boyd also claims that these sites give young people a platform on which to experiment with identities, voice their opinions, and practice how they present themselves through personal data, pictures, and music placed in their profiles (Bowley). OSNs also assist them in learning more about people they've met offline. Used as an investigative tool, OSNs offer quick ways to get additional background information on someone. For example, a student could use an OSN to decide whom to partner with for

Gardiner 3

a class project, to learn more about a new roommate, or to find out more about someone he or she just met at a party, all by browsing classmates' profiles.

Despite these benefits, OSNs have a downside. One potential harm is that OSNs could have a negative effect on grades. One study shows a direct connection between the amount of time spent on the networks and declining grades in school. A college newspaper article entitled "Research Links *MySpace* Use to Drop in Grades" reports a survey of high school students conducted by Fresno State University professor Tamyra Pierce. Pierce found that students with *MySpace* accounts were significantly more likely than students without *MySpace* accounts to report a decline in grades since the previous year. According to Pierce, "We can't know for sure that *MySpace* caused the lower grades, but when compared to other after-school activities (work, sports, video games, etc.), only *MySpace* showed significance" (qtd. in "Research Links"). Pierce's research also revealed that 42 percent of polled students said they often had *MySpace* open while doing homework, and 34 percent stated that they would delay homework to spend time on social networking sites. Pierce adds that 59 percent of students reported spending "between 30 minutes and six hours daily on *MySpace*." Such heavy usage significantly takes time away from school work, extracurricular activities, and sleep. Although this specific study focused on high school students, it would be safe to assume that the results would be generally similar for college students. In fact, the results of the Fresno State study were reported in other college newspapers (Scrabis; Jimenez); the writers for these college newspapers usually included anecdotes from their own campuses about college students obsessed with OSNs. One Penn State student said of *MySpace*, "I keep getting rid of it and then getting it back again because I'm addicted. It's like cocaine" (qtd. in Scrabis).

Another potential problem with OSNs is their tendency to promote superficial or unsatisfying relationships. According to Chou, Condron, and

Use quotation marks for article titles.

Use "qtd. in" for a source quoted in another source.

Gardiner 4

Belland, for some users "over-dependence on online relationships may result in significant problems with real-life interpersonal and occupational functioning" (381). When logged on to the network, students may believe that they are "in touch" with people, when actually they are physically alone with their computers. In a controversial 1998 article cited by Matsuba, Kraut and his colleagues suggested that extensive Internet use "was associated with declines in participants' communication with family members in the household, declines in the size of their social circle, and increases in their depression and loneliness" (qtd. in Matsuba 275). Matsuba conducted an extensive study to test Kraut's conclusions. Matsuba found that persons who scored high on measures of loneliness spent more time on the Internet than persons who scored low on the loneliness measures. In another facet of his study, Matsuba found that for persons who established online friendships, these friendships did not seem "as rich and diverse in quality compared to face-to-face friendships" (283). Matsuba concludes that while online communication can be used to enhance relationships, it can become a problem when it begins to replace offline interaction. He found that face-to-face friendships scored higher for both positive and negative aspects of relationships than did online friendships. He then speculates, "While it is possible that the internet is helping [lonely] people in their search, the possibility remains that the internet is hindering them in facing life in the 'real' world and thus preventing them from developing an adult identity" (283).

Matsuba's finding that face-to-face friendships are more "rich and diverse in quality" than online friendships has led me to speculate that a possible problem with OSNs is the complete lack of nonverbal communication exchanged between users. According to communications professor Julia T. Woods, "Scholars estimate that nonverbal behaviors account for 65 percent to 93 percent of the total meaning of communication" (132). Since the people

Gardiner 5

interacting on OSNs are unable to view each other, they are unable to gauge the other's subtle body language, facial expressions, and voice tones that are such vital ingredients of effective communication. Part of achieving the "adult identity" called for by Matsuba is learning to communicate nonverbally as well as verbally in an environment requiring real contact.

For me, a particularly interesting yet subtle danger of OSNs is their contribution to a rise in narcissism. In an article with the subtitle "Study Says Many Students Are Narcissists," journalist E. Hoover reports on the unpublished research of Jean M. Twenge, a psychology professor at San Diego State University, who says that new technologies such as OSNs have "stoked the self-loving tendencies of modern students" (qtd. in Hoover). Twenge's recent research shows that college kids today are more narcissistic than college kids were in the 1980s; she labels the current generation of youth as "the most narcissistic in recent history" (Hoover). According to Hoover, Twenge defines narcissism as "excessive vanity and a sense of entitlement." Narcissists, Hoover reports, "tend to lack empathy for others, behave aggressively when insulted, and ignore the needs of those around them."

According to Twenge, narcissism finds expression on OSNs in the way that young people on *MySpace* and *Facebook* compete with each other to be heard. In another article reporting Twenge's research, Melissa Ludwig states that OSNs have "gone beyond touching base with friends to an arena where people vie for the most digital friends, the best videos, the coolest sites, and the biggest audience" (A15). She then quotes Twenge: "Now it all becomes a competition, seeking attention and seeking status rather than a true connection between people, or a meaningful connection." The work of Twenge and others suggests that the popularity of OSNs is partly the result of young people's finding an online way to express their narcissistic tendencies. The sites may contribute to self-expression more than to connection and friendship.

Gardiner 6

A final danger of OSNs is that persons will place on their sites material that they will later regret. Young people tend to think that their audiences are only their like-minded friends and classmates. They often don't imagine their professors, their potential employers, or even their parents reading their sites. One journalist describes a *MySpace* profile in which a college student has posted photos of herself in "a skin-tight black leather Catwoman costume, two triangles of vinyl struggling to cover her silicone-enhanced breasts" (Ludwig A15). Ludwig continues:

> Much of the stuff floating around in cyberspace is tame, mundane even. But there also is plenty that's racy, embarrassing or squeamishly intimate. Bad or good, Generation Next is living out loud and doing it online, before a global audience, in a medium where digital archives may linger for a long, long time.... [Generation Nexters] still are too young to fully grasp the permanence of their online actions, and the possible consequences down the road. (A15)

One indication of this danger has already surfaced in the case of some sports teams. The University of Minnesota Duluth recently barred all athletes from creating profiles on *MySpace*, *Facebook*, and similar sites, a policy that, according to journalist Chao Xiong, aims to shield students and the school from bad press that might occur from the posting of inappropriate material. Xiong reports that athletic departments across the country are considering similar bans. One coach at the UM-Duluth campus said, "It was amazing to me how revealing people are with their lives on the Internet" (qtd. in Xiong 1A). (This coach had established her own *Facebook* profile in order to police the activities of her team members.) Xiong reports that across the country athletes have embarrassed their programs by posting pictures of themselves drinking blindfolded at parties or making disparaging comments about coaches or teammates. It is unclear

Indent longer quotations 10 spaces or 1 inch.

Use ellipsis to show omitted words.

Use brackets when inserting explanatory words in quotation.

Cite page number after period.

Gardiner 7

whether coaches have the legal right to forbid their team members to place profiles on OSNs (some students are claiming violation of free speech rights). However, the fact that athletic programs are concerned about the impact of these social networks shows the potential negative consequence of posting embarrassing material on OSNs.

Although I don't support the banning of *Facebook* or *MySpace* profiles for athletes or other students, I do think that young people should be aware of some of the problems associated with them. Two of the problems I have noted here— decline in grades and narcissistic competition for the coolest sites—could be avoided by students' simply limiting their time online. Knowing that OSNs can promote a superficial view of friendships might encourage people to use OSNs to stay in touch face-to-face with friends rather than try to find online substitutes for real friendships. Finally, young people should be aware that the materials they post on their profiles might one day come back to haunt them. To gain the maximum benefits of online social networks and avoid the pitfalls associated with them, my advice to today's students would be to use them as an advanced e-mail-type communication tool rather than as a place to loiter and waste valuable hours that they will never get back.

Gardiner 8

Works Cited

Bowley, Graham. "The High Priestess of Internet Friendship." *Financial
Times Weekend Magazine* 27 Oct. 2006. *LexisNexis Academic*.
Web. 22 Feb. 2007.

Chou, Chien, Linda Condron, and John C. Belland. "A Review of the Research on
Internet Addiction." *Educational Psychology Review* 17.4 (2005): 363–89.
Academic Search Complete. Web. 22 Feb. 2007.

Copeland, Libby. "Click Clique: *Facebook's* Online College Community."
Washingtonpost.com. Washington Post, 28 Dec. 2004. Web. 24 Feb. 2007.

George-Cosh, David. "Social Net: Thousands of Local Students Build
Friendships on *Facebook*." *TheStar.com*. Toronto Star, 20 Jan. 2007.
Web. 15 Apr. 2007.

Hoover, E. "Here's You Looking at You, Kid: Study Says Many Students Are
Narcissists." *Chronicle of Higher Education* 53.29 (9 Mar. 2007): A41.
Academic Search Complete. Web. 14 Apr. 2007.

Jimenez, Eddie. "*MySpace* Adds to Overload for Teens." *Fresno Bee* 9 Mar. 2007.
Newspaper Source. Web. 14 Apr. 2007.

Joly, Karine. "*Facebook, MySpace*, and Co." *University Business*. Professional
Media Group, Apr. 2007. Web. 5 May 2007.

Lenhart, Amanda, and Mary Madden. "Social Networking Websites and Teens:
An Overview." *Pew Internet and American Life Project*. Pew Research
Center, 3 Jan. 2007. Web. 19 Feb. 2007.

Ludwig, Melissa. "LOOK@ME: Generation Next Is Living Out Loud and
Online." *MySanAntonio.com*. San Antonio Express News, 15 Mar. 2007.
Web. 15 Apr. 2007.

Matsuba, M. Kyle. "Searching for Self and Relationships Online."
CyberPsychology and Behavior 9.3 (2006): 275–84. *Academic Search
Complete*. Web. 14 Apr. 2007.

Gardiner 9

"Research Links *MySpace* Use to Drop in Grades." *FresnoStateNews.com*. California State U, 9 Mar. 2007. Web. 2 May 2007.

Scrabis, J. "*MySpace* Usage May Lower Grades in Both High School, College Students." *Daily Collegian*. Pennsylvania State U, 23 Mar. 2007. Web. 15 Apr. 2007.

"Top Sites for United States." *alexia.com*. N.p., n.d. Web. 2 May 2007. <http://www.alexia.com/site/ds/ top_sites?cc=US&ts_mode=country&lang=none>.

Woods, Julia T. *Interpersonal Communication*: *Everyday Encounters*. 5th ed. New York: Wadsworth, 2007. Print.

Xiong, Chao. "Not Their Space." *Minneapolis Star Tribune* 16 Apr. 2007. *LexisNexis*. Web. 2 May 2007.

Put URLs in angle brackets.

Italicize book titles.

Check that everything cited in paper is in Works Cited list.

SKILL 13.4   **Cite and document sources using APA style.**

In many respects, the APA style and the MLA style are similar and the basic logic is the same. In the APA system, the list where readers can find full bibliographic information is titled "References"; as in MLA format, it includes only the sources cited in the body of the paper. The distinguishing features of APA citation style are highlighted in the following sections.

In-Text Citations in APA Style

A typical APA-style in-text citation contains three elements: (1) the last name of the author, (2) the date of the publication, and (3) the page number of the quoted or paraphrased passage. Table 13.3 identifies some typical variations and shows again the one-to-one connection between the in-text citation and the References list.

TABLE 13.3   In-Text Citations in APA Style

Type of Source	References Entry at End of Paper	In-Text Citation in Body of Paper
One author	Pollan, M. (2006). *The omnivore's dilemma: A natural history of four meals*. New York, NY: Penguin.	…(Pollan, 2006, p. 256). OR According to Pollan (2006), … (p. 256).
Two authors	Kwon, O., & Wen, Y. (2010). An empirical study of the factors affecting social network service use. *Computers in Human Behavior, 26*, 254–263. doi:10.1016 /j.chb.2009.04.011	…(Kwon & Wen, 2010, p. 262). OR Kwon and Wen (2010) claim that…(p. 262).
Three to five authors	Pollay, R. W., Lee, J. S., & Carter-Whitney, D. (1992). Separate, but not equal: Racial segmentation in cigarette advertising. *Journal of Advertising, 21*(1), 45–57.	…race" (Pollay, Lee, & Carter-Whitney, 1992, p. 52). OR Pollay, Lee, and Carter-Whitney have argued that "advertisers… race" (1992, p. 52). *For subsequent citations, use Pollay et al. For a quotation, use the specific page number, not the whole range of pages.*

(*continued*)

TABLE 13.3   *continued*

Type of Source	References Entry at End of Paper	In-Text Citation in Body of Paper
Author has more than one work in References list	Dombrowski, D. A. (1984). *The philosophy of vegetarianism.* Amherst, MA: University of Massachusetts Press. Dombrowski, D. A. (1997). *Babies and beasts: The argument from marginal cases.* Urbana: University of Illinois Press.	…(Dombrowski, 1984, p. 207). …(Dombrowski, 1997, p. 328). OR Dombrowski (1984) claims that…(p. 207). According to Dombrowski (1997),…(p. 328).
Indirect citation of a source that you found in another source *You use a quotation from Peter Singer from a book by Dombrowski. Include Dombrowski, not Singer, in References.*	Dombrowski, D. A. (1997). *Babies and beasts: The argument from marginal cases.* Urbana: University of Illinois Press.	Animal rights activist Peter Singer argues that…(as cited in Dombrowski, 1997, p. 429). *Singer is used for the attributive tag, but the in-text citation is to Dombrowski.*

References List in APA Style

The APA References list at the end of a paper presents entries alphabetically. If you cite more than one item for an author, repeat the author's name each time and arrange the items in chronological order, beginning with the earliest. In cases where two works by an author appeared in the same year, arrange them in the list alphabetically by title, and then add a lowercase "a" or "b" (etc.) after the date so that you can distinguish between them in the in-text citations:

Smith, R. (1999a). *Body image in non-Western cultures, 1750–present.* London, England: Bonanza Press.

Smith, R. (1999b). Eating disorders reconsidered. *Journal of Appetite Studies, 45,* 295–300.

APA Citation Models

Print Articles in Scholarly Journals

General Format for Print Article in Scholarly Journal

Author. (Year of Publication). Article title. *Journal Title, volume number,* page numbers.

doi: xx.xxxx/x.xxxx.xx

If there is one, include the **DOI** (digital object identifier), a number that is uniquely assigned to many journal articles. Note the style for capitalizing article titles and for italicizing the volume number.

One author

Herrera-Sobek, M. (2006). Border aesthetics: The politics of Mexican immigration in
film and art. *Western Humanities Review, 60,* 60–71. doi:10.1016/j.chb.2009.04.011

Two to seven authors

Kwon, O., & Wen, Y. (2010). An empirical study of the factors affecting social network
service use. *Computers in Human Behavior, 26,* 254–263.

When a source has more than seven authors, list the first six and the last one
by name. Use ellipses (. . .) to indicate the authors whose names have been
omitted.

Scholarly journal that restarts page numbering with each issue

Pollay, R. W., Lee, J. S., & Carter-Whitney, D. (1992). Separate, but not equal: Racial
segmentation in cigarette advertising. *Journal of Advertising, 21*(1), 45–57.

Note that the issue number and the parentheses are *not* italicized.

Print Articles in Magazines and Newspapers

General Format for Print Article in Magazine or Newspaper

Author. (Year, Month Day). Article title. *Periodical Title, volume number,* page numbers.

If page numbers are discontinuous, identify every page, separating numbers with
a comma.

Magazine article with named author

Hall, S. S. (2001, March 11). Prescription for profit. *The New York Times Magazine,* 40–45,
59, 91–92, 100.

Magazine article without named author

Daddy, daddy. (2001, July 30). *New Republic, 225,* 12–13.

Review of book or film

Schwarz, B. (2001, November). A bit of bunting: A new history of the British empire
elevates expediency to principle [Review of the book *Ornamentalism: How the
British saw their empire*]. *Atlantic Monthly, 288,* 126–135.

Kaufman, S. (2001, July 30). Polishing a gem [Review of the motion picture *The blue
angel*]. *New Republic, 225,* 28–29.

Newspaper article

Henriques, D. B. (1998, September 27). Hero's fall teaches Wall Street a lesson. *Seattle
Times,* pp. A1, A24.

Newspaper editorial

Dr. Frankenstein on the hill [Editorial]. (2002, May 18). *The New York Times,* p. A22.

Letter to the editor of a magazine or newspaper

Tomsovic, K. (1998, July 13). Culture clash [Letter to the editor]. The New Yorker, 7.

Print Books

General Format for Print Books

Author. (Year of publication). *Book title: Subtitle.* City, State [abbreviated]: Name of
    Publisher.

Brumberg, J. J. (1997). *The body project: An intimate history of American girls.* New York,
    NY: Vintage.

If the publisher's name indicates the state in which it is located, list the city but
omit the state.

Reid, H., & Taylor, B. (2010). *Recovering the commons: Democracy, place, and global justice.*
    Champaign: University of Illinois Press.

Second, later, or revised edition

Montagu, A. (1986). *Touching: The human significance of the skin* (3rd ed.). New York, NY:
    Perennial Press.

*Republished book (for example, a paperback published after the original hardback
edition or a modern edition of an older work)*

Wollstonecraft, M. (1995). *The vindication of the rights of woman, with strictures on
    political and moral subjects.* Rutland, VT: Tuttle. (Original work published 1792)

The in-text citation should read: (Wollstonecraft, 1792/1995).

Multivolume work

Churchill, W. S. (1956–1958). *A history of the English-speaking peoples* (Vols. 1–4). New
    York, NY: Dodd, Mead.

Citation for all the volumes together. The in-text citation should read: (Churchill,
1956–1958).

Churchill, W. S. (1957). *A history of the English-speaking peoples: Vol. 4. The great
    democracies.* New York, NY: Dodd, Mead.

Citation for a specific volume. The in-text citation should read: (Churchill, 1957).

Article in reference work

Ling, T. O. (1970). Buddhism in Burma. In S. G. F. Brandon (Ed.), *Dictionary of
    comparative religion.* New York, NY: Scribner's.

Translation

De Beauvoir, S. (1961). *The second sex* (H. M. Parshley, Trans.). New York, NY: Bantam
    Books. (Original work published 1949)

The in-text citation should read: (De Beauvoir, 1949/1961).

Corporate author (a commission, committee, or other group)

American Red Cross. (1993). *Standard first aid*. St. Louis, MO: Mosby Lifeline.

Anonymous author

The New Yorker cartoon album: 1975–1985. (1987). New York, NY: Penguin Books.
The in-text citation is (*New Yorker*, 1987).

Whole anthology

O'Connell, D. F., & Alexander, C. N. (Eds.). (1994). *Self recovery: Treating addictions using transcendental meditation and Maharishi Ayur-Veda*. New York, NY: Haworth Press.

Anthology article

Royer, A. (1994). The role of the transcendental meditation technique in promoting smoking cessation: A longitudinal study. In D. F. O'Connell & C. N. Alexander (Eds.), *Self recovery: Treating addictions using transcendental meditation and Maharishi Ayur-Veda* (pp. 221–239). New York, NY: Haworth Press.

Articles or Books from an Online Database

Article from database with digital object identifier (DOI)

Scharrer, E., Daniel, K. D., Lin, K.-M., & Liu, Z. (2006). Working hard or hardly working? Gender, humor, and the performance of domestic chores in television commercials. *Mass Communication and Society, 9*(2), 215–238. doi:10.1207/s15327825mcs0902_5

Omit the database name. If an article or other document has been assigned a digital object identifier (DOI), include the DOI at the end. To see where the information in the Scharrer citation came from, refer to Figure 13.4.

Article from database without DOI

Highland, R. A., & Dabney, D. A. (2009). Using Adlerian theory to shed light on drug dealer motivations. *Applied Psychology in Criminal Justice, 5*(2), 109–138. Retrieved from http://www.apcj.org

Omit the database name. Instead, use a search engine to locate the publication's home page, and cite that URL. If you need to break a URL at the end of a line, do not use a hyphen. Instead, break it *before* a punctuation mark or *after* http://.

Other Internet Sources

General Format for Web Documents

Author, editor, director, narrator, performer, compiler, or producer of the work, if available. (Year, Month Day of posting). *Title of web document, italicized*. Retrieved from Name of website if different from author or title: URL of home page

Barrett, J. (2007, January 17). *MySpace is a natural monopoly*. Retrieved from ECommerce Times website: http://www.ecommercetimes.com

APA Style

FIGURE 13.4 Scholarly Journal Article with a Digital Object Identifier (DOI) with Elements Identified for an APA-Style Citation

Scharrer, E., Daniel, K. D., Lin, K.-M., & Liu, Z. (2006). Working hard or hardly working?
Gender, humor, and the performance of domestic chores in television commericals.
Mass Communication and Society, 9(2), 215–238. doi:10.1207/s15327825mcs0902_5

To see where each element of the Barrett citation comes from, refer to Figure 13.2. If there is no posting date for the document you cite, use *n.d.* (for "no date").

Marks, J. (n.d.). "Overview: Letter from the president." Retrieved June 3, 2010, from
the Search for Common Ground website: http://www.sfcg.org

Entire Web site
BlogPulse. (n.d.). Retrieved September 3, 2010, from the Intelliseek website:
http://www.intelliseek.com

Article from a newspaper site
Bounds, A. (2007, June 26). Thinking like scientists. *Daily Camera* [Boulder]. Retrieved
from http://www.dailycamera.com

Article from a scholarly e-journal
Welch, J. R., & Riley, R. (2001). Reclaiming land and spirit in the western Apache
homeland. *American Indian Quarterly, 25,* 5–14. Retrieved from
http://muse.jhu.edu/journals/american_indian_quarterly

Reference material
Cicada. (2004). In *Encyclopaedia Britannica.* Retrieved from http://www.britannica.com

E-book

Hoffman, F. W. (1981). *The literature of rock: 1954–1978.* Retrieved from
    http://www.netlibrary.com

E-mail, interviews, and personal correspondence

Cite personal correspondence in the body of your text, but not in the References
list: "Daffinrud (personal communication, December 12, 2001) claims that...."

Blog Posting

Dyer, B., & Barnes, E. (2008, October 7). The "greening" of the Arctic [Web log post].
    Retrieved from http://blog.epa.gov/blog/2008/10/07/the-greening-of-the-arctic

To see where each element of this citation comes from, refer to Figure 13.3.

Web video

Beck, R. (2006, November 2). Immigration gumballs [Video file]. Retrieved from
    http://www.youtube.com/watch?v=n7WJeqxuOfQ

Podcast

Funke, E. (Host). (2007, June 26). *ArtScene* [Audio podcast]. National Public Radio.
    Retrieved from http://www.npr.org

Miscellaneous Sources

Television program

Bochco, S., & Milch, D. (Directors). (2001, November 6). Lie like a rug [Television series
    episode]. In *NYPD blue*. New York, NY: American Broadcasting Company.

Film

Madden, J. (Director). (1998). *Shakespeare in love* [Motion picture]. United States:
    Universal Miramax.

Sound recording

Dylan, B. (1966). Rainy day women #12. On *Blonde on blonde* [Record]. New York, NY:
    Columbia.

Government publications

O'Toole, M. (2000). *The school shooter: A threat assessment perspective.* Washington,
    DC: U.S. Federal Bureau of Investigation. Retrieved from http://www.fbi.gov/
    publications/school/school2.pdf

14 | PUNCTUATION

CONCEPT 1 **End Punctuation**

FAQs
- Which is correct, *FBI* or *F.B.I.*?
- Should a question mark go inside or outside quotation marks?
- What is an "indirect question," and how do I punctuate it?

It is important to end sentences with proper punctuation so that readers know what types of statements are being made and what kinds of silent intonation to give each one. There are three ways to punctuate a sentence: with a period, a question mark, or an exclamation point.

The Period

The period is used for several purposes: to indicate the end of a statement, to punctuate initials and abbreviations, and to mark basic divisions in units and computer names.

Use a period to mark the end of a statement Sometimes called a "full stop," the period is most commonly used to mark the end of a sentence. Just make sure before you place the period that the words form a *complete grammatical sentence,* or else you will be creating a sentence fragment.

If the sentence ends with a quotation mark, place the period *inside* the quotation mark:

> One commentator said that "rainforest destruction, overpopulation, and the global arms trade are problems for the entire world."

If the sentence ends with a parenthesis, place the period *outside* the parenthesis unless the entire sentence is a parenthetical comment:

> Mexicans voted Sunday in elections that could weaken the power of the world's longest ruling political party, the Institutional Revolutionary Party (PRI).

Use periods to punctuate initials and many abbreviations Initials that stand for middle names or first names take periods:

Mary W. Shelley   O. J. Simpson   F. Scott Fitzgerald

Leave one space after each period when punctuating initials in names.
Most abbreviations ending in lowercase letters take periods:

Ms.	a.m.	St.	Jan.
Mrs.	p.m.	Ave.	i.e.
Mr.	etc.	Rd.	Jr.
Dr.	e.g.	apt.	Inc.

Use periods to mark basic divisions in units and computer names Basic divisions in money, measurements, email addresses, and file names are indicated by periods:

$99.50   3.2 meters   13.5 gallons
English.paper.com   michael.okiwara@u.c.utah.edu

Avoid common misuses of periods

1. **Do not use a period to mark just any pause.** If you insert a period whenever you want readers to pause, you risk creating sentence fragments. Consider this example:

> Attempts to challenge reactionary political views are often branded as "politically correct" by those same reactionaries. Who support only their own versions of "free speech."

The second statement is a fragment; the writer has incorrectly set it off as a separate sentence. The correct way to signal a pause is to insert a comma, thus turning the fragment into a relative clause:

> Attempts to challenge reactionary political views are often branded as "politically correct" by those same reactionaries, who support only their own versions of "free speech."

2. **Do not use periods with acronyms and other all uppercase abbreviations.** The recent trend is not to use periods with common abbreviations for states, countries, organizations, computer programs, famous people, and other entities:

CA	NJ	USA	UN	FBI
NOW	NAACP	MS-DOS	CD-ROM	HTML
MIT	NBA	JFK	FDR	AAA

3. **Do not use periods at the end of stand-alone titles or headings.** The title of this chapter and its numbered headings are examples of stand-alone titles and headings, respectively.

4. **Do not use periods at the end of sentences within sentences.** Here is an example of a sentence within a sentence:

   The famous statement "I think, therefore I am" originated in an essay by the French philosopher Descartes.

5. **Do not use periods after items in a formatted list (except for full sentences).** The table of contents for this handbook is an example of a formatted list. Only when the items in the list are full sentences is it acceptable to end them with periods.

The Question Mark

Question marks are placed after direct questions, whereas periods follow indirect questions. Do not use a comma or a period after a question mark unless the question mark is part of a title.

Use a question mark after a direct request

Requesting Information	Who wrote *Jesus Christ, Superstar*?
Asking for Confirmation	It's a complicated situation, isn't it?
Making a Polite Request	Could you please be a little quieter?

Using question marks with quotation marks If the quotation is a question and it is at the end of the sentence, put the question mark inside the quotation marks.

   The police officer asked me, "Do you live here?"

If the quotation is a statement embedded within a question and it comes at the end of the sentence, put the question mark outside the quotation marks.

   Who said, "Those who forget history are condemned to repeat it"?

Using question marks in a series It is acceptable to put a question mark after each independent item, even if it is not a full sentence.

   Will our homeless population continue to grow? Stay about the same? Get smaller?

If the question is an either/or type, put a question mark only at the end.

   Are you coming with us or staying here?

Do not use a question mark after an indirect question An indirect question is the writer's rewording of a question posed by someone else.

> A tourist asked me where the Lincoln Memorial was.

The Exclamation Point

Exclamation points are used to show strong emotion, including amazement and sarcasm. Do not use a comma or a period after an exclamation point. (The one exception is when the exclamation point is part of a title.)

Use an exclamation point to signal a strong statement The statement marked with an exclamation point does not have to be a full sentence.

An Outcry or Command	Oh! Watch out!
Strong Emphasis	People before profits!
Astonishment	Imagine reading this news report and not getting upset!
Sarcasm	And the cigarette companies claim that smoking is not addictive!

Using exclamation points with quotation marks If the quotation itself is an exclamation, put the exclamation point inside the quotation marks.

> It is not a good idea to go into a crowded movie theater and shout "Fire!"

Otherwise, the exclamation point should be placed outside the quotation marks.

> I can't believe he said, "Alice doesn't live here"!

Avoiding overuse of exclamation points Exclamation points are rarely used in college papers, essays, and other kinds of formal writing. Try not to use them except in highly unusual circumstances. Any kind of writing—even informal writing—that has too many exclamations sounds juvenile. There are better ways to express your enthusiasm.

EXERCISE

The following email message contains a number of errors in end punctuation. Make the appropriate corrections.

> Guess what
>
> I just found the Web site for NoF.X. Which I have been meaning to search out. It's NoF.X.@www.nofxofficialwebsite.com.
>
> I just got their new C.D. it was a real deal At WEJones Music downtown—$12 99 I'm listening to it now—it rules.
>
> That's it for now I have to write a paper (yuck) due Tues It's on F.D.R. and W.W.II Got to go
>
> Later :)

> ### EXERCISE
>
> The end punctuation marks have been deleted from the following paragraphs. Supply the appropriate punctuation marks.
>
> 1. How long have human beings been concerned about population growth If you believe the warnings, we have long been on the verge of overpopulating the earth In a warning written around AD 200, a Roman writer named Tertullian lamented that "we are burdensome to the world and the resources are scarcely adequate to us" The population at the time is believed to have been 200 million, barely 3 percent of today's 5.8 billion He thought *he* had reason for concern
> 2. Can a program ever be believed once it stages an incident Sometimes it can NBC's *Dateline* was not the first network to fake a car crash when it used igniters in its dramatization of the hazards of GM trucks; all three networks had done the same Unfortunately, the public was not told that program personnel "helped" ignite the fire Why did the network do it They did it because of competition for viewers The line between entertainment and news was badly blurred What was the reason for the media error *Dateline* anchor Jane Pauley replied, "Because on one side of the line is an Emmy; the other, the abyss"

CONCEPT 2 **The Comma**

FAQs

- Should I use a comma before *and* or *but*?
- How should I punctuate a series of items?
- In addresses, is there a comma between the state and the zip code?
- Should I put a comma after *such as*?

The comma is the most common and most useful punctuation mark in academic writing—and also the most difficult to master. Commas are used mainly to indicate sentence structure and thereby clarify meaning. This chapter provides some guidelines (not absolute rules) for the use of commas.

Use a comma to set off an introductory phrase or clause When readers start to read a sentence, one of the first things they do (unconsciously) is try to locate the grammatical subject. Help them do this by setting off with a comma any potentially distracting words that *precede* the subject. In the following excerpt, note how the commas allow the reader to identify easily the sentence subjects that follow them: *cultural relativism, most US citizens,* and *bullfighting.*

> *Because we tend to use our own culture to judge others,* cultural relativism presents a challenge to ordinary thinking.

> *For example,* most US citizens appear to have strong feelings against raising bulls for the sole purpose of stabbing them to death in front of crowds shouting "Olé!"

According to cultural relativism, however, bullfighting must be viewed strictly within the context of the culture in which it takes place—its history, its folklore, its ideas of bravery, and its ideas of sex roles.

The writer has put a comma after an introductory subordinate clause (*Because we tend to use our own culture to judge others*), a transitional phrase (*For example*), and a prepositional phrase and conjunctive adverb (*According to cultural relativism, however*). In each sentence, the comma marks off everything preceding the subject, allowing the reader to locate the subject easily.

Using a comma after an introductory element is sometimes necessary to prevent possible confusion.

Confusing   Soon after starting the car began making funny noises.

Clear   Soon after starting, the car began making funny noises.

Exception: If the introductory element is short and unemphatic, you do not need to insert a comma.

Today I have class from 9:00 a.m. to 1:00 p.m.

On most days the mail does not get here until late afternoon.

Use a comma before a coordinating conjunction to separate independent clauses

The combination of a comma and a coordinating conjunction (*and, but, or, nor, for, so, yet*) is one of the most common ways of connecting independent clauses.

Members of a mainstream culture often feel threatened by a counterculture, *and* they sometimes move against it in the attempt to affirm their own values.

Conflict theorists acknowledge that social institutions were originally designed to meet basic survival needs, *but* they do not see social institutions as working harmoniously for the common good.

Using a comma before a coordinating conjunction to separate independent clauses, as in these examples, clarifies for the reader that each clause is making a separate statement.

When the two clauses are closely linked, however, you may want to omit the comma, as in this example.

It was very hot and the men had marched a long way. They slumped under the weight of their packs and the curiously black faces were glistening with sweat.

—George Orwell, "Marrakech"

When you are using a coordinating conjunction to link phrases rather than clauses, you generally do not insert a comma.

Incorrect   Acupuncture has proved effective for treating chronic pain, and for blocking acute pain briefly.

Correct   Acupuncture has proved effective for treating chronic pain and for blocking acute pain briefly.

However, writers sometimes insert a comma to create more separation between the two parts.

> Acupressure is similar to acupuncture, but does not use needles.

Here the writer has put a comma between the two verb phrases in order to emphasize the contrast in meaning between them.

EXERCISE

Correct the comma errors in the following sentences:

1. In comparison with ordinary soap the production of detergents exerts a more intense environmental impact.
2. Three out of four Americans claim to believe in God and four out of ten go to church regularly.
3. If a typical book contains 500 pages the information content of a single chromosome corresponds to some 4,000 volumes.
4. There are numerous private daycare centers in the United States but the employees are often underpaid and weary from looking after too many children.
5. In many countries people cannot conceive of themselves apart from the family or group they belong to. In the United States on the other hand self-reliance is the fundamental virtue.
6. The English language surrounds us like a sea and like the waters of the deep it is full of mysteries.
7. Of all the world's languages (which now number some 2,700) English is arguably the richest in vocabulary.
8. For most people body temperature drops at night, and then rises in the morning.
9. Enjoyment and appreciation are related terms but they are not synonymous.
10. Although one can enjoy music without understanding it appreciation of music requires some knowledge.

Use commas between items in a series A series of three or more items generally has commas after all but the last item.

> My super-patriotic neighbor says *red, white, and blue* are his favorite colors.

> Each day, cigarettes contribute to over 1,000 deaths from *cancer, heart disease, and respiratory diseases.*

Some writers, however, drop the final comma (or **serial comma**), especially in fields such as journalism, advertising, and business.

> My uncle used to work for *Pierce, Fenner and Smith.*

Using the serial comma is never wrong, however; and sometimes it helps clarify the meaning of a sentence.

> **Unclear**   The three balls were colored red, blue and white and green.
>
> **Clear**   The three balls were colored red, blue and white, and green.
>
> OR
>
> **Clear**   The three balls were colored red, blue, and white and green.

Use commas to separate coordinate adjectives When the adjectives in a series could be arranged in any order or could be (but are not) strung together with the use of *and,* they are termed **coordinate adjectives**. To show their loose relationship and to avoid confusion with adjectives that cumulate in a particular order to modify each other, separate coordinate adjectives with commas.

> A *rusty, dented, broken-down* car was left behind.

In this example, each adjective modifies the word car, and the string of adjectives could be rearranged:

> A *broken-down, dented, rusty* car was left behind.

Use commas to set off nonessential elements A **nonessential element**, or **nonrestrictive element**, provides an extra piece of information that can be left out without changing the basic meaning of the sentence. Always use punctuation to set off nonessential, or nonrestrictive, elements from the rest of the sentence. (By contrast, elements that are essential, or restrictive, are always integrated into the sentence without separating punctuation.) Nonessential elements are most commonly set off with commas; however, dashes or parentheses may also be used.

> Lung cancer, *the leading cause of cancer deaths in the United States,* kills more than 153,000 Americans each year. [A nonessential appositive is set off with commas.]
>
> Many other illnesses, *like the common cold and even back strain,* are self-limiting and will improve in time. [A nonessential phrase is set off with commas.]
>
> Universal health care, *which guarantees every citizen at least basic medical benefits,* is found in every industrialized country in the world except the United States and South Africa. [A nonessential clause is set off with commas.]

In each of these sentences, the writer could have omitted the italicized elements without affecting the basic meaning:

> Lung cancer . . . kills more than 153,000 Americans each year.
>
> Many other illnesses . . . are self-limiting and will improve in time.
>
> Universal health care . . . is found in every industrialized country in the world except the United States and South Africa.

Instead, she chose to insert extra information to help the reader.

Unless the nonessential element ends the sentence, be sure to use *two* commas to set it off, not just one.

Incorrect	Alzheimer's disease, *a progressive impairment of the brain* strikes over 4 million older Americans every year.
Correct	Alzheimer's disease, *a progressive impairment of the brain*, strikes over 4 million older Americans every year.

When should you use commas instead of dashes or parentheses to set off nonrestrictive elements? Commas represent less of a break in the flow of thought, so the elements they enclose are a bit more closely attached to the main part of the sentence. Dashes give more emphasis to the nonrestrictive element, while parentheses can make the nonrestrictive element seem almost like an afterthought.

EXERCISE

Correct the comma errors in the following sentences.

1. The antitax group collected 65,202 signatures, on a petition, in support of an immediate tax cut.
2. Although this is more than the required 64,928 signatures it still may not be enough.
3. Because of duplications, illegible signatures and people improperly signing for other family members a minimum margin of at least 2,000 is usually needed, to withstand challenges experts say.
4. At one time many states often barred the sale of contraceptives to minors prohibited the display of contraceptives or, even, banned their sale altogether.
5. Today condoms are sold in the grocery store and some television stations, even air ads for them.
6. The capital campaign which was off to a great start, hoped to net $1.2 million.
7. When we shop we want to get the most for our money.
8. Herbalists practice herbal medicine which is based on the medicinal qualities of plants or herbs.
9. Economically and culturally overshadowed by the United States Canada has nonetheless managed to carve out a feisty independent identity since World War II.
10. The participants who had been carefully chosen by Akron's political and community establishment expressed a range of views.

Grammar Checkers: Comma Errors   **TechALERT!**

Do not expect your grammar checker to catch comma errors. The previous Exercise contains twenty such errors, and our grammar checker failed to detect any of them.

Use commas to set off conjunctive adverbs **Conjunctive adverbs** include such words and phrases as *however, therefore, consequently, thus, furthermore, on the other hand, in general,* and *in other words.* They serve as useful transitional devices, helping the reader to follow the flow of the writer's thinking. By setting off conjunctive adverbs with commas, you give them more prominence, clearly marking a shift in thinking.

> Over eighty million people in the United States suffer from chronic health conditions. Their access to health care, *however,* is largely determined by whether or not they have health insurance.

> Resistance training exercises cause microscopic damage to muscle fibers, which take twenty-four to forty-eight hours to heal; *therefore,* resistance training programs require at least one day of rest between workouts.

Use commas with dates, place names and addresses, titles and degrees, and numbers

Using commas with dates When writing a date in the traditional American format—month, day, and year—set off the year by placing a comma after the day.

> John F. Kennedy died on November 22, 1963, in Dallas, Texas.

Do not use a comma if only the month and year are given.

> John F. Kennedy died in November 1963 in Dallas, Texas.

Do not use a comma when writing the date in inverse order (day, month, year).

> John F. Kennedy died on 22 November 1963 in Dallas, Texas.

Using commas in place names and addresses Use commas after all major elements in a place name or address. However, do not put a comma before a zip code.

> Aretha Franklin was born in Memphis, Tennessee, on March 25, 1942.

> Alfredo's new address is 112 Ivy Lane, Englewood, NJ 07631.

Using commas with titles and degrees Use commas to set off a title or degree following a person's name.

> Stella Martinez, MD, was the attending physician.

> Ken Griffey, Jr., will never break Barry Bonds's home run record.

Using commas in numbers Use a comma in numbers having five digits or more, to form three-digit groups. In a number with four digits, the comma is optional.

2,400 or 2400

56,397

1,000,000

Exceptions: Do not use commas in street numbers, zip codes, telephone numbers, account numbers, model numbers, or years.

Use commas with speaker tags If you are quoting someone and using a speaker tag (such as *he said, according to Freud,* or *notes Laurel Stuart*), put a comma between the tag and the quotation.

Thomas Edison said, "Genius is 1 percent inspiration and 99 percent perspiration."

"The only thing about the fishing industry that has not changed much," *she writes,* "is the fishermen themselves."

Note that if a quotation ends in a comma, the comma goes inside the quotation marks.
    A comma is not used if the quotation ends in another punctuation mark.

"What a marvelous performance!" exclaimed the Queen.

A comma is not used if the quotation is introduced with *that.*

Rush Limbaugh claims that "the poorest people in America are better off than the mainstream families in Europe."

Use commas with markers of direct address Put commas around words that indicate that you are talking directly to the reader: words such as *yes* or *no,* the reader's name (*Bob*), a question tag (*don't you agree?*), or a mild initiator (*Well* or *Oh*).

Yes, the stock market is likely to turn around.

Do you really think, *Grace,* that Professor Wilson will postpone the test?

Intelligence is impossible to measure with just one type of test, *don't you think?*

Some people say we should all have guns to protect ourselves. *Well,* I do not agree.

EXERCISE

Correct the comma errors in the following sentences.

1. One fictitious address used by advertisers is John and Mary Jones 100 Main Street Anytown USA 12345.
2. We are a nation of shoppers aren't we?
3. Easy access to birth control however, was not always the case.

4. "It would be good to have this question on the ballot" the governor said.
5. Dr. Martin Luther King Jr. often quoted lines from the Bible.
6. For example, he would sometimes say "Let justice roll down like the waters."
7. A Renoir exhibition organized and first shown by the National Gallery of Canada in Ottawa Ontario opened at the Art Institute of Chicago, on October 21 1997 and ran through January 4th, of the next year.
8. Much to the irritation of its neighbor, for instance Canada keeps friendly ties with Fidel Castro's Cuba.
9. Lee surrendered to Grant at Appomattox Court House Virginia on April 9 1865.
10. According to the police there were more than 10000 protestors at the rally.

Avoid misuse of commas

1. **Never use a single comma between the subject and predicate.** When a complex subject begins a sentence, writers sometimes feel inclined to add an inappropriate comma that splits the subject and predicate.

   Incorrect   Numerous psychological and social factors, have a strong influence on how people age.

   Correct   Numerous psychological and social factors have a strong influence on how people age.

This mistake arises only if you insert a *single* comma between subject and predicate. A nonrestrictive element between the subject and the predicate may be set off by two commas.

   Police discretion, the decision as to whether to arrest someone or even to ignore a matter, is a routine part of police work.

2. **Never put commas around essential elements. Essential** (or **restrictive**) elements are phrases or clauses that help define some other element in the sentence. Unlike nonessential elements, they should not be set off with commas.

   Incorrect   Consumers, who are considering using a hospital or clinic, should scrutinize the facility's accreditation.

   Correct   Consumers who are considering using a hospital or clinic should scrutinize the facility's accreditation. [Omitting the commas makes it clear that the writer is referring only to those consumers who are considering using a hospital or clinic.]

Incorrect	Be sure to use a filtration system, which will destroy all harmful bacteria in the water.
Correct	Be sure to use a filtration system which will destroy all harmful bacteria in the water. [Omitting the comma before the modifying phrase makes it clear that the writer is referring only to a certain type of filtration system, not just any filtration system.]

Essential elements include names that come immediately after a common noun and define what the noun refers to:

The film *Citizen Kane* is an all-time classic. [The name *Citizen Kane* serves as a restrictive appositive, identifying a specific film.]

The Chilean novelist Isabel Allende is an acclaimed defender of human rights. [The name Isabel Allende is a restrictive appositive, identifying a particular Chilean novelist.]

3. **Avoid using commas with cumulative adjectives.** Adjectives that accumulate before a noun, each one modifying those that follow, are called **cumulative adjectives**. Their modifying relationships, which depend on their order, are likely to be confused by the separating commas that are common with adjectives in a coordinate series.

Incorrect	The suspect was seen driving a *small, new, Italian, luxury* car.
Correct	The suspect was seen driving a *small new Italian luxury* car.

Cumulative adjectives follow a certain order. Therefore, one way of identifying such adjectives is to see whether they can be reordered. If the result sounds awkward (*a luxury Italian new small car*), the original ordering is cumulative.

Coordinate adjectives are different. Instead of modifying the following adjectives, they each modify the noun directly. Therefore, it is appropriate to separate them with commas.

4. **Avoid putting a comma before** *than*. Resist the urge to heighten a comparison or contrast by using commas to separate the *than* phrase from the rest of the sentence.

Incorrect	Beating our arch rival was more important, than getting to the state playoffs.
Correct	Beating our arch rival was more important than getting to the state playoffs.

Using Commas

Use commas to separate or set off

- Introductory phrases or clauses, especially if they tend to obscure the subject
- Independent clauses connected with a coordinating conjunction
- Three or more items in a series
- A string of adjectives that could be rearranged or linked by *and*
- Nonessential phrases or clauses that add to but do not restrict the sentence's basic meaning
- Conjunctive adverbs used as transitional devices
- Speaker tags
- Markers of direct address

Do not use commas to separate or set off

- A subject and a predicate that would be split with a single comma
- Restrictive phrases or clauses that are essential to a sentence's basic meaning
- Adjectives that depend on their order to show modification in meaning
- Items in a series of only two items
- Phrases beginning with *than*
- Subordinating conjunctions
- Independent clauses that are not connected with a coordinating conjunction

5. **Avoid using a comma after a subordinating conjunction.** A comma should not be used to separate a subordinating conjunction from its own clause.

Incorrect	Although, the car is fifteen years old, it seems to be in good shape.
Correct	Although the car is fifteen years old, it seems to be in good shape.

6. **Do not use a comma before parentheses or after a question mark or exclamation point.** A comma is superfluous with an opening parenthesis, a question mark, or an exclamation point, unless the punctuation mark is part of a title.

Incorrect	Muhammad was born in Mecca, (now in Saudi Arabia) and founded the religion of Islam around AD 610.
Correct	Muhammad was born in Mecca (now in Saudi Arabia) and founded the religion of Islam around AD 610.
Incorrect	"Where are you going?," he asked.
Correct	"Where are you going?" he asked.
But	According to the book *Culture Shock!*, 57% of Americans are Protestants.

7. **Do not insert a comma before a list.** Resist the urge to punctuate before a listed series.

Incorrect	Some countries, such as, Holland, Sweden, and Denmark, have very compassionate welfare systems.
Correct	Some countries, such as Holland, Sweden, and Denmark, have very compassionate welfare systems.
Incorrect	My toughest subjects are, math, biology, and physics.
Correct	My toughest subjects are math, biology, and physics.

8. **Do not use a comma in a two-item series.** While commas are needed to separate three or more items in a series, separating two items with a comma is unnecessary and distracting.

Incorrect	Her outfit used strong contrasts between red, and blue.
Correct	Her outfit used strong contrasts between red and blue.

EXERCISE

Remove commas where necessary from the following sentences.

1. Tiger Woods has more competition, than he did five years ago.
2. My favorite sports are team sports such as, basketball and football.
3. Anyone, who appreciates classic art, would enjoy a visit to the Prado museum in Madrid.
4. The cues of daylight and darkness, help to keep plants and animals synchronized with the environment.
5. Someday, when we begin to assemble a kind of time map of the body's various rhythms, everyone will be surprised and perhaps delighted to recognize rhythms already observed in themselves.
6. Although, they often find Americans welcoming, and friendly, this is not altogether an easy country for foreigners to travel in.
7. Rodney gave his girlfriend a necklace with a beautiful, large, black, gemstone in it.
8. I normally use the Internet portal, *Yahoo!*, but my mother prefers *Excite*.
9. The objective of the US school system, is to bestow a broad education on every youngster.
10. Unless, they frequently trade in their car for a new one, people normally search for a car, that will last many years.

EXERCISE

Insert or remove commas where appropriate in the following sentences.

1. Length area and volume, are properties that can be measured.
2. Many plants are poisonous and others can be toxic if used in high doses.

3. We spend more on health care than does any other nation yet, unlike the rest of the industrialized world we do not provide access to health care for our entire population.
4. Stereotypes concerning inevitable intellectual decline among the elderly, have largely been refuted.
5. Classified advertisements are lists of ads set in small, type sizes, that advertise jobs items for sale and garage sales.
6. Long detailed explanations, can put a listener to sleep.
7. People, who are good shoppers, spend many hours planning their purchases.
8. They check sale circulars, from the newspaper and use the telephone to compare prices.
9. When they, finally, find an item at the best possible price they make their purchase.
10. Celebrations, marking the year 2000, were held in cities and towns across the continent.

EXERCISE

The following passage contains a number of comma errors (not in the original). Make the appropriate corrections.

To survive on the Earth human beings require the stable continuing existence of a suitable environment. Yet the evidence is overwhelming, that the way, in which we now live on the Earth is driving its thin life-supporting skin, and ourselves with it to destruction. To understand this calamity we need to begin with a close look, at the nature of the environment itself. Most of us find this a difficult thing to do for there is a kind of ambiguity, in our relation to the environment. Biologically human beings *participate* in the environmental system as subsidiary parts of the whole. Yet, human society is designed to *exploit* the environment as a whole to produce wealth. The paradoxical role we play in the natural environment—at once participant, and exploiter—distorts our perception of it.

Among primitive people a person is seen as a dependent part of nature, a frail reed in a harsh world governed by natural laws, that must be obeyed if he is to survive. Pressed by this need primitive peoples can achieve a remarkable knowledge of their environment. The African Bushman lives in one of the most stringent habitats on earth; food and water are scarce and the weather is extreme. The Bushman survives, because he has an incredibly intimate understanding of this environment. A Bushman can, for example return after many months, and miles of travel to find a single underground tuber noted in his previous wanderings when he needs it, for his water supply in the dry season.

—Barry Commoner, *The Closing Circle*

> *For Collaboration:* Share your corrected paragraphs with a friend or member of your group. Notice which revisions do the most to improve the paragraphs.

CONCEPT 3 **The Semicolon**

FAQs

* When should I use a semicolon?
* Do semicolons go inside or outside quotation marks?

Semicolons have three main functions: (1) linking closely related independent clauses without an intervening *and, but, or, nor, for, so, or yet*; (2) linking closely related independent clauses with an intervening *however, therefore*, or other conjunctive adverb; and (3) punctuating a complex list of items.

Use a semicolon to link independent clauses without a coordinating conjunction There are three ways to show a close relationship between independent clauses: with a *comma* and coordinating conjunction, with a *colon*, or with a *semicolon*. A semicolon is used when the two clauses have a coordinate relationship—that is, when they convey equally important ideas—but do not have a coordinating conjunction (*and, but, or, nor, for, so, yet*) between them.

> The first panacea for a mismanaged nation is inflation of the currency; the second is war. Both bring a temporary prosperity; both bring a permanent ruin.
>
> —Ernest Hemingway, *Notes on the Next War*

Use a semicolon to connect independent clauses separated by a conjunctive adverb If you separate two independent clauses with a conjunctive adverb like *however, therefore*, or *nevertheless*, you must use a semicolon.

> More than 185 countries belong to the United Nations; *however,* only five of them have veto power.

> Japan and Germany are now among the five most-powerful nations in the world; *therefore,* they would like to have veto power, too.

Use semicolons in a series with internal punctuation A **complex series** is one that has internal punctuation. Normally, commas are used to separate items in a series; however, if the individual items themselves contain commas, it can be difficult for readers to determine what the items are. In these cases, semicolons are used to separate the items.

> I have lived in Boulder, Colorado; Corpus Christi, Texas; and Vero Beach, Florida.

Place semicolons outside quotation marks Semicolons are always positioned outside quotation marks.

> Those who feel abortion is not a woman's prerogative say they are "pro-life"; those who feel it is say they are "pro-choice."

Grammar Checkers: Semicolon Errors

A grammar checker is unlikely to identify semicolon errors with any reliability. You'll do better to learn the principles laid out in this chapter and apply them on your own.

Avoid common semicolon errors Most errors with semicolons occur as a result of confusing semicolons with commas or with colons.

1. **Do not use a semicolon between an independent clause and a dependent clause or phrase.** Dependent clauses or phrases are linked to independent clauses most often by commas, not semicolons.

Incorrect	When we say that a country is "underdeveloped"; we imply that it is backward in some way.
Correct	When we say that a country is "underdeveloped," we imply that it is backward in some way.
Incorrect	In *MS Word*, you can remove several items from a document and then insert them as a group into another document by using the Spike; a scrapbook-like feature.
Correct	In *MS Word*, you can remove several items from a document and then insert them as a group into another document by using the Spike, a scrapbook-like feature.

2. **Do not use a semicolon to introduce a list.** Use a colon instead of a semicolon to introduce a list.

Incorrect	Utah has five national parks; Arches, Bryce, Canyonlands, Capitol Reef, and Zion.
Correct	Utah has five national parks: Arches, Bryce, Canyonlands, Capitol Reef, and Zion.

EXERCISE

Correct the punctuation errors in the following sentences.

1. Socrates disliked being called a "teacher," he preferred to think of himself as an intellectual midwife.
2. Tests will be given on the following dates; Monday, November 2, Friday, November 20, and Monday, December 7.
3. The scientific naming and classification of all organisms is known as *taxonomy*, both living and extinct organisms are taxonomically classified.
4. A single category of a species is called a *taxon*, multiple categories are *taxa*.
5. Since laughter seems to help the body heal; many doctors and hospitals are prescribing humor for their patients.
6. Beethoven was deaf when he wrote his final symphonies, nevertheless, they are considered musical masterpieces.
7. Some people think that watching a video at home is more fun than going to a movie, movie theaters are often crowded and noisy.
8. The lifeguards closed the beach when a shark was spotted, a few hours later some fishermen reported seeing the shark leave; so the beach was re-opened.
9. The feeling of balance is controlled by the ears, inside each ear are three small tubes filled with fluid.
10. Since its opening in 1955; Disneyland has been an important part of American culture, it has the ability to reflect and reinforce American beliefs, values, and ideals.

CONCEPT 4 **The Colon**

FAQs

- How does the colon differ from the semicolon?
- What punctuation mark should I use to introduce a quotation?

In formal writing, the colon is used mainly at the end of a general statement to announce details related in some way to the statement. These details may be given in a list of items, an appositive, an explanatory statement, or a quotation.

Use a colon to introduce a list or an appositive

In creating a macro, you can assign it to any one of three places: the toolbar, the keyboard, or a menu.

One principle should govern your choice: which one is most convenient?

In using a colon to introduce a list or an appositive, be sure that the introductory part of the sentence is a grammatically complete independent clause.

Faulty Colon Use

The four main parts of a memo are: header, introduction, summary, and details.

Faulty Colon Use Revised

A memo has four main parts: header, introduction, summary, and details.

OR

There are four main parts to a memo: header, introduction, summary, and details.

In academic writing, the phrase *as follows* is often used. It directly precedes the colon.

There are four main parts to a memo, as follows: header, introduction, summary, and details.

TechALERT!

Electronic Language: Punctuation-Based Emoticons

Emoticons using colons, semicolons, and other punctuation marks, such as :-o, :-/, and ;-), are not appropriate in formal or academic writing, including email to an instructor or on the job.

Use a colon to set off a second independent clause that explains the first

Rock climbing is like vertical chess: in making each move up the wall, you should have a broad strategy in mind.

Eighteenth century French philosophers were the godfathers of American democracy: Their writings, which influenced many of the Founders, advocated religious tolerance, individual liberty, majority rule, and checks and balances in government.

Note: You may begin the clause after the colon with either an uppercase letter or a lowercase letter.

Use a colon to introduce a quotation When a colon is used to introduce a quotation, the part of the sentence that precedes the colon should be grammatically independent.

In *Against Empire*, Michael Parenti states his concern about American foreign policy: "We should pay less attention to what US policymakers profess as their motives—for anyone can avouch dedication to noble causes—and give more attention to what they actually do."

If the part introducing the quotation is not an independent clause, use a comma instead of a colon.

In *Against Empire*, Michael Parenti states, "We should pay less attention. . . ."

> *Note:* If the quotation serves only as an example and is set off from the sentence that introduces it, a colon is not required. For instance, the sentence about *Against Empire* is set apart, by indentation and extra spacing, as an example. That is why there is no colon following the preceding sentence, which introduces it.

Use colons in titles Colons are often used in the titles of academic papers and reports. The part of the title that follows the colon is called the *subtitle*. It usually provides a more explicit description of the topic than does the title.

Nature and the Poetic Imagination: Death and Rebirth in "Ode to the West Wind"

Use colons in business letters and memos In business letters and memos, colons are used with salutations (*Dear Ms. Townsend:*), to separate the writer's initials from the typist's initials (*TH:ab*), and in memo headings (*To:, From:, Date:, Subject:, Dist:*).

Use colons in numbers and addresses Colons are used in Biblical citations to distinguish chapter from verse (*Matthew 4:11, Genesis 3:9*), in clock times to separate hours from minutes and minutes from seconds (*5:44 p.m.*), in ratios (*3:1*), and in Web site addresses (*http://www.fray.com*).

EXERCISE

Correct the punctuation errors in the following sentences.

1. There are several steps involved in writing an effective summary; read the original carefully, choose the material for your summary rewrite the material in a concise manner, identify the source of the original text.
2. We need to buy several ingredients in order to bake the cookies, brown sugar, chocolate chips eggs, and milk.
3. In *Becoming a Critical Thinker*, Ruggiero states, "Truth is not something we create to fit our desires. Rather, it is a reality to be discovered."
4. There are three important characteristics that all critical thinkers possess; the ability to be honest with themselves, the ability to resist manipulation, and the ability to ask questions.
5. Experts say swimming is one of the best forms of exercise, it burns as many calories as running but is low-impact.

6. The hacker apparently logged on to <http//www.au.org> at 9.03 a.m.
7. There are four qualities of a diamond that a prospective buyer should be aware of, color, clarity, cut, and carat weight.
8. In *The Language Instinct*, Steven Pinker discusses the inherent nature of language, "We are all born with the instinct to learn, speak, and understand language."
9. There are six major speech organs which are used to articulate sounds; the larynx, soft palate, tongue body, tongue tip, tongue root, and lips.
10. Denise titled her paper "Howls of Delight; Reintroduction of the Wolf into Yellowstone National Park."

CONCEPT 5 **The Apostrophe**

FAQs

* What is the difference between *its* and *it's*?
* How do I show possession with two names, like *Maria and Roberto*?
* Should I write *1990's* or *1990s*?

The apostrophe is used to indicate possession, to signal contractions and omitted letters, and to form certain plurals.

Use apostrophes with nouns to indicate possession In its grammatical sense, *possession* refers to ownership or some other special relationship between two nouns, such as that between an amount and the noun it quantifies. With singular nouns, possession is usually indicated by attaching *'s* to the end of the noun.

Sue Ellen's jacket	everyone's dream
my mother's photo	yesterday's bad weather
the club's treasurer	Gandhi's place in history
Ahmad's smile	a week's worth of work
Mr. Linder's class	

There are two exceptions to this rule:

1. If the rule would lead to awkward pronunciation, the extra *s* may be omitted: *Euripides' plays, Moses' laws, Mister Rogers' Neighborhood*.
2. In names of places, companies, and institutions, the apostrophe is often omitted: *Robbers Roost, Kings County, Starbucks, Peoples Republic*.

For plural nouns ending in *s*, form the possessive by just adding an apostrophe at the end:

the Browns' car	the Yankees' star pitcher	my parents' friends

For plural nouns not ending in *s*, form the possessive by adding *'s*:

women's rights   children's section   sheep's wool

Avoiding apostrophes with possessive pronouns Pronouns never take apostrophes to indicate possession. They have their own possessive forms: *its, his, her/hers, your/yours, their/theirs, our/ours, my/mine.*

Be careful not to confuse *its* and *it's*. The former is possessive; the latter is a contraction for *it is*.

Possessive   The university has revised its policy on hate speech.

Contraction   If you fall way behind in your studies, it's hard to catch up.

Showing possession with multiple nouns With multiple nouns, use apostrophes according to your intended meaning. If you want to indicate joint possession, add an apostrophe only to the last of the nouns:

Bill and Hillary's wedding

Siskel and Ebert's recommendations

If you want to show *separate* possession, put an apostrophe after each of the nouns:

Julie's and Kathy's weddings

Omar's, Gretchen's, and Mike's birthdays

TechALERT!

Grammar Checkers: Apostrophe Errors

Your grammar checker should flag most of the apostrophe errors described in this chapter, including all three of the common errors listed in the box. However, it may not tell you exactly how to fix the problem. For example, in the sentence "TV news reporting *seem's* like yet another form of entertainment," our grammar checker identified *seem's* as problematic but offered five different alternatives, only one of which was correct. You will have to exercise your own judgment in such cases. The guidelines in this chapter should help you.

Use apostrophes to indicate contractions and omitted letters In casual speech, syllables are sometimes omitted from common word combinations. For example, *cannot* becomes *can't*. In formal writing, such contractions are generally inappropriate. In much informal writing, however, such as email messages and personal letters, contractions are quite common. Just be sure to punctuate them correctly with an apostrophe.

will not → won't	should not → shouldn't	it is → it's
I am → I'm	you have → you've	they are → they're

The apostrophe also can be used for less common contractions, especially if you are trying to create a colloquial, slangy tone.

the 1990s → the '90s	magazine → 'zine
underneath → 'neath	neighborhood → 'hood

Use apostrophes to mark certain plural forms When a letter or symbol is used as a noun, the usual way of pluralizing nouns (adding an *-s* or *-es*) does not work well: "There are four *ss* in *sassafras*." In such cases, an apostrophe can help out: "There are four *s's* in *sassafras*."

Forming the plurals of letters, symbols, and words referred to as words Adding *'s* instead of *s* clarifies the plural forms of unusual nouns.

How can she have two @'s in her email address?

My instructor said I have too many *there*'s in my paper.

Apostrophes

Using an apostrophe for the possessive form of it

No   Her dog lost *it's* collar.

Yes   Her dog lost *its* collar.

Using an apostrophe with a nonpossessive noun

No   This report discusses four major *features'* of modern mass media.

No   This report discusses four major *feature's* of modern mass media.

Yes   This report discusses four major *features* of modern mass media.

Using an apostrophe with a present-tense verb

No   TV news reporting *seem's* like yet another form of entertainment.

Yes   TV news reporting *seems* like yet another form of entertainment.

Forming the plurals of numbers and abbreviations Both the Modern Language Association and the American Psychological Association recommend omitting the apostrophe in forming plurals like the following:

the 1990s   several IOUs

a pair of 6s   a shipment of PCs

Avoid misusing the apostrophe Be careful not to use apostrophes where they do not belong. The box below lists some of the most common apostrophe errors.

EXERCISE

Each of the following sentences contains at least one error involving the use of apostrophes. Make the appropriate correction(s).

1. Its unfortunate that Bobs' birthday falls on February 29.
2. I wanted to go to Maria's and Roberto's party, but I wasnt able to.
3. The snake sheds it's skin many times during its life.
4. Does the mens' group meet here?
5. No, its a womens' group that meets in this room on Thursdays.
6. I can't wait til my vacation comes!
7. Im taking my lawyers advice on such matter's.
8. All of the orchestra member's instruments seemed to be out of tune.
9. The driver and passenger's airbags both deployed after the accident.
10. Kevin's and Lauren's older sister is in high school now.

For Collaboration: Take note of apostrophe errors that you see on campus or in your neighborhood; share your examples with your group.

CONCEPT 6 **Quotation Marks**

FAQs
- Should I use quotation marks if I am only paraphrasing someone's words?
- Should a comma go inside or outside the quotation mark?
- How do I introduce a quotation?

The primary use of quotation marks is to acknowledge other people's words and statements. Using quotation marks is especially important in academic writing, which puts a premium on the ownership of ideas.

Use quotation marks for exact direct quotations Quotation marks should be placed around any words, phrases, or sentences that you have borrowed from someone else (unless the quotations are so lengthy that you prefer to set them off as an indented block).

> In *The End of Work*, Jeremy Rifkin said, "In the years ahead, more than 90 million jobs in a labor force of 124 million are potentially vulnerable to replacement by machines."

> One reviewer called it "a very readable and timely book."

> Some years ago, a group of artists designed a "space bridge" between Los Angeles and New York.

Paraphrasing or quoting indirectly A summarization, restatement, or paraphrase of a statement made by someone else is a form of **indirect discourse**, and quotation marks are not used. Putting quotation marks around words that were not those of the speaker or writer would be extremely misleading.

> Rifkin argues that in the future more than two-thirds of the American workforce could be displaced by automation.

Setting off long quotations in block form A long quotation (more than four lines) should be set off as an indented block without quotation marks.

> Rifkin sees this reduction of the workforce as having profound social effects:

> > The wholesale substitution of machines for workers is going to force every nation to rethink the role of human beings in the social process. Redefining opportunities and responsibilities for millions of people in a society absent of mass formal employment is likely to be the single most pressing social issue of the coming century. (Rifkin xv)

Use quotation marks to suggest skepticism about a term Sometimes you may find yourself writing about a concept that you think does not deserve the respect other people are giving it. In such cases, you can convey your skepticism by putting the concept name in quotation marks.

> Some politicians who claim to support "family values" have been found to be unfaithful to their spouses and abusive of their children.

In this example, the quotation marks around *family values* suggest that the writer has a skeptical view of the term.

This application of quotation marks (sometimes referred to as "scare quotes") should be reserved for cases where you believe that a term is being misused by others. Only on rare occasions should you use quotation marks simply to make ironic or sarcastic comments.

Incorrect	Action films are very "intellectual," aren't they?
Correct	Action films are not very intellectual, are they?

Use quotation marks to indicate shifts of register Quotation marks can be used occasionally to set off a colloquial term from the more formal discourse surrounding it.

One should always try to avoid an inflexible, "cookie-cutter" approach to rhetorical criticism.

Note: Colloquialisms should be used sparingly in formal writing, even when punctuated with quotation marks.

Use quotation marks when citing titles of short works When referring by title to short stories, book chapters, poems, essays, songs, and other brief works, enclose the titles in quotation marks.

I will never forget the first time I read Shirley Jackson's short story "The Lottery."

"Smells Like Teen Spirit" is a musical classic.

Chapter 20, "Design Principles and Graphics," talks about the functionality and aesthetics of formatting.

Titles of longer or more encompassing works are italicized or underlined.

Follow standard practice in using other punctuation with quotations Quoted material is commonly combined and mixed with a writer's original material. Here are common guidelines for using other punctuation with quotations.

1. **Put commas and periods inside the end quotation mark.** Standard American editorial practice calls for commas and periods to be placed as shown in the following passage:

   "The definition of community implicit in the market model," argues Patricia Hill Collins, "sees community as arbitrary and fragile, structured fundamentally by competition and domination."

   Note: Readers of British publications may see exceptions to this rule, as the British style is to place commas and periods outside quotation marks. When quoting from British sources, you should standardize punctuation for consistency with modern American usage, placing periods and commas inside quotation marks.

2. **Put colons and semicolons outside the end quotation mark.**

One critic called 1990 "the year in which rock and roll was reborn"; the fusing of metal and rap by groups like Living Colour and Faith No More broke down racial barriers in a way reminiscent of early rock and roll.

One of the things that distinguished Snoop Doggy Dogg from other rappers was his style, which was described in the *New York Times* as "gentle"; "where many rappers scream," said *Times* reporter Touré, "he speaks softly."

3. **Put other punctuation marks inside the end quotation mark if they are part of the quotation; otherwise, put them outside the end quotation mark.** Question marks, exclamation points, dashes, parentheses, and other punctuation marks should be positioned according to meaning.

Part of Quoted Title
Whitney Houston's "How Will I Know?" entered the pop charts at number one.

Part of Sentence
What do you think of controversial songs like "Deep Cover" and "Cop Killer"?

4. **Use single quotation marks (' ') for quotation marks within quotation marks.**

Garofalo notes that "on cuts like 'JC' and 'Swimsuit Issue,' Sonic Youth combined an overt sexuality with uncompromisingly feminist lyrics about women's issues."

The last line of the stanza reads, "Quoth the raven, 'Nevermore.'"

Quotation Marks

Using quotation marks just to call attention to something
No Pete Sampras won the Wimbledon championship "seven" times.
Yes Pete Sampras won the Wimbledon championship seven times.

Using quotation marks for indirect discourse
No President Bush said "he was a compassionate conservative."
Yes President Bush said he was a compassionate conservative.

Putting quotation marks around the title of your paper on a title page or at the head of the paper
If your title contains within it the title of *another* short work, however, that work's title should be enclosed in quotation marks.

Death and Rebirth in "Ode to the West Wind"

5. **Introduce quotations with the punctuation standard grammar calls for.** If the introduction to a quotation is not a full clause, do not use any punctuation.

> The conservative Parents Music Resource Center said that heavy metal was "the most disturbing element in contemporary music."

If the introduction to a quotation is a full clause, use a colon.

> The conservative Parents Music Resource Center said that heavy metal was harmful to society: "It's the most disturbing element in contemporary music."

Exception: If the introduction to a quotation is a speaker tag such as *she said* or *he notes*, use a comma.

> *Rolling Stone* noted, "Beneath the 'save the children' rhetoric is an attempt by a politically powerful minority to impose its morality on the rest of us."

TechHelp

Using Smart Quotation Marks

To use the more elegant smart (curly) quotation marks, instead of straight ones, click on TOOLS > AUTOCORRECT > AUTOFORMAT and then check "replace straight quotes with smart quotes."

EXERCISE

Correct the punctuation errors in the following sentences.

1. The question is not "why some rappers are so offensive, but rather, why do so many fans find offensive rappers appealing"?
2. "When you hear your record company has been sold for 20 or 30 times its earnings", said Tim Collins, Aerosmith's manager, "you think, "I want a piece of that"."
3. According to one critic, the 2006 Lollapalooza summer tour was, "way too male and way too guitar-oriented."
4. The biggest lottery prize in history, shared by eight workers in a Nebraska meatpacking plant, was worth "$365 million."
5. PMRC's Pam Howar expressed the concern that Madonna was teaching young girls: "how to be porn queens in heat".
6. In announcing that US superskier Picabo Street would miss the World Cup races because of a knee injury, her coach told the press", When the mind is ready but the body is not [. . .] there is danger of another injury".
7. The citation for the 2004 Nobel Peace Prize given to Kenyan activist Wangari Maathai reads, in part: She represents an example and a source of inspiration for everyone in Africa fighting for sustainable development, democracy and peace.

8. There are people who really enjoy line dances like "YMCA" and "The Electric Slide", although there are others who think those dances are silly.
9. Older people are often labeled "old and sick", "old and helpless", old and useless, or old and dependent:" in fact, the general image of old age is negative.
10. The Celtic tune "Greensleeves" is the melody used for the carol "What Child Is This"?

CONCEPT 7 **Other Punctuation Marks**

FAQs

- When should I use dashes instead of parentheses?
- How should I use brackets and ellipses in quotations?

Parentheses, dashes, brackets, ellipses, or slashes can be used, in moderation and in the proper contexts, to clarify meaning and add interest to writing.

Parentheses ( )

Use parentheses to insert extra information Parenthetical comments—clarifications, asides, examples, or other extra pieces of information—are often embedded within sentences. They can be as short as a single word or as long as an entire sentence.

Many components of biological diversity (biodiversity) are dwindling.

You can get a free annual credit report from any of the nation's three largest agencies (visit *annualcreditreport.com*).

For most right-handed people, the left hemisphere of the brain controls manual skill and language. (The opposite is true for most left-handed people.)

Manual skill (that is, the skill associated with making and using tools) is usually localized in the same hemisphere as speech.

Another common use of parentheses is in documentation. The scientific reference style calls for inserting reference citations in parentheses within sentences. This parenthetical style is the preferred method of the MLA and APA.

We need to think about the implications of our future liberation (Eastman and Hayford).

In antiquity and through the Middle Ages, memory was a valued skill (Hacking, 1995).

Do not overuse parentheses Parentheses are so handy that you may be tempted to overuse them. Resist the temptation. Too many parentheses can make it difficult for readers to follow the main train of thought. If you find yourself developing a parenthesis habit, look for ways to rewrite some of the parenthetical comments as modifiers or as subordinate clauses.

Use parentheses around letters or numbers to set off embedded lists
Listed phrases or clauses embedded in a longer sentence may be itemized with numbers or letters placed within parentheses.

> Socialism has three essential components: **(1)** the public ownership of the means of production, **(2)** central planning, and **(3)** distribution of goods without a profit motive.

Use parentheses to acknowledge editorial emphasis within a quotation
When you quote a passage, you may want to emphasize a certain part of it that is not emphasized in the original. You can do so by underlining or italicizing that part and then, at the end of the passage, acknowledging the change by writing *emphasis added* or *italics mine* between parentheses.

> Scheuer states, "Our popular and political cultures are dominated by money and profit, imagery and spin, hype and personality—and there can be no doubt that *the chief culprit* is commercial television." (emphasis added)

EXERCISE

The following passage has too many parentheses. Rewrite it, using the suggestions given in this chapter.

Abatement of water pollution in the United States (like that of air pollution) has been largely a success story. It also is one of the longest running (its legislative origins go back to the turn of the century). Until the 1970s, most legislation addressed public health issues and included provisions for helping communities build treatment plants (specifically, for water and sewage). With passage of the Water Pollution Control Act in 1972 (later called the Clean Water Act), the federal government turned its attention to cleaning up the nation's waterways (they had become badly polluted from industrial effluents and inadequately treated sewage).

For Collaboration: If you feel that you have a parenthesis habit, give a sample piece of writing to a friend or member of your group, and ask him or her for suggestions for revision.

Dashes —

Although dashes are a slightly less formal kind of punctuation than parentheses, they have several good uses. You can create a dash by typing two consecutive hyphens, which most word processors will then convert into a solid dash. If you first type a space before the hyphens, you'll get a short *en dash*; if you don't type such a space, you'll get a longer *em dash*. (The former is preferred for narrow-column writing such as in newspapers, the latter for full-page columns such as in college papers.)

Use dashes to highlight extra informational comments Dashes set off internal, informational comments in a more emphatic way than parentheses do.

> The first great American myth—the myth of the Chosen People—emerged among the Puritans in the colonial period.

> The modern industrial food chain has been unrivaled for its productivity—on average, a single US farmer today grows enough food each year to feed 100 people.

> Public decision makers have a tendency to focus mostly on the more obvious and immediate environmental problems—usually described as "pollution"—rather than on the deterioration of natural ecosystems upon whose continued functioning global civilization depends.

Dashes are particularly useful for setting off an internal list of items.

> Particularly resistant to increased pollution controls have been small businesses in California—paint dealers, gas stations, and dry-cleaning establishments—which the state began regulating in 1990.

Use dashes to set off important or surprising points If not overused, dashes can be a dramatic way to set off an inserted comment.

> While the Marshall Islanders continue to wrestle with the consequences of nuclear testing, a new proposal is on the table that will make the islands a dumping ground for American garbage—literally.

> A US waste disposal company, Admiralty Pacific, proposes to ship household waste from the west coast of the United States to the Pacific islands—an estimated 34 billion pounds of waste in the first five years of the program alone.

Confine yourself to one pair of dashes per sentence Dashes, like parentheses, can be overused. If you need to add more than one informational comment to a sentence, use commas or parentheses around the other comments. Too many dashes in a paragraph are a sign of poorly integrated ideas.

EXERCISE

Insert appropriate punctuation if needed (parentheses, dashes, or commas) in the places marked in the following sentences.

1. In 1987, officials in the Guatemalan government and the US Drug Enforcement Agency___DEA___entered into an agreement to defoliate vast areas of Guatemala's north and northwest___a region that contains a wildlife refuge and the largest area of unplundered rainforest remaining in Central America.

2. On the Internet are thousands of Usenet newsgroups, made up of people who communicate about almost any conceivable topic___from donkey racing and bird watching to sociology and quantum physics___.

3. People look forward to communicating almost daily with others in their newsgroup, with whom they share personal, sometimes intimate, matters about themselves___even though they have "met" only electronically___.

4. There is no theory that would have led anyone to expect that after World War II, Japan___with a religion that stressed fatalism, with two major cities destroyed by atomic bombs, and stripped of its colonies___would become an economic powerhouse able to turn the Western world on its head.

5. Although the distinction between race and ethnicity is clear___one is biological, the other cultural___people often confuse the two.

6. The United Nations defines seven basic types of families, including single-parent families, communal families___unrelated people living together for ideological, economic, or other reasons___, extended families, and others.

7. By the late 1980s, the proportion of adult Americans who were single by choice or by chance___often after failed marriages___had increased to slightly over 25 percent of adult men and over 20 percent of adult women.

8. If you were to go on a survival trip, which would you take with you___food or water___?

9. The key to a successful exercise program is to begin at a very low intensity, progress slowly___and stay with it___!

10. The three branches of the US government___the executive, the legislative, and the judicial___are roughly equal in power and authority.

Brackets [ ]

Use brackets to insert editorial comments or clarifications into quotations Quotations represent someone's exact words. If you choose to alter those words (because of a misspelling in the original quotation or to add explanatory information, for example), you must indicate that you have done so by putting brackets around the alterations.

> "One of the things that will produce a stalemate in Rio [the site of the 1992 UN conference on the environment] is the failure of the chief negotiators, from both the

north and the south, to recognize the contradictions between the free market and environmental protection."

The reference to Rio in this quotation might not be understood out of context, so the author has inserted a brief clarification between brackets.

Whenever you insert a quotation from your reading into your writing, be aware that you may need to give the reader important information that was located in the sentences immediately preceding or following it in the original. Any necessary clarification may be added either outside the actual quotation or within it, in which case it should be in brackets. Say, for example, that you have come across this passage in your reading and want to quote the final sentence:

> Sea snails are the source of highly refined painkilling chemicals now being tested for human use. One scientist describes these as "little chemical factories" that are in essence doing what drug companies are trying to do. They have created thousands of chemical compounds and refined them to be exquisitely sensitive and potent.

If you just quoted the final sentence word for word, readers would not know what *They* referred to. Therefore, you should write the sentence in one of the following two ways:

> Sea snails "have created thousands of chemical compounds and refined them to be exquisitely sensitive and potent."

OR

> "[Sea snails] have created thousands of chemical compounds and refined them to be exquisitely sensitive and potent."

Use brackets with the word *sic* The Latin word *sic* (meaning "so" or "thus") indicates a mechanical error—for example, an error of grammar, usage, or spelling—in a quotation. You may want to use it to show both that you recognize an error in a quote and that you did not introduce the error when transposing the quote into your writing. Place it in brackets in the quotation, immediately following the error.

> "Any government that wants to more and more restrict freedoms will do it by financial means, by creating financial vacums [*sic*]."

If you frequently quote Internet messages like this one, you may have many opportunities to use *sic*. Overusing it, though, may make your writing sound snobbish.

Use brackets for parenthetical comments within parentheses If one parenthetical comment is nested within another, the inner one should be punctuated with brackets to distinguish it from the outer one.

> The spectacular palace that King Louis XIV built at Versailles (which is located 19 kilometers [12 miles] west of Paris) required 35,000 workers and 27 years to construct.

Ellipses . . .

An **ellipsis** (plural: *ellipses*) is a series of three periods, used to indicate a deletion from a quotation or a pause in a sentence. An ellipsis consists of three *spaced* periods (. . .), not three bunched ones (...).

Use an ellipsis to indicate a deletion from a quotation The sentence with an ellipsis should not be significantly different in meaning from the original sentence, nor should it be ungrammatical.

> "Practically any region on earth will harbor some insect
>
> species—native or exotic—that are functioning near the limits of their temperature or moisture tolerance."

If you end a sentence with an ellipsis, use a fourth period to indicate the end of the sentence.

> "The notion of literature as a secular scripture extends roughly from Matthew Arnold to Northrop Frye. . . ."

Use an ellipsis to indicate a pause in a sentence To mark a pause for dramatic emphasis in your own writing, use an ellipsis.

> I was ready to trash the whole thing . . . but then I thought better of it.

Beware, however, of overusing ellipses to indicate pauses.

EXERCISE

Reduce the following passage to a two-sentence quotation, using at least one set of brackets and one ellipsis.

Preserving the planet's remaining natural areas is one of our most urgent responsibilities. Such places are fundamental to every economy in the world, no matter how divorced from "nature" it might appear to be, and no conceivable development will lessen that dependence. There is no substitute for a stable hydrological cycle, healthy pollinator populations, or the general ecological stability that only natural areas can confer. We need these places in ways that are direct enough to satisfy even the most hard-nosed economist, but we also need them for reasons that are harder to quantify.

Use brackets around ellipses in quotations to differentiate them from the author's ellipses MLA style recommends that you place brackets around your ellipsis marks if necessary to differentiate them from ellipsis marks the original author used. One space should be inserted before the opening bracket and one space after the closing bracket, unless it is followed by another punctuation mark. There should be no space between a bracket and the ellipsis mark itself. Thus, someone quoting the example sentence above might insert additional ellipsis marks as follows:

> "The writer states: 'I was ready to trash the whole thing . . . but [. . .] thought better of it.' "

Note that this bracketing applies only to quotations. It is *not* done with statements of your own.

Slashes /

Use slashes to separate lines of poetry quoted within a sentence If you are quoting lines of poetry without setting them off in separate lines as they appear in the poem, put a slash (surrounded by spaces) between the lines.

> Gerard Manley Hopkins's poetry features what he called "sprung rhythms," as can be heard in these lines from "The Windhover": "No wonder of it: sheer plod makes plow down sillion / Shine, and blue-bleak embers, ah my dear, / Fall, gall themselves, and gash gold-vermilion."

Use a slash to show alternatives Slashes (with no surrounding spaces) are used in expressions such as *either/or, pass/fail, on/off, win/win* and *writer/editor*. Readers may object, though, if you overuse them. The expressions *he/she, his/her,* and *s/he* are admirable attempts at gender neutrality, but many people dislike their phonetic clumsiness. We suggest you use *he or she* and *his or her* or find other ways of avoiding sexist pronouns.

Use a slash to indicate a fraction Fractions that would be set in formal mathematics on separate lines also can be shown on one line, with a slash dividing the numerator from the denominator:

   1/3   3/8   2 2/5

Your word-processing program may automatically convert fractions into more elegant versions like $\frac{1}{2}$ and $\frac{1}{4}$, but first you have to type them with slashes. (Check under AUTOFORMAT to see whether your program will format fractions for you.)

Use slashes in Internet addresses Slashes are indispensable components of URLs (Web site addresses), such as <http://mediachannel.org/views/>. Include the last slash if it brackets a directory, but not if it brackets an HTML file. (Tip: If your browser automatically adds a final slash to the address, that tells you the final term names a directory, not a file.)

Use slashes in writing dates informally Instead of writing out a date like June 16, 2006, you can write the date informally: 6/16/06. (Note: In many other countries, this date would be written 16/06/06.)

PUNCTUATION

15

CONCEPT 1 **End Punctuation**

End a sentence with one of three punctuation marks: a period (.), a question mark (?), or an exclamation point (!).

Use a period after most sentences and with some abbreviations.

Statements, mild commands, and indirect questions

Statement
The airline went bankrupt.   It no longer flies.

Mild command
Think of the possibilities.   Please consider others.

Indirect question

An **indirect question** reports what someone asked but not in the exact form or words of the original question:

The judge asked why I had been driving with my lights off.

No one asked how we got home.

CULTURE LANGUAGE

In standard American English, an indirect question uses the wording and subject-verb order of a statement: *The reporter asked why* the negotiations failed [not *why* did the negotiations fail].

Abbreviations Use periods with abbreviations that consist of or end in small letters. Otherwise, omit periods from abbreviations.

Dr.	Mr., Mrs.	e.g.	Feb.	ft.
St.	Ms.	i.e.	p.	a.m., p.m.
PhD	BC, BCE	USA	IBM	AM, PM
BA	AD, CE	US	USMC	AIDS

Note: When a sentence ends in an abbreviation with a period, don't add a second period: *My first class is at 8 a.m.*

EXERCISE

Revising: Periods

Revise the following sentences so that periods are used correctly. If a sentence is correct as given, circle the number preceding it.

Example

Several times I wrote to ask when my subscription ended?

Several times I wrote to ask when my subscription ended.

1. Cut the flowers and put them in the vase
2. The office manager asked whose computer was broken?
3. The championship game begins at 7:30 PM sharp.
4. The area of the new athletic complex is almost 8200 sq ft.
5. Plato wrote *Republic* in about 370 BC.

Use a question mark after a direct question and sometimes to indicate doubt.

Direct questions

Who will follow her**?**

What is the difference between these two people**?**

After indirect questions, use a period: *We wondered who would follow her*. (See the preceding page.)

Questions in a series are each followed by a question mark:

The officer asked how many times the suspect had been arrested. Three times**?** Four times**?** More than that**?**

> **Note:** Do not combine question marks with other question marks, periods, commas, or other punctuation.

Doubt A question mark within parentheses can indicate doubt about a number or date.

The Greek philosopher Socrates was born in 470 (**?**) BC and died in 399 BC from drinking poison. [Socrates's birthdate is not known for sure.]

Use sentence structure and words, not a question mark, to express sarcasm or irony.

| **Not** | Stern's friendliness (?) bothered Crane. |
| **But** | Stern's <u>insincerity</u> bothered Crane. |

EXERCISE

Revising: Question marks

Add, delete, or replace question marks as needed in the following sentences.

Example

"When will it end?," cried the man dressed in rags.
"When will it end**?**" cried the man dressed in rags.

1. I often wonder whether I will remember any of my French when I'm sitting in a café in Paris?
2. Why does the poem end with the question "How long?"?
3. "What does *ontogeny* mean?," the biology instructor asked?
4. The candidate for Congress asked whether there was anything he could do to help us?
5. Ulysses and his mariners took seven years to travel from Troy to Ithaca. Or was it six. Or eight?

Use an exclamation point after a strong statement, interjection, or command.

No**!** We must not lose this election**!**

Come here immediately**!**

> *Note:* Do not combine exclamation points with periods, commas, or other punctuation marks. And use exclamation points sparingly, even in informal writing. Overused, they'll fail to impress readers, and they may make you sound overemphatic.

interjection A word that expresses feeling or commands attention, either alone or within a sentence: *Oh! Hey! Wow!*

EXERCISE

Revising: Exclamation points

Add or replace exclamation points as needed in the following sentences. If a sentence is correct as given, circle the number preceding it.

Example

What a shock it was to hear her scream "Stop"

What a shock it was to hear her scream "Stop**!**"

1. I was so late returning from lunch that I missed the three o'clock meeting!
2. Look both ways before you cross the street.
3. "Well, now!," he said loudly.
4. The child's cries could be heard next door: "Don't go. Don't go."
5. As the firefighters moved their equipment into place, police walked through the crowd shouting, "Move back!."

EXERCISE

Revising: End punctuation

Insert appropriate end punctuation (periods, question marks, or exclamation points) where needed in the following paragraph.

When Maureen approached Jesse with her idea for a class gift to the school, he asked if she knew how much it would cost "Forget it if it's over $500," he said "Do you think the class can come up with even that much" Both of them knew the committee treasury contained only the $200 given by Dr Wheeler Maureen said that she thought they could raise the rest with a talent show "That's ridiculous" exclaimed Jesse "What talent Dr Wheeler's Whose" But he softened when Maureen asked him if he would perform his animal imitations Jesse loved to do animal imitations.

CONCEPT 2 The Comma

The comma (,) is the most common punctuation mark inside sentences. It is also the most misused punctuation mark. If you omit a comma when one is needed or add an unnecessary comma, your sentences will be confusing. Here is a sentence that is confusing at first because it lacks an important comma:

Confusing	While very tall Abraham Lincoln was not an overbearing man.
Clear	While very tall, Abraham Lincoln was not an overbearing man.

Overall, the comma is used to separate parts of a sentence from one another, as shown in the box on the next page.

Use a comma with independent clauses linked by *and, but, or, nor, for, so, yet.*

When a coordinating conjunction links words or phrases, do not use a comma: *Dugain plays and sings Irish and English folk songs.* However, *do* use a comma when a coordinating conjunction joins independent clauses, as in the next examples.

Caffeine can keep coffee drinkers alert, and it may elevate their mood.

Caffeine was once thought to be safe, but now researchers warn of harmful effects.

Coffee drinkers may suffer sleeplessness, for the drug acts as a stimulant to the nervous system.

> ***Note:*** The comma goes before, not after, the coordinating conjunction.

independent clause A word group that can stand alone as a sentence because it contains a subject and a predicate and does not begin with a subordinating word: *Water freezes at temperatures below 32°F.*

KEY TERM

Success
Using the comma

- **Separate independent clauses linked by a coordinating conjunction** (facing page and next page).

Main clause $,$ { or and or / so but nor / yet } main clause .

The building is finished, but it has no tenants.

- **Set off most introductory elements** (p. 399).

Introductory element $,$ main clause .

Unfortunately, the only tenant pulled out.

- **Set off nonessential elements** (p. 401).

Main clause $,$ nonessential element .

The empty building symbolizes a weak local economy, which affects everyone.

Beginning of main clause $,$ nonessential element $,$ end of main clause .

The primary cause, the decline of local industry, is not news.

- **Separate items in a series** (p. 404).

... item 1 $,$ item 2 $,$ { and / or } item 3 ...

The city needs healthier businesses, new schools, and improved housing.

- **Separate adjectives that equally modify the same word** (p. 361).

... first adjective $,$ second adjective word modified ...

A tall, sleek skyscraper is not needed.

Other uses of the comma:

Separate parts of dates, addresses, long numbers (p. 406).

Separate quotations and signal phrases (p. 407).

See also pp. 408–409 for when *not* to use the comma.

EXERCISE

Revising: Comma with linked independent clauses

Insert a comma before each coordinating conjunction that links independent clauses in the following sentences.

Example

I would have attended the concert but I had to baby-sit for my niece.

I would have attended the concert, but I had to baby-sit for my niece.

1. I have auditioned for many lead roles but I have been offered only one minor speaking part and two walk-on parts.
2. Flat screen televisions continue to come down in price so more people are buying them.
3. Kampala is Uganda's capital and largest city and it serves as the nation's social and economic center.
4. He wanted to wear his black leather jacket but his roommate had borrowed it.
5. We had driven all night and all day to get to the town and we were too tired to sightsee or search for a cozy inn.

EXERCISE

Sentence combining: Linked independent clauses

Combine each of the following pairs of sentences into one sentence by using the coordinating conjunction in parentheses. Then insert a comma between the clauses.

Example

The circus had just come to town. Everyone wanted to see it. (*and*)

The circus had just come to town, and everyone wanted to see it.

1. The police must have based the accusation on the polygraph test. They would not have made it at all. (*or*)
2. We once thought cell phones were a faultless invention. Now we know they can create problems. (*but*)
3. We caught Sam in his lie. He refused to tell the truth. (*yet*)
4. Parents sometimes combine their last names. Their children bear both their names. (*so*)
5. In many bird species the female builds the nest. The male defends it. (*and*)

Use a comma after most introductory elements.

An introductory element begins a sentence and modifies something in the independent clause. The element is usually followed by a comma.

Word
Fortunately, the news was good.

Phrase
As predicted, the rain began at 4:00 PM.

Dependent clause
Even when they are raised apart, identical twins grow up very alike.

Transitional word or phrase
After a while, the child became bored with the expensive toy.

> ***Note:*** The subject of a sentence is not an introductory element but a part of the independent clause. Thus, do not use a comma to separate the subject and its verb.
>
> **Not**   Some tourists, may be disappointed.
>
> **But**   Some tourists, may be disappointed.

KEY TERMS

phrase A word group that lacks a subject or a verb or both: *Words can do damage by hurting feelings.*

transitional word or phrase A word or phrase that shows the relationship between sentences: *for example, however, after a day,* etc.

subject Who or what the sentence is about: *Biologists often study animals.*

EXERCISE

Revising: Commas with introductory elements

Insert commas where needed after introductory elements in the following sentences. If a sentence is punctuated correctly as given, circle the number preceding it.

Example

After the new library opened the old one became a student union.

After the new library opened, the old one became a student union.

1. Giggling to themselves the children ran behind the barn.
2. Before you proceed to your argument state your thesis.
3. Running water is a luxury in some of the distant villages.
4. Even when employees have been laid off they may still be entitled to health insurance from the company.
5. Predictably the lawyer was late for the meeting.

EXERCISE

Sentence combining: Introductory elements

Combine each pair of sentences below into one sentence that begins with an introductory phrase or clause as specified in parentheses. Follow the introductory element with a comma. You will have to add, delete, change, and re-arrange words.

Example

The girl was humming to herself. She walked up the stairs. (*Phrase beginning Humming.*)

<u>Humming to herself,</u> the girl walked up the stairs.

1. The government cut back on its student loan program. Students and their parents have had to rely more on banks. (*Clause beginning Since.*)
2. More than five hundred people signed the petition. The mayor did not respond. (*Clause beginning Although.*)
3. One needs information to vote wisely. One needs objective information about the candidates' backgrounds and opinions. (*Phrase beginning To.*)
4. The flags were snapping in the wind. They made the speaker's message seem even more urgent. (*Phrase beginning Snapping.*)
5. Rhode Island has approximately 1200 square miles. It is the smallest state in the country. (*Phrase beginning With.*)

Use a comma or commas to set off many interrupting and concluding elements.

Commas around part of a sentence often signal that the element is not necessary to the meaning. This **nonessential element** may modify or rename the word it refers to, but it does not limit the word to a particular individual or group. The meaning of the word would still be clear if the element were deleted:

Nonessential element

The company, <u>which is located in Oklahoma,</u> has a good reputation.

(Because it does not restrict meaning, a nonessential element is also called a **non-restrictive element**.)

In contrast, an **essential** (or **restrictive**) **element** *does* limit the word it refers to: the element cannot be omitted without leaving the meaning too general. Because it is essential, such an element is *not* set off with a comma or commas.

Essential element

The company rewards employees <u>who work hard.</u>

Omitting the underlined words would distort the meaning: the company doesn't necessarily reward *all* employees, only the hardworking ones.

> **Note:** When optional information falls in the middle of the sentence, be sure to use one comma *before* it and one *after* it.

Here are additional examples of nonessential elements:

Nonessential modifiers

Hai Nguyen, who emigrated from Vietnam, lives in Denver.

His company, which is ten years old, studies the pollution of air and water.

Nguyen's family lives in Chicago, even though he lives in Denver.

Nonessential appositives

Hai Nguyen's work, research into air pollution, keeps him in Denver.

His wife, Tina Nguyen, writes stories for a newspaper in Chicago.

KEY TERMS

modifier A word or word group that describes another word or word group: *sweet candy, running in the park*.

appositive A noun or noun substitute that renames another noun immediately before it.

Success
Testing for nonessential and essential elements

Step	Example
1. **Identify the element.**	Hai Nguyen who lives in Denver was born in Vietnam.
	The teacher gives awards to students who work hard.
2. **Remove the element. Does the basic meaning of the sentence change?**	**No.** Hai Nguyen was born in Vietnam.
	Yes. The teacher gives awards to students.
3. **If *no*, the element is *nonessential* and should be set off with punctuation.**	Hai Nguyen, who lives in Denver, was born in Vietnam.
If *yes*, the element is *essential* and should not be set off with punctuation.	The teacher gives awards to students who work hard.

Commas with transitional words or phrases or with parenthetical expressions

A transitional word or phrase such as *however*, *for example*, and *of course* forms a link between ideas. The word or phrase is nonessential and is usually set off with a comma or commas.

Most students at the city colleges, for example, have no health insurance.

A parenthetical expression provides additional information not essential for meaning—for instance, *fortunately*, *all things considered*, and *published in 1990*. It can be enclosed in parentheses or, with more emphasis, in commas.

Some schools, it seems, do not offer group insurance.

Commas with phrases of contrast

Students may focus on the cost of health care, not on their health as they should.

Commas with *yes* and *no*

All schools should agree that, yes, they will provide at least minimal insurance at low cost.

Commas with words of direct address

Heed this lesson, readers.

EXERCISE

Revising: Punctuation of nonessential and essential elements

Insert commas in the following sentences to set off nonessential elements, and delete any commas that incorrectly set off essential elements. If a sentence is correct as given, circle the number preceding it.

Example

Elizabeth Blackwell who attended medical school in the 1840s was the first American woman to receive a medical degree.

Elizabeth Blackwell, who attended medical school in the 1840s, was the first American woman to receive a medical degree.

1. *The Time Machine* a novel by H. G. Wells is a haunting portrayal of Darwin's evolutionary theory carried to a terrible conclusion.
2. The report concluded that Americans who pay property taxes are the most disgruntled citizens.
3. All people, over six feet tall, can join the Boston Beanstalks Club.
4. Jarratt studies the eating disorder bulimia researching its causes and treatment.
5. Those of us, who hadn't seen the concert, felt we had missed something.

Use commas between items in a series.

A **series** consists of three or more items of equal importance (words, phrases, or clauses). Separate series items with commas. Do not use commas around series.

> The names Belial, Beelzebub, and Lucifer sound ominous.

> I plan to take math, psychology, and biology next semester.

The comma before the last item in a series (before *and*) is optional, but it is never wrong and it is usually clearer.

EXERCISE

Revising: Commas within a series

Insert commas in the following sentences to separate elements in a series. If a sentence is correct as given, circle the number preceding it.

Example

Anna Spingle worked as a secretary a baby-sitter and a crossing guard.

Anna Spingle worked as a secretary, a baby-sitter, and a crossing guard.

1. The tedious work absence of people her own age and low salary depressed Debra.
2. She was a Miamian by birth a farmer by temperament and a worker to the day she died.
3. For his second birthday I'd like to buy my son a plastic hammer a punching bag and a stuffed animal.
4. Television newscasters rarely work full-time as reporters investigate only light stories if any and rarely write the copy they read on the air.
5. Commuting by bus gives me time to do the reading for my courses and saves me money on gas and car upkeep.

Use commas between some adjectives.

Use a comma between two or more adjectives when each one modifies the same word equally. As a test, such adjectives could be joined by *and*.

> The book had a worn, cracked binding.

> The beach had a desolate, windswept atmosphere.

Do not use a comma between adjectives when the second one forms a unit with the modified word. As a test, the two adjectives could not sensibly be joined by *and*.

> The house overflowed with ornate electric fixtures.

> Among the junk in the attic was one lovely vase.

Success
Testing for commas with adjectives

Step	Examples
1. **Identify the adjectives.**	She was a faithful sincere friend.
	They are dedicated medical students.
2. **Can the two adjectives be sensibly joined by the word** *and*?	**Yes.** She was a faithful and sincere friend.
	No. They are dedicated and medical students.
3. **If** *yes*, **use a comma to separate the adjectives.**	She was a faithful, sincere friend.
If *no*, **do not use a comma to separate the adjectives.**	They are dedicated medical students.

EXERCISE

Revising: Commas between adjectives

Insert commas in the following sentences as needed to separate adjectives. If a sentence is correct as given, circle the number preceding it.

Example

Automakers need to offer more small fuel-efficient cars.

Automakers need to offer more small, fuel-efficient cars.

1. The manager bought new pine bar stools for the restaurant.
2. The first boats were probably crude heavy canoes made from hollowed-out logs.
3. We bought a heavy waterproof tarp to cover the campsite.
4. The comedian's outrageous offensive monologue was not broadcast.
5. I called the police when I received a third crank phone call.

EXERCISE

Revising: Punctuation of series and adjectives

Insert commas as needed in the following paragraph to separate series items or adjectives. If a sentence is correct as given, circle the number preceding it.

Example

The daring provocative groundbreaking performance earned an Oscar.

The daring, provocative, groundbreaking performance earned an Oscar.

1 Shoes with high heels were originally designed to protect the wearer's feet from mud garbage and animal waste in the streets. **2** The first high heels worn strictly for fashion, however, appeared in the sixteenth century. **3** They were made popular when the short powerful King Louis XIV of France began wearing them. **4** At first, high heels were worn by men and were made of colorful silk fabrics soft suedes or smooth leathers. **5** But Louis's influence was so strong that men and women of the court priests and cardinals and even household servants wore high heels. **6** By the seventeenth and eighteenth centuries, only wealthy fashionable French women wore high heels. **7** At that time, French culture represented the one true standard of elegance and refinement. **8** High-heeled shoes for women spread to other courts of Europe among the Europeans of North America and to all social classes. **9** Now high heels are common, though depending on the fashion they range from short squat thick heels to tall skinny spikes. **10** A New York boutique recently showed a pair of purple satin pumps with tiny jeweled bows and four-inch stiletto heels.

Use commas with dates, addresses, place names, and long numbers.

When they appear within sentences, elements punctuated with commas are also ended with commas.

Dates

July 4, 1776, was the day the Declaration was signed. [Note that commas appear before *and* after the year.]

The United States entered World War II in December 1941. [No comma is needed between a month or season and a year.]

Addresses and place names

Use the address 806 Ogden Avenue, Swarthmore, PA 19081, for all correspondence. [No comma is needed between a state abbreviation or name and a zip code.]

Numbers

The new assembly plant cost $7,525,000.

A kilometer is 3,281 feet [*or* 3281 feet].

EXERCISE

Revising: Punctuation of dates, addresses, place names, and numbers

Insert commas as needed in the following sentences.

Example

The house cost $87000 fifteen years ago.

The house cost $87,000 fifteen years ago.

1. The novel opens on February 18 2054 in Montana.
2. The world's population exceeds 4762000000.
3. Boulder Colorado sits at the base of the Rocky Mountains.
4. Whoever writes PO Box 725 Asheville NC 28803 will get a quick response.
5. The police discovered that the call was made on September 28 2007 from Ames Iowa.

Use commas with most quotations.

A comma or commas usually separate a quotation from a signal phrase that identifies the source, such as *she said* or *he replied*.

Eleanor Roosevelt said, "You must do the thing you think you cannot do."

"Knowledge is power," wrote Francis Bacon.

"You don't need a weatherman," Bob Dylan sings, "to know which way the wind blows."

Do not use a comma when the signal phrase interrupts the quotation between independent clauses. Instead, follow the signal phrase with a semicolon or a period, depending on the punctuation used in the source.

"That part of my life was over," she wrote; "his words had sealed it shut."

"That part of my life was over," she wrote. "His words had sealed it shut."

EXERCISE

Revising: Punctuation of quotations

Insert commas or semicolons in the following sentences to correct punctuation with quotations.

Example

When asked to open her bag, the shoplifter said "I didn't steal anything."

When asked to open her bag, the shoplifter said, "I didn't steal anything."

1. "Having chicken pox as an adult" the doctor explained "is much more serious than having it as a child."
2. "We are not only a Latin-American nation" Fidel Castro said in 1977 "we are also an Afro-American nation."
3. "The mass of men lead lives of quiet desperation" Henry David Thoreau wrote in *Walden*.
4. "I'll be on the next bus for Cleveland" the woman promised.
5. "I think of the open-ended writing process as a voyage in two stages" Peter Elbow says.

Delete commas where they are not required.

Commas can make sentences choppy and even confusing if they are used more often than needed.

No comma between subject and verb, verb and object, or preposition and object

Faulty	The returning <u>soldiers, received</u> a warm welcome. [Separated subject and verb.]
Revised	The returning <u>soldiers received</u> a warm welcome.
Faulty	They had <u>chosen, to fight</u> for their country <u>despite, the risks</u>. [Separated verb *chosen* and its object; separated preposition *despite* and its object.]
Revised	They had <u>chosen to fight</u> for their country <u>despite the risks</u>.

No comma in most compound constructions
Compound constructions consisting of two elements almost never require a comma. The only exception is the sentence consisting of two independent clauses linked by a coordinating conjunction: *The computer failed, but employees kept working.*

Faulty	┌─── compound subject ───┐ <u>Banks, and other financial institutions</u> have helped older people ┌── compound object of preposition ──┐ with <u>money management, and investment</u>.
Revised	<u>Banks and other financial institutions</u> have helped older people with <u>money management and investment</u>.
Faulty	┌─── compound predicate ───┐ One bank <u>created</u> special accounts for older people, <u>and held</u> ┌compound object of verb┐ <u>classes, and workshops</u>.
Revised	One bank <u>created</u> special accounts for older people <u>and held classes and workshops</u>.

No comma after a conjunction

Faulty   Parents of adolescents notice increased conflict at puberty, <u>and,</u> they complain of bickering.

Revised   Parents of adolescents notice increased conflict at puberty, <u>and</u> they complain of bickering.

Faulty   <u>Although,</u> other primates leave the family at adolescence, humans do not.

Revised   <u>Although</u> other primates leave the family at adolescence, humans do not.

KEY TERMS

compound construction Two or more words, phrases, or clauses connected by a coordinating conjunction, usually *and, but, or, nor: man and woman, old or young, leaking oil and spewing steam.*

conjunction A connecting word such as a **coordinating conjunction** (*and, but, or,* and so on) or a **subordinating conjunction** (*although, because, when,* and so on).

No commas around essential elements

Faulty   Hawthorne's work, *The Scarlet Letter,* was the first major American novel. [The title is essential to distinguish the novel from the rest of Hawthorne's work.]

Revised   Hawthorne's work *The Scarlet Letter* was the first major American novel.

Faulty   The symbols<u>, that Hawthorne uses,</u> have influenced other novelists. [The clause identifies which symbols have been influential.]

Revised   The symbols <u>that Hawthorne uses</u> have influenced other novelists.

No commas around a series Commas separate the items *within* a series but do not separate the series from the rest of the sentence.

Faulty   The skills of<u>, hunting, herding, and agriculture,</u> sustained the Native Americans.

Revised   The skills of <u>hunting, herding, and agriculture</u> sustained the Native Americans.

No comma before an indirect quotation

Faulty   The report <u>concluded, that</u> dieting could be more dangerous than overeating.

Revised   The report <u>concluded that</u> dieting could be more dangerous than overeating.

KEY TERMS   **essential element** A word or word group that limits the word it refers to.

indirect quotation A report of what someone has written or said, but not in the exact words and not enclosed in quotation marks.

EXERCISE

Revising: Needless and misused commas

Revise the following sentences to eliminate needless or misused commas. If a sentence is correct as given, circle the number preceding it.

Example

The portrait of the founder, that hung in the dining hall, was stolen.

The portrait of the founder that hung in the dining hall was stolen.

1. Classes were canceled for five days because, of the heat.
2. My sister was furious, when I dragged her out of bed.
3. The students, having finished their exams, drove home for the holidays.
4. The guidebook suggested a visit to the Smithsonian, and to the Kennedy Center.
5. The 5 percent rent decrease for all rent-controlled units, reflects this year's lower property taxes.
6. Of all the novels by Charles Dickens, his tale, *David Copperfield*, is still a favorite of readers.
7. The coach said, that next year the team would have a winning season.
8. Mary bought some of her books used, and borrowed the rest.
9. Forest fires are destructive, but they can benefit the woods they burn.
10. One Internet provider created special accounts for senior citizens and, offered workshops.

EXERCISE

Revising: Commas

Insert commas as needed in the following paragraphs, and delete any misused commas. If a sentence is correct as given, circle the number preceding it.

1 Ellis Island New York reopened for business in 1990 but now the visitors are tourists not immigrants. **2** This spot which lies in New York Harbor was the first American soil seen, or touched by many of the nation's immigrants. **3** Though other places also served as ports of entry for foreigners none has the symbolic power of, Ellis Island. **4** Between its opening in 1892 and its closing in 1954, over 20 million people about two-thirds of all immigrants were detained there before taking up their new lives in the United States. **5** Ellis Island processed over 2000 newcomers a day when immigration was at its peak between 1900 and 1920.

6 As the end of a long voyage and the introduction to the New World Ellis Island must have left something to be desired. **7** The "huddled masses" as the Statue of Liberty calls them indeed were huddled. **8** New arrivals were herded about kept standing in lines for hours or days yelled at and abused. **9** Assigned numbers they submitted their bodies to the pokings and proddings of the silent nurses and doctors, who were charged with ferreting out the slightest sign, of sickness disability or insanity. **10** That test having been passed, the immigrants faced interrogation by an official through an interpreter. **11** Those, with names deemed inconveniently long or difficult to pronounce, often found themselves permanently labeled with abbreviations, of their names, or with the names, of their hometowns. **12** But, millions survived the examination humiliation and confusion, to take the last short boat ride to New York City. **13** For many of them and especially for their descendants Ellis Island eventually became not a nightmare but the place where a new life began.

CONCEPT 3 The Semicolon

The semicolon (;) separates equal and balanced sentence elements, usually independent clauses.

Success
Using the semicolon

Use a semicolon . . .	Examples
. . . **to separate two related independent clauses not joined by a comma and a coordinating conjunction.**	Yolanda had a 99 average in math; she earned an A in the course.
. . . **to separate two independent clauses joined by a conjunctive adverb or a transitional word or phrase.**	Marguerite earned an A on her term paper; consequently, she was exempt from the final exam.
. . . **to separate items in a series when they contain commas.**	The play's characters included Marianne Loundsberry, the heroine; Ellen and Sarah, her children; Barry, her ex-husband; and Louise, Marianne's best friend.

Use a semicolon between independent clauses not joined by *and, but, or, nor,* etc.

Use a semicolon between independent clauses that are not connected by *and, but, or, nor, for, so,* or *yet* (the coordinating conjunctions).

> Recycling trash is one way to help the environment; conserving energy is another.

> People who recycle rarely complain about the extra work; they believe they have a responsibility to the earth.

KEY TERM

independent clause A word group that can stand alone as a sentence because it contains a subject and a verb and does not begin with a subordinating word: *Parks help cities breathe.*

EXERCISE

Revising: Semicolons between independent clauses

Insert semicolons or substitute them for commas to separate independent clauses in the following sentences.

Example

One man at the auction bid prudently another did not.

One man at the auction bid prudently; another did not.

1. Steve spent an evening writing the paper he spent an entire day typing it.
2. Pet rocks and bongo boards were once immensely popular today they are forgotten objects.
3. Karate is not just a technique for self-defense, like a religion, it teaches inner calm.
4. The Himalayas are the world's loftiest mountain range, they culminate in the world's highest mountain, Mount Everest.
5. Subways in New York City are noisy, dirty, and sometimes dangerous they are also a superbly efficient means of transportation.

Use a semicolon between independent clauses related by *however, for example,* and so on.

Use a semicolon between independent clauses that are related by two kinds of words and phrases:

- **Conjunctive adverbs,** such as *however, indeed, therefore,* and *thus.*

  conjunctive adverb

  Blue jeans have become fashionable all over the world; however, the

  American originators still wear more jeans than anyone else.

- **Transitional words and phrases,** such as *after all, for example, in fact,* and *of course.*

  transitional phrase

  Blue jeans are very popular; in fact, more than half a billion pairs were sold in North America last year.

  A conjunctive adverb or transitional word or phrase may move around within its clause, so the semicolon will not always come just before the adverb or transitional expression. The adverb or transitional expression itself is usually set off with a comma or commas.

  Blue jeans have become fashionable all over the world; the American originators, however, still wear more jeans than anyone else.

KEY TERM

conjunctive adverb A modifier that describes the relation of ideas in two clauses, such as *consequently, hence, however, indeed, instead, nonetheless, otherwise, still, then, therefore, thus.*

EXERCISE

Revising: Semicolons between independent clauses with conjunctive adverbs and transitional words or phrases

Insert a semicolon in each sentence below to separate independent clauses related by a conjunctive adverb or a transitional word or phrase, and insert a comma or commas to set off the adverb or transitional word or phrase.

Example

He knew that tickets for the concert would sell quickly therefore he arrived at the box office hours before it opened.

He knew that tickets for the concert would sell quickly; therefore, he arrived at the box office hours before it opened.

1. Door-to-door salespeople are less common than they once were even so they still turn up from time to time.
2. It was 11 PM on his twentieth birthday still his family had not acknowledged the day.
3. The music suddenly went quiet consequently everyone could hear their argument.

4. The elevator shakes when it goes down the inspector says it is safe however.
5. We must cut down on our fuel consumption otherwise we'll find ourselves with *no* fuel, not just less.

EXERCISE

Sentence combining: Related independent clauses

Combine each numbered set of sentences into one sentence containing only two independent clauses. Connect the clauses with a semicolon plus the word given in parentheses, setting off the added word with a comma or commas. You will have to add, delete, change, and rearrange words. Each item has more than one possible answer.

Example

The Albanians censored their news. We got little news from them. And what we got was unreliable. (*therefore*)

The Albanians censored their news; therefore, the little news we got from them was unreliable.

1. She was disappointed with the conclusion of the novel. It seemed anticlimactic. She went on to read the author's other two books. (*nonetheless*)
2. Most young children did not enjoy the movie. The jokes went over their heads. The characters' adventures frightened them. (*furthermore*)
3. My grandfather grew up in Italy. But he never spoke Italian in the United States. He always spoke English. (*instead*)
4. Peanuts thrive in light, sandy soil. They are an ideal crop for the South. In the South such soil is common. (*thus*)
5. The speaker's nervousness showed in his damp brow. His trembling voice also indicated nervousness. His hands shook so badly that he could barely hold his notes. (*moreover*)

KEY TERM

transitional word or phrase A word or phrase that shows the relationship between ideas. Transitional words and phrases include conjunctive adverbs as well as *for example, in fact,* and many others.

Use semicolons between series items containing commas

Use semicolons (rather than commas) to separate items in a series when the items contain commas.

The custody case involved Amy Dalton, the child; Ellen and Mark Dalton, the parents; and Ruth and Hal Blum, the grandparents.

Delete or replace unneeded semicolons.

Too many semicolons can make writing choppy. And semicolons are often misused in certain constructions that call for other punctuation or no punctuation.

No semicolon between a main clause and a subordinate clause or phrase The semicolon does not separate unequal parts, such as main clauses and subordinate clauses or phrases.

Faulty	Pygmies are in danger of extinction; because of encroaching development.
Revised	Pygmies are in danger of extinction because of encroaching development.
Faulty	According to African authorities; only about 35,000 Pygmies exist today.
Revised	According to African authorities, only about 35,000 Pygmies exist today.

No semicolon before a series or explanation Colons and dashes, not semicolons, introduce series, explanations, and so forth.

Faulty	Teachers have heard all sorts of reasons why students do poorly; psychological problems, family illness, too much work, too little time.
Revised	Teachers have heard all sorts of reasons why students do poorly: psychological problems, family illness, too much work, too littletime.

EXERCISE

Revising: Semicolons

In the following paragraph, insert semicolons as needed and eliminate any misused semicolons, substituting other punctuation as appropriate. If a sentence is correct as given, circle the number preceding it.

1 The set, sounds, and actors in the movie captured the essence of horror films. **2** The set was ideal; dark, deserted streets, trees dipping their branches over the sidewalks, mist hugging the ground and creeping up to meet the trees, looming shadows of unlighted, turreted houses. **3** The sounds, too, were appropriate, especially terrifying was the hard, hollow sound of footsteps echoing throughout the film. **4** But the best feature of the movie was its actors; all of them tall, pale, and thin to the point of emaciation. **5** With one exception, they were dressed uniformly in gray and had gray hair. **6** The exception was an actress who dressed only in black as if to set off her pale yellow, nearly white, long hair; the only color in the film. **7** The glinting black eyes of another actor stole almost every scene, indeed, they were the source of the film's mischief.

CONCEPT 4 **The Colon**

The colon (:) is mainly a mark of introduction. It signals that the words following will explain or add information. The colon also has several conventional uses, such as in expressions of time.

Use a colon for introduction.

As an introducer, a colon always ends an independent clause. It may or may not be followed by an independent clause.

Concluding explanation
Soul food has a deceptively simple definition: the ethnic cooking of African Americans.

Concluding series
At least three soul food dishes are familiar to most Americans: fried chicken, barbe-cued spareribs, and sweet potatoes.

Concluding appositive
Soul food has one disadvantage: fat.

Concluding quotation after an independent clause
One soul food chef has a solution: "Instead of using ham hocks to flavor beans, I use smoked turkey wings. The soulful, smoky taste remains, but without all the fat of pork."

Success
Using the colon

Use a colon . . .	Examples
. . . **to introduce an explanation.**	Mathematics is enjoyable: it requires concentration and accuracy.
. . . **to introduce items in a series.**	The purposes of speeches vary: to inform, to persuade, or to entertain.
. . . **to introduce an appositive.**	Judo has another name: jujitsu.
. . . **after an independent clause that introduces a quotation.**	My brother stated his point loudly: "Never borrow my car without asking first!"
. . . **to separate titles and subtitles and divisions of time and to set off the salutation of a business letter.**	*Biology: The Study of Life* 5:47 PM Dear Dr. Rodriguez:

KEY TERMS

independent clause A word group that can stand alone as a complete sentence because it contains a subject and a verb and does not begin with a subordinating word: *Soul food is a varied cuisine.*

appositive A noun or noun substitute that renames another noun immediately before it: *my brother, Jack.*

Use colons with salutations of business letters, titles and subtitles, and divisions of time.

Salutation of a business letter
Dear Ms. Burak:

Title and subtitle
Anna Freud: Her Life and Work

Time
12:26   6:00

Delete or replace unneeded colons.

Use the colon only at the end of a main clause, not in the following situations:

- **Delete a colon after a verb:**

  Faulty   The best-known soul food dish is: fried chicken.

  Revised   The best-known soul food dish is fried chicken.

- **Delete a colon after a preposition:**

  Faulty   Soul food recipes can be found in: mainstream cookbooks as well as specialized references.

  Revised   Soul food recipes can be found in mainstream cookbooks as well as specialized references.

- **Delete a colon after *such as* or *including*:**

  Faulty   Many Americans have not tasted delicacies such as: chitlins and black-eyed peas.

  Revised   Many Americans have not tasted delicacies such as chitlins and black-eyed peas.

KEY TERM

preposition *In, on, outside,* or another connecting word that takes a noun or pronoun as its object: *in the house.*

EXERCISE

Revising: Colons

Insert colons as needed in the following sentences, or delete colons that are misused.

Example

Mix the ingredients as follows sift the flour and salt together, add the milk, and slowly beat in the egg yolk.

Mix the ingredients as follows: sift the flour and salt together, add the milk, and slowly beat in the egg yolk.

1. During the interview she detailed: her impressions of the job, her own qualifications, and her career hopes.
2. He concluded with a threat "Either rehire me, or I will go to the labor board."
3. Three breeds of dogs are very popular collies, poodles, and golden retrievers.
4. She left her cottage at 8:00 in the morning with only one goal in mind to murder the man who was blackmailing her.
5. The pilgrims had one major reason for coming to the New World they sought religious freedom.

EXERCISE

Revising: Colons and semicolons

In the following paragraph, insert colons and semicolons as needed and delete or replace them where they are misused. If a sentence is correct as given, circle the number preceding it.

1 Sunlight is made up of three kinds of radiation: visible rays; infra-red rays, which we cannot see; and ultraviolet rays, which are also invisible. **2** Infrared rays are the longest; measuring 700 nanometers and longer; while ultraviolet rays are the shortest; measuring 400 nanometers and shorter. **3** Especially in the ultraviolet range; sunlight is harmful to the eyes. **4** Ultraviolet rays can damage the retina: furthermore, they can cause cataracts on the lens. **5** The lens protects the eye by: absorbing much of the ultraviolet radiation and thus protecting the retina. **6** Protecting the retina, however, the lens becomes a victim; growing cloudy and blocking vision. **7** The best way to protect your eyes is: to wear hats that shade the face and sunglasses that screen out ultraviolet rays. **8** Many sunglass lenses have been designed as ultraviolet screens; many others are extremely ineffective. **9** People who spend much time outside in the sun; owe it to themselves to buy and wear high-quality sunglasses that shield their eyes.

CONCEPT 5 **The Apostrophe**

The apostrophe (') is used as part of a word mainly to indicate possession (below) and the omission of one or more letters.

Use the apostrophe to show possession.

A noun or indefinite pronoun shows possession with an apostrophe and, usually, -*s*: *the <u>dog's</u> hair, <u>everyone's</u> hope*. Only the pronouns *mine, yours, his, hers, its, ours, theirs*, and *whose* do not use apostrophes for possession.

For singular words, add -'s.

Bill <u>Boughton's</u> skillful card tricks amaze children.

<u>Anyone's</u> feet would be tired from the walk.

Honesty will win the average <u>voter's</u> respect.

When a singular word ends in -*s*, you should still add -'*s*:

Henry <u>James's</u> novels reward the patient reader.

The <u>business's</u> customers filed suit.

> *Exception:* An apostrophe alone may be added to a singular word ending in -*s* when another *s* would make the word difficult to say: *Moses' mother, Joan Rivers' jokes*. But the added -*s* is never wrong (*Moses's, Rivers's*).

For plural words ending in -s, add only an apostrophe.

<u>Workers'</u> incomes have fallen slightly over the past year.

Many students benefit from several <u>years'</u> work after high school.

The <u>Jameses'</u> talents were extraordinary.

---

indefinite pronoun A pronoun that does not refer to a specific person or thing, such as *anyone, each, everybody, no one,* or *something*.

KEY TERM

Notice the difference in the possessives of singular and plural words ending in -*s*. The singular form usually takes -'*s*: *James's*. The plural takes only the apostrophe: *Jameses'*.

For plural words not ending in -s, add -'s.

<u>Children's</u> educations are at stake.

We need to attract the <u>media's</u> attention.

Success
Using and not using the apostrophe

Use the apostrophe . . .	Examples	
. . . to show possession for nouns and indefinite pronouns.	*Singular*	*Plural*
	Ms. Park's	the Parks'
	lawyer's	lawyers'
	everyone's	two weeks'
. . . to form contractions.	It's a girl. [It is a girl.]	
	you're [you are]	
	won't [will not]	

Do not use an apostrophe . . .		
. . . to form plurals of nouns.	*Incorrect:* book's are	
	Correct: books are	
	Incorrect: the Freed's	
	Correct: the Freeds	
. . . with verbs ending in -s.	*Incorrect:* swim's	
	Correct: swims	
. . . to form the possessives of personal pronouns.	*Incorrect:* it's toes	
	Correct: its toes	
	Incorrect: your's	
	Correct: yours	

For compound words, add -'s only to the last word.

The brother-in-law's business failed.

Taxes are always somebody else's fault.

For two or more owners, add -'s depending on possession.

Individual possession
Bale's and Mason's styles are similar. [Each man has his own style.]

Joint possession
The child recovered despite her mother and father's neglect. [The mother and father were jointly neglectful.]

EXERCISE

Forming possessives

Form the possessive of each word or word group in brackets.

Example

The [men] blood pressures were higher than the [women].

The men's blood pressures were higher than the women's.

1. The [treasurer] resignation was expected.
2. My [brother-in-law] attitude was predictable.
3. The [Smiths] car alarm went off at midnight.
4. [Laura and Jane] landlord was totally unreasonable.
5. They visited [Keats] house on Hampstead Heath.
6. An [hour] exercise was plenty.
7. She studied the [goddesses] roles in Greek myths.
8. Higher pay and three [weeks] vacation were the focus of the [sanitation workers] strike.
9. John [Adams] letters to his wife illuminate his character.
10. [Everyone] books were stolen from the gym.
11. [Children] clothes are ridiculously expensive.
12. [Emily and Sarah] husbands are both out of work.
13. The [utility companies] recent price increases are unlawful.
14. Sam [Prince] speech won special praise.
15. The [Hickses] decision to move upset their children.

Do not use the apostrophe to form a plural noun, a singular verb, or a possessive personal pronoun.

Plural nouns The plurals of nouns are generally formed by adding *-s* or *-es*, never with an apostrophe: *boys, families, Joneses, Murphys*.

Faulty	The Jones' controlled the firm's until 2001.
Revised	The Joneses controlled the firms until 2001.

Singular verbs Verbs ending in *-s* never take an apostrophe:

Faulty	The subway break's down less often now.
Revised	The subway breaks down less often now.

Possessives of personal pronouns *His, hers, its, ours, yours, theirs,* and *whose* are possessive forms of *he, she, it, we, you, they,* and *who*. They do not take apostrophes:

Faulty	The house is her's. It's roof leaks.
Revised	The house is hers. Its roof leaks.

Don't confuse possessive pronouns with contractions. See the next page.

EXERCISE

Revising: Apostrophes with possessives

In the following paragraph, insert or reposition apostrophes as needed and delete any needless apostrophes. If a sentence is correct as given, circle the number preceding it.

Example

Its not fair that the companys policy left employees vacation days unpaid.

It's not fair that the company's policy left employees' vacation days unpaid.

1 The eastern coast of Belize was once a fishermans paradise, but overfishing caused the fishing industrys sharp decline in this Central American country. **2** The country's government is now showing the world that leaders' foresight can turn a problem into an opportunity. **3** Belize is capitalizing on something that can capture tourists interest: whale sharks. **4** Huge but harmless to people, whale sharks regularly visit Belizes coast to feed on smaller fishes eggs. **5** The predictable gatherings of the shark's attract large numbers of scuba diver's and snorkeler's, so that the fishs' fascinating beauty has become an economic treasure. **6** A tourists eagerness to spend money for an up-close view of whale sharks is Belizes renewable and reliable resource.

EXERCISE

Distinguishing between plurals and possessives

Revise the following sentences to correct mistakes in the formation of plurals or of the possessive case of personal pronouns. If a sentence is correct as given, circle the number preceding it.

Example

Was the raincoat her's?

Was the raincoat hers?

1. Radio talk-show host's all sound the same.
2. Its unfairness was clear.
3. We could hear the shouts of the boys playing basketball down the street.
4. The designer bag's, each with it's own distinctive look, went on sale.
5. The responsibility was your's.
6. The Russian's high prices make our's seem reasonable.
7. Its shocking color made the car easy to spot.
8. Theirs was far messier.
9. Book's can be good friend's.
10. Street crime was a particular focus of their's.

EXERCISE

Revising: Misuses of the apostrophe

Revise the following paragraph by deleting or repositioning apostrophes or by repairing incorrect possessive pronouns or contractions. If a sentence is correct as given, circle the number preceding it.

Example

The dog wagged it's tail.

The dog wagged <u>its</u> tail.

1 Research is proving that athlete's who excel at distance running have physical characteristics that make them faster than most people. **2** For example, they're hearts are larger. **3** An average adult's heart pump's about fifteen liters of blood per minute, but a competitive distance runner's heart circulate's twice as much. **4** Elite runners are also more efficient: they're able to run with less effort than less talented runners must exert. **5** In addition, competitive runner's are able to keep running for long time's at high levels of exertion. **6** Although these abilities can be honed in training, they cannot be acquired by a runner: they are his' or her's from birth.

Use the apostrophe to form contractions.

A contraction replaces one or more letters, numbers, or words with an apostrophe, as in the following examples:

it is, it has	it's	you are	you're
they are	they're	who is, who has	who's
cannot	can't	were not	weren't
does not	doesn't	class of 2009	class of '09

Note: Don't confuse contractions with personal pronouns:

Contractions	Personal pronouns
It's a book.	Its cover is green.
They're coming.	Their car broke down.
You're right.	Your idea is good.
Who's coming?	Whose party is it?

EXERCISE

Forming contractions

Form contractions from each set of words below. Use each contraction in a complete sentence.

Example

we are: we're

We're open to ideas.

1. she would
2. could not
3. they are
4. he is

5. do not
6. she will
7. hurricane of 1962

8. is not
9. it is
10. will not

EXERCISE

Revising: Contractions and personal pronouns

Revise the following sentences to correct mistakes in the use of contractions and personal pronouns. Circle the number preceding any sentence that is correct as given.

Example

The company gives it's employees their birthdays off.

The company gives its employees their birthdays off.

1. They're reasons for the merger were questioned.
2. Its important to review you're notes before taking an exam.
3. I can begin work whenever your ready for me.
4. After spending two weeks on vacation, their now looking for jobs.
5. When it's team won the championship, the city celebrated.
6. The investigators wondered whose gun it was.
7. Its a wonder that any rivers remain unspoiled.
8. Business is a good major because it's certain that corporations will always need competent managers.
9. The Soltis, who's daughter was married last year, retired to Florida.
10. The only way of avoiding a fine is to pay you're taxes on time.

CONCEPT 6 Quotation Marks

Quotation marks—either double (" ") or single (' ')—mainly enclose direct quotations from speech or writing. This chapter treats the main uses of quotation marks. Additional information on using quotations appears elsewhere in this book:

- **Using commas with signal phrases such as *she said* to introduce quotations.**
- **Using the ellipsis mark and brackets to indicate changes in quotations.**
- **Quoting sources versus paraphrasing or summarizing them.**
- **Integrating quotations into your text.**
- **Acknowledging the sources of quotations to avoid plagiarism.**
- **Formatting long prose quotations and poetry quotations.**

Use quotation marks with direct quotations.

A **direct quotation** reports what someone said or wrote, in the exact words of the original.

Double quotation marks

"Life," said the psychoanalyst Karen Horney, "remains a very efficient therapist."

> *Note:* Do not use quotation marks with an **indirect quotation**, which reports what someone said or wrote but not in the exact words of the original: *Karen Horney remarked that life is a good therapist.*

Single quotation marks Use single quotation marks to enclose a quotation within a quotation.

"In formulating any philosophy," Woody Allen writes, "the first consideration must always be: What can we know? Descartes hinted at the problem when he wrote, 'My mind can never know my body, although it has become quite friendly with my leg.'"

EXERCISE

Revising: Double and single quotation marks

Insert double and single quotation marks as needed in the following sentences. Circle the number preceding any sentence that is correct.

Example

The bus driver always says Go get 'em, tiger! to my five-year-old.

The bus driver always says "Go get 'em, tiger!" to my five-year-old.

1. Why, the lecturer asked, do we say Bless you! or something else when people sneeze but not acknowledge coughs, hiccups, and other eruptions?
2. She said that sneezes have always been regarded differently.
3. Sneezes feel more uncontrollable than some other eruptions, she said.
4. Unlike coughs and hiccups, she explained, sneezes feel as if they come from inside the head.
5. She concluded, People thus wish to recognize a sneeze, if only with a Gosh.

Set off quotations of dialog according to standard practice.

When quoting conversations, begin a new paragraph for each speaker.

> "What shall I call you? Your name?" Andrews whispered rapidly, as with a high squeak the latch of the door rose.
> "Elizabeth," she said. "Elizabeth."
>
> —Graham Greene, *The Man Within*

When you quote a single speaker for more than one paragraph, put quotation marks at the beginning of each paragraph but at the end of only the last paragraph.

Put quotation marks around the titles of works that are parts of other works.

Use quotation marks to enclose the titles of works that are published or released within larger works. (See the following box.) Use single quotation marks for a quotation within a quoted title, as in the article title and essay title in the box. And enclose all punctuation in the title within the quotation marks, as in the article title.

Titles to be enclosed in quotation marks

Titles	Examples
Song	"The Star-Spangled Banner"
Short story	"The Gift of the Magi"
Short poem	"Mending Wall"
Article in periodical	"Does 'Scaring' Work?"
Essay	"Joey: A 'Mechanical Boy'"
Page or document on a Web site	"Readers' Page" (on the site *Friends of Prufrock*)
Episode of a television or radio program	"The Mexican Connection" (on *60 Minutes*)
Subdivision of a book	"The Mast Head" (Chapter 35 of *Moby-Dick*)

Use italics or underlining for other titles.

Note: Some academic disciplines do not require quotation marks for titles within source citations.

EXERCISE

Revising: Quotation marks for titles

Insert quotation marks as needed for titles and words in the following sentences. If quotation marks should be used instead of italics, insert them.

Example

In the movie *Dead Poet's Society,* Whitman's poem O Captain! My Captain! is often recited.

In the movie *Dead Poet's Society,* Whitman's poem "O Captain! My Captain!" is often recited.

1. In Chapter 8, titled *How to Be Interesting,* the author explains the art of conversation.
2. The Beatles' song Let It Be reminds Martin of his uncle.
3. The article that appeared in *Mental Health* was titled *Children of Divorce Ask,* "Why?"
4. In the encyclopedia the discussion under Modern Art fills less than a column.
5. One prizewinning essay, *Cowgirls on Wall Street,* first appeared in *Entrepreneur* magazine.

Use quotation marks to enclose words being used in a special sense.

On movie sets movable "wild walls" make a one-walled room seem four-walled on film.

Note: Use italics or underlining for defined words.

Delete quotation marks where they are not required.

Title of your paper

Faulty	"The Death Wish in One Poem by Robert Frost"
Revised	The Death Wish in One Poem by Robert Frost
Or	The Death Wish in "Stopping by Woods on a Snowy Evening"

Common nickname

| **Faulty** | As President, "Jimmy" Carter preferred to use his nickname. |
| **Revised** | As President, Jimmy Carter preferred to use his nickname. |

Slang or trite expression

Quotation marks will not excuse slang or a trite expression that is inappropriate to your writing. If slang is appropriate, use it without quotation marks.

Faulty   We should support the President in his "hour of need" rather than "wimp out on him."

Revised   We should give the President the support he needs rather than turn away like cowards.

Place other punctuation marks inside or outside quotation marks according to standard practice.

Commas and periods: Inside quotation marks

Swift uses irony in his essay "A Modest Proposal**.**"

Many first-time readers are shocked to see infants described as "delicious**.**"

"'A Modest Proposal**,**'" writes one critic, "is so outrageous that it cannot be believed**.**"

> ***Exception:*** When a parenthetical source citation immediately follows a quotation, place any period or comma *after* the citation.
>
> One critic calls the essay "outrageous" (Olms 26)**.**
>
> Partly because of "the cool calculation of its delivery" (Olms 27)**,** Swift's satire still chills a modern reader.

Colons and semicolons: Outside quotation marks

A few years ago the slogan in elementary education was "learning by playing**";** now educators are concerned with basic skills.

We all know what is meant by "inflation**":** more money buys less.

Dashes, question marks, and exclamation points: Inside quotation marks only if part of the quotation When a dash, question mark, or exclamation point is part of the quotation, place it *inside* quotation marks. Don't use any other punctuation, such as a period or comma.

"But must you**—**" Maria hesitated, afraid of the answer.

"Go away**!**" I yelled.

Did you say, "Who is she**?**" [When both your sentence and the quotation would end in a question mark or exclamation point, use only the mark in the quotation.]

When a dash, question mark, or exclamation point applies only to the larger sentence, not to the quotation, place it *outside* quotation marks—again, with no other punctuation.

One evocative line in English poetry—"After many a summer dies the swan"—comes from Alfred, Lord Tennyson.

Who said, "Now cracks a noble heart"?

The woman called me "stupid"!

EXERCISE

Revising: Quotation marks

Revise the following sentences for the proper use of quotation marks. Insert quotation marks where they are needed, remove them where they are not needed, and be sure that other marks of punctuation are correctly placed inside or outside the quotation marks. If a sentence is correct as given, circle the number preceding it.

Example

The award-winning story was titled *How to Say I'm Sorry to a Child*.

The award-winning story was titled "How to Say 'I'm Sorry' to a Child."

1. The reading included Virginia Woolf's essay The Anatomy of Fiction.
2. "No smoking on this bus!" the driver shouted.
3. The commercial says, Lite Beer is a third less filling than your regular beer; but how do they measure that?
4. Wearing coveralls and work boots, she looked like a "hick."
5. How can we answer children who ask, Is there a Santa Claus?
6. In America the signs say, Keep off the grass; in England they say, Please refrain from stepping on the lawn.
7. In *King Richard II* Shakespeare called England "This precious stone set in the silver sea".
8. The doctors gave my father an "electrocardiogram."
9. Our forests—in Longfellow's words, The murmuring pines and the hemlocks—are slowly succumbing to land development.
10. Must we regard the future with what the philosopher Kierkegaard called fear and trembling?

EXERCISE

Revising: Quotation marks

Insert quotation marks as needed in the following paragraph. If a sentence is correct as given, circle the number preceding it.

1 In one class we talked about a passage from I Have a Dream, the speech delivered by Martin Luther King, Jr., on the steps of the Lincoln Memorial on August 28, 1963:

> **2** When the architects of our republic wrote the magnificent words of the Constitution and the Declaration of Independence, they were signing a promissory note to which every American was to fall heir. **3** This note was a promise that all men would be guaranteed the unalienable rights of life, liberty, and the pursuit of happiness.

4 What did Dr. King mean by this statement? the teacher asked. **5** Perhaps we should define promissory note first. **6** Then she explained that a person who signs such a note agrees to pay a specific sum of money on a particular date or on demand by the holder of the note. **7** One student suggested, Maybe Dr. King meant that the writers of the Constitution and Declaration promised that all people in America should be equal. **8** He and over 200,000 people had gathered in Washington, DC, added another student. **9** Maybe their purpose was to demand payment, to demand those rights for African Americans. **10** The whole discussion was an eye-opener for those of us (including me) who had never considered that those documents make promises that we should expect our country to fulfill.

CONCEPT 7 **Other Marks**

The other marks of punctuation are the dash, parentheses, the ellipsis mark, brackets, and the slash.

Use the dash or dashes to indicate shifts and to set off some sentence elements.

The dash (—) is mainly a mark of interruption: it signals a shift, insertion, or break. In your papers, form a dash with two hyphens (--) or use the character called an em dash on your word processor. Do not add extra space around or between the hyphens or around the em dash.

> **Note:** Be sure to use a pair of dashes when a shift or interruption falls in the middle of a sentence.

Shifts in tone or thought
The novel—if one can call it that—appeared in 2005.

Nonessential elements
The qualities Monet painted—sunlight, rich shadows, deep colors—abounded near the rivers and gardens he used as subjects.

Though they are close together—separated by only a few blocks—the two neighborhoods could be in different countries.

Introductory series
Shortness of breath, skin discoloration or the sudden appearance of moles, persistent indigestion, the presence of small lumps—all these symptoms may signify cancer.

Concluding series or explanation
The patient may undergo a battery of tests—CAT scan, bronchoscopy, perhaps even a biopsy.

Many patients are disturbed by the CAT scan—by the need to keep still for long periods in an exceedingly small space.

---

nonessential element Gives added information but does not limit the word it refers to.

KEY TERM

EXERCISE

Revising: Dashes

Insert dashes as needed in the following sentences.

Example
What would we do if someone like Adolf Hitler that monster appeared among us?

What would we do if someone like Adolf Hitler—that monster—appeared among us?

1. The exuberant I should say outlandish quality of his ravings electrified the crowd.
2. The two brothers one tall and thin, the other short and stocky look nothing alike.
3. The difficulties of city living they hardly need explaining can undermine the most cheerful spirit.
4. The movie theater business is undergoing dramatic changes changes that affect what movies are made and shown.
5. To feed, clothe, and shelter the needy these are real achievements.

Use parentheses to enclose parenthetical expressions and labels for lists within sentences.

Note: Parentheses *always* come in pairs, one before and one after the punctuated material.

Parenthetical expressions Parenthetical expressions include explanations, facts, and examples that may be helpful or interesting but are not essential to meaning. Parentheses de-emphasize parenthetical expressions. (Commas emphasize them more than parentheses do, and dashes emphasize them still more.)

The population of Philadelphia (now about 1.5 million) has declined since 1950.

> **Note:** Don't put a comma before a parenthetical expression enclosed in parentheses. Punctuation after the parenthetical expression should be placed outside the closing parenthesis.

Incorrect   The population of Philadelphia compares with that of Phoenix, (just over 1.6 million.)

Correct   The population of Philadelphia compares with that of Phoenix (just over 1.6 million).

When a complete sentence falls within parentheses, place the period *inside* the closing parenthesis.

In general, coaches will tell you that scouts are just guys who can't coach. (But then, so are brain surgeons.)   —Roy Blount

Labels for lists within sentences

Outside the Middle East, the countries with the largest oil reserves are (1) Venezuela (63 billion barrels), (2) Russia (57 billion barrels), and (3) Mexico (51 billion barrels).

Do not enclose such labels in parentheses when you set a list off from your text.

EXERCISE

Revising: Parentheses

Insert parentheses as needed in the following sentences.

Example

Students can find good-quality, inexpensive furniture for example, desks, tables, chairs, sofas, even beds in junk stores.

Students can find good-quality, inexpensive furniture (for example, desks, tables, chairs, sofas, even beds) in junk stores.

1. T. S. Eliot's *The Waste Land* 1922 is one of the most analyzed poems in the English language.
2. The Golden Gate Bridge actually it's closer to red is a famous landmark of San Francisco.
3. Our present careless use of coal and oil will lead to a series of unpleasant events: 1 all of us will have to cut back drastically on our use of resources; 2 only the rich will have access to these resources; and 3 no one will have access to them, for they will be exhausted.

4. Some exotic pets monkeys and fragile breeds of dog require too much care to be enjoyable.
5. The Hundred Years' War 1337–1453 between England and France was actually a series of widely spaced battles, not a continuous war.

Use the ellipsis mark to indicate omissions from quotations.

The ellipsis mark, consisting of three periods separated by space (. . .), generally indicates an omission from a quotation. All the following examples quote from this passage about environmentalism:

Original quotation
At the heart of the environmentalist world view is the conviction that human physical and spiritual health depends on sustaining the planet in a relatively unaltered state. Earth is our home in the full, genetic sense, where humanity and its ancestors existed for all the millions of years of their evolution. Natural ecosystems—forests, coral reefs, marine blue waters—maintain the world exactly as we would wish it to be maintained. When we debase the global environment and extinguish the variety of life, we are dismantling a support system that is too complex to understand, let alone replace, in the foreseeable future.

—Edward O. Wilson, "Is Humanity Suicidal?"

1. Omission of the middle of a sentence
"Natural ecosystems . . . maintain the world exactly as we would wish it to be maintained."

2. Omission of the end of a sentence, without source citation
"Earth is our home. . . ." [The sentence period, closed up to the last word, precedes the ellipsis mark.]

3. Omission of the end of a sentence, with source citation
"Earth is our home . . ." (Wilson 27). [The sentence period follows the source citation.]

4. Omission of parts of two or more sentences
Wilson writes, "At the heart of the environmentalist world view is the conviction that human physical and spiritual health depends on sustaining the planet . . . where humanity and its ancestors existed for all the millions of years of their evolution."

5. Omission of one or more sentences
As Wilson puts it, "At the heart of the environmentalist world view is the conviction that human physical and spiritual health depends on sustaining the planet in a relatively unaltered state. . . . When we debase the global environment and extinguish the variety of life, we are dismantling a support system that is too complex to understand, let alone replace, in the foreseeable future."

6. Omission from the middle of a sentence through the end of another sentence
"Earth is our home. . . . When we debase the global environment and extinguish the variety of life, we are dismantling a support system that is too complex to understand, let alone replace, in the foreseeable future."

7. Omission of the beginning of a sentence, leaving a complete sentence
a. Bracketed capital letter

"[H]uman physical and spiritual health," Wilson writes, "depends on sustaining the planet in a relatively unaltered state." [No ellipsis mark is needed because the bracketed *H* indicates that the letter was not capitalized originally and thus that the beginning of the sentence has been omitted.]

b. Small letter

According to Wilson, "human physical and spiritual health depends on sustaining the planet in a relatively unaltered state." [No ellipsis mark is needed because the small *h* indicates that the beginning of the sentence has been omitted.]

c. Capital letter from the original

Hami comments, ". . . Wilson argues eloquently for the environmentalist world view." [An ellipsis mark is needed because the quoted part of the sentence begins with a capital letter and it's otherwise not clear that the beginning of the original sentence has been omitted.]

8. Use of a word or phrase
Wilson describes the earth as "our home." [No ellipsis mark needed.]

Note these features of the examples:

- **Use an ellipsis mark when it is not otherwise clear that you have left out material from the source,** as when you omit one or more sentences (examples 5 and 6) or when the words you quote form a complete sentence that is different in the original (examples 1–4 and 7c).
- **You don't need an ellipsis mark when it is obvious that you have omitted something,** such as when a bracketed or small letter indicates omission (examples 7a and 7b) or when a phrase clearly comes from a larger sentence (example 8).
- **Place an ellipsis mark after a sentence period** *except* when a parenthetical source citation follows the quotation, as in example 3. Then the sentence period comes after the citation.

When you omit one or more lines of poetry or paragraphs of prose from a displayed quotation, use a separate line of ellipsis marks across the full width of the quotation to show the omission.

> In "Song: Love Armed" from 1676, Aphra Behn contrasts two lovers' experiences of a romance:
>
> > Love in fantastic triumph sate,
> >   Whilst bleeding hearts around him flowed,
> >
> > . . . .
> > But my poor heart alone is harmed,
> >   Whilst thine the victor is, and free. (lines 1-2, 15-16)

EXERCISE

Using ellipsis marks

Use ellipsis marks and any other needed punctuation to follow the numbered instructions for quoting from the following paragraph.

Women in the sixteenth and seventeenth centuries were educated in the home and, in some cases, in boarding schools. Men were educated at home, in grammar schools, and at the universities. The universities were closed to female students. For women, "learning the Bible," as Elizabeth Joceline puts it, was an impetus to learning to read. To be able to read the Bible in the vernacular was a liberating experience that freed the reader from hearing only the set passages read in the church and interpreted by the church. A Protestant woman was expected to read the scriptures daily, to meditate on them, and to memorize portions of them. In addition, a woman was expected to instruct her entire household in "learning the Bible" by holding instructional and devotional times each day for all household members, including the servants.

—Charlotte F. Otten, *English Women's Voices, 1540–1700*

1. Quote the fifth sentence, but omit everything from *that freed the reader* to the end.
2. Quote the fifth sentence, but omit *was a liberating experience that*.
3. Quote the first and sixth sentences.

Use brackets to indicate changes in quotations.

Brackets have specialized uses in mathematical equations, but their main use for all kinds of writing is to indicate that you have altered a quotation to explain, clarify, or correct it.

"That Texaco station [just outside Chicago] is one of the busiest in the nation," said a company spokesperson.

Use the slash between options and between lines of poetry run into the text.

Option
Some teachers oppose pass/fail courses.

Poetry
Many readers have sensed a reluctant turn away from death in Frost's lines "The woods are lovely, dark and deep, / But I have promises to keep" (13–14).

When separating lines of poetry in this way, leave a space before and after the slash.

EXERCISE

Revising: Other punctuation marks

Insert dashes, parentheses, brackets, ellipsis marks, or slashes as needed in the following sentences, or remove them where they are not needed. When different marks would be appropriate in the same place, be able to defend the choice you make. Circle the number preceding any sentence that is already correct.

Example

The residents of the neighborhood including many who grew up there signed a petition against further development.

The residents of the neighborhood—including many who grew up there—signed a petition against further development. [The dashes emphasize the parenthetical expression.]

1. I read about Emma Goldman (or Red Emma), an American anarchist who died in 1940.
2. From the reviewer's sentence "The acting is amazingly incompetent, given that these actors can be powerful," the advertisement extracted praise by using an ellipsis mark: "The acting is amazingly powerful."
3. The bikers—tattooed and draped in chains look more threatening than they really are.
4. James Joyce's *Ulysses* first published in 1922 is a beautiful, shocking novel.
5. Paying taxes one of life's certainties is only a little less painful than the other certainty.

REVISING, EDITING, AND PROOFREADING

16

Because so much of what we read is in a final, published form, we cannot appreciate how many hours the author spent **revising**—considering and reconsidering content and structure, tearing out whole sections and redrafting them, honing and refining paragraphs, polishing the style, and finding just the right words to express a thought. Revision is not simply **editing,** a fine tuning for style, grammar, and problems with sentences and wording. Nor is it **proofreading,** a final-stage cleaning up of typographical errors or a search for missing commas and apostrophes. *Revision* means stepping outside a draft to assess its strengths and weaknesses and then deciding what to expand, clarify, elaborate, illustrate, reword, restructure, modify, or cut.

Revision Highlights for Three Communities of Readers

Academic Settings	Public Settings	Work Settings
Pay special attention to:	**Pay special attention to:**	**Pay special attention to:**
Clarity of conclusions and thesis statement	Clear statement of policy, cause, or position	Clear statement of problems, solutions, tasks, and goals
Topic sentences and section headings	Relevant and accurate supporting evidence	Explanations and proposals presented concisely and directly
Integration of quotations and supporting information	Direct and clear presentation of ideas and explanations	Factual accuracy
Acknowledgment of competing viewpoints	Fairness of reasoning and in treatment of opposing points of view	Section headings and conventional elements of document
Critical analysis and fresh insight	Focus on actions or solutions	

Major Revisions

When you begin revising, concentrate on **major revisions,** large-scale changes in your draft. For example, if you've left out a major point, you may need to draft some new material and change your conclusion.

Redraft unworkable material

Read through your draft as if you were seeing it for the first time. It helps if you have left your draft alone for a short while so that you can see it afresh. As you read, place a question mark next to sections that seem confusing or garbled. You may need to **redraft** these parts entirely. Go back to the parts you've marked and bracket the specific places where your writing seems to lose its vitality, meaning, or style. Ask yourself what you're trying to accomplish in a particular passage. Then, without even looking at the draft, try again on a new sheet of paper to write what you mean.

Jessica DiGregorio shared with her classmates a draft of her essay reflecting on her father's professional sports contract. They felt the first paragraph didn't capture much tension or create interest, and they placed brackets around sentences that seemed particularly weak. After changing a few words, DiGregorio realized she really needed to redraft the entire paragraph.

Original Draft with Brackets from Peer Group

[A few days ago I decided to go through the musty old cedar chest in my living room and dig up some of the old documents that I had read years earlier.] I came across the Contract marked NBA (National Basketball Association) [that I had looked at before, but remembered that it was very confusing.] It contained words such as: hereunder, however, notwithstanding, and hereof, but when I read this over for the second time it made me realize that my father, [for a total of five years was bound to this document,] and chose to live his life according to what it said.

Jessica's revised introduction appears on page 445.

Reorganize poorly arranged paragraphs or sections

Structural problems are common in early drafts. Often you find that you've written your way into your main point, discovering later what you want to say earlier in the draft. Or you may recognize that two paragraphs are making the same point and should be consolidated.

STRATEGY

Summarize your paragraphs

Number each paragraph in your draft. Then, on a piece of paper, explain in a single sentence what each numbered paragraph says (its main point). When you've finished, look back at your list of statements.

- Could any paragraphs be consolidated?
- Are any paragraphs ineffectively ordered?
- Could you arrange the paragraphs or parts of the paper to yield a clearer, smoother flow of ideas?

Keyshawn Williams drafted a section of his paper on the problems of electronic archives. Reading over his draft, he identified the main points of the paragraphs and then arranged the paragraphs in a more logical order. Having done this, he realized that his new paragraphs needed considerable elaboration. He also added a sentence that helped to focus his next two paragraphs.

Original

Although most people think that electronic archives can store written documents permanently, they would be surprised to learn that medieval parchment makes a far more lasting medium than computers. In fact, electronic media will begin decaying rapidly.

To create a digital archive that will last without being recopied, you would have to preserve the original system software, hardware, operating manuals, recording devices, and all the other apparatus that did the original archive.

decay

The decay is so rapid that the federal government requires its records to be recopied every ten years and "exercised" once a year. A congressional report notes that there are now only two machines in the world that can read the electronically stored information from the 1960 U.S. Census.

obsolescence

Another problem concerns the fact that some records are written in programs that are obsolete, making it impossible to read the data even if the disk is in good shape.

Revision

Although most people think that electronic archives can store written documents permanently, they would be surprised to learn that medieval parchment makes a far more lasting medium than computers. **There are two main reasons why electronic document storage is highly questionable even as our society plunges into the electronic age.**

First, electronic media will begin decaying rapidly. [Explain why the magnetic medium decays.] The decay is so rapid that the federal government requires its records to be recopied every ten years and "exercised" once a year.

Another problem concerns the fact that some records are written in programs that are obsolete, making it impossible to read the data even if the disk is in good shape. A congressional report notes that there are now only two machines in the world that can read the electronically stored information from the 1960 U.S. Census. To create a digital archive that will last without being recopied, you would have to preserve the original system software, hardware, operating manuals, recording devices, and all the other apparatus that created the original archive.

Add new material

Because you may write your first draft quickly, just to get it down on the page, you may find places where something is missing. As you reread your paper, mark any paragraph or sentence that doesn't connect clearly enough to the one before it. Also note any gaps in information or detail. Make a list if you need to add information to your draft.

Looking over her draft Web page telling employees how to transfer to a new email system, Gina White noticed some gaps and filled them in.

Your new email address is listed below. It should be easy to remember **because it consists of the first four letters of your name and the last four numbers of your Social Security number.** Our company's address is the same: @Wishfactory.com. You may send your new address to people or discussion groups that send you frequent email, but you don't need to. **Our server will automatically forward any mail directed to your old address.**

Delete unnecessary or redundant material

Reread your draft as if an editor has accepted it for publication in a magazine with the stipulation that you trim at least ten percent. Too much prose can be just as distracting or frustrating to a reader as too little. What can you cut? Could some paragraphs be eliminated, perhaps by merging just the essential material from them into another paragraph?

EXERCISE

Compare the following drafts of Maureen Lagasse's paper on racism. Describe the nature of Lagasse's changes did she redraft, reorganize, add, or cut? What do you think motivated her revisions?

First Draft

In setting out to write this paper my concept to explain was racism, and in doing some reading and thinking, I realized that racism can't be defined or explained in one simple definition. In the dictionary the definition of racism is "the practice of racial discrimination or segregation, etc." Although this is what racism is, this doesn't fully explain racism. What exactly are races, and how do people actually develop these discriminations against people of different races?

Revised Draft

Have you ever wondered why people view interracial relationships as unacceptable? Have you wondered whether there really is a difference between you and someone of another race? In the dictionary the definition of racism is "the practice of racial discrimination or segregation." Although this is a legitimate definition, it doesn't fully explain racism.

Minor Revisions

Minor revisions are fairly small changes, mostly in the individual sentences of your prose, with the goal of refining and polishing. Most minor revisions are made for three reasons: *sense* (how clear and understandable is your prose?), *style* (how elegant and smooth is your prose?), and *economy* (how much can you say in the least space?).

Revise for sense

Read each sentence of your paper individually and test its clarity: does the statement *make sense* in the context of the paper? Don't let your mind float back into your own construction of ideas; instead, imagine yourself as your intended reader. If you have peer readers, ask them to place question marks next to any statement or group of statements they find confusing or garbled.

Revise for style

When you revise for style, you're concerned with the way your prose "sounds"— that is, with its rhythm, complexity, and diction or word choice. When you read a rough draft, some parts will usually sound better to you than others. Use your intuition as a reader.

In his report on the environmentally threatened wild mustangs of Nevada, Paul Tichey placed an asterisk next to a paragraph he had already revised for sense. Paul liked the clarity of his revision, but the end of his new sentence seemed awkward because so many words began with a *d* ("dehydration and death during the duration of the drought"). He also thought that "during the duration" seemed redundant. Here's his further revision.

> The Air Force, which was partly responsible for the demise of the wild mustangs on the Tonopah missile range, has now joined forces with the Bureau of Land Management and a group of wild-horse preservationists to help save the mustangs from **fatal** dehydration and death during the duration of the drought, **while the drought persists.**

Mark paragraphs in need of revision

Place an asterisk in the margin next to any paragraph that seems to need polishing. Then go back to the first paragraph you marked and code each sentence according to what you feel about it: + (positive), ✓ (neutral), − (negative), ? (unsure). Now concentrate on revising the sentences you do not like in that paragraph. Move on to revising the questionable sentences. Reread the entire paragraph. When you are satisfied, go to the next paragraph you marked with an asterisk. If you're still uncertain about any sentence, ask peer readers for their impressions. When in doubt, try an alternative.

Revise for economy

To revise for economy, read your writing and think about what you can cut from it *without causing it to lose sense or coherence*. In the middle of Paul Tichey's paper, one paragraph included too much material. He decided that half of it could be cut.

Second Draft

> A serious problem confronting groups who want to manage wild mustangs on military sites in Nevada is the relative inaccessibility of the sites, since many require security passes or are fenced off, and environmentalists can't come and go as they please, as they can on public or even some private land. It's simply harder to study or help horses on restricted military installations. Open rangeland has easier access, and inspectors can simply move in and out at will.

Third Draft

Restricted access to Nevada military sites presents a serious obstacle to successful horse management. In contrast to open rangeland, where inspectors can come and go as they please, military sites are often fenced off and require security clearance.

In the revised paragraph, Tichey said essentially the same thing in thirty-eight words that he had said before in seventy-eight—a cut of over 50 percent!

EXERCISE

Examine the following paragraphs from Anita Jackson's paper on Buddhism. Then characterize the sorts of minor revisions Jackson made. Did she revise for sense, style, or economy? What sorts of changes did she make? How successful were the changes?

Early Draft

The man who became the first Buddha was named Siddhartha. Siddhartha was a prince in northern India who lived in a large palace. His father didn't allow him outside the palace because he wanted to spare Siddhartha from the miseries of the world.

Siddhartha became curious and one day he went riding outside the palace. What he saw would forever change his life and influence the lives of many thereafter. That which Siddhartha saw has since been named the Four Sights.

Revised Draft

The man who became the first Buddha was Siddhartha, a pampered prince of northern India who lived in a lavish palace. Yet for all his riches his father would not allow him to venture beyond the castle walls because he wanted to spare Siddhartha the miseries of life. Siddhartha grew extremely curious about the outside world and one day went riding beyond the limits of the palace. What he saw that day would forever change his life and influence the lives of many thereafter.

What Siddhartha saw has since been named the Four Sights.

Collaborative Revising

Professional writers rarely produce a good piece of writing without getting responses from many readers along the way. Follow their lead: *make sure to ask at least one person you respect to read your papers and give you some honest feedback, and promise you'll do the same in return.* Here are tips for getting and giving helpful feedback in **collaborative revision.**

Respond helpfully

When you're reading someone else's writing in order to offer constructive criticism, remember that your most helpful role is not as proofreader or editor but as real, warm-blooded *reader.*

- Find out the writer's purpose for the paper. What is the writer trying to accomplish? What sort of paper is this?
- Who is the writer's intended reader?
- What are the writer's main concerns at this point? What would the writer most like to learn from you?

When you have answers to those questions, read the paper through, jotting comments in the margins and keeping track of your thoughts and impressions. Remember you'll need to balance praise with helpful criticism. Don't just say, "I liked it" or give directions like "Move this paragraph up to page 3." Instead, offer diplomatic advice; ask, "What would happen if you moved this paragraph?" or suggest, "I wonder whether that paragraph would fit better on page 3."

Make the most of responses

Remember, you're not out to collect pats on the back; you want the most useful, constructive commentary you can get from astute, honest readers. This means accepting even hard-hitting reactions and suggestions with grace and diplomacy. If you react defensively to a peer reader's criticism, that person is not likely to keep giving you much feedback. If a reader questions something you especially like in your draft, *remember that no one can force you to make a change.* You have the final say.

- Give your readers a list of specific concerns you have about your draft. Do you want them to comment on tone? style? structure? logic?
- Keep your apologies to a minimum. You may feel anxious about sharing a first draft, but all writers face the same situation.
- If all of your group members are working on papers at the same time, forming a writer's group and spending time on each of your drafts can be an especially valuable experience.
- Using your readers' responses, *spend some time planning your changes.* A few minutes planning your revisions may save you from fruitlessly experimenting.

Workplace collaboration

Collaborative revision is often the norm outside the school setting. However, workplace collaboration may be somewhat different from sharing your draft with classmates.

- In the workplace, many people will have a stake in your text. They are more likely than fellow students to be willing—even eager—to review it for you.
- Supervisors, in particular, may be direct and insistent about making certain changes.
- It helps to solicit responses from individuals with a range of perspectives and kinds of knowledge about your topic or problem.

Revising with a Peer Reader

ESL
ADVICE

If you are worried about your grammar or spelling, you might want to review these items quickly before sharing your rough draft. Look for a peer reader who is willing to ignore these details. Ask this reader to focus on specific issues (such as the order or development of your ideas) or on problems you often have in your papers (such as weak first paragraphs). Consider sharing your draft with several readers, including native speakers of English, to get a range of responses.

EXERCISE

A. If you haven't done so, form a small revision group and circulate rough drafts of your papers in progress. Using the tips in this section as well as the techniques for major and minor revision, comment on your partners' drafts. Then meet in a revision group to discuss your drafts. Keep track of the group's comments on your own paper.

B. Analyze your group experience. What was helpful? What comments will lead (or have led) to specific revisions? What comments did you choose not to act on? Why?

Revising: Paper in Progress

After semidrafting several paragraphs about items on her list of particulars, Jessica DiGregorio wrote the following full rough draft of her paper about her father's sports contract.

First Draft of Sports Contract Paper

Jessica DiGregorio

A few days ago I decided to go through the musty old cedar chest in

my living room and dig up some of the old documents that I had read years

earlier. I came across the Contract marked NBA (National Basketball

Association) that I had looked at before, but remembered that it was very confusing. It contained words such as: hereunder, however, notwithstanding, and hereof, but when I read this over for the second time it made me realize that my father, for a total of five years was bound to this document, and chose to live his life according to what it had said. This twelve-page "AGREEMENT" caught my attention from the time I was young, but it did not make sense to me until now.

When I was younger I never took interest in my father's past mainly because I was tired of hearing people telling me "Did you know your father was the best basketball player?!" and "If you could have seen him play!" I used to just smile and not say anything because I never thought my father could be an athlete as good as Michael Jordan or Larry Bird. My perspective on his basketball career changed as I got older, I became interested in watching videos of him and asked him questions on what it was like to be a basketball legend.

"CLUB DOES HEREBY EMPLOY PLAYER

AS A SKILLED BASKETBALL PLAYER"

This statement which was said on the first page of his contract set the setting for all of the other statements that followed. Since the NBA decided that my father was good enough to play the sport, a contract was made to fit the needs of both the Club (the Buffalo Braves) and the Player (my father). After my father read the first line he was honored and knew that all of his hard work and determination had paid off. The Club which drafted him in 1973 knew that he was a person of great charisma and talent including basketball legend Red Auerbach. This contract was the beginning of a five-year long agreement which was taken very seriously.

"HE WILL TO THE BEST OF HIS ABILITY MAINTAIN
HIMSELF IN PHYSICAL CONDITION SUFFICIENT
TO PLAY SKILLED BASKETBALL"

This rule stated in the contract meant that my father had to keep himself fit for the next five years, and not allow himself to overindulge in bad habits. The Club made up this rule to insure themselves that they were signing someone who was serious about the game. This meant that my father had to stay physically fit and never stop playing basketball. He was advised to stay clear of skiing, ice-skating, or any other strenuous activity not related to basketball so that he would not get injured. If my father, or any other player disobeyed this part of the contract it stated that, "the club shall have the right to suspend the player for a period of one week . . . and will be examined by a physician."

"IN THE EVENT OF THE DEATH OF THE PLAYER PRIOR
TO THE TERMINATION OF ANY SEASON . . .
THE CLUB SHALL PAY TO THE PLAYER'S HEIRS . . ."

This particular part of the contract interested me the most. It stated that if my father had died, all of the money which was already promised to my father within the contract went to my mother. This was very important to my father since my mother was a housewife and stayed home with my older sisters. The Club added this statement to the contract to give the player's family the proper amount of financial help after the loss of their loved one. Basically after the death of a player the money which was promised throughout the five year term is terminated and the family only received what the player lived for. If there was to be a breach in the contract then lawyers would have had to be appointed to the family of the deceased, and determining where money goes can be a sticky situation if it is not written down and documented properly.

"THE CLUB SHALL HAVE THE OPTION IN ITS
SOLE DISCRETION TO TERMINATE THIS AGREEMENT
AND RENDER IT NULL AND VOID"

This final part in this contract stated that the Club had the final say in any of the decisions that would have come along. This meant my father had to follow all of the requirements made within the document which he had signed. If he or anyone else did not follow any of the regulations, then they would have no say if their contract was to be null and void. This left the final power up to the Club and gave them the upper hand in everything that dealt with the players. This was an important part of his contract because it allowed the Club to demonstrate how powerful it really was in the make or break of a person's professional basketball career.

Contracts and legal documents shape our everyday life. Some people underestimate the power of legal documents which bind and connect us to different things. A single piece of paper can determine where we live or how we live our lives. The contract which bound my father to the NBA shaped his life in a major way. For five years he lived by rules and regulations created by the Club to which he belonged. He became a basketball legend and lives in the memories of some people, but to me he is just my dad.

EXERCISE

A. Study Jessica DiGregorio's first draft. Assuming that she has drafted with a loose structure in mind, how would you describe that structure? What is your impression of the draft as a whole, and what suggestions would you make for its organization and its supporting points relative to the main goal of examining her father's NBA contract?

B. In a small group, compare your analyses of DiGregorio's first draft, and try to reach some consensus about what she should focus on in her revision.

Editing Your Own Writing

After making major and minor revisions in your writing, you should turn your attention to editing. **Editing** means fine-tuning your work for a reader—adjusting sentences and words for clarity, for precise meaning and effect, and for correctness. It means identifying problems in grammar and sentence structure as well as glaring omissions or repetitions. And it means looking for consistency in style, punctuation, word usage, and tone.

Successful editing also means recognizing and using the conventions of specific communities. For example, a scientist would use numerals (such as *12* or *84*) for the numbers in a lab report, while an art historian might spell out *twelve* or *eighty-four* in an interpretive paper. Many workplace communities use particular "local" conventions, and you'll need to adapt your writing to those contexts.

Often, editing requires you to keep in mind a certain concern (commas, for example, or sexist language) while you scour your entire text for specific cases. It's hard to look for too many kinds of problems at once. Sometimes you may need to read your text four, five, six, or more times, keeping in mind a different cluster of concerns for each reading.

Editing for style and correctness calls for a special kind of reading, one that shifts away from content (what's being said) and toward form (how it's being said). Focus on each sentence, and scrutinize it for smaller stylistic concerns, grammar, and punctuation. Problems, inconsistencies, and errors will emerge, and you *must* fix them before your paper can be considered finished.

Final editing for economy and style

Even after major and minor revisions have tightened the focus, most papers can still profit from some final cosmetic surgery. If any part of a sentence adds little or nothing to style or meaning, eliminate it during a final check for redundancy or wordiness.

Near-Final Draft	In actual fact, the aligned pulleys are lined up so that they are located up above the center core of the machine.
	Reader's Reaction: This seems repetitive and confusing.
Edited	The aligned pulleys are **positioned** above the **machine's core.**

Edit for economy and style

STRATEGY

- **Are my sentences reasonably easy to read?** Try reading out loud. Whenever you stumble over wording, try rephrasing or restructuring.
- **Do any words stand out as odd or inappropriate for my purpose?** Try to choose a more appropriate word. Consider turning to a dictionary or a thesaurus for help.
- **Have I used some sentence structures too often?** Try varying sentence structures. For example, do almost all sentences begin with nouns or

with a pronoun like *I?* Then try starting some sentences with prepositional phrases or subordinate clauses.

• **If I had to cut ten words from each page, which ones could I eliminate?** Cut if you can do so without creating new problems in style (such as short, choppy sentences) or meaning.

EXERCISE

In a brochure-writing assignment, Kim Francis drafted the following paragraph for a pamphlet describing tourist attractions and accommodations near her Wisconsin home. Read the paragraph once for meaning and then a second time for editing. During the second reading, ask some of the questions listed in the preceding Strategy. Then edit the paragraph to make it more effective.

After spending a day exploring the countryside, rest and relax at a quaint country inn, relaxing by the fire and sipping on some mulled wine. After spending a quiet night in a room decorated with beautiful old antiques, wake up to a country breakfast. Then after your pleasant stay at the inn, explore the quaint towns and roads that have made Door County, Wisconsin, such an attractive vacation destination for people who like to escape and get away from it all.

Editing for grammatical problems

When you edit for grammatical problems, first you need to *identify* or *recognize* a problem, and then you must *edit* your prose to fix the problem.

Identifying known errors. Read your paper slowly from start to finish but don't become immersed in the ideas. Instead, look carefully and deliberately at each paragraph, circling or marking any errors in grammar, punctuation, and sentence logic. If you can quickly correct an error along the way, do so. If you're not certain how to correct the error, wait until you've finished identifying problems; then refer to the appropriate sections in this handbook or ask a teacher or a knowledgeable peer for advice.

"Before" and "after" passages from Jim Tollefson's newsletter article on the Endangered Species Act for his local conservancy group show his circled errors (labeled in the margins) and his edited version.

Draft with Errors Identified

Critics of the endangered species act think it is too broad. Because some specie's may be less vital to environmental balance than others. They want to protect species selectively, however, scientists still do not know which species are more important.

Edited

Critics of the Endangered Species Act think it is too broad because some species may be less vital to environmental balance than others. These critics want to protect species selectively. However, scientists still do not know which species are more important.

Serious mistakes. Here is a list of the ten mistakes many instructors are likely to consider quite serious because they confuse or irritate readers. Refer to the section of the text listed in parentheses for more information on identifying or correcting the mistake.

Ten Serious Mistakes

1. **Fragment**
   The heavy rain turned the parking lot to mud. **And stranded thousands of cars.**

2. **Fused Sentence**
   The promoters called **the insurance company they discovered** their coverage for accidents was limited.

3. **Unclear Pronoun Reference**
   After talking with the groundskeeper, the security chief said **he** would not be responsible for the safety of the crowd.

4. **Lack of Subject-Verb Agreement**
   Away from the microphone, the mayor said, "I hope the security chief or the promoters **has** a plan to help everyone leave safely."

5. **Dangling Modifier**
   After announcing the cancellation from the stage, the crowd began complaining to the promoters.

6. **Shift**
   If **people** left the arena quickly, **you** could get to **your** car without standing in the rain.

Ten Serious Mistakes

7. **Misused or Missing Apostrophe**
   Even the **promoters promise** to reschedule and honor tickets did little to stop the crowd's complaints.

8. **Unnecessary Commas**
   Although, the muddy lot caused problems, all the cars and **people, began** to leave.

9. **Missing or Misused Quotation Marks**
   "The grounds are **slippery, the** mayor repeated, "so please walk carefully."

10. **Double Negative**
    The authorities were relieved because they **hadn't scarcely** enough resources to cope.

Identifying suspected errors. You may suspect that you've made an error but aren't sure. *Don't take a risk.* Check the rule or convention, and edit accordingly.

STRATEGY

Create an editing checklist

Create an editing checklist of problems or errors that you often encounter in your writing. Apply the checklist to each paper you write. Begin by analyzing your own papers and by giving samples of your writing to a teacher or expert writer. Ask that person to identify *patterns* of errors in your writing, and also look for them on your own. Using this handbook, study the errors and try to identify their causes. Then create your own strategies for recognizing the errors, and turn them into a personalized editing checklist for your papers and other writing.

After editing her paper on the effects of loud music, Carrie Brehe added three items to her editing checklist.

1. A lot—sounds like one word but is actually two. Think of an entire "lot" full of whatever. Think of the opposite of a little. Search for all cases of alot.

2. Their vs. there. Sound the same. I usually write "there" for "their" when I make this mistake, but not the reverse. "Their" is possessive only, and "there" is location. Search for all cases of there/their.

3. If they would have known. I say this a lot (ha!). I'm still not sure what the subjunctive means, but this problem shows up when I write "if." Correct to "if they had" or "if they were." Search for all cases of "if + would."

Identifying unknown errors. A final category of mistakes consists of those you have no idea you're making.

Read your writing, preferably aloud. Sometimes this will help you to locate problems intuitively. Or you may recognize them because you encounter difficulty reading a passage. Circle everything you question; then use the Strategy on page 452 to check suspected errors. Add *all* previously unknown errors to your editing checklist (see above).

Ask someone to read your paper and to mark or circle any problems he or she encounters. Your reader doesn't need to be a grammarian to call attention to problems with sentences, usage, and the like. Because they're not as close to the text as you are, these readers may find problems you overlooked.

Collaborative Editing

When you edit collaboratively, you identify and talk about specific problems in a paper with one or more consulting readers, usually friends or peers. Your goal is not just to rid your paper of errors but to learn to identify and correct errors on your own.

EXERCISE

On the day your teacher returns drafts or finished papers with comments, look for any errors he or she has noted. Working in groups of three or four, read each other's papers, looking for patterns of error. Compare these patterns and, as a group, try to write "rules" explaining how to fix them. In creating the rules, feel free to use your own terms and ways of explaining. Add any new items to your editing checklist.

Collaborative Editing Guidelines

Guidelines for Writers

- Revise content and organization first to prepare your draft for editing. (Or ask your reader for feedback on larger revisions instead.)
- Supply a clean draft; don't waste your reader's time on sloppiness.
- Share your requirements or writing concerns with your reader.

Guidelines for Readers

- Use familiar labels and symbols for comments. (The terms in this handbook are generally accepted in academic, public, and work communities. See the list of symbols on the inside back cover.)
- Just note possible errors. Let the writer use a dictionary, a style guide, or this handbook to identify and repair each problem.
- Be specific; *awkward* or *unclear* may not tell the writer exactly what's wrong. Briefly tell why something does or doesn't work.
- Identify outright errors, but don't "take over" the draft. Rewriting sentences and paragraphs is the writer's job.
- Look for patterns of error, noting repetition of the same mistakes.

Editing on the Computer

Editing has its share of "quick fix" remedies. Among the most attractive are computer programs that "read" a piece of prose and then tell you how to correct or improve it. Before using or buying such a program, learn something about what it can and can't do.

What computer editors can do

When examining an editing program, see whether it will meet your specific needs. Use the following questions as a guide.

- Does the program identify errors in spelling, punctuation, capitalization, and usage? Does it identify incorrect sentence structure? How reliable are the identifications?
- Will the program alert you to unclear sentences, problems with subject-verb agreement or modifiers, sexist or discriminatory language, and vague expressions?
- Is it linked to a spell checker, thesaurus, dictionary, synonym finder, or other utility? Will it identify clichéd or vague expressions and commonly misused words?
- Does it allow you to design and add your own rules, tailoring the program to your editorial needs and to meet the conventions of use within your writing community? Does it reflect the expectations of a particular community, such as business readers and writers?

What computer editors can't do

Although they may claim to answer most of your writing problems, computerized editing programs are no match for human readers and editors. Most programs will alert you to a potential problem but leave you to identify and repair it yourself. The programs provide few options for different kinds of writing or for audiences that differ in sophistication and background knowledge. Beware, therefore, of blanket pronouncements from the program. They may be inappropriate for your writing situation.

Proofreading

After you've made as many conscious decisions about your writing as possible and you are ready to submit it, it's time for **proofreading**, looking for errors you may have missed during the editing process. No writer produces an absolutely flawless document every single time. As the slips accumulate, however, your credibility diminishes, and that can ruin the effectiveness of your ideas and lead to a poor assessment of your work.

When proofreading, you submit a piece of writing to a meticulous reading. Focus consciously on every word of your document. Don't let your eyes blur; move from word to word, fixing your eyes on each word to be sure it doesn't contain transposed letters, typographical errors, and the like. Use a spell checker. Or try reading your writing out loud. Every error you identify is a prize catch that increases your credibility.

When working in public settings, it also helps to have several people proofread separately to catch as many errors as possible.

EXERCISE

Two versions of a paragraph follow—one in an unedited form, the other partly edited. Without looking at the edited version, read the unedited draft as an editor would. Scrutinize the passage ruthlessly, making any corrections you wish and explaining them in a notebook. Then compare your editing with the changes made in the second paragraph. What differences do you find between your editing and the writer's editing?

Unedited Draft

At the start of her career, historian Barbara Smithey, felt forced to choose between a life of: public service vs. research. As curator of the Westville Museum of New England culture in Westville, Ct, she was passionately devoted to preserving or restoring old houses in disrepair and seeing to it that they were entered if they qualified into the National Register of Historical Places. At the same time, she had a kean interest in research on the town of Westville which had been settled in the early 17th-Century. She manfully seized control of all public documents on the area, that were not already protected and got them housed in the local historical archives. These included, some early notes about the Indian savages that the White men encountered when they settled the land. Also some personal diaries lady settlers kept.

Edited Draft

At the start of her career, ~~the~~ historian Barbara Smithey, felt forced to choose between a life of public service ~~vs.~~ *and* research. As curator of the Westville Museum of New England Culture in Westville, ~~Ct~~ *Connecticut,* she was passionatly *passionately* devoted to preserving or resto~~r~~ing *e* old houses in disrepair and seeing to it that they were entered *(*if they qualified*)* into the National Register of Historical Places. At the same time, she had a ke~~a~~n *e* interest in research on the town of Westville, which had been settled in the early ~~17th Century~~ *seventeenth century.* She ~~manfully~~ seized control of all public documents on the area, that were not already protected and ~~got~~ *had placed* them ~~housed~~ in the local historical archives. These included, some early notes about, ~~the Indian savages that the White men encountered~~ *settlers' local Native Americans, as well as* ~~when they settled the land. Also~~ some personal diaries ~~lady settlers kept.~~ *of women settlers.*

 Visit **www.mycomplab.com** for more resources and exercises on revising, editing, and proofreading.